MICROSOFT® PROGRAMMING SERIES

P9-AFK-465

Developing
XML
Solutions

Jake Sturm

PUBLISHED BY
Microsoft Press
A Division of Microsoft Corporation
One Microsoft Way
Redmond, Washington 98052-6399

Library of Congress Cataloging-in-Publication Data
Sturm, Jake, 1961-
    Developing XML Solutions / Jake Sturm.
        p. cm.
    Includes index.
    ISBN 0-7356-0796-6
    1. XML (Document markup language) 2. Electronic data processing--Distributed
processing.   3. Web sites--Design.   I. Title.
    QA76.76.H94 S748 2000
    005.7'2--dc21   00-031887

Printed and bound in the United States of America.

1 2 3 4 5 6 7 8 9   MLML   5 4 3 2 1 0

Distributed in Canada by Penguin Books Canada Limited.

A CIP catalogue record for this book is available from the British Library.

Microsoft Press books are available through booksellers and distributors worldwide. For further information about international editions, contact your local Microsoft Corporation office or contact Microsoft
Press International directly at fax (425) 936-7329. Visit our Web site at mspress.microsoft.com. Send
comments to mspinput@microsoft.com.

Intel is a registered trademark of Intel Corporation. ActiveX, BackOffice, BizTalk, JScript, Microsoft,
Microsoft Press, Visual Basic, Visual C++, Visual Studio, Windows, and Windows NT are either
registered trademarks or trademarks of Microsoft Corporation in the United States and/or other countries.
Other product and company names mentioned herein may be the trademarks of their respective owners.

Unless otherwise noted, the example companies, organizations, products, people, and events depicted
herein are fictitious. No association with any real company, organization, product, person, or event is
intended or should be inferred.

Acquisitions Editor: Eric Stroo
Project Editor: Denise Bankaitis
Technical Editor: Julie Xiao
Manuscript Editors: Denise Bankaitis, Jennifer Harris

Contents

Contents

Contents

Acknowledgements

I would like to begin by recognizing the work of the two primary editors of this book: Denise Bankaitis and Julie Xiao. A book is created by a team consisting of the author and the editors, and my two editors have made this one of the best book teams I have worked with. Denise has reviewed the grammar, flow, and content of this book, and she has greatly improved the book's readability. Julie, the technical editor, has carefully checked the technical content of this book. Julie's job has been especially difficult due to the constantly changing W3C specifications, the new releases of products, and the lack of documentation on the most current XML technologies. Julie has consistently looked through the text and has located errors and inconsistencies, and in this way has made a substantial contribution to this book. I also want to thank Marc Young, who did the technical editing in the earlier chapters of the manuscript, and Jennifer Harris, who served as the manuscript editor at the beginning of the project. I would also like to thank the following individuals for their contributions to the book: Gina Cassill, principal compositor; Patricia Masserman, principal proofreader/copy editor; Joel Panchot, interior graphic artist; and Richard Shrout, indexer.

I would like to acknowledge Dan Rogers and Kevin McCall, who are in charge of Microsoft's BizTalk Server group and who have answered numerous questions for me.

Writing this book has required the use of numerous XML tools. I would like to acknowledge the people at Extensibility, Inc., who have answered many questions and provided me with their tool XML Authority. I would also like to acknowledge Vervet for the use of XML Pro, Microstar for Near and Far, and Icon Information-Systems for XML Spy. These are all great XML tools that often work together and have helped me build the examples in this book. In addition to the tools I just mentioned, the wide range of products and tools created by Microsoft—from IE 5 to BizTalk server—are making XML part of corporate solutions today. Without these tools and products, this book could never have been completed.

I would also like to acknowledge my family—Gwen, Maya, William, Lynzie, and Jillian—who once again had to sacrifice their time with me so that I could complete this book.

Finally, I would like to acknowledge you, the reader. Thank you for purchasing this book, and may this book help you understand XML and how to use it in your future work.

Introduction

This book is intended for anyone who wants a glimpse into the next generation of enterprise development. If you want to develop an understanding of Extensible Markup Language (XML) and learn how to use XML for business-to-business (B2B) communications, learn what the Simple Object Access Protocol (SOAP) and BizTalk extensions are, and learn how to use Microsoft Internet Explorer 5 with XML, this book will provide the information you need. You are assumed to have a basic understanding of Microsoft Visual Basic and the Visual Basic Integrated Development Environment (IDE). Developers will find code samples, a discussion of the Internet Explorer 5 document object model, and many more topics. Web developers will find material on using XML to build Web pages. Senior developers and managers will find discussions on how XML can be integrated into the enterprise. Some of the World Wide Web Consortium (W3C) specifications discussed in this book are not final, and they are changing constantly. It is recommended that you visit the W3C Web site at *http:// www.w3.org* often for the updated specifications.

WHAT IS IN THIS BOOK

This book provides a detailed discussion of what XML is and how it can be used to build a Digital Nervous System (DNS) using the Microsoft Windows DNA framework with SOAP 1.1, BizTalk Framework 2.0, and Internet Explorer 5. The book is divided into two parts. Part I covers all the essential elements of XML and enterprise development using SOAP and BizTalk. Part II covers XML and Windows DNA. It discusses how to use Internet Explorer 5 and the Windows DNA framework to build enterprise systems. Throughout the book, you will find code samples that will bring all the ideas together.

Part I: Introducing XML

Chapter 1 discusses how XML fits within the enterprise. It provides an overview of DNS, XML, and knowledge workers and includes a discussion of where XML solutions fit into the DNS.

Chapter 2 gives a general overview of markup languages. The chapter begins with a brief history of markup languages. Next, the three most important markup languages are discussed: Standard Generalized Markup Language (SGML), Hypertext Markup Language (HTML), and XML.

Chapter 3 covers the basic structure of an XML document. Topics include XML elements, attributes, comments, processing instructions, and well-formed documents. Some of the more common XML tools will be discussed and demonstrated in this chapter.

Chapter 4 introduces the *document type definition (DTD)*. The DTD is an optional document that can be used to define the structure of XML documents. This chapter provides an overview of DTDs, discusses the creation of valid documents, and describes the DTD syntax and how to create XML document structures using DTDs.

Chapter 5 examines DTD entities. This chapter shows you how to declare external, internal, general, and parameter entities and how these entities will be expanded in the XML document and the DTD.

Chapter 6 covers four of the specifications that support XML: XML Namespaces, XML Path Language (XPath), XML Pointer Language (XPointer), and XML Linking Language (XLink). This chapter provides an overview of namespaces, including why they are important and how to declare them. The chapter will also cover how XPath, XLink, and XPointers can be used to locate specific parts of an XML document and to create links in an XML document.

Chapter 7 covers XML schemas. This chapter discusses some of the shortcomings of DTDs, what a schema is, and the elements of a schema.

Chapter 8 is all about SOAP, version 1.1. This chapter covers the problems associated with firewalls and procedure calls and using SOAP for interoperability. Examples demonstrate how to use SOAP in enterprise solutions.

Chapter 9 examines the BizTalk Framework 2.0. A detailed discussion of BizTalk tags and BizTalk schemas is provided. The next generation of products that will support BizTalk is also discussed. The rest of the chapter focuses on using BizTalk in enterprise solutions.

Part II: XML and Windows DNA

Chapter 10 provides an overview of the Windows DNA framework and the two fundamental models of the Windows DNA framework: the logical and physical models. This chapter focuses on the logical three-tier model, which is defined by the services performed by components of the system. These services fall into three basic categories: user services components, business services components, and data services components. The chapter ends with a discussion of Windows DNA system design.

Chapter 11 covers the majority of the objects in the XML Document Object Model (DOM). This chapter examines how to use the DOM and provides numerous code samples showing how to work with the DOM objects. The DOM objects not covered in Chapter 11 are discussed in Chapter 12.

Chapter 12 discusses how to present XML data in a Web browser using Extensible Stylesheet Language (XSL), how to transform XML documents using XSL Transformations (XSLT), and how to build static user services components using XML. The rest of the chapter examines XSL and XSLT support in the XML DOM and programming with XSL and XSLT.

Chapter 13 covers the creation of dynamic Web-based user services components using Dynamic HTML (DHTML) and the XML Data Source Object (DSO) available in Internet Explorer 5. This chapter will discuss how to use DHTML to create user services components that can respond directly to input from users. The rest of the chapter covers how to use the XML DSO to work directly with XML data embedded in HTML code.

Chapter 14 examines how XML can be used to build business services components. This chapter shows you how to create business services components using HTML Components (HTC).

Chapter 15 explores using XML in the data services component. This chapter discusses using ActiveX Data Objects (ADO) with XML, the Microsoft XML SQL Server Internet Server Application Programming Interface (ISAPI) extension, and the XSL ISAPI extension. The SQL ISAPI extension allows data in a SQL Server 6.5 or 7.0 database to be retrieved directly through Microsoft Internet Information Server (IIS) as XML. The XSL ISAPI extension allows XSL documents to be automatically converted to XML when a browser other than Internet Explorer 5 requests data.

Chapter 16 introduces Microsoft BizTalk Server 2000. BizTalk Server 2000 allows corporations to pass information within the corporation and between the corporation and its partners using XML.

XML TOOLS

There are a number of XML tools available to assist you in developing XML applications. You will find some of these tools used in examples throughout this book. The tools I use are XML Authority from Extensibility, Inc., XML Spy from Icon Informations-System, and XML Pro from Vervet Logic. XML Authority provides a comprehensive design environment that accelerates the creation, conversion, and management of XML schemas. XML Spy is a tool for viewing and editing an XML document. XML Pro is an XML editing tool that enables you to create and edit XML documents using menus and screens. You can download Extensibility's tools from *www.extensibility.com*, XML Spy from *http://xmlspy.com*, and XML Pro from *www.vervet.com*.

Please note these products are not under the control of Microsoft Corporation, and Microsoft is not responsible for their content, nor should their reference in this book be construed as an endorsement of a product or a Web site. Microsoft does not make any warranties or representations as to third party products.

USING THE COMPANION CD

The CD included with this book contains all sample programs discussed in the book, Microsoft Internet Explorer 5, third-party software, and an electronic version of the book. You can find the sample programs in the Example Code folder.

To use this companion CD, insert it into your CD-ROM drive. If AutoRun is not enabled on your computer, run StartCD.exe in the root folder to display the Start menu.

Installing the Sample Programs

You can view the samples from the companion CD, or you can install them onto your hard disk and use them to create your own applications.

Installing the sample programs requires approximately 162 KB of disk space. To install the sample programs, insert the companion CD into your CD-ROM drive and run Setup.exe in the Setup folder. Some of the sample programs require that the full version of Internet Explorer 5 be installed to work properly. If your computer doesn't have Internet Explorer 5 installed, run ie5setup.exe in the MSIE5 folder to install Internet Explorer 5. If you have trouble running any of the sample files, refer to the Readme.txt file in the root directory of the companion CD or to the text in the book that describes the sample program.

You can uninstall the samples by selecting Add/Remove Programs from the Microsoft Windows Control Panel, selecting Developing XML Solutions Example Code, and clicking the Add/Remove button.

Electronic Version of the Book

The complete text of *Developing XML Solutions* has been included on the companion CD as a fully searchable electronic book. To view the electronic book, you must have a system running Microsoft Windows 95, Microsoft Windows 98, Microsoft Windows NT 4 Service Pack 3 (or later), or Microsoft Windows 2000. You must also have Microsoft Internet Explorer 4.01 or later and the latest HTML Help components installed on your system. If you don't have Internet Explorer 4.01 or later, the setup wizard will offer to install a light version of Internet Explorer 5, which is located in the Ebook folder. The Internet Explorer setup has been configured to install the minimum files necessary and won't change your current settings or associations.

System Requirements

The XML samples in this book can be run using a computer that has at least the following system requirements.

- 486 or higher processor
- Windows 95, Windows 98, Windows NT 4.0, or Windows 2000
- Visual Basic 6 (If you want to perform the Visual Basic examples in the book, you will need to have this installed on your computer.)

MICROSOFT PRESS SUPPORT INFORMATION

Every effort has been made to ensure the accuracy of this book and the contents of the companion CD. Microsoft Press provides corrections for books through the World Wide Web at the following address: *http://mspress.microsoft.com/support/*.

If you have comments, questions, or ideas regarding this book or the companion CD, please send them to Microsoft Press using either of the following methods:

Postal Mail:
Microsoft Press
Attn: Developing XML Solutions Editor
One Microsoft Way
Redmond, WA 98052-6399
E-mail:
MSPINPUT@MICROSOFT.COM

Please note that product support is not offered through these addresses.

Part I

Introducing XML

Chapter 1

XML Within the Enterprise

The last four decades of the twentieth century witnessed the birth of the Computer Age. Computers have become an essential tool for nearly every corporate worker. Personal computers are now found in over 50 percent of U.S. households, and with this proliferation has come the explosion of the Internet. The Internet has not only changed the way consumers gather information and make their purchases, but it has also completely changed the way corporations must do business.

Today corporations must be able to respond quickly to market pressures and must be able to analyze large quantities of data to make appropriate decisions. To be of any use to the corporation, this data must be accurate, relevant, and available immediately. As we will see in this chapter, a *Digital Nervous System (DNS)* will provide the corporation with a computer and software infrastructure that will provide accurate, relevant data in a timely manner. One of the most important elements of the DNS is the movement of data. In many circumstances, the ideal way to move this data will be in *Extensible Markup Language (XML)* format.

XML can be used to create text documents that contain data in a structured format. In addition to the data, you can include a detailed set of rules that define the structure of the data. The author of the XML document defines these rules. For example, you could create a set of rules that can be used for validating Microsoft Exchange e-mail documents, Microsoft SQL Server databases, Microsoft Word documents, or any type of data that exists within the corporation.

An industry initiative called *BizTalk,* which was started by Microsoft and supported by many other organizations such as CommerceOne and Boeing, provides a standard set of rules that are agreed upon by different corporate communities and individual corporations. These rules are stored in a central repository and can be used to build standardized XML messages that can be sent between applications within the corporation and to applications belonging to the corporation's partners. Both large and small corporations can benefit from using these XML messages because it allows them to do business with a wider range of partners.

XML can do a great deal more than just move data. Data can be included in an XML document and then an *Extensible Stylesheet Language (XSL)* page can be used with the XML document to present the data in Microsoft Internet Explorer 5 (and hopefully other Web browsers in the near future). Using an XML document and an XSL page allows Web developers to separate data and presentation. Chapter 2 will examine why this technique is essential for corporate Web development.

Another initiative, the *Simple Object Access Protocol (SOAP),* enables you to use XML to call methods on a remote computer on the Internet, even through a firewall. The SOAP initiative is being developed by Developmentor, Microsoft, and others. For more information on SOAP, visit *http://www.develop.com/soap/.*

BizTalk, Internet Explorer 5, and SOAP address three of the most important issues facing corporations today:

■ Creating standardized messages that can be moved inside and outside the corporation (BizTalk)

■ Separating data and presentation when building Web pages (Internet Explorer 5)

■ Calling methods through firewalls and between different platforms (SOAP)

The focus of this book will be on the features of XML and how it can be used to address these three issues.

KNOWLEDGE WORKERS

A DNS is built to deliver information to the workers that require this information to perform their jobs. These *knowledge workers* focus on using information to make decisions for the corporation. Ideally, over the next decade most workers in the corporation should become knowledge workers as computers take over mundane, repetitious tasks.

Knowledge workers can be any of the following:

■ Managers who review data to make corporate decisions

■ Analysts who create detailed reports of the health of the corporation

- Workers who take orders and assist the customer in choosing a product

- Workers who create documents that contain information valuable to the corporation, such as project design documents, project schedules, and e-mail documents

To be able to do their jobs, these knowledge workers will need to access the vast quantity of information stored on the computers inside and outside the corporation. For the most part, this information will be accessed by workers through the intranet or Internet, creating a Web workstyle. During the first decade of the twenty-first century, we will see a major revolution: corporations will build DNS's to overcome the challenges of managing, sharing, and using information important to the knowledge worker.

DNS CORPORATE MODEL

The DNS supports and connects the four functions of a corporation:

- **Basic operations**   Basic operations include accounting, order entry, purchasing, inventory, human resources, and so on. The majority of the applications in the corporation are built to maintain and promote the basic operations.

- **Strategic thinking**   Strategic thinking centers on long-term profit, growth forecasts, marketing strategies, analysis of sales, business direction, vision and scope of projects that will create the DNS, and so on.

- **Customer interaction**   Customer interaction involves anything that has to do with how the corporation interfaces with the customer, including customer feedback, analysis of customer satisfaction, and so on.

- **Business reflexes**   Business reflexes determine how quickly a corporation can respond to bad news and correct the situation. Production or inventory shortfalls or overruns, downturn in a market, failure to reach projected goals, and so on must all reach the appropriate knowledge worker quickly.

The DNS is at the center of the corporate functions; all information can flow through the DNS. The most difficult part of creating this system is providing a means to pass messages through the DNS. As has been discussed previously, and will be discussed throughout this book, the means for the most part is XML.

The DNS vision is that digital storage, retrieval, and delivery of information will radically improve the efficiency, effectiveness, and responsiveness of corporations that use it correctly. The role of the DNS in linking these corporate functions is illustrated in Figure 1-1.

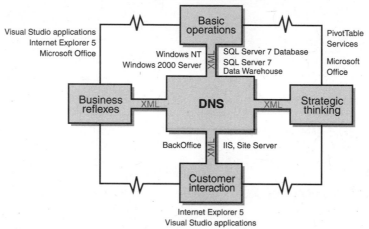

Figure 1-1. *Microsoft products that support the four corporate functions and the DNS.*

As the figure illustrates, each of the corporate functions and the DNS are supported by Microsoft products. The heart of the DNS is Microsoft's server products: Microsoft BackOffice, SQL Server 7, Internet Information Services, Site Server, Microsoft Windows NT, and so on. All of the functions of the enterprise will be able to connect to these server products through the DNS.

Site Server will eventually be replaced by Business Server. You could also include Microsoft SNA Server as part of the DNS if you need to connect to mainframe systems. The upgrades of SNA Server, which will be released soon, and Business Server will both be XML based. The new versions of IIS and SQL Server 7.5 will also have added XML functionality. Thus, XML will become a critical element in every part of the DNS.

GOALS OF A DNS

Let's take a more detailed look at the DNS itself. The primary goal of the DNS is to provide business-critical information to the right place at the right time. To accomplish this, the DNS will have to perform the following tasks:

- Provide scalability
- Enable creation of Microsoft Windows Distributed interNet Application Architecture (DNA) systems
- Facilitate Internet use
- Create corporate memory

- Eliminate paper forms
- Allow self-service applications, which will enable users to perform tasks independently
- Capture customer feedback
- Provide business partner communication
- Respond to crises

All of these topics will be discussed in detail in the sections that follow.

Provide Scalability

One of the basic realities of our time is that everything changes very quickly. A system that needs to support only 10,000 users today might have to support 100,000 users tomorrow. Scalability must be built into every DNS and is one of the most important elements in creating an effective DNS. Scalability can be created through either hardware or software solutions. We'll look briefly here at hardware solutions, but this chapter, and this book as a whole, will focus on software solutions.

Hardware solutions

Intel and Microsoft are developing products that support a much higher capacity by using faster processors, more memory, more clustered computers, and multiple processors. Ultimately, Microsoft's vision is to create scalable computing using clusters of smaller computers that cooperate via software. These clusters will provide redundancy and scalability and will offer an alternative to monolithic mainframes. With the release of Windows 2000, PCs with 32 processors connected in a cluster consisting of up to four PCs should become a possibility.

Software solutions

Windows DNA provides a framework for designing, building, and reusing software components to build a DNS. Large, distributed systems can be built using the Windows DNA framework. These Windows DNA systems are distributed because they can have components that are located anywhere in the enterprise—that is, on the client machine; on a Web, database, or middle-tier server; on a mainframe computer; or on any computer within the enterprise.

The XML extensions proposed in BizTalk are being developed to overcome some of the barriers that currently exist with *extranets*. Extranets are networks created by connecting computer systems from two different corporations. Usually, the two corporations are corporate partners. Using BizTalk, information can flow in a standardized format through the extranet.

The XML extensions proposed in SOAP are being developed to solve the problems of communication between platforms (UNIX, Windows, and so on). SOAP also addresses the difficulty of calling methods through a firewall by using XML and Hypertext Transfer Protocol (HTTP) to pass messages to methods behind a firewall.

The combination of XML and the Internet will allow the actual physical locations of the different elements of a Windows DNA system to span the entire globe. The Windows DNA systems that use the Internet and XML will be capable of moving messages across international boundaries inside and outside the corporations of the world.

These Windows DNA systems can be created using Component Object Model (COM) components, such as those built from Microsoft Visual Studio in C++, Microsoft Visual Basic, or Java; ASP pages; and Web browsers such as Internet Explorer 5. They will be supported by the full range of Microsoft's software, including BackOffice, Office, Exchange Server, Site Server, SQL Server 7, and so on. Essentially, Microsoft provides all of the support and development products to create a customized enterprise solution that meets the specific needs of any corporation.

Enable Creation of Microsoft Windows DNA Systems

A Windows DNA system cannot be built without careful foresight and planning. For the system to work properly, you will need to be sure that all of the components of the system can work together. Many of the components in the system will depend on other components to perform services for them. Each component can have *methods* and *properties* associated with it. The methods are the services the component performs, and the properties are the attributes of the component.

For example, suppose we have a component named DataServices. The DataServices component communicates directly with the database and performs all of the Create, Read, Update, and Delete (CRUD) services with the database. The DataServices component will have the following methods: *Create*, *Read*, *Update*, and *Delete*. Another component, called the UserServices component, will interact with the user. The UserServices component will allow the user to review, update, add, and delete records from the database through the DataServices component.

Tightly bound systems

Currently, the usual way to create a system of interdependent components is to design all of the components together and have one component call the methods and properties of another component directly. In our example, the user would request a service from the UserServices component and the UserServices component would make a direct request to the DataServices component to actually perform this service. Figure 1-2 illustrates this process for a request to update a record.

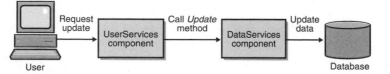

Figure 1-2. *Request to update a record in a tightly bound system.*

As you can see, the UserServices component will be coded such that it will call the *Update* method in the DataServices component. If you change the *Update* method, you will also have to change the code within the UserServices component. This is called a *tightly bound system,* meaning that components in the system are directly dependent on other components in the system.

This type of system requires you to design all of its components at the same time. You can build the UserServices component first, but you'll need to know what methods the DataServices component will have—in other words, you will need to design the DataServices component at the same time as the UserServices component. When you are creating a Windows DNA system, which spans an entire enterprise that consists of hundreds of components, the task of designing all of the components at the same time can become nearly impossible. Add to this the capability of communicating with components outside the system through extranets, and you may now have a system that cannot be built using tightly bound components.

Corporations usually have many existing tightly bound systems. These systems do not always need to be replaced, but might need to be upgraded with newer components that can communicate with the older components. Tightly bound components can be appropriate in systems that have few components. XML can be used to build or augment tightly bound systems by using SOAP. Using SOAP, one component can call the methods or set the properties of another component using XML and HTTP.

Loosely bound systems

To solve the problems of the tightly bound system, we must do some rethinking. We need to allow components to request services without knowing in advance which component will actually perform that service—in other words, we need to create a loosely bound system.

A request for a service can be considered as a message. When a component requests a service, it sends a message to another component specifying what it wants the other component to do. A request for a service can also contain additional information that is required to perform the service (such as the ID of the record that is about to be updated and the updated values for the record).

To request a service in a loosely bound system, a component packages the request in a message that is passed to a messaging component. The messaging component will then be responsible for determining the message type and identifying which component will provide the services associated with the message. Our update request will now look like the one shown in Figure 1-3 on the following page.

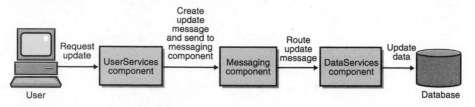

Figure 1-3. *Request to update a record in a loosely bound system.*

In the loosely bound system, the UserServices component does not need any information about the DataServices component; it needs to know only the format of the update message. The DataServices component, including its interface, can be completely and repeatedly rewritten, and nothing will have to change in the UserServices component as long as the DataServices component still works with the same message format.

Building on this example, suppose we have two corporations: Corporation A and its partner, Corporation B. As you can see in Figure 1-3, it's quite possible that the UserServices component is running in Corporation A and the DataServices component is running in Corporation B. Neither corporation has to be concerned about using the same platforms or the same types of components or about any of the details of the components running in the other corporation. As long as both corporations can agree on a standard format for messages, they will be able to request services on each other's systems. BizTalk is all about creating these standard formats for messages used in business-to-business (B2B) communications. Thus, BizTalk will allow the creation of large Windows DNA systems that support both the internal DNS for the corporation's knowledge workers and the extranet for the corporate partners.

Facilitate Internet Use

The Internet has changed everything. It has become a way of doing business for nearly every corporation. The number of people surfing the Internet has reached epic proportions. The use of the Internet to do research, make purchases, download software, and so on has created a new Web lifestyle.

Corporations will need to do more than simply throw together a corporate Web site. Consumers and business partners expect sophisticated, easy-to-use sites that fulfill their needs. The Internet creates entirely new markets and allows small and large corporations to compete on an even playing field. This competition can be fierce, as we've seen in the rivalry between corporations such as Amazon.com and Barnes & Noble.

Changes in technology will affect the way Web sites are created and presented. Corporations will need to develop sites that reflect current trends and technology or they might lose their business to competitors. The backbone of a successful DNS will be an intranet or the Internet or both. XML can be used to move data over the Internet using the HTTP protocol. Using SOAP, HTTP can also be used to invoke methods.

Create Corporate Memory

Corporate memory refers to how well the corporation as a whole learns from previous problems and the associated solutions. The creation of corporate memory will require documentation, storage, organization, and retrieval of these solutions so that any member of the corporation can share this knowledge and not have to "reinvent the wheel."

Ideally, a manager should be able to locate and access the correct information he or she needs to make business decisions within one minute—this is called the one-minute manager. It might not be possible to achieve this level of performance at the present time, but it should be the goal for the Windows DNA systems being designed today.

XML can be used to translate data into a standard format and move it through the corporation using the DNS. A standard format will allow a diverse range of information formats, from e-mail documents to database fields, to be treated as a single entity.

Eliminate Paper Forms

As you know, using paper forms rather than electronic media to store and analyze corporate information is inefficient. Electronic storage of corporate information allows that information to be searched efficiently and shared across the enterprise. In addition, using electronic data entry allows information to be packaged in XML format and transported inside and outside the enterprise. Ideally, any form should be able to be completed within about three minutes. This is called the "soft-boiled egg" rule.

Allow Self-Service Applications

In many corporations, a great deal of personnel resources are used to respond to routine requests such as order status, simple help questions, employee information, and so on. An essential part of the DNS is providing Internet and intranet sites that allow users to perform these services without the help of corporate personnel. Well-designed sites allow the user to access information quickly and easily, and allow workers to focus on dealing with only the more critical issues. XML can be used to package and deliver the information to and from the user.

Capture Customer Feedback

A corporation's marketing department requires detailed information about the corporation's customers. Normally, surveys, sales analyses, and third-party marketing results are used to gather information about current and future customers. Today's technology allows an in-depth analysis of customer usage of Web sites that can provide detailed information about buying practices, customer needs, the success of sales promotions, and so on. In addition, users can provide direct feedback by being allowed to customize the way they navigate the Web site or through survey forms. The information obtained from these forms can be formatted using XML into a standard BizTalk format for analysis by the corporation's marketing department.

Creating Web sites is an iterative process. Every new iteration is based on careful analysis of previous iterations. In this way, Web sites and the corporation's definition of the needs of its customers are constantly refined and updated as the customers' needs change and technology evolves.

Provide Business Partner Communication

Extranets provide a powerful means of sharing information among business partners. Critical information that must be shared between corporate partners can pass easily through a DNS that spans corporate boundaries. XML and BizTalk provide a workable solution that can allow this transfer of messages.

The creation of advanced real-time business transactions that can be transmitted across extranets using XML will allow for just-in-time (JIT) delivery of goods between suppliers and consumers.

Respond to Crises

The quick flow of critical business information to the knowledge workers capable of making crucial decisions will be essential for the success of any corporation. An event-driven DNS provides the conduit through which business events are published to the DNS; those interested in certain types of events subscribe to them and are automatically notified. Once again, XML can be used to package the messages that are published.

Chapter 2

Markup Languages

As you saw in Chapter 1, XML is becoming an essential part of the corporate Digital Nervous System (DNS). Microsoft's focus is on using XML to accomplish three goals: creating messages in a standard format (using BizTalk), separating data and presentation when building Web pages (using Microsoft Internet Explorer 5), and calling methods through firewalls and between different platforms (using the Simple Object Access Protocol [SOAP]). In this chapter, we will look at some of the reasons XML is better suited to accomplish these goals than other markup language options, such as Hypertext Markup Language (HTML) or Standard Generalized Markup Language (SGML).

A *markup language* uses special notation to mark the different sections of a document. In HTML documents, for example, angle brackets (<>) are used to mark the different sections of text. In other kinds of documents, you can have comma-delineated text, in which commas are used as special characters. You can even use binary code to mark up the text, as could be done in a Microsoft Office document. For every markup language, software developers can build an application to read documents written in that markup language. Web browsers will read HTML documents and Microsoft Office will read Office documents. Documents written in XML can be read by customized applications using various parsing objects, or they can be combined with Extensible Stylesheet Language (XSL) and presented in a Web browser.

Documents created using a markup language consist of markup characters and text. The markup characters define the way the text should be interpreted by an application reading this document. For example, in HTML *<h1>Introduction</h1>* contains the markup characters *<h1>* and *</h1>* and the text *Introduction*. When read by an application that reads HTML—say, a Web browser—the markup characters tell the application that the text *Introduction* should be displayed using the h1 (heading 1) font.

Thus, when you are using a markup language, you should consider the following three elements:

- The markup language, which defines the markup characters
- The markup document, which uses the markup language and consists of markup characters and text
- The interpreted document, which is a markup document that has been read and interpreted by an application

However, in XML the markup language itself is the only element that is predefined—the designer of an XML document defines the structure of the document and the markup characters. This feature makes XML flexible and allows the data in the interpreted document to be used for a wide variety of purposes. For example, the formatted data in an XML document could be parsed and then displayed to a user, placed in a database, or used by another application.

This chapter focuses on three markup languages: XML, HTML, and SGML. Let's begin with SGML, the parent language of both HTML and XML.

SGML

As mentioned, you can think of a Microsoft Office document as being built from a type of markup language. However, Microsoft Office documents can be read only by Microsoft Office or by an application that can convert a Microsoft Office document. Thus, Microsoft Office documents are not application-independent and can be shared only with people who have Microsoft Office or a converter. Because corporations need to share data with a large number of partners, customers, and different departments within the corporation, they need documents that are application-independent. SGML was designed to meet this need; it is a markup language that is completely independent of any application.

SGML uses a document type definition (DTD) to define the structure of the document. The DTD specifies the elements and attributes that can be used within the document and specifies what characters will be used to mark the text. In SGML, you can use brackets (<>), dashes (-), or any other character to mark up your document as long as the special character is properly defined in the DTD.

SGML has existed for more than a decade and is older than the Web. It is a metalanguage that was created to maintain repositories of structured documentation in an electronic format. As a metalanguage, SGML describes the document structures for other markup languages. SGML is used to define the markup characters and structure for XML. An SGML definition for HTML has also been created. Both HTML and XML can be considered applications of SGML.

SGML is an extremely versatile, powerful language. Unfortunately, these features come with a price: SGML is difficult to use. Training people to use SGML documents and creating applications that read SGML documents requires a great deal of time and energy. Because of these difficulties, SGML is not suited for Web development. The specification for SGML is over 500 pages long, with over 100 pages of annexes. It is a very complex specification designed for large, complex systems—overkill for our three goals of standardized messages, separation of data and presentation, and method calling.

HTML

Nearly every computer user is familiar with HTML. HTML is a fairly simple language that has helped promote the wide usage of the Internet. HTML has come a long way since it was originally designed so that scientists could use hyperlinked text documents to share information. Let us begin by looking at HTML's original version.

Early HTML

In its original conception, HTML was supposed to include elements that could be used to mark information within the HTML document according to meaning. Tags such as <title>, <h1>, <h2>, and so on were created to represent the content of the HTML document.

How the marked text would actually be interpreted and displayed would depend on the Web browser's settings. Theoretically, any two browsers with the same user settings would present the same HTML document in the same way. This flexibility would enable users with special needs or specific preferences to customize their Web browsers to view HTML pages in their preferred format—an especially useful feature for people with impaired vision or who are using older Web browsers.

In this scenario, the HTML developer uses tags based on an HTML standard that are displayed according to the user's preferences. For this to work, it must be based on a standard for HTML. The current Web standard can be found at *http:// www.w3.org*.

Problems with HTML

HTML has proved to be a great language for the initial development of the Internet. As the Internet matures, the need has developed for a language that can be used for more complex and large-scale purposes such as fulfilling corporate functions, and HTML quickly fails to meet the mark. Let's look at some of the problems with HTML.

Conflicting standards

In 1994, Netscape created a set of HTML extensions that worked only in Netscape's Web browser. This was the beginning of the browser wars, and the first casualty was the HTML standard. Using these extensions, Netscape could now allow the author of the HTML document to specify font size, font and background color, and other features. Eventually, Netscape added frames. Of course, all of these extensions would not display properly in any other browser. The HTML extensions were so popular that by 1996 Netscape was the number one browser.

Although Netscape won a major victory, Web developers and users suffered a major loss. In addition to the problem of handling nonstandard extensions, different browsers handle the standard tags in different ways. This means that Web designers now have to create different versions of the same HTML document for different Web browsers. The extensions force users to accept pages that are formatted according to the author's wishes.

> **NOTE**   In most browsers, you can create default settings that will override the settings in the HTML pages. Unfortunately, most users do not know how to use these settings, and if you do set your own defaults, most pages will not display correctly.

Creating HTML documents that will appear approximately the same in all browsers is a difficult, and at times impossible, task. For information about this topic, see the Web Standards Project at *http://www.webstandards.org*.

> **NOTE**   It is beyond the scope of this book to go into the details of HTML standardization, but the Web Standards Project site will provide you with the information and resources you need.

No international support

The Internet has created a global community and made the world a much smaller place. Corporations are expanding their businesses into this global marketplace, and they are extending their partners and corporations around the globe, linking everything through the Internet. A few proposals to create an international HTML standard have been put forward, but no standard has actually materialized. There are no HTML tags that can identify what language an HTML document is written in.

Inadequate linking system

When you create HTML documents, links are hard-coded into the document. If a link changes, the Web developer must search through all the HTML documents to find all references to the link and then update them. With Web sites that are dynamic and constantly evolving and growing to meet the needs of the users, this lack of a linking system can create substantial problems. We need a much more sophisticated method of linking documents than can be provided by HTML. HTML does not allow you to associate links to any element, nor does it allow you to link to multiple locations, whereas the linking system in XML does provide these features. In Chapter 6, you will learn more about XML's linking capability.

Faulty structure and data storage

HTML does have a structure, but this structure is not extremely rigid. For example, you can place heading 3 (<h3>) tags before heading 1 (<h1>) tags. Within the <body> tag, you can place any legitimate tag anywhere you want. You can validate HTML documents, but this validation only confirms that you have used the tags properly. Even worse, if you leave off end tags, the browser will try to figure out where the end tags should be and add them in. Thus, you can create HTML code that is not properly written but will still be interpreted properly by the browser.

Another problem arises if you try to put data into an HTML document. You will find it very difficult to do so. For example, suppose we are trying to put information from a database into an HTML document. We have a database table named Customer with the following fields: *customerID*, *customerName*, and *customerAddress*. When we create an HTML document with this data, every customer should have a *customerID* and a *customerName* value. The *customerAddress* value is optional. We could present this data in HTML in a table, as follows:

```
<body>

<table border="1" width="100%">
    <tr>
        <th width="33%">Name</th>
        <th width="33%">Address</th>
        <th width="34%">ID</th>
    </tr>
    <tr>
        <td width="33%">John Smith</td>
        <td width="33%">125 Main St. Anytown NY 10001</td>
        <td width="34%">001</td>
    </tr>
```

(continued)

```
<tr>
    <td width="33%">Jane Doe</td>
    <td width="33%">2 Main St. Anytown NY 10001</td>
    <td width="34%">002</td>
</tr>
<tr>
    <td width="33%">Mark Jones</td>
    <td width="33%">35 Main St. Anytown NY 10001</td>
    <td width="34%"></td>
</tr>
</table>
</body>
```

In a browser, this table would appear as shown in Figure 2-1.

Name	Address	ID
John Smith	125 Main St. Anytown NY 10001	001
Jane Doe	2 Main St. Anytown NY 10001	002
Mark Jones	35 Main St. Anytown NY 10001	

Figure 2-1. *Database table created using HTML.*

This document is completely valid HTML code. There are no errors in the HTML code for the table; it is syntactically correct. Yet in terms of the validity of the data, the information is invalid. The third entry, Mark Jones, is missing an ID. Although it is possible to write applications that perform data validation on HTML documents, such applications are complex and inefficient. HTML was never designed for data validation.

HTML was also not designed to store data. The table is the most common way of both presenting and storing data in HTML. You can use <div> tags to create more complex structures to store data, but once again you are left with the task of writing your own data validation code.

What we need instead is something that enables us to put the data in a structured format that can be automatically validated for syntactical correctness and proper content structure. Ideally, the author of the document will want to define both the format of the document and the correct structure of the data. As you will see in Chapters 4 and 5, this is exactly what XML and DTDs do.

XML

In 1996, the World Wide Web Consortium (W3C) began to develop a new standard markup language that would be simpler to use than SGML but with a more rigid structure than HTML. The W3C established the XML Working Group (XWG) to begin the process of creating XML.

Goals of XML

The goals of XML as given in the version 1.0 specification (*http://www.w3.org/TR/WD-xml-lang#sec1.1*) are listed here, followed by a description of how well these have been implemented in the current XML standard:

- **XML shall be straightforwardly usable over the Internet.** Currently, only minimal support for XML is provided in most Web browsers. Internet Explorer 4 and Netscape Navigator 4 both provide minimal support. Internet Explorer 5 provides additional support for XML, which will allow Web developers to use XSL pages to present XML content.

- **XML shall support a wide variety of applications.** With the introduction of BizTalk and SOAP, XML will be used in a wider range of applications. Other applications, such as Lotus Domino, also use XML. Many applications are now available for viewing and editing XML content and DTDs.

- **XML shall be compatible with SGML.** Many SGML applications and SGML standard message formats are currently in existence. By making XML compatible with SGML, many of these SGML applications can be reused. Although the conversion process can be complex, XML is compatible with SGML.

- **It shall be easy to write programs that process XML documents.** For XML to become widely accepted, the applications that process XML documents must be easy to build. If these applications are simple, it will be cost-effective to use XML. The current specification does meet this goal, especially when you use a parser such as the ones provided by Microsoft and IBM.

- **The number of optional features in XML is to be kept to the absolute minimum, ideally zero.** The more optional features, the more difficult it will be to use XML. The more complex a language, the more it costs to develop with it and the less likely anyone will be to use it. The XML standard has met this goal.

- **XML documents should be human-legible and reasonably clear.** Ideally, you should be able to open an XML document in any text editor and determine what the document contains. With a basic understanding of XML, you should be able to read an XML document.

- **The XML design should be prepared quickly.** It is essential that the standard be completed quickly so that XML can be used to solve current problems.

- **The design of XML shall be formal and concise.** It is essential that computer applications be able to read and parse XML. Making the language formal and concise will allow it to be easily interpreted by a computer application. XML can be expressed in Extended Backus-Naur Form (EBNF), which is a notation for describing the syntax of a language. EBNF in turn can be easily parsed by a computer software program. SGML cannot be expressed in EBNF. For more information about EBNF, refer to *http://nwalsh.com/docs/articles/xml/index.html#EBNF*.

- **XML documents shall be easy to create.** Several XML editors are now available that make it easy to create XML documents; these editors will be discussed in Chapter 3. You can also create your own custom XML editor.

- **Terseness in XML markup is of minimal importance.** Making the XML markup extremely concise is less important than keeping the XML standard concise. You could include an entire set of acceptable shortcuts in the standard (as SGML does) and avoid putting them in the markup, but this will make XML much more complex. XML has successfully done this.

These goals are geared toward making XML the ideal medium for creating Web applications. As an added bonus, XML will also be perfect for creating standard messages and passing messages to call methods.

Four specifications define XML and specify how it will achieve these goals:

- The XML specification defines XML syntax. It is available at *http://www.w3.org/TR/WD-xml-lang*.

- The XLL specification defines the Extensible Linking Language. It is available at *http://www.w3.org/TR/xlink*.

- The XSL specification defines Extensible Style Sheets. It is available at *http://www.w3.org/TR/NOTE-XSL.html*.

- The XUA specification defines the XML User Agent. This specification will define an XML standard similar to SOAP; it has not yet been created.

The current XML specification is only 26 pages long—as opposed to several hundred pages for the SGML specification. XML is easy to use and, with BizTalk, can be used to create messages in a standardized format. XML allows you to separate content and presentation using XML documents and XSL pages. Using SOAP, you can package a request for a method on a remote server in an XML document, which can be used by a server to call the method. Thus, XML can fulfill the three basic goals perfectly.

Advantages of XML

The following features of XML make it well suited for the corporate DNS:

- **XML is international.** XML is based on Unicode. Unicode allows for a larger amount of storage space for each character, which in turn makes it possible for Unicode to include characters for foreign alphabets. SGML and HTML are based on ASCII, which does not work well with many foreign languages.

- **XML can be structured.** Using DTDs, XML can be structured so that both the content and syntax can be easily validated. This enhanced structure will enable you to create standardized valid XML documents.

- **XML documents can be built using composition.** Using the more powerful linking methods of XML, documents can be created from a composite of other documents. This enhanced linking system will enable you to create customized documents by selecting only the pieces of other documents you need.

- **XML can be a data container.** XML is ideally suited to be a container for data. Using DTDs, you can efficiently represent almost any data so that it can be read by humans, computer parsers, and applications.

- **XML offers flexibility.** XML allows you either to not use a DTD (a default one will be used) or to define the structure of your document to the smallest detail using a DTD. With a DTD, you can define the exact structure of your document so that both the structure of the data and the content can be easily validated.

- **XML is easy to use.** XML is only slightly more complicated than HTML. As more browsers support XML and more tools are available for working with XML, it is likely that more developers will take advantage of XML.

- **XML has standard formats.** Standard formats for XML documents can be easily produced.

With these advantages, XML can be used to cater to the more complex corporate needs.

SUMMARY

HTML was well suited for the birth of the Internet, but the Internet has become a center for commerce and information and a central focus of business operations, and HTML is no longer capable of meeting its needs. The failure of Internet browsers to meet the HTML standards, the difficulty of validating HTML documents, a poor linking system, and a lack of international support has made HTML a poor choice for the future. SGML is an excellent, powerful tool capable of documenting complex systems, but unfortunately, SGML is far too complex for the current needs of the Internet.

XML is ideally suited for the next generation of Internet applications, for e-commerce, and for the corporate DNS. XML is a simpler, lighter markup language, which is flexible, is easy to use, and can be used for international documents. XML is ideal for storing data and sending messages, and XML documents can be validated.

At the time this book is being written, a large portion of the XML standard is complete, and it's likely to remain the same for some time. The XML 1.0 specification, defining the syntax of the XML language and XML DTDs, is well accepted and is not likely to change in the near future. Other elements of XML are still evolving, including schemas, which are similar to DTDs, and XML Path Language (XPath), which is a replacement for some of the current XML linking mechanisms. Over the next few years, XML will be refined to become an incredibly powerful tool that will create the next evolution of the Internet. This book will present both the current XML standard and a glimpse into the XML, and applications, of the future.

Chapter 3

Structure of an XML Document

The structure of an XML document can be defined by two standards. The first standard is the XML specification, which defines the default rules for building all XML documents. You can see the specification at the following Web site: *http://www.w3.org/TR/1998/ REC-xml-19980210*. Any XML document that meets the basic rules as defined by the XML specification is called a *well-formed XML document*. An XML document can be checked to determine whether it is well formed—that is, whether the document has the correct structure (syntax). For example, one of the rules for a well-formed document is that every XML element must have a begin tag and an end tag. If an element is missing either tag in an XML document, the document is not well formed. Whether an XML document conforms to the XML specification can be easily verified by an XML-compliant computer application such as Microsoft Internet Explorer 5.

The second standard, which is optional, is created by the authors of the document and defined in a document type definition (DTD). When an XML document meets the rules defined in the DTD, it is called a *valid XML document*. A valid XML document can be checked for proper content. For example, suppose you have created an XML DTD that constrains the *body* element to only one instance in the entire document. If the document contained two instances of the *body* element, it would not be valid. Thus, using the DTD and the rules contained in the XML specification, an application can verify that an XML document is valid and well formed. *Schemas* are similar to DTDs, but they use a different format. DTDs and schemas are useful when the content of a group of documents shares a common set of rules. Computer applications can be written that produce documents that are valid according to the DTD and well formed according to the current XML standard.

Many industries are currently writing standard DTDs and schemas. These standards will be used to create XML documents that will share information among the members of the industry. For example, a committee of members from the medical community could determine the essential information for a patient and then use that information to build a patient record DTD. Patient information could be sent from one medical facility to another by writing applications that create messages containing an XML document built according to the patient record DTD. When an XML patient message was received, the patient record DTD would then be used to verify that the patient record was valid—that is, that it contained all of the required information. If the XML patient message was invalid, the message would be sent back to the sending facility for correction. The patient record DTD and schema could be stored in a repository accessible through the Internet, allowing any medical facility to check the validity of incoming XML documents. One of the goals of BizTalk is to create a repository of schemas.

In this chapter, we will begin the process of creating an XML document that can be used to build Internet applications. Ideally, you will want to create an XML document that can be read as an XML document by an XML-compliant browser, as an HTML document using style sheets for non-XML-compliant browsers that understand cascading style sheets (CSS), and as straight HTML for browsers that do not recognize CSS or XML.

We will focus here on the process of creating a well-formed document. We'll review the rules that must be met by a well-formed document and create a well-formed document that can be used to display XML over the Internet in any HTML 4–compliant Web browser. In Chapter 4, you'll learn how to create a DTD for this well-formed document, and in Chapter 5, we will rework the DTD to make it more concise.

BASIC COMPONENTS OF AN XML DOCUMENT

The most basic components of an XML document are *elements, attributes,* and *comments*. To make it easier to understand how these components work in an XML document, we will look at them using Microsoft XML Notepad. XML Notepad is included in the Microsoft Windows DNA XML Resource Kit, which can be found at Microsoft's Web site (*msdn.microsoft.com/vstudio/xml/default.asp*).

Elements

Elements are used to mark up the sections of an XML document. An XML element has the following form:

```
<ElementName>Content</ElementName>
```

The content is contained within the XML tags.

Although XML tags usually enclose content, you can also have elements that have no content, called *empty elements*. In XML, an empty element can be represented as follows:

```
<ElementName/>
```

> **NOTE** The *<ElementName/>* XML notation is sometimes called a *singleton*. In HTML, the empty tag is represented as *<ElementName></ElementName>*.

In a patient record XML document, for example, *PatientName*, *PatientAge*, *PatientIllness*, and *PatientWeight* can all be elements of the XML document, as shown here:

```
<PatientName>John Smith</PatientName>
<PatientAge>108</PatientAge>
<PatientWeight>155</PatientWeight>
```

This *PatientName* element marks the content *John Smith* as the patient's name, *PatientAge* marks the content *108* as the patient's age, and *PatientWeight* marks the content *155* as the patient's weight. Elements provide information about the content in the document and can be used by computer applications to identify each content section. The application can then manipulate the content sections according to the requirements of the application.

In the case of the patient record document, the content sections could be placed into fields for a new record in a patient database or presented to a user in text boxes in a Web browser. The elements will determine what fields or text boxes each content section belongs in—for example, the content marked by the *PatientName* element will go into the PatientName field in the database or in the txtPName text box in the Web browser. Using elements, the presentation, storage, and transfer of data can be automated.

Nesting elements

Elements can be nested. For example, if you wanted to group all the patient information under a single *Patient* element, you might want to rewrite the patient record example as follows:

```
<Patient>
    <PatientName>John Smith</PatientName>
    <PatientAge>108</PatientAge>
    <PatientWeight>155</PatientWeight>
</Patient>
```

When nesting elements, you must not overlap tags. The following construction would not be well formed because the </Patient> end tag appears between the tags of one of its nested elements:

```
<Patient>
    <PatientName>John Smith</PatientName>
    <PatientAge>108</PatientAge>
    <PatientWeight>155</Patient>
</PatientWeight>
```

Thus XML elements can contain other elements. However, the elements must be strictly nested: each start tag must have a corresponding end tag.

Naming conventions

Element names must conform to the following rules:

■ Names consist of one or more nonspace characters. If a name has only one character, that character must be a letter, either uppercase (A–Z) or lowercase (a–z).

■ A name can only begin with a letter or an underscore.

■ Beyond the first character, any character can be used, including those defined in the Unicode standard (*http://www.unicode.org/*).

■ Element names are case sensitive; thus, *PatientName*, *PATIENTNAME*, and *patientname* are considered different elements.

For example, the following element names are well formed:

```
Fred
_Fred
Fredd123
FredGruß
```

These element names would not be considered well formed:

```
Fred 123
-Fred
123
```

Here the first element name contains a space, the second begins with a dash, and the third begins with a numeral instead of a letter or an underscore.

Attributes

An attribute is a mechanism for adding descriptive information to an element. For example, in our patient record XML document, we have no idea whether the patient's weight is measured in pounds or kilograms. To indicate that *PatientWeight* is given in pounds, we would add a *unit* attribute and specify its value as *LB*:

```
<PatientWeight unit="LB">155</PatientWeight>
```

Attributes can be included only in the begin tag, and like elements they are case-sensitive. Attribute values must be enclosed in double quotation marks (").

Attributes can be used with empty elements, as in the following well-formed example:

```
<PatientWeight unit="LB"/>
```

In this case, this might mean that the patient weight is unknown or it has not yet been entered into the system.

An attribute can be declared only once in an element. Thus, the following element would not be well formed:

```
<PatientWeight unit="LB" unit="KG">155</PatientWeight>
```

This makes sense because the weight cannot be both kilograms and pounds.

Comments

Comments are descriptions embedded in an XML document to provide additional information about the document. Comments in XML use the same syntax as HTML comments and are formatted so that they are ignored by the application processing the document, as shown here:

```
<!-- Comment text -->
```

UNDERSTANDING HTML BASICS

Before we begin using the basic components of an XML document to create Web applications, we must cover some basics of HTML documents. Unlike XML, HTML markup does not always define content within the markup. For example, HTML includes a set of tags that do not contain anything, such as <hr>, <img>, and <br>. These elements do not have end tags in HTML; if you include end tags with these elements, the Web browser will ignore them.

Logical and Physical HTML Elements

For the most part, elements and attributes in HTML can be divided into two groups: *physical* and *logical*. A logical HTML element or attribute is similar to an XML element. Logical elements and attributes describe the format of the content enclosed within the tags. For example, here the text *Hello, world* should be displayed with a font size of 3:

```
<font size="3">Hello, world</font>
```

The actual size of the font will depend on the browser settings and the user's preferences. With logical elements, the Web browser will use the markup elements and attributes to identify what the content is and then display the content accordingly.

Physical elements and attributes do not give the user any options as to how content is displayed—they define exactly what the content will look like. Rewriting our font size example using a physical attribute, we have:

```
<font size="12 pt">Hello, world</font>
```

The *Hello, world* text will now always be displayed in 12 point type, regardless of the user's preferences. The attribute no longer defines the content as being of a certain format that the application will interpret; it simply sets the attribute to a value that the application will use.

When you develop XML applications, you will want to define elements and attributes that give the user more control, such as logical HTML elements and attributes. These elements and attributes will be used by the application to identify the content contained within the element. Once the application understands what the content is, it can determine how to use the content based on user preferences (for example, setting the default size 3 text to 14 point text in the browser), the structure of the database (for example, in one corporation a customer's last and first names might be saved as a single entity called *CustomerName*, and in another corporation the same information might be saved as *LName* and *FName*), and so on. As we create Web applications using XML throughout this book, we will use logical elements and attributes whenever possible.

The main problem we will have with building Web applications using XML is that most people are working with browsers that only understand HTML. We'll need some way to get the non-XML browsers to view XML code as HTML code so that the pages will render properly in the browser. When cascading style sheets (CSS) were introduced, they also faced the same problem: how to render documents properly in non-CSS browsers. The ingenious solution that was used for CSS documents can also be used for XML. Let's take a look at how CSS can work in both browsers that understand style sheets and browsers that do not.

CSS and Non-CSS Browsers

When the CSS standard was created, a great number of people were still using browsers that did not support style sheets (many still are). Web developers need to be able to create Web applications using style sheets for the new browsers and yet still have these applications present properly in browsers that do not support style sheets.

This might sound like an impossible task, but it is actually quite simple. Web browsers will ignore any tag or attribute they do not recognize. Thus, you could put the following tag in your HTML code without causing any errors:

```
<Jake>This is my tag</Jake>
```

The browser will ignore the <Jake> tag and output *This is my tag* to the browser. Taking advantage of this browser characteristic is the key to using style sheets.

A style sheet is a document that defines what the elements in the document will look like. For example, we can define the <h1> tag as displaying the normal font at 150 percent of the default *h1* size, as shown here:

```
<style>
    h1 {font: normal 150%}
</style>
```

> **NOTE** The style definitions do not have to be contained in a separate document; you can place the style definitions in the same document as the HTML code that will use these definitions. To support both CSS browsers and non-CSS browsers, it's recommended that the style sheet be referred to as a separate document.

In browsers that support style sheets, this definition will display all content within <h1> tags in the document in the normal font at 150 percent of the default *h1* size. If the style definition is saved in a document named MyStyle.css, you can use this style in your HTML page by including the following line of code:

```
<link rel=MyStyle.css>
```

Browsers that do not support style sheets will not know what the <link> tag is, nor will they know what the *rel* attribute is. These browsers will simply ignore the <link> tag and use the default settings associated with the *h1* element. Browsers that do support style sheets will recognize the tag, access and read the style sheet, and present the *h1* elements as defined in the style sheet (unless the style definition is overridden locally in the HTML page).

A detailed discussion of style sheets is beyond the scope of this book. The specification for the latest version for CSS can be found at *http://www.w3.org/TR/REC-CSS2/*. You can use style sheets to do much more than simply override the standard HTML tags.

XMLizing HTML Code

To "XMLize" your HTML code, that is to convert HTML to XML, you will begin by creating a Web document using XML elements that will default to standard HTML tags. To do this, you will have to close all HTML tags. For example, if you use the tag <br> that does not have an end tag in the document, you will have to add one, as shown here:

```
<br></br>
```

Because the Web browser does not know what the </br> tag is, it will ignore it. You could not use the following empty element XML notation, however, because non-XML browsers would not be able to identify the tag:

```
<br/>
```

Adding end tags is one of several tasks that will need to be performed to create a well-formed document—in other words, the first step in XMLizing your HTML is to make the document well formed.

HTML Quirks

HTML contains many features that can make it a difficult language to use. For example, the following code would work but probably would not give you the results you wanted:

```
<h1>Hello, world
<p>How are you today?</p>
```

The missing end tag </h1> is added implicitly at the end of the document, meaning that both lines would be presented in the *h1* style, not just the first line. Another problem with HTML is that there is no easy way to create an application to validate HTML documents to find errors such as the one shown above.

Keeping your document well formed will help prevent these types of problems. When you create a document, you will need to make sure that tags are positioned correctly so that you get the results you want. With these HTML basics in mind, you are ready to build an XML Web application using XML Notepad.

BUILDING AN XML WEB DOCUMENT TEMPLATE

The information needed to create a complete XML document that will work in an XML-compliant browser such as Internet Explorer 5 is presented over the course of several chapters in this book. We will begin in this chapter by building a well-formed XML document that will always default to standard HTML. Any browser can read this document. We will use XML Notepad to create an XML Web document using a simple user interface.

Using XML Notepad

XML Notepad enables us to focus on working with elements, attributes, and comments and to properly position them in the document structure. XML Notepad will handle the complexities of writing the XML document in a well-formed manner. In the section "The Final XML Document" later in this chapter, you'll find a review of the code created by XML Notepad. To create the initial document structure, follow these steps:

1. To open XML Notepad, choose Program Files from the Start menu, and then choose Microsoft XML Notepad.

2. XML Notepad will be displayed with a *root element,* which will contain all the other elements of the XML document. Every XML document must have a single root element to be well formed. Click on the root element (Root_Element), and rename it *html.*

3. We will create two main child elements for our HTML document, *body* and *head.* Change the name of the default child element (Child_Element) to *head.*

4. To add a second child element, click on *head* and choose Element from the Insert menu. Name the new child element *body*.

Figure 3-1 shows XML Notepad after you've made these changes.

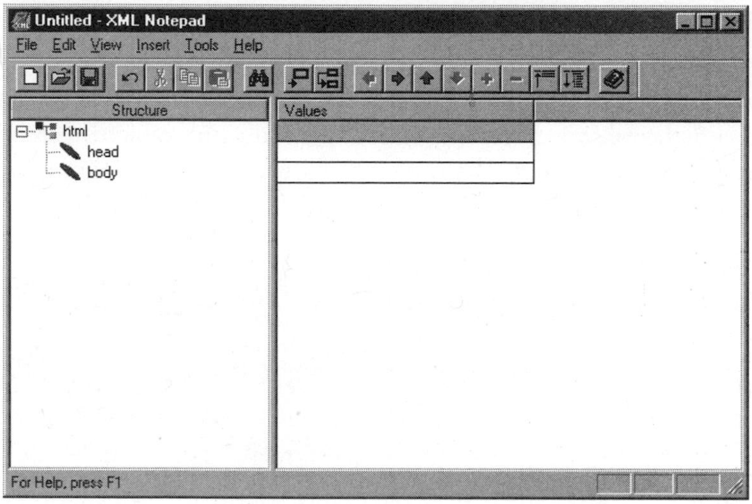

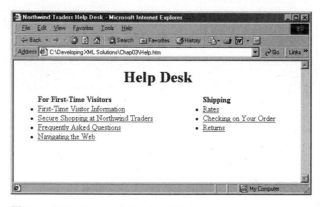

Figure 3-1. *XML Notepad, showing the root element and two child elements.*

In this example, we will build a simple help desk Web page that uses a table to properly place the page elements in the Web browser. The Web page is shown in Figure 3-2.

Figure 3-2. *Sample help desk Web page.*

The table consists of two rows and two columns, for a total of four table cells, as shown in Figure 3-3. Notice that the title spans the two columns in the first row.

Help	Desk
For First-Time Visitors • First-Time Visitor Information • Secure Shopping at Northwind Traders • Frequently Asked Questions • Navigating the Web	**Shipping** • Rates • Checking on Your Order • Returns

Figure 3-3. *The four table cells.*

In the following section, we'll create a generic template for producing Web pages that follow this design. These pages will use tables for formatting text and lists for presenting information.

The *head* Section

To complete the *head* element, follow these steps:

1. To add a child element to the *head* section, click on the *head* element and choose Child Element from the Insert menu. Name the new child element *title*.

2. To add another child element, click on *title* and choose Element from the Insert menu. Name this element *base*.

3. In HTML, the *base* element has an attribute named *target*. The *target* attribute defines the default page to which a link will go when no link is specified in an *a* element. To add an attribute to this element, click on *base* and choose Attribute from the Insert menu. Name the attribute *target*.

   The completed *head* element is shown in Figure 3-4.

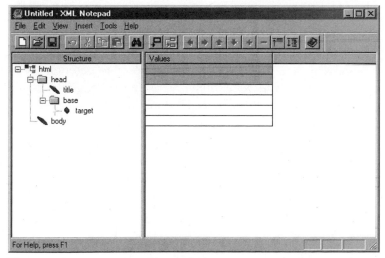

Figure 3-4. *The completed* head *element in XML Notepad.*

4. Choose Source from the View menu to display the source code, shown in Figure 3-5.

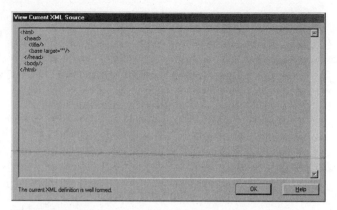

Figure 3-5. *Source code for the completed* head *element.*

As you can see, this source code looks a lot like HTML. This document meets the requirements for a well-formed XML document, but it can also be used as an HTML document with a little work. Three of the elements are empty elements: <title/>, <base target=""/>, and <body/>. XML uses the singleton format to denote an empty element, which is not recognized by HTML. To modify these elements so that HTML Web browsers can read them, they should be written as follows:

```
<title></title>
<base target=""></base>
<body></body>
```

We could leave the *title* and *body* elements as singletons since a Web browser reading this as an HTML document will simply ignore them. However, we don't want a Web browser to ignore the empty *base* element because it has the *target* attribute associated with it. The *base* element is supposed to be empty because it exists only as a container for its *target* attribute. We should change the *base* element to *<base target=""></base>*, but this cannot be done in XML Notepad. If you edit the document in a regular text editor and change this element, XML Notepad will change it back to the singleton when it reads the file.

We can prevent XML Notepad from converting the element back to a singleton by adding a comment to the element. To do so, click on *base* and choose Comment from the Insert menu, and then add the following comment value in the right pane of XML Notepad:

```
Default link for page
```

The source code will now look as follows:

```
<base target=""><!--Default link for page--></base>
```

This added comment solves the empty element problem without having to resort to any ugly hacks.

These problems are caused by the fact that HTML doesn't understand singletons. You will encounter these difficulties when you XMLize currently existing HTML document structures.

The *body* Section

Now that we have completed the *head* section, we can next make the *body* section. The *body* section will contain the information that will be displayed in the browser. To complete the *body* element, follow these steps:

1. Add the following attributes to the *body* element: *text, bgcolor, link, alink,* and *vlink*. Then add the following child elements: *basefont, a,* and *table*.

2. Click on *vlink*, and add the following comment below the attribute:

    ```
    Default display colors for entire body
    ```
    Figure 3-6 shows the modified *body* element.

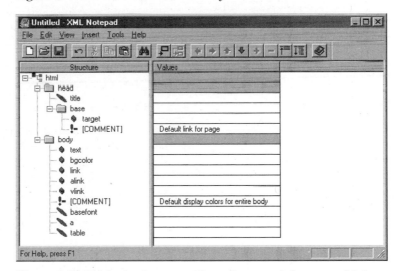

Figure 3-6. *The* body *element, with attributes and elements added.*

Completing the *basefont* element

To complete the *basefont* element, you need to add a size attribute and the following comment:

```
Size is default font size for body; values should be 1 through 7
(3 is usual browser default).
```

Once again, the comment solves the problem of the empty tag.

NOTE   Although we have placed constraints on the possible values for *size*, you will not be able to verify whether the correct values are used unless you create a DTD. You'll learn how to do this in Chapter 4.

Completing the *a* element

This *a* element will act as an anchor for the top of the page. Add the following attributes to the *a* element: *name*, *href*, and *target*, and then add the following comment to the *name* attribute:

```
Anchor for top of page
```

Completing the *table* element

To complete the *table* element, follow these steps:

1. Add the following attributes to the *table* element: *border*, *frame*, *rules*, *width*, *align*, *cellspacing*, and *cellpadding*. Add the following comment below *cellpadding*:

   ```
   Rules/frame is used with border.
   ```

2. Next you will need to add a *tr* child element to the *table* element to create rows for the table. The result is shown in Figure 3-7.

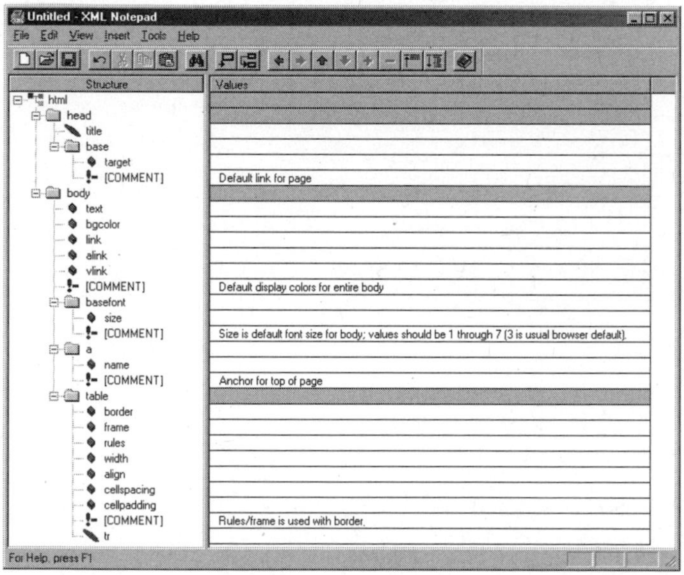

Figure 3-7. *Adding a* tr *element to the* table *element.*

3. Add the following attributes to the *tr* element: *align*, *valign*, and *bgcolor*.

4. Add a *td* child element to the *tr* element. The *td* element represents a table cell. Each cell will contain the content that will go into the Web page.

5. Add the following attributes to the *td* element: *rowspan, colspan, align, valign,* and *bgcolor*. Then add the following comments:

```
Either rowspan or colspan can be used, but not both.
Valign: top, bottom, middle
```

Next we will add a child element to *td* named *CellContent*. *CellContent* is not recognized by HTML, so HTML Web browsers will ignore the tag. We will use *CellContent* to identify the type of information being stored in the cell. This information can be used later by applications to help identify the content in the Web site.

The *CellContent* element will contain a series of tags that can be used as a template to create the content that will go into the cell. To keep things organized, *h1, h2, h3,* and *h4* headers could be used. To keep this example simple, we will use only an *h1* child element. Below each header will be a paragraph. Within the paragraph will be a series of elements that can be arranged as necessary to build the cell.

Completing the *CellContent* element

To complete the *CellContent* element, follow these steps:

1. Add an attribute named *cellname* below the *CellContent* element.

2. Add an *h1* child element to the *CellContent* element, and add an *align* attribute to the *h1* element.

3. Add a *p* child element to the *CellContent* element, and add an *align* attribute to the *p* element. Add the following comments to the *p* element:

```
All of the elements below can be used in any order
within the p element.
You must remove the li elements from ul and ol if they
are not used.
```

4. Add the following child elements to the *p* element: *font, font, img, br, a, ul,* and *ol*. Two *font* elements are needed because one will be used to create sections of text that are marked to be displayed in a different font than the default font and one will be used with the *b* element to display any content within the *b* tags in boldface.

5. Click on *p*, and then choose Text from the Insert menu to create an object that you can use for adding content to the *p* element.

6. In the first *font* element, add the following attributes: *face*, *color*, and *size*. In the second *font* element, add the same attributes and a *b* child element.

7. In the *img* element, add the following attributes: *src*, *border*, *alt*, *width*, *height*, *lowsrc*, *align*, *hspace*, and *vspace*. Add the following comments after *vspace*:

    ```
    Border is thickness in pixels.
    Align = right, left
    ```

    ```
    The hspace and vspace attributes represent padding between
    image and text in pixels.
    ```

8. The *br* element prevents text wrapping around images. Add an attribute to the *br* element named *clear*. Add the following comment after the *clear* attribute:

    ```
    Clear = left, right, all; used to prevent text
    wrapping around an image
    ```

    Figure 3-8 shows what the structure of your XML document should look like at this point.

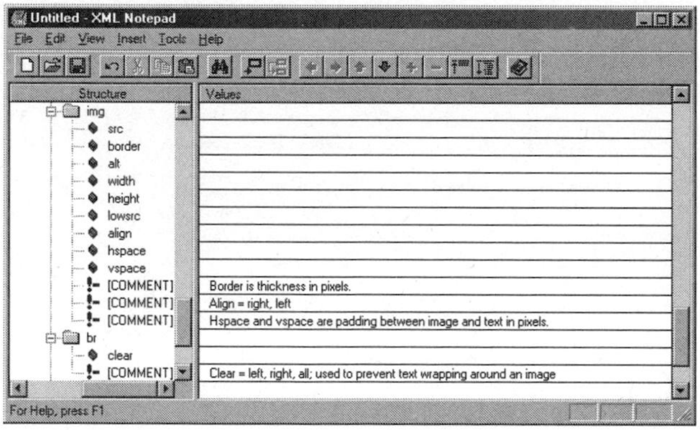

Figure 3-8. *The structure of the* img *and* br *elements.*

9. Add a *type* attribute to the *ul* element, and add the following comment:

    ```
    Type: circle, square, disk
    ```

10. To create text that appears in boldface at the top of the list as a heading, click on the *font* element that contains the *b* element, and choose Copy from the Edit menu. Click on the *ul* element, and then choose Paste from the Edit menu. Next add an *li* child element to the *ul* element. An *li* element represents an item in the list. Copy the *font* element that does not contain the *b* element into the *li* element. Copy the *a* element into the *li* element. Add a text object to the *li* element.

11. Finally, add the following attributes to the *ol* element: *type* and *start*. Add the following comment:

```
Type: A for caps, a for lowercase, I for capital roman
numerals, i for lowercase roman numerals, 1 for numeric
```

12. Copy the *font* element that contains the *b* element from the *p* element into the *ol* element. Copy the *li* element from the *ul* element into the *ol* element.

Figure 3-9 shows the completed *CellContent* element.

Figure 3-9. *XML Notepad, showing the* CellContent *element.*

NOTE Several elements in Figure 3-9, such as the *img* and *br* elements, are collapsed.

You have now created a basic XML template that can be used to build Web pages. In the next section, we will build a Web help page using this XML document.

CREATING A WEB HELP PAGE

You can insert values for elements, text, and attributes in the right pane of the XML Notepad just as you did when you entered values for the comments. Save the document we have just created as Standard.xml. Next choose Save As from the File menu and save the file as Help.htm. You can now begin to add values to the template.

You can also add copies of existing elements if you do not alter the overall structure of the document. For the most part, the structure will be maintained as long as a new element is added at exactly the same level in the tree as the item that was copied. Thus, we could add many copies of the *li* element if all of the new *li* elements are located under a *ul* element or the *ol* element. You could not position an *li* element under any other element without changing the structure of the document.

Adding the Values for the *head* and *body* Elements

Now that we have created the template, we can use it to build a Web document. We can now add content for the elements and values for the attributes. To add values to the *head* and *body* elements, follow these steps:

1. Expand the *body* element, and enter the following value for the *title* element of the *head* element: *Northwind Traders Help Desk.*

2. Next add values for the *body* element attributes as shown in the following table:

Attribute	Value
Text	#000000
Bgcolor	#FFFFFF
Link	#003399
Alink	#FF9933
Vlink	#996633

3. Expand the *a* element and give the *name* attribute a value of *Top*.

4. Enter the values for the *table* element attributes shown in the following table:

Attribute	Value
Border	*0*
Width	*100%*
Cellspacing	*0*
Cellpadding	*0*

Completing the first row

As shown in Figure 3-3, the first row of our sample table contains the title centered on the page. To accomplish this, follow these steps:

1. Expand the *tr* element, and set its *valign* attribute to *Center*. Then expand the *td* element and set its *align* attribute to *Center*.

2. For the *colspan* attribute of the *td* element, enter *2* (meaning that the title will span the two columns).

3. Expand the *CellContent* element, and enter *Table Header* for the *cellname* attribute. Enter *Help Desk* for the value of the *h1* element and *Center* for the value of its *align* attribute.

    Figure 3-10 shows what the document should look like at this point. You can now collapse this *tr* section because we have finished with this row.

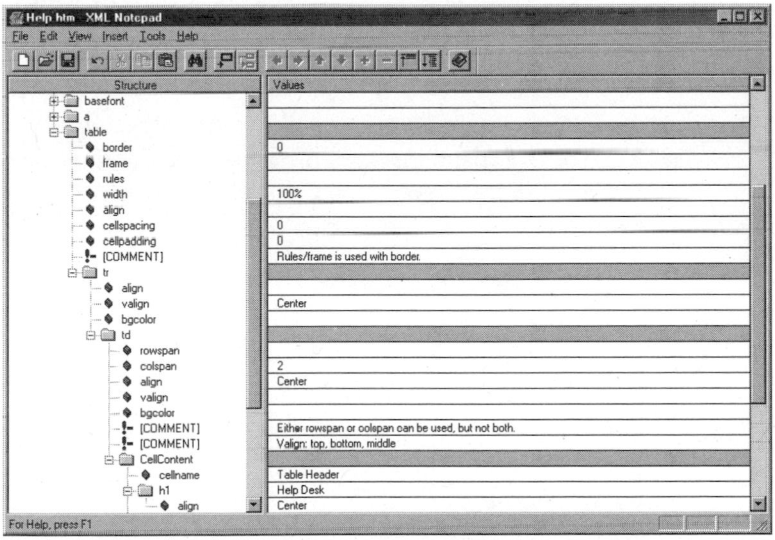

Figure 3-10. *XML Notepad, showing the completed first row.*

Completing the second row

To add a second row, follow these steps:

1. Click on *tr*, and then choose Duplicate Subtree from the Insert menu. This will add another *tr* element, complete with all of its subtrees. Expand the new *tr* element, and set its *valign* attribute to *Top*.

2. We need two cells in the second row to allow two sets of hyperlink lists in two separate columns. To accomplish this, click on the *td* element and choose Duplicate Subtree from the Insert menu to add a second *td* element and all of its subtrees.

3. We'll begin by working with the first *td* element. For the *align* attribute of the first *td* element, enter *Left*. Expand the *CellContent* element, and enter *Help Topic List* for the *cellname* attribute. Expand the *p* element, expand the *ul* element, and then expand the *font* element. Enter *3* for the *size* attribute. For the *b* element, enter *For First-Time Visitors*.

4. Because we want to make hyperlinks to help pages, we will use the *a* element. Expand the *li* element, and then expand the *a* element and enter the value *First-Time Visitor Information*. For the *href* attribute of the *a* element, enter *FirstTimeVisitorInfo.htm*.

5. Click on *li*, and then choose Duplicate Subtree from the Insert menu to add an *li* element and all of its subtrees. Expand the new *li* element, and then expand the *a* element and enter the value *Secure Shopping at Northwind Traders*. For the *href* attribute of this *a* element, enter *SecureShopping.htm*.

6. Click on *li*, and choose Duplicate Subtree from the Insert menu to add a third *li* element. Expand this *li* element, expand the *a* element, and enter the value *Frequently Asked Questions*. Enter the value *FreqAskedQ.htm* for the *href* attribute.

7. Click on *li*, and choose Duplicate Subtree from the Insert menu to add a fourth *li* element. Expand this *li* element, expand the *a* element, and enter the value *Navigating the Web*. Enter the value *NavWeb.htm* for the *href* attribute. Figure 3-11 on the following page shows the document at this point.

8. Expand the second *td* element, and set its *align* attribute to *Left*. Expand the *CellContent* element, and enter the value *Shipping Links* for the *cellname* attribute. Expand the *p*, *ul*, and *font* elements, and enter the value *Shipping* for the *b* element.

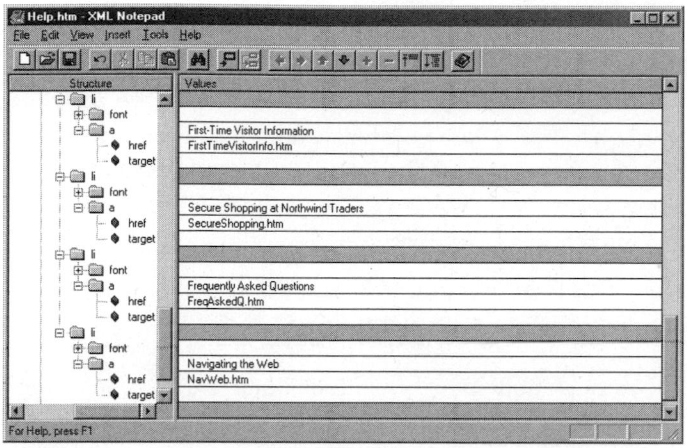

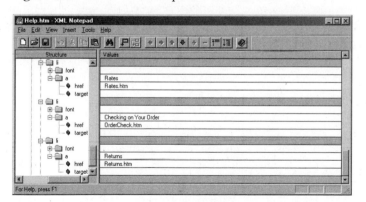

Figure 3-11. *XML Notepad, showing the completed first list.*

9. Expand the *li* element, expand the *a* element, and enter the value *Rates*. Enter the value *Rates.htm* for the *href* attribute.

10. Click on *li*, and choose Duplicate Subtree from the Insert menu to insert a second *li* element. Expand the new *li* element, expand the *a* element, and enter the value *Checking on Your Order*. For the *href* attribute, enter the value *OrderCheck.htm*.

11. Click on *li*, and choose Duplicate Subtree from the Insert menu to insert a third *li* element. Expand the new *li* element, expand the *a* element, and enter the value *Returns*. For the *href* attribute, enter the value *Returns.htm*. Figure 3-12 shows the completed second row.

Figure 3-12. *XML Notepad, showing the completed second list.*

Cleaning Up

Many of the available elements in our template have not been used—for example, we have not used the *ol* elements, several *h1* elements, the *base* element, and so on. There's no need to keep these elements, and some of them will affect the output when the document is viewed as HTML. Go through the template and delete any elements that have not been used. When you have finished, save the document. When you view the document in a Web browser, it should look like Figure 3-2.

WHAT HAVE YOU GAINED?

We've gone through quite a bit of work building this standard template and using it to create a simple Web page. The obvious question is, "Have you gained anything by doing this?" In this section, we'll look at some of the advantages of the standard template.

Manipulating the Content Automatically

Our ultimate goal is to be able to write computer applications that catalog, present, and store content in documents. Ideally, these applications should perform these tasks as an automatic process, without human intervention. You should always be able to create a computer application that automatically processes a well-formed XML document.

Ordinary HTML documents cannot be processed automatically because they are not well formed. It is extremely difficult to create HTML code according to a uniform standard. If you sketch out a design for a Web page and give it to ten different Web developers, it is likely they will create ten documents containing completely different HTML code. Even with a standard, it is likely that the code will still differ.

An automated computer application needs a standard format to work with. If every HTML document can have only a certain set of tags and these tags can appear only in a certain order, you can write an application to process the content. You could define a set of rules and pass them to your developers. In our sample XML template, we used XML and the XML Notepad to define these rules.

These rules could have simply been written in a document, but you would then have no way to verify that the ten developers all built their HTML pages according to the rules. By defining the rules as XML, you can quickly verify whether the document meets the requirements by verifying whether the document is well formed (which it must be if it is built in an XML editor). You will also need a DTD to check all the rules. (You'll learn how to build this DTD in Chapter 4.) Using XML Notepad to create the document in XML thus helps prevent errors when an application reads the document.

The elements of our sample Web page could be stored in a database. You could then create tables and fields based on the information stored in the database. Because an XML-aware computer application can identify the content of each element, the application can automatically put the correct element in the correct table and field.

Interpreting the Content

You can also define the content in any manner you see fit. In our sample document, we added a *CellContent* element. You could have added numerous elements throughout the document to identify the content of each section. You could also have added attributes to existing elements. For example, you could have defined the *ul* element as follows:

```
<ul type="" comment=""></ul>
```

These additional attributes and elements can then be used by an application to catalog the content of your documents. Imagine using these tags to build the search indexes for your Web site.

These extra tags and attributes also make the document much more readable to humans. When you are designing a Web site, you can define the content of different elements rather than just drawing what the page should look like. Certain components, such as the navigation bars at the top and sides of the page and the footer section, are likely to be shared by many pages. These components can be identified and can be added to the standard template. The developer will need to change only the elements on the page that differ from one page to the next.

Reusing Elements

In our sample template, you created elements that could be used to build a Web document. When it came time to add a new row, you copied the row structure and pasted a new row into the document. This new row had the entire structure already built into it. The same technique was used to duplicate several other elements, including the *li* element, the *font* element, the *p* element, and the *a* element.

Reusing elements that contain attributes and child elements guarantees that the entire document will be uniform. When you are building documents, this uniformity will help ensure that you are following the rules for the document. Reusable elements will also make it easier to build the entire document since you are building the document from predefined pieces. For example, it would be easy to include the additional *h* elements by reusing the *p* element. You would only need to insert the *h2, h3*, and *h4* elements and copy and paste three *p* elements. In this example, you are reusing the *p* element. Figure 3-13 illustrates this.

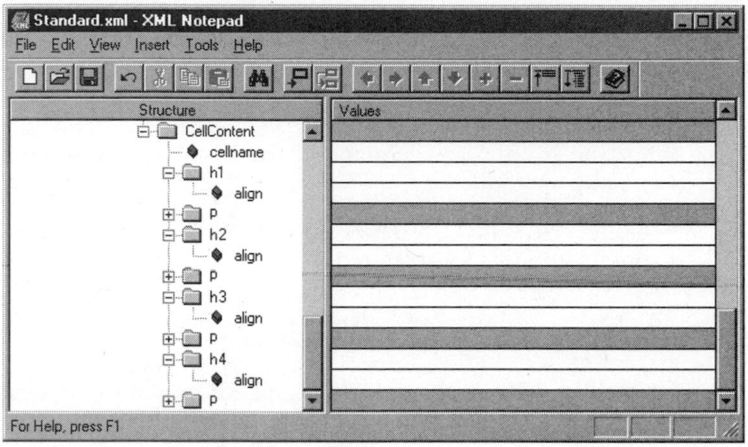

Figure 3-13. *XML Notepad, showing added* h2, h3, *and* h4 *elements.*

OTHER XML VIEWERS

Other programs are available that allow you to view XML documents. Some of these applications will work with DTDs and are discussed in Chapter 4. For viewing and editing an XML document, you can use XML Spy (*http://xmlspy.com*). Figure 3-14 shows the final Help.htm file displayed in XML Spy.

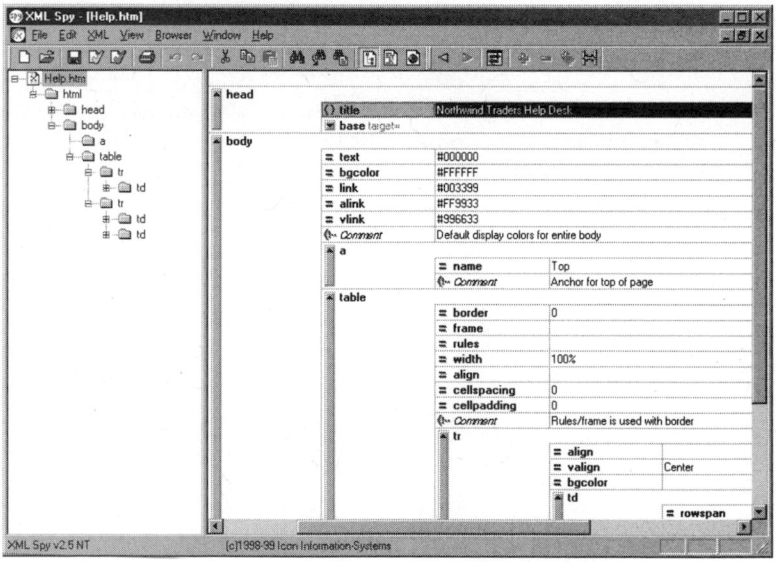

Figure 3-14. *The Help.htm file displayed in XML Spy.*

You can also view XML documents using XML Pro (*http://www.vervet.com*). XML Pro provides a window that lists the elements you can insert. Figure 3-15 shows the final Help.htm file displayed in XML Pro.

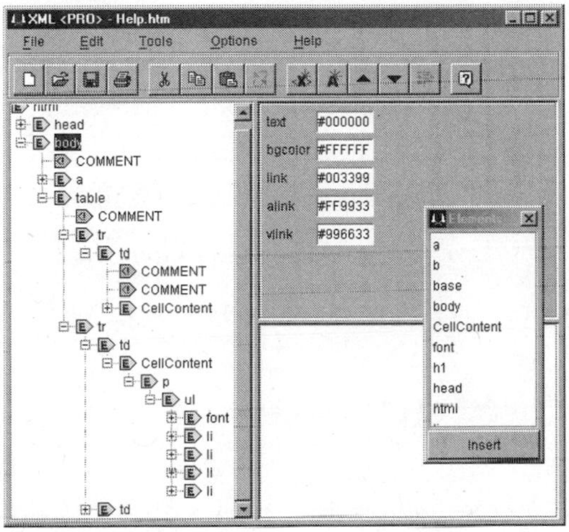

Figure 3-15. *The Help.htm file displayed in XML Pro.*

You can download trial versions of these programs from their Web sites. Use the tool that works best for you.

CRITERIA FOR WELL-FORMED XML DOCUMENTS

To be well formed, your XML document must meet the following requirements:

1. The document must contain a single root element.

2. Every element must be correctly nested.

3. Each attribute can have only one value.

4. All attribute values must be enclosed in double quotation marks or single quotation marks.

5. Elements must have begin and end tags, unless they are empty elements.

6. Empty elements are denoted by a single tag ending with a slash (/).

7. Isolated markup characters are not allowed in content. The special characters <, &, and > are represented as &gt, &amp, &lt in content sections.

8. A double quotation mark is represented as &quot, and a single quotation mark is represented as &apos in content sections.

9. The sequence <[[and]]> cannot be used.

10. If a document does not have a DTD, the values for all attributes must be of type CDATA by default.

Rules 1 through 6 have been addressed in this chapter. If you need to use the special characters listed in rules 7 and 8, be sure to use the appropriate replacement characters. The sequence in rule 9 has a special meaning in XML and so cannot be used in content sections and names. We will discuss this sequence in Chapter 5. The CDATA type referred to in rule 10 consists of any allowable characters. In our sample document, the values for the attributes must contain characters, which they do.

ADDING THE XML DECLARATION

XML Notepad does not add the XML declaration to an XML document. The XML declaration is optional, and should be the first line of the XML document if provided. The syntax for the declaration is shown here:

```
<?xml version="version_number" encoding="encoding_declaration"
    standalone="standalone status"?>
```

The *version* attribute is the version of the XML standard that this document complies with. The *encoding* attribute is the Unicode character set that this document complies with. Using this encoding, you can create documents in any language or character set. The *standalone* attribute specifies whether the document is dependent on other files (*standalone = "no"*) or complete by itself (*standalone = "yes"*).

THE FINAL XML DOCUMENT

The final XML document is shown here:

```
<?xml version="1.0" standalone="yes"?>
<html>
    <head>
        <title>Northwind Traders Help Desk</title>
        <base target=""><!--Default link for page--></base>
    </head>
    <body text="#000000" bgcolor="#FFFFFF" link="#003399"
        alink="#FF9933" vlink="#996633">
        <!--Default display colors for entire body-->
        <a name="Top"><!--Anchor for top of page--></a>
```

```
<table border="0" frame="" rules="" width="100%" align=""
    cellspacing="0" cellpadding="0">
  <!--Rules/frame is used with border.-->
  <tr align="" valign="Center" bgcolor="">
    <td rowspan="" colspan="2" align="Center" valign=""
        bgcolor="">
      <!--Either rowspan or colspan can be used,
      but not both.-->
      <!--Valign: top, bottom, middle-->
      <CellContent cellname="Table Header">
        <h1 align="Center">Help Desk</h1>
      </CellContent>
    </td>
  </tr>
  <tr align="" valign="Top" bgcolor="">
    <td rowspan="" colspan="" align="Left" valign=""
        bgcolor="">
      <CellContent cellname="Help Topic List">
        <p align="">
        <ul type="">
        <font face="" color="" size="3">
          <b>For First-Time Visitors</b>
        </font>
        <li>
        <a href="FirstTimeVisitorInfo.htm" target="">
          First-Time Visitor Information
        </a>
        </li>
        <li>
        <a href="SecureShopping.htm" target="">
          Secure Shopping at Northwind Traders
        </a>
        </li>
        <li>
        <a href="FreqAskedQ.htm" target="">
          Frequently Asked Questions
        </a>
        </li>
        <li>
        <a href="NavWeb.htm" target="">
          Navigating the Web
        </a>
        </li>
        </ul>
        </p>
      </CellContent>
```

(continued)

```
                </td>
                <td rowspan="" colspan="" align="Left" valign=""
                    bgcolor="">
                    <CellContent cellname="Shipping Links">
                        <p align="">
                        <ul type="">
                        <font face="" color="" size="">
                            <b>Shipping</b>
                        </font>
                        <li>
                        <a href="Rates.htm" target="">
                            Rates
                        </a>
                        </li>
                        <li>
                        <a href="OrderCheck.htm" target="">
                            Checking on Your Order
                        </a>
                        </li>
                        <li>
                        <a href="Returns.htm" target="">
                            Returns
                        </a>
                        </li>
                        </ul>
                        </p>
                    </CellContent>
                </td>
            </tr>
        </table>
    </body>
</html>
```

The final document looks basically like an HTML document and works like one, but it meets the criteria for being a well-formed XML document. Notice that all of the tags nest properly, all tags are closed, and the root element (<html></html>) encloses all the other elements.

You could have written all of this XML code manually, but it would have been more difficult and you would have been more likely to make a syntax error. There are various XML editors such as XML Authority, XML Instance, and XML Spy that allow you to focus on the structure of your document and the elements that will go into your document without being concerned about the syntax. Of course, once you have finished with the XML editor, you should review the final document to verify that the XML code is actually what you want.

SUMMARY

Well-formed XML documents can be created by using elements, attributes, and comments. These components define content within the document. Using these definitions, applications can be created that will manipulate the content.

The requirements for well-formed documents that have been addressed in this chapter include having a single root element, having properly nested elements, having no duplicate attribute names in an element, and enclosing all attribute values in single and double quotation marks. Using XML editors to create XML documents will allow you to focus on defining the structure of your document, the first step in building a well-formed XML document.

To make a class of documents with the same format as the one we created in this chapter, you will want to create a DTD to validate the entire class of documents. In the next chapter, you will learn how to create DTDs, and you will create one specifically for this document.

Chapter 4

An Introduction to Document Type Definitions

In Chapter 3, we developed a document template for creating XML documents that can be viewed in Web browsers as HTML documents. In this chapter, we will create a document type definition (DTD) for this template. This DTD defines a set of rules that are associated with all of the XML documents created using the template. This DTD can be used to create and validate the XML documents that conform to the rules defined in the DTD.

Many tools are available for creating and editing DTDs—for example, XML Authority, XML Spy, and Near and Far. We will use XML Authority to create and edit our DTD. You can download a trial version of XML Authority from *http://www. extensibility.com*. Microsoft XML Notepad cannot be used to edit DTDs (although it can validate a document that has a DTD).

BUILDING A DTD

In this chapter, we will build a DTD that defines a set of rules for the content of the sample Web document template we created in Chapter 3. The DTD can be used to verify that a set of XML documents is created according to the rules defined in the DTD by checking the validity of the documents.

> **NOTE**   If you are building a large Internet system, you can define a set of rules that all developers must use when creating Web pages. If the Web pages are written using XML, a DTD can be used to verify that all the pages follow the rules. XML can also be used to pass information from one corporation to another or from one department to another within a corporation. The DTD can be used to verify that the incoming information is in the correct format.

To open the sample document in XML Authority, follow these steps:

1. Open XML Authority, select New from the File menu, and then select New (DTD) from the submenu. If a default UNNAMED element appears at the top of the document, delete it.

2. Choose Import from the File menu, and then choose XML Document from the submenu.

3. Select the Standard.xml document you created in Chapter 3. XML Authority will import the document as a DTD.

   Figure 4-1 shows Standard.xml displayed in XML Authority.

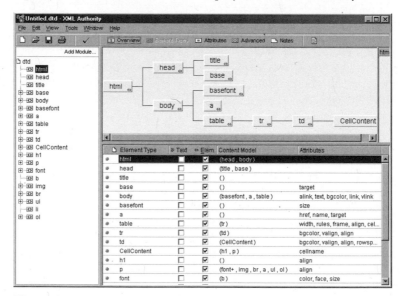

Figure 4-1. *The Standard.xml template displayed in XML Authority.*

4. Choose Source from the View menu.

XML Authority automatically builds a DTD for the XML document, so in this case, the source is a DTD for the Standard.xml XML document. The complete source code that XML Authority generated is shown here:

```
<!ELEMENT html  (head, body)>

<!ELEMENT head  (title, base)>

<!ELEMENT title  ( )>

<!ELEMENT base  ( )>
<!ATTLIST base  target CDATA  #REQUIRED>
<!ELEMENT body  (basefont, a, table)>
<!ATTLIST body  alink   CDATA  #REQUIRED
                text    CDATA  #REQUIRED
                bgcolor CDATA  #REQUIRED
                link    CDATA  #REQUIRED
                vlink   CDATA  #REQUIRED>
<!ELEMENT basefont  ( )>
<!ATTLIST basefont  size CDATA  #REQUIRED>
<!ELEMENT a  ( )>
<!ATTLIST a  href    CDATA  #IMPLIED
             name    CDATA  #IMPLIED
             target  CDATA  #IMPLIED>
<!ELEMENT table  (tr)>
<!ATTLIST table  width        CDATA  #REQUIRED
                 rules        CDATA  #REQUIRED
                 frame        CDATA  #REQUIRED
                 align        CDATA  #REQUIRED
                 cellpadding  CDATA  #REQUIRED
                 border       CDATA  #REQUIRED
                 cellspacing  CDATA  #REQUIRED>
<!ELEMENT tr  (td)>
<!ATTLIST tr  bgcolor CDATA  #REQUIRED
              valign  CDATA  #REQUIRED
              align   CDATA  #REQUIRED>
<!ELEMENT td  (CellContent)>
<!ATTLIST td  bgcolor CDATA  #REQUIRED
              valign  CDATA  #REQUIRED
              align   CDATA  #REQUIRED
              rowspan CDATA  #REQUIRED
              colspan CDATA  #REQUIRED>
<!ELEMENT CellContent  (h1, p)>
<!ATTLIST CellContent  cellname CDATA  #REQUIRED>
<!ELEMENT h1  ( )>
```

(continued)

```
<!ATTLIST h1  align CDATA  #REQUIRED>
<!ELEMENT p  (font+, img, br, a, ul, ol)>

<!ELEMENT font  (b)>
<!ATTLIST font  color CDATA  #REQUIRED
                face  CDATA  #REQUIRED
                size  CDATA  #REQUIRED>
<!ELEMENT b  ( )>

<!ELEMENT img  ( )>
<!ATTLIST img  width  CDATA  #REQUIRED
               height CDATA  #REQUIRED
               hspace CDATA  #REQUIRED
               vspace CDATA  #REQUIRED
               src    CDATA  #REQUIRED
               alt    CDATA  #REQUIRED
               align  CDATA  #REQUIRED
               border CDATA  #REQUIRED
               lowsrc CDATA  #REQUIRED>
<!ELEMENT br  ( )>
<!ATTLIST br  clear CDATA  #REQUIRED>
<!ELEMENT ul  (font, li)>
<!ATTLIST ul  type CDATA  #REQUIRED>
<!ELEMENT li  (font, a)>

<!ELEMENT ol  (font, li)>
<!ATTLIST ol  type  CDATA  #REQUIRED
              start CDATA  #REQUIRED>
```

As you can see, the DTD consists of two basic components: !ELEMENT and !ATTLIST. In this chapter, we will look at these two statements in detail.

NOTE   The DTD that has been generated here is only the first approximation. In this chapter, you will refine this DTD so that it defines a set of rules for your XML documents.

THE !ELEMENT STATEMENT

Every element used in your XML documents has to be declared by using the <!ELEMENT> tag in the DTD. The format for declaring an element in a DTD is shown here:

<!ELEMENT *ElementName Rule*>

The *Rule* component defines the rule for the content contained in the element. These rules define the logical structure of the XML document and can be used to check the document's validity. The rule can consist of a generic declaration and one or more elements, either grouped or unordered.

The Predefined Content Declarations

Three generic content declarations are predefined for XML DTDs: PCDATA, ANY, and EMPTY.

PCDATA

The PCDATA declaration can be used when the content within an element is only text—that is, when the content contains no child elements. Our sample document contains several such elements, including *title*, *a*, *h1*, and *b*. These elements can be declared as follows. (The pound sign identifies a special predefined name.)

```
<!ELEMENT title (#PCDATA)>
<!ELEMENT a (#PCDATA)>
<!ELEMENT h1 (#PCDATA)>
<!ELEMENT b (#PCDATA)>
```

> **NOTE** PCDATA is also valid with empty elements.

ANY

The ANY declaration can include both text content and child elements. The *html* element, for example, could use the ANY declaration as follows:

```
<!ELEMENT html  ANY>
```

This ANY declaration would allow the *body* and *head* elements to be included in the *html* element in an XML document:

```
<html><head/><body/></html>
```

The following XML would also be valid:

```
<html>This is an HTML document.<head/><body/></html>
```

And this XML would be valid with the ANY declaration in our sample DTD:

```
<html>This is an HTML document.<head/><body/><AnotherTag/></html>
```

The ANY declaration allows any content to be marked by the element tags, provided the content is well-formed XML. Although this flexibility might seem useful, it defeats the purpose of the DTD, which is to define the structure of the XML document so that the document can be validated. In brief, any element that uses ANY cannot be checked for validity, only for being well formed.

EMPTY

It is possible for an element to have no content—that is, no child elements or text. The *img* element is an example of this scenario. The following is its definition:

```
<!ELEMENT img EMPTY>
```

The *base*, *br*, and *basefont* elements are also correctly declared using EMPTY in our sample DTD.

One or More Elements

Instead of using the ANY declaration for the *html* element, you should define the content so that the *html* element can be validated. The following is a declaration that specifies the content of the *html* element and is the same as the one given by XML Authority:

```
<!ELEMENT html  (head, body)>
```

This (*head, body*) declaration signifies that the *html* element will have two child elements: *head* and *body*. You can list one child element within the parentheses or as many child elements as are required. You must separate each child element in your declaration with a comma.

For the XML document to be valid, the order in which the child elements are declared must match the order of the elements in the XML document. The comma that separates each child element is interpreted as *followed by*; therefore, the preceding declaration tells us that the *html* element will have a *head* child element *followed by* a *body* child element. Building on the preceding declaration, the following is valid XML:

```
<html><head></head><body/></html>
```

However, the following statement would not be valid:

```
<html><body></body><head/></html>
```

This statement indicates that the *html* element *must* contain two child elements—the first is *body* and the second is *head*—and there can only be one instance of each element.

The following two statements would also be invalid:

```
<html><body></body></html>
<html><head/><body/><head/><body/></html>
```

The first statement is missing the *head* element, and in the second statement the *head* and *body* elements are listed twice.

Reoccurrence

You will want every *html* element to include one *head* and one *body* child element, in the order listed. Other elements, such as the *body* and *table* elements, will have child elements that might be included multiple times within the main element or might not be included at all. XML provides three markers that can be used to indicate the reoccurrence of a child element, as shown in the following table:

XML ELEMENT MARKERS

Marker	Meaning
?	The element either does not appear or can appear only once (0 or 1).
+	The element must appear at least once (1 or more).
*	The element can appear any number of times, or it might not appear at all (0 or more).

Putting no marker after the child element indicates that the element must be included and that it can appear only one time.

The *head* element contains an optional *base* child element. To declare this element as optional, modify the preceding declaration as follows:

```
<!ELEMENT head  (title, base?)>
```

The *body* element contains a *basefont* element and an *a* element that are also optional. In our example, the *table* element is a required element used to format the page, so you want to make *table* a required element that appears only once in the *body* element. You can now rewrite the *Body* element as follows:

```
<!ELEMENT body (basefont?, a?, table)>
```

The *table* element can have as many rows as are needed to format the page but must include at least one row. The *table* element should now be written as follows:

```
<!ELEMENT table (tr+)>
```

The same conditions hold true for the *tr* element: the row element must have at least one column, as shown here:

```
<!ELEMENT tr (td+)>
```

The *a*, *ul*, and *ol* elements might not be included in the *p* element, or they might be included many times, as shown here:

```
<!ELEMENT p (font+, img, br, a*, ul*, ol*)>
```

Because the *br* element formats text around an image, the *img* and *br* tags should always be used together.

Grouping child elements

Fortunately, XML provides a way to group elements. For example, you can rewrite the *p* element as follows:

```
<!ELEMENT p (font*, (img, br?)*, a*, ul*, ol*)>
```

This declaration specifies that an *img* element followed by a *br* element appears zero or more times in the *p* element.

One problem remains in this declaration. As mentioned, the comma separator can be interpreted as the words *followed by*. Thus, each *p* element will have *font, img, br, a, ul,* and *ol* child elements, in that order. This is not exactly what you want; instead, you want to be able to use these elements in any order and to use some elements in some paragraphs and other elements in other paragraphs. For example, you would like to be able to write the following code:

```
<p>
    <font size=5>
        <b>Three Reasons to Shop Northwind Traders</b>
    </font>
    <ol>
        <li>
            <a href="Best.htm">Best Prices</a>
        </li>
        <li>
            <a href="Quality.htm">Quality</a>
        </li>
        <li>
            <a href="Service.htm">Fast Service</a>
        </li>
    </ol>
    <!--The following img element is not in the correct order.-->
    <img src="Northwind.jpg"></img>
</p>
```

As you can see, the *img* element is not in the correct order—it should precede the *ol* element, since the declaration imposes a strict ordering on the elements.

> **NOTE** Also, numerous elements are declared but are not included (for example, *ul*). The missing elements are not a problem because you have declared each element with an asterisk (*), indicating that there can be zero or more of each element.

To allow a "reordering" of elements, you could rewrite the declaration as follows:

```
<!ELEMENT p (font*, (img, br?)*, a*, ul*, ol*)+>
```

The plus sign (+) at the very end of the declaration indicates that one or more copies of these child elements can occur within a *p* element.

The preceding XML code could thus be interpreted as two sets of child elements, as shown here:

```
<p>
    <!--The elements that follow are the first set of
        (font*, (img, br?)*, a*, ul*, ol*) elements (missing
        the (img, br), a, and ul elements).-->

    <font  size=5>
        <b>Three Reasons to Shop Northwind Traders</b>
    </font>
    <ol>
        <li>
            <a href="Best.htm">Best Prices</a>
        </li>
        <li>
            <a href="Quality.htm">Quality</a>
        </li>
        <li>
            <a href="Service.htm">Fast Service</a>
        </li>
    </ol>
    <!--The img element that follows is a second set of
        (font*,(img, br?)*, a*, ul*, ol*) elements containing
        only an img element.-->
    <img src="Northwind.jpg"></img>
</p>
```

This new declaration is better, but it still does not allow you to choose any element in any order. All of the elements have been declared as optional and yet at least one member of the group must still be included (as indicated by the plus sign at the end of the list of elements). There is another option.

Creating an unordered set of child elements

In addition to using commas to separate elements, you can use a vertical bar (|). The vertical bar separator indicates that one child element or the other child element but not both will be included within the element—in other words, one element or the other must be present. The preceding declaration can thus be rewritten as follows:

```
<!ELEMENT p  (font | (img, br?) | a | ul | ol)+>
```

This declaration specifies that the *p* element can include a *font* child element, an *(img, br?)* child element, an *a* child element, a *ul* child element, *or* an *ol* child element, but only one of these elements. The plus sign (+) indicates that the element must contain one or more copies of one or several child elements. With this declaration, you can use child elements in any order, as many times as needed.

NOTE   The additional markers (?, +, *) can be used to override the vertical bar (I), which limits the occurrences of the child element to one or none.

According to the new declaration, our XML code will be interpreted as follows:

```
<p>
    <!--First group, containing single font element-->
    <font size=5>
        <b>Three Reasons to Shop Northwind Traders</b>
    </font>
    <!--Second group, containing the single child element ol-->
    <ol>
        <li>
            <a href="Best.htm">Best Prices</a>
        </li>
        <li>
            <a href="Quality.htm">Quality</a>
        </li>
        <li>
            <a href="Service.htm">Fast Service</a>
        </li>
    </ol>
    <!--Third group, containing a single child element img-->
    <img src="Northwind.jpg"></img>
</p>
```

Suppose you also want to include text within the *p* element. To do this, you will need to add a PCDATA declaration to the group. You will have to use the vertical bar separator because you cannot use the PCDATA declaration if the child elements are separated by commas. You also cannot have a subgroup such as *(img, br?)* within a group that includes PCDATA. We can solve this problem by creating a new element named *ImageLink* that contains the subgroup and add it to the *p* element as follows:

```
<!ELEMENT ImageLink  (img, br?)>
<!ELEMENT p  (#PCDATA | font | ImageLink | a | ul | ol)+>
```

Web browsers that do not understand XML will ignore the *ImageLink* element. When you use PCDATA within a group of child elements, it must be listed first and must be preceded by a pound sign (#).

You can use the DTD to make certain sections of the document appear in a certain order and include a specific number of child elements (as was done with the *html* element). You can also create sections of the document that contain an unspecified number of child elements in any order. DTDs are extremely flexible and can enable you to develop a set of rules that matches your requirements.

THE !ATTLIST STATEMENT

Every element can have a set of attributes associated with it. The attributes for an element are defined in an !ATTLIST statement. The format for the !ATTLIST statement is shown here:

<!ATTLIST *ElementName AttributeDefinition*>

ElementName is the name of the element to which these attributes belong.
AttributeDefinition consists of the following components:

AttributeName AttributeType DefaultDeclaration

AttributeName is the name of the attribute. *AttributeType* refers to the data type of the attribute. *DefaultDeclaration* contains the default declaration section of the attribute definition.

Attribute Data Types

XML DTD attributes can have the following data types: CDATA, enumerated, ENTITY, ENTITIES, ID, IDREF, IDREFS, NMTOKEN, and NMTOKENS.

CDATA

The CDATA data type indicates that the attribute can be set to any allowable character value. For our sample DTD used for creating Web pages, the vast majority of the elements will have attributes with a CDATA data type. The following *body* attributes should all be CDATA:

```
<!ATTLIST body  alink   CDATA  #REQUIRED
                text    CDATA  #REQUIRED
                bgcolor CDATA  #REQUIRED
                link    CDATA  #REQUIRED
                vlink   CDATA  #REQUIRED>
```

Notice that you can list multiple attributes for a single element.

Enumerated

The enumerated data type lists a set of values that are allowed for the attribute. Using an enumerated data type, you can rewrite the *font* element to limit the *color* attribute to *Cyan*, *Lime*, *Black*, *White*, or *Maroon*; limit the *size* attribute to *2, 3, 4, 5,* or *6*; and limit the *face* attribute to *Times New Roman* or *Arial*. The new *font* declaration would look as follows:

```
<!ATTLIST font  color (Cyan | Lime | Black | White | Maroon) #REQUIRED
                size  (2 | 3 | 4 | 5 | 6)  #REQUIRED
                face  (&apos;Times New Roman&apos;|Arial)  #REQUIRED>
```

NOTE Keep in mind that this declaration is case sensitive. Thus, entering *cyan* as a *color* value would cause an error. Also notice the use of *'* as a place-holder for a single quotation mark and the use of the parentheses to group the collection of choices.

In the section "The Default Declaration" later in this chapter, you'll learn how to declare a default value for the *color* and *size* attributes.

ENTITY and ENTITIES

The ENTITY and ENTITIES data types are used to define reusable strings that are represented by a specific name. These data types will be discussed in detail in Chapter 5.

ID, IDREF, and IDREFS

Within a document, you may want to be able to identify certain elements with an attribute that is of the ID data type. The name of the attribute with an ID data type must be unique for all of the elements in the document. Other elements can reference this ID by using the IDREF or IDREFS data types. IDREFS can be used to declare multiple attributes as IDREF.

When you work with HTML, you use anchor (*a*) elements to bookmark sections of your document. These bookmarks can be used to link to sections of the document. Unlike the ID data type, the *a* element does not have to be unique. In XML, IDs are used to create links to different places in your document. When we examine linking in detail in Chapter 6, you'll see that the ID data type offers other advantages.

Our example document includes an *a* element at the top of the document as an anchor that can be used to jump to the top of the page. You can modify the *a* element definition in the DTD as follows:

```
<!ATTLIST a  linkid  ID     #REQUIRED
             href    CDATA  #IMPLIED
             name    CDATA  #IMPLIED
             target  CDATA  #IMPLIED>
```

Now when you create an XML document, you can define an *a* element at the top of the page and associate a unique ID with it using the *linkid* attribute. To reference this ID from another element, you first have to add an IDREF attribute to that element, as shown here:

```
<!ATTLIST ul   headlink IDREF  #IMPLIED
               type     CDATA  #REQUIRED>
```

In your XML document, you can associate the *linkid* attribute of the *a* element with the *headlink* attribute of the *ul* element by assigning the same value (*HeadAnchor*, for example) to these two attributes. If a second ID attribute, named *footlink*, was added to an element at the bottom of the XML document, you could define references to both of these elements. In this case, you would need to use IDREFS, as shown here:

```
<!ATTLIST ul    headlink footlink   IDREFS  #IMPLIED
                type                CDATA   #REQUIRED>
```

The actual XML document would contain the following code:

```
<a linkid="HeadAnchor" name="head">
    <!--Head anchor-->
</a>
<!--Some HTML code here-->
<a href="#head">
    <ul headlink="HeadAnchor">
        <!--li elements here-->
    </ul>
</a>
<a href="#foot">
    <ul footlink="FootAnchor">
        <!--li elements here-->
    </ul>
</a>
<!--Some more HTML code here-->
<a linkid="FootAnchor" name="foot">
    <!--Foot anchor-->
</a>
```

This code will work with non-XML browsers and with browsers that support XML.

NMTOKEN and NMTOKENS

The NMTOKEN and NMTOKENS data types are similar to the CDATA data type in that they represent character values. The *name tokens* are strings that consist of letters, digits, underscores, colons, hyphens, and periods. They cannot contain spaces. A declaration using these data types could look as follows:

```
<!ATTLIST body
    background NMTOKEN "Blue"
    foreground NMTOKENS "Green, Yellow, Orange"
>
```

The Default Declaration

The default declaration can consist of any valid value for your attributes, or it can consist of one of three predefined keywords: #REQUIRED, #IMPLIED, or #FIXED. The #REQUIRED keyword indicates that the attribute must be included with the element and that it must be assigned a value. There are no default values when

#REQUIRED is used. The #IMPLIED keyword indicates that the attribute does not have to be included with the element and that there is no default value. The #FIXED keyword sets the attribute to one default value that cannot be changed. The default value is listed after the #FIXED keyword. If none of these three keywords are used, a default value can be assigned if an attribute is not set in the XML document.

THE REVISED DTD

Based on this information about the components of the !ELEMENT and !ATTLIST statements, we can rewrite our original DTD as follows:

```
<!ELEMENT html  (head, body)>

<!ELEMENT head  (title, base?)>

<!ELEMENT title  (#PCDATA)>

<!ELEMENT base EMPTY>
<!ATTLIST base  target CDATA  #REQUIRED>
<!ELEMENT body  (basefont?, a?, table)>
<!ATTLIST body  alink   CDATA  #IMPLIED
                text    CDATA  #IMPLIED
                bgcolor CDATA  #IMPLIED
                link    CDATA  #IMPLIED
                vlink   CDATA  #IMPLIED>
<!ELEMENT basefont EMPTY>
<!ATTLIST basefont  size CDATA  #REQUIRED>
<!ELEMENT a  (#PCDATA)>
<!ATTLIST a  linkid ID      #IMPLIED
             href   CDATA  #IMPLIED
             name   CDATA  #IMPLIED
             target CDATA  #IMPLIED>
<!ELEMENT table  (tr+)>
<!ATTLIST table  width       CDATA  #IMPLIED
                 rules       CDATA  #IMPLIED
                 frame       CDATA  #IMPLIED
                 align       CDATA  'Center'
                 cellpadding CDATA  '0'
                 border      CDATA  '0'
                 cellspacing CDATA  '0'>
<!ELEMENT tr  (td+)>
<!ATTLIST tr  bgcolor (Cyan | Lime | Black | White | Maroon)  'White'
              valign  (Top | Middle | Bottom)  'Middle'
              align   (Left | Right | Center)  'Center'>
<!ELEMENT td  (CellContent)>
```

```
<!ATTLIST td  bgcolor (Cyan | Lime | Black | White | Maroon)  'White'
              valign  (Top | Middle | Bottom)  'Middle'
              align   (Left | Right | Center)  'Center'
              rowspan CDATA  #IMPLIED
              colspan CDATA  #IMPLIED>
<!ELEMENT CellContent  (h1?| p?)+>
<!ATTLIST CellContent  cellname CDATA  #REQUIRED>
<!ELEMENT h1  (#PCDATA)>
<!ATTLIST h1  align CDATA  #IMPLIED>
<!ELEMENT ImageLink  (img, br?)>

<!ELEMENT p  (#PCDATA | font | ImageLink | a | ul | ol)+>
<!ATTLIST p  align CDATA  #IMPLIED>
<!ELEMENT font  (#PCDATA | b)*>
<!ATTLIST font  color (Cyan | Lime | Black | White | Maroon)  'Black'
                face  (&apos;Times New Roman &apos;| Arial) #REQUIRED
                size  (2 | 3 | 4 | 5 | 6)  '3'>
<!ELEMENT b  (#PCDATA)>

<!ELEMENT img EMPTY>
<!ATTLIST img  width  CDATA  #IMPLIED
               height CDATA  #IMPLIED
               hspace CDATA  #IMPLIED
               vspace CDATA  #IMPLIED
               src    CDATA  #IMPLIED
               alt    CDATA  #IMPLIED
               align  CDATA  #IMPLIED
               border CDATA  #IMPLIED
               lowsrc CDATA  #IMPLIED>
<!ELEMENT br EMPTY>
<!ATTLIST br  clear CDATA  #REQUIRED>
<!ELEMENT ul  (font?, li+)>
<!ATTLIST ul  type CDATA  #IMPLIED>
<!ELEMENT li  (font?| a?)+>

<!ELEMENT ol  (font?, li+)>
<!ATTLIST ol  type  CDATA  #REQUIRED
              start CDATA  #REQUIRED>
```

The *body* element contains two optional child elements, *basefont* and *a*, and one required element, *table*. For this example, because you are using a table to format the page and all information will go into the table, the *table* element is required. The *a* element is used to create an anchor to the top of the page, and the *basefont* element specifies the default font size for the text in the document. Because all of the attributes associated with the *body* element are optional, they include the keyword #IMPLIED.

In the *base* element, the *target* attribute is required. It would make no sense to include a *base* element without specifying the *target* attribute, as the specification of this attribute is the reason you would use the *base* element. Therefore, the *target* attribute is #REQUIRED.

In the *font* element, the *color* and *size* attributes have enumerated data types and are assigned default values (*Black* and *3*). The *face* attribute remains unchanged.

ASSOCIATING THE DTD WITH AN XML DOCUMENT

Now that the DTD has been created, it can be used to validate the Help.htm document we created in Chapter 3. There are two ways to associate a DTD with an XML document: the first is to place the DTD code within the XML document, and the second is to create a separate DTD document that is referenced by the XML document. Creating a separate DTD document allows multiple XML documents to reference the same DTD. We will take a look at how to declare a DTD first, and then examine how to place a DTD within the XML document.

The !DOCTYPE statement is used to declare a DTD. For an internal DTD, called an *internal subset,* you can use the following syntax:

```
<!DOCTYPE DocName [ DTD ]>
```

The new XML document that combines Help.htm and the DTD would look like this:

```
<!DOCTYPE HTML
[
<!ELEMENT html  (head, body)>

<!ELEMENT head  (title, base?)>

<!ELEMENT title  (#PCDATA)>

<!ELEMENT base EMPTY>
<!ATTLIST base  target CDATA  #REQUIRED>
<!ELEMENT body  (basefont?, a?, table)>
<!ATTLIST body  alink   CDATA  #IMPLIED
                text    CDATA  #IMPLIED
                bgcolor CDATA  #IMPLIED
                link    CDATA  #IMPLIED
                vlink   CDATA  #IMPLIED>
<!ELEMENT basefont EMPTY>
<!ATTLIST basefont  size CDATA  #REQUIRED>
<!ELEMENT a  (#PCDATA)>
```

```
<!ATTLIST a    linkid ID      #IMPLIED
               href   CDATA   #IMPLIED
               name   CDATA   #IMPLIED
               target CDATA   #IMPLIED>
<!ELEMENT table (tr+)>
<!ATTLIST table  width        CDATA   #IMPLIED
                 rules        CDATA   #IMPLIED
                 frame        CDATA   #IMPLIED
                 align        CDATA   'Center'
                 cellpadding CDATA   '0'
                 border       CDATA   '0'
                 cellspacing CDATA   '0'>
<!ELEMENT tr  (td+)>
<!ATTLIST tr  bgcolor (Cyan | Lime | Black | White | Maroon) 'White'
              valign  (Top | Middle | Bottom) 'Middle'
              align   (Left | Right | Center) 'Center'>
<!ELEMENT td  (CellContent)>
<!ATTLIST td  bgcolor (Cyan | Lime | Black | White | Maroon) 'White'
              valign  (Top | Middle | Bottom) 'Middle'
              align   (Left | Right | Center) 'Center'
              rowspan CDATA #IMPLIED
              colspan CDATA #IMPLIED>
<!ELEMENT CellContent (h1? | p?)+>
<!ATTLIST CellContent cellname CDATA #REQUIRED>
<!ELEMENT h1 (#PCDATA)>
<!ATTLIST h1 align CDATA #IMPLIED>
<!ELEMENT ImageLink (img, br?)>

<!ELEMENT p (#PCDATA | font | ImageLink | a | ul | ol)+>
<!ATTLIST p align CDATA #IMPLIED>
<!ELEMENT font (#PCDATA | b)*>
<!ATTLIST font color (Cyan | Lime | Black | White | Maroon) 'Black'
               face  (&apos;Times New Roman &apos;| Arial)#REQUIRED
               size  (2 | 3 | 4 | 5 | 6) '3'>
<!ELEMENT b (#PCDATA)>

<!ELEMENT img EMPTY>
<!ATTLIST img  width  CDATA  #IMPLIED
               height CDATA  #IMPLIED
               hspace CDATA  #IMPLIED
               vspace CDATA  #IMPLIED
               src    CDATA  #IMPLIED
               alt    CDATA  #IMPLIED
               align  CDATA  #IMPLIED
               border CDATA  #IMPLIED
               lowsrc CDATA  #IMPLIED>
<!ELEMENT br EMPTY>
```

(continued)

```
<!ATTLIST br   clear CDATA   #REQUIRED>
<!ELEMENT ul   (font?, li+)>
<!ATTLIST ul   type CDATA   #IMPLIED>
<!ELEMENT li   (font? | a?)+>

<!ELEMENT ol   (font?, li+)>
<!ATTLIST ol   type  CDATA   #REQUIRED
               start CDATA   #REQUIRED>
]>

<html>
    <head>
        <title>Northwind Traders Help Desk</title>
        <base target=""><!--Default link for page--></base>
    </head>
    <body text="#000000" bgcolor="#FFFFFF" link="#003399"
          alink="#FF9933" vlink="#996633">
        <!--Default display colors for entire body-->
        <a name="Top"><!--Anchor for top of page--></a>
        <table border="0" frame="" rules="" width="100%" align=""
               cellspacing="0" cellpadding="0">
            <!--Rules/frame is used with border-->
            <tr valign="Center">
                <td rowspan="" colspan="2" align="Center">
                    <!--Either rowspan or colspan can be used, but
                        not both-->
                    <!--Valign: top, bottom, middle-->
                    <CellContent cellname="Table Header">
                        <h1 align="Center">Help Desk</h1>
                    </CellContent>
                </td>
            </tr>
            <tr valign="Top">
                <td rowspan="" colspan="" align="Left">
                    <CellContent cellname="Help Topic List">
                        <p align="">
                        <ul type="">
                        <font face="" color="" size="3">
                            <b>For First-Time Visitors</b>
                        </font>
                        <li>
                        <a href="FirstTimeVisitorInfo.htm" target="">
                            First-Time Visitor Information
                        </a>
                        </li>
                        <li>
                        <a href="SecureShopping.htm" target="">
                            Secure Shopping at Northwind Traders
                        </a>
                        </li>
```

```
                    <li>
                    <a href="FreqAskedQ.htm" target="">
                        Frequently Asked Questions
                    </a>
                    </li>
                    <li>
                    <a href="NavWeb.htm" target="">
                        Navigating the Web
                    </a>
                    </li>
                    </ul>
                    </p>
                </CellContent>
            </td>
            <td rowspan="" colspan="" align="Left">
                <CellContent cellname="Shipping Links">
                    <p align="">
                    <ul type="">
                    <font face="">
                        <b>Shipping</b>
                    </font>
                    <li>
                    <a href="Rates.htm" target="">
                        Rates
                    </a>
                    </li>
                    <li>
                    <a href="OrderCheck.htm" target="">
                        Checking on Your Order
                    </a>
                    </li>
                    <li>
                    <a href="Returns.htm" target="">
                        Returns
                    </a>
                    </li>
                    </ul>
                    </p>
                </CellContent>
            </td>
        </tr>
    </table>
  </body>
</html>
```

The marked-up text has remained the same with one exception. Any element that uses an enumerated data type cannot have an attribute set to an empty string (""). For example, if a *tr* element does not use the *align* attribute, the attribute must be removed from the element. Because a default value (*Center*) has been assigned in the DTD for the *align* attribute of the *tr* element, the default value will be applied only when the attribute is omitted.

If you open this document in the browser, you will find that it almost works. The closing brackets (]>) belonging to the !DOCTYPE statement will appear in the browser, however, which is not acceptable. To solve this problem, save the original DTD in a file called StandardHTM.dtd, remove the empty attributes that have an enumerated data type, and reference the external file StandardHTM.dtd in the new file named HelpHTM.htm. The format for a reference to an external DTD is as follows:

<!DOCTYPE *RootElementName* SYSTEM | PUBLIC [Name]

DTD-URI>

RootElementName is the name of the root element (in this example, *html*). The SYSTEM keyword is needed when you are using an unpublished DTD. If a DTD has to be published and given a name, the PUBLIC keyword can be used. If the parser cannot identify the name, the DTD-URI will be used. You must specify the location of the *Uniform Resource Identifier (URI)* of the DTD in the DTD-URI. A URI is a general type of system identifier. One type of URI is the *Uniform Resource Locator* (URL) you're familiar with from the Internet.

For our example, we would need to add the following line of code to the beginning of the document HelpHTM.htm:

```
<!DOCTYPE html SYSTEM "StandardHTM.dtd">
```

A browser that does not understand XML will ignore this statement. Thus, by using an external DTD, you not only have an XML document that can be validated, but also one that can be displayed in any browser.

SUMMARY

You now know how to build a DTD to define a set of rules that can be used to validate an XML document. Using DTDs, a standard set of rules can be developed that can be used to create standard XML documents. These documents can be exchanged between corporations or internally within a corporation and validated using the DTD. The DTD can also be used to create standard documents within a group, such as a group that is building an e-commerce site.

In Chapter 5, we'll look at entities. Entities enable you to create reusable strings within a DTD.

Chapter 5

Entities and Other Components

In Chapter 4, we examined the two principal components of a document type definition (DTD): elements and attributes. In this chapter, we will look at some additional components that can be added to the DTD. The focus of this chapter will be *entities,* which are used to represent text that can be part of either the DTD or the XML document. You can use a single entity to represent a lengthy declaration and then use the entity in the DTD. You can also use entities to make one common file that contains a set of standard declarations that can be shared by many DTDs.

OVERVIEW OF ENTITIES

Entities are like macros in the C programming language in that they allow you to associate a string of characters with a name. This name can then be used in either the DTD or the XML document; the XML parser will replace the name with the string of characters. All entities consist of three parts: the word ENTITY, the name of the entity (called the *literal entity value*), and the replacement text—that is, the string of characters that the literal entity value will be replaced with. All entities are declared in either an internal or an external DTD.

Entities come in several types, depending on where their replacement text comes from and where it will be placed. *Internal entities* will get their replacement text from within the DTD, inside their declaration. *External entities* will get their replacement text from an external file. Both internal and external entities can be broken down into *general entities* and *parameter entities*. General entities are used in XML documents, and parameter entities are used in DTDs.

Internal general entities, internal parameter entities, and external parameter entities always contain text that should be parsed. Because external general entities go within the body of a document and because you might want to insert a nontext file (such as an image) into the body of the document, external general entities can be parsed or unparsed. External parsed general entities are used to insert XML statements from external files into the XML document. External unparsed general entities are used to insert information into the XML document that is not text-based XML and should not be parsed. Thus, we have five basic entity categories: internal general entities, internal parameter entities, external parsed general entities, external unparsed general entities, and external parameter entities.

Figure 5-1 illustrates the source of the replacement text for each of the entity categories (the closed circles) and where the replacement text will go (the arrows).

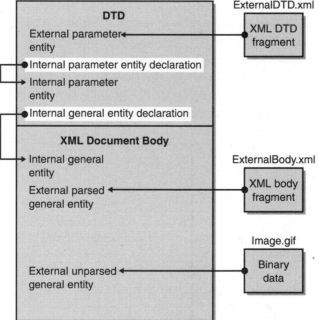

Figure 5-1. *Source and destination of the replacement text for the five entity categories.*

INTERNAL ENTITIES

Let's begin by looking at internal entities. An entity that is going to be used in only one DTD can be an internal entity. If you intend to use the entity in multiple DTDs, it should be an external entity. In this section, you'll learn how to declare internal entities, where to insert them, and how to reference them.

Internal General Entities

Internal general entities are the simplest among the five types of entities. They are defined in the DTD section of the XML document. First let's look at how to declare an internal general entity.

Declaring an internal general entity

The syntax for the declaration of an internal general entity is shown here:

```
<!ENTITY name "string_of_characters">
```

NOTE As you can see from the syntax line above, characters such as angle brackets(<>) and quotation marks (" ") are used specifically for marking up the XML document; they cannot be used as content directly. So to include such a character as part of your content, you must use one of .XML's five predefined entities. The literal entity values for these predefined entities are &, <, >, ", and '. The replacement text for these literal entity values will be &, <, >, ", and '.

You can create your own general entities. General entities are useful for associating names with foreign language characters, such as *ü* or *ß*, or escape characters, such as <, >, and *&*. You can use Unicode character values in your XML documents as replacements for any character defined in the Unicode standard. These are called *character references*.

To use a Unicode representation in your XML document, you must precede the Unicode character value with *&#*. You can use either the Unicode characters' hex values or their decimal values. For example, in Unicode, *ü* is represented as *xFC* and *ß* is represented as *xDF*. These two characters' decimal values are *252* and *223*. Thus, in your DTD you could create general entities for the preceding two characters as follows:

```
<!ENTITY u_um "&#xFC">
<!ENTITY s_sh "&#xDF">
```

The two entities could also be declared like this:

```
<!ENTITY u_um "&#252">
<!ENTITY s_sh "&#223">
```

Using internal general entities

To reference a general entity in the XML document, you must precede the entity with an ampersand (&) and follow it with a semicolon (;). For example, the following XML statement references the two general entities we declared in the previous section:

```
<title>Gr&u_um;&s_sh;</title>
```

When the replacement text is inserted by the parser, it will look like this:

```
<title>Grüß</title>
```

Internal general entities can be used in three places: in the XML document as content for an element, within the DTD in an attribute with a #FIXED data type declaration as the default value for the attribute, and within other general entities inside the DTD. We used the first location in the preceding example: (<title>Gr&u_um;&s_sh;</title>).

The second place you can use an internal general entity is within the DTD in an attribute with a #FIXED data type declaration or as the default value for an attribute. For example, you can use the following general entities in your DTD declaration to create entities for several colors:

```
<!ENTITY Cy "Cyan">
<!ENTITY Lm "Lime">
<!ENTITY Bk "Black">
<!ENTITY Wh "White">
<!ENTITY Ma "Maroon">
```

Then if you want the value of the *bgcolor* attribute for *tr* elements to be *White* for all XML documents that use the DTD, you could include the following line in the previous DTD declaration:

```
<!ATTLIST tr align (Left | Right | Center) 'Center'
       valign (Top | Middle | Bottom) 'Middle'
       bgcolor CDATA #FIXED "&Wh;">
```

The internal general entities must be defined before they can be used in an attribute default value since the DTD is read through once from beginning to end. In this case, internal general entities for several colors have been created. The *bgcolor* attribute is declared with the keyword #FIXED, which means that its value cannot be changed by the user—the value will always be *White*. The color general entities could also be used as content for the elements in the *body* section of the XML document.

You can use the internal general entity as a default value—for example, *bgcolor CDATA "&Wh;"*. In this case, if no value is given, *&Wh;* is substituted for *bgcolor* when the XML attribute is needed in the document body, and that reference will be converted to *White*.

NOTE   You can use an internal general entity in a DTD for a #FIXED attribute, but the attribute value will be assigned in the XML document's body only when the attribute is referenced. You cannot use an internal general entity in an enumerated type attribute declaration because the general entity would have to be interpreted in the DTD, which cannot happen.

The third place you can use internal general entities is within other general entities inside the DTD. For example, we could use the preceding special character entities as follows:

```
<!ENTITY u_um "&#252>
<!ENTITY s_sh "&#223">
<!ENTITY greeting "Gr&u_um;&s_sh;">
```

At this point, it's not clear whether *greeting* will be replaced with *Gr&u_um;&s_sh;* in the XML document's body and then converted to *Grüß* or whether *greeting* will be replaced directly with *Grüß* when the entity is parsed. The order of replacement will be discussed in the section "Processing Order" later in this chapter.

CAUTION   When you include general entities within other general entities, circular references are not allowed. For example, the following construction is not correct:

```
<!ENTITY greeting "&hello;! Gr&u_um;&s_sh;">
<!ENTITY hello "Hello &greeting;">
```

In this case, *greeting* is referencing *hello*, and *hello* is referencing *greeting*, making a circular reference.

Internal Parameter Entities

Internal parameter entities are interpreted and replaced within the DTD and can be used only within the DTD. While you need to use an ampersand (&) when referencing general entities, you need to use a percent sign (%) when referencing parameter entities.

NOTE   If you need to use a quotation mark, percent sign, or ampersand in your parameter or general entity strings, you must use character or general entity references—for example, &#x22, &#x25, &#x26, or ", and &. (There is no predefined entity for the percent sign, but you could create a general or parameter entity for it.)

Declaring an internal parameter entity

The syntax for declaring an internal parameter entity is shown here:

```
<!ENTITY % name "string_of_characters">
```

As you can see, the syntax for declaring an internal parameter entity is only slightly different from that used for declaring internal general entities—a percent sign is used in front of the entity name. (The percent sign must be preceded and followed by a white space character.)

In Chapter 4, we created a sample DTD for a static HTML page. If you want to create a dynamic page, you will probably want to add forms and other objects to your DTD. There is a standard set of events associated with all of these objects, but instead of listing the events for every declaration of every object, you could use the following parameter entity in your DTD:

```
<!ENTITY % events
    "onclick     CDATA      #IMPLIED
    ondblclick   CDATA      #IMPLIED
    onmousedown  CDATA      #IMPLIED
    onmouseup    CDATA      #IMPLIED
    onmouseover  CDATA      #IMPLIED
    onmousemove  CDATA      #IMPLIED
    onmouseout   CDATA      #IMPLIED
    onkeypress   CDATA      #IMPLIED
    onkeydown    CDATA      #IMPLIED
    onkeyup      CDATA      #IMPLIED"
    >
```

This code declares a parameter entity named *events* that can be used as an attribute for all of your objects that have these attributes.

> **NOTE**   You could have also declared a parameter entity named *Script*, and then used it within the *events* parameter entity declaration, as shown here:
>
> ```
> <!ENTITY % Script "CDATA">
> <!ENTITY % events
>         "onclick     %Script;      #IMPLIED
>          ondblclick  %Script;      #IMPLIED
>          ⋮
> >
> ```
>
> The *Script* parameter entity allows you to use data type names that are more readable than just using CDATA. Although this code is more readable, some XML tools (such as XML Authority) cannot accept parameter entities used in this way. Be aware of this limitation if you use this technique.

Using internal parameter entities

The *events* parameter entity will be used in the attribute declaration of the form objects and in other elements, such as *body*. To reference a parameter entity, you must precede the entity with a percent sign and follow it with a semicolon. For example, you could now make this declaration:

```
<!ATTLIST body
    alink    CDATA    #IMPLIED
    text     CDATA    #IMPLIED
    bgcolor  CDATA    #IMPLIED
    link     CDATA    #IMPLIED
    vlink    CDATA    #IMPLIED
    %events;
    onload   CDATA    #IMPLIED
    onunload CDATA    #IMPLIED
  >
```

In this case, the internal parameter entity *%events;* has been added to the *body* element's attribute declaration. The parameter entity *events* could be used in any declaration in which these events are allowed.

The XHTML Standard and Internal Parameter Entities

Now would be a good time to introduce a new standard that is being created for HTML. This new standard is called XHTML; it is also represented in a new version of HTML (version 4.01). The World Wide Web Consortium (W3C) standards committee is currently working out the last details of the standard, which is all about doing what we've done in the last few chapters, XMLizing HTML. You can find information about this standard by visiting *http://www.w3.org*.

Basically, the XHTML standard introduces two content models: inline and block. The inline elements affect individual text elements, whereas the block elements affect entire blocks of text. These two elements are then used as child elements for other elements.

Inline entities and elements

The XHTML standard provides the following declarations for defining a series of internal parameter entities to be used to define the inline elements:

```
<!ENTITY % special "br
                    | span
                    | img">
<!ENTITY % fontstyle "tt
                      | i
                      | b
                      | big
```

(continued)

```
                                 | small">
<!ENTITY % phrase "em
                    | strong
                    | q
                    | sub
                    | sup">
<!ENTITY % inline.forms "input
                         | select
                         | textarea
                         | label
                         | button">
<!ENTITY % inline "a
                   | %special;
                   | %fontstyle;
                   | %phrase;
                   | %inline.forms;">
<!-- Entities that can occur at block or inline level. -->
<!ENTITY % misc "script
                 | noscript">
<!ENTITY % Inline " (#PCDATA
                    | %inline;
                    | %misc; )*">
```

This declaration fragment builds the final *Inline* parameter entity in small pieces. Notice that the *Inline* entity definition contains the *inline* and *misc* entities and uses the technique described in Chapter 4 for including an unlimited number of child elements in any order—in this example, using *(#PCDATA | %inline; | %misc;)**.

In the example DTD created in Chapters 3 and 4, the *p* element was used to organize the content within a cell. Although that usage makes sense, the purpose of the *p* element is to make text that is not included in a *block* element (such as text within an *h* element) word-wrap properly. Therefore, putting the *h* element or any of the block elements within a *p* element is not necessary because text within a *block* element is already word-wrapped. On the other hand, if any of the *inline* elements are used outside of a *block* element, they should be placed inside a *p* element so that the text element wraps properly. Therefore, you could rewrite the definition for the *p* element as follows:

```
<!ELEMENT p %Inline;>
```

This shows exactly the way the definition for the *p* element appears in the XHTML specification.

Block entities and elements

The XHTML standard also declares a set of internal parameter entities that can be used in the declarations of the *block* elements. These internal parameter entities appear as follows:

```
<!ENTITY % heading "h1
                  | h2
                  | h3
                  | h4
                  | h5
                  | h6">
<!ENTITY % lists "ul
                  | ol">
<!ENTITY % blocktext "hr
                     | blockquote">
<!ENTITY % block "p
                  | %heading;
                  | div
                  | %lists;
                  | %blocktext;
                  | fieldset
                  | table">
<!ENTITY % Block " (%block;
                  | form
                  | %misc; )*">
```

Notice that the *Block* entity contains the *block* entity, the *misc* entity, and the *form* element and also includes an unlimited number of these child elements in any order. Using the *Block* parameter entity, the declaration for the *body* element becomes the following:

```
<!ELEMENT body %Block;>
```

As you can see, using the parameter entities, you can give your document a clear structure.

Using parameter entities in attributes

The XHTML standard also uses parameter entities in attributes, as we saw earlier with the *events* entity. You could use this *events* entity and two additional entities to create an internal parameter entity for attributes shared among many elements, as shown here:

```
<!-- Internationalization attributes
    lang          Language code (backward-compatible)
    xml:lang      Language code (per XML 1.0 spec)
    dir           Direction for weak/neutral text
-->
<!ENTITY % i18n " lang      NMTOKEN  #IMPLIED
                xml:lang NMTOKEN  #IMPLIED
                dir      (ltr | rtl )  #IMPLIED">
<!ENTITY % coreattrs
                " id      ID       #IMPLIED
                class   CDATA    #IMPLIED
                style   CDATA    #IMPLIED
                title   CDATA    #IMPLIED">

<!ENTITY % attrs " %coreattrs;
                %i18n;
                %events;">
```

The language entity *i18n* can be understood by XML and non-XML compliant browsers and is used to mark elements as belonging to a particular language.

> **NOTE**   For more information about language codes, visit the Web site *http://www.oasis-open.org/cover/iso639a.html.*

The *attrs* parameter entity can be used for the most common attributes associated with the HTML elements in the DTD. For example, the *body* element's attribute can now be written as follows:

```
<!ATTLIST body   %attrs;
                onload   CDATA  #IMPLIED
                onunload CDATA  #IMPLIED>
```

Rewriting the sample DTD using parameter entities

Ideally, you want your XML Web documents to be compatible with the new XHTML standard. Using entities and with other changes, the DTD example from Chapter 4 can be rewritten as follows:

```
<!-- Entities that can occur at block or inline level. ====-->

<!ENTITY % misc " script
                  | noscript">
<!ENTITY % Inline "(#PCDATA | %inline; | %misc;)*">

<!-- Entities for inline elements =================-->
<!ENTITY % special "br
                    | span
                    | img">

<!ENTITY % fontstyle "tt
                      | i
                      | b
                      | big
                      | small">

<!ENTITY % phrase "em
                   | strong
                   | q
                   | sub
                   | sup">

<!ENTITY % inline.forms "input
                         | select
                         | textarea
                         | label
                         | button">

<!ENTITY % inline "a
                   | %special;
                   | %fontstyle;
                   | %phrase;
                   | %inline.forms;">

<!ENTITY % Inline  "(#PCDATA
                    | %inline;
                    | %misc;)*">

<!-- Entities used for block elements ============-->
<!ENTITY % heading "h1
                    | h2
                    | h3
                    | h4
                    | h5
```

(continued)

```
                               | h6">

<!ENTITY % lists "ul
                     | ol">

<!ENTITY % blocktext "hr
                         | blockquote">

<!ENTITY % block "p
                   | %heading;
                   | div
                   | %lists;
                   | %blocktext;
                   | fieldset
                   | table">

<!ENTITY % Block " (%block;
                   | form
                   | %misc; )*">

<!-- Mixed block and inline ===========================-->
<!-- %Flow; mixes block and inline and is used for list
     items and so on. -->
<!ENTITY % Flow " (#PCDATA
                   | %block;
                   | form
                   | %inline;
                   | %misc; )*">
<!ENTITY % form.content " #PCDATA
                            | p
                            | %lists;
                            | %blocktext;
                            | a
                            | %special;
                            | %fontstyle;
                            | %phrase;
                            | %inline.forms;
                            | table
                            | %heading;
                            | div
                            | fieldset
                            | %misc; ">

<!ENTITY % events " onclick     CDATA   #IMPLIED
                    ondblclick  CDATA   #IMPLIED
                    onmousedown CDATA   #IMPLIED
                    onmouseup   CDATA   #IMPLIED
                    onmouseover CDATA   #IMPLIED
```

```
                                   onmousemove CDATA   #IMPLIED
                                   onmouseout  CDATA   #IMPLIED
                                   onkeypress  CDATA   #IMPLIED
                                   onkeydown   CDATA   #IMPLIED
                                   onkeyup     CDATA   #IMPLIED">

<!ENTITY % i18n " lang      NMTOKEN  #IMPLIED
                  xml:lang NMTOKEN  #IMPLIED
                  dir       (ltr | rtl )  #IMPLIED">

<!-- Core attributes common to most elements
 id      Document-wide unique ID
 class   Space-separated list of classes
 style   Associated style info
 title   Advisory title/amplification
-->
<!-- Style sheet data -->
<!ENTITY % StyleSheet "CDATA">
<!ENTITY % coreattrs " id     ID   #IMPLIED
                       class CDATA  #IMPLIED
                       style CDATA  #IMPLIED">

<!ENTITY % attrs " %coreattrs;
                   %i18n;
                   %events;">

<!-- End Entity Declarations  =====================-->
<!ENTITY % URI "CDATA">
<!--a Uniform Resource Identifier, see [RFC2396]-->
<!ELEMENT html  (head, body)>
<!ATTLIST html  %i18n;
                xmlns CDATA  #FIXED 'http://www.w3.org/1999/xhtml'>

<!ELEMENT head  (title, base?)>
<!ATTLIST head  %i18n;
                profile CDATA  #IMPLIED>

<!ELEMENT title  (#PCDATA )>
<!ATTLIST title  %i18n; >

<!ELEMENT base EMPTY>
<!ATTLIST base  target CDATA  #REQUIRED >

<!ELEMENT body  (basefont? , (p )? , table )>
<!ATTLIST body  alink   CDATA  #IMPLIED
                text    CDATA  #IMPLIED
                bgcolor CDATA  #IMPLIED
```

(continued)

```
                    link    CDATA   #IMPLIED
                    vlink   CDATA   #IMPLIED >

<!ELEMENT basefont EMPTY>
<!ATTLIST basefont  size CDATA  #REQUIRED >

<!-- Generic language/style container ===============-->
<!ELEMENT a   (#PCDATA )>
<!ATTLIST a   %attrs;
            href   CDATA  #IMPLIED
            name   CDATA  #IMPLIED
            target CDATA  #IMPLIED >

<!ELEMENT table   (tr )+>
<!ATTLIST table   %attrs;
                width       CDATA  #IMPLIED
                rules       CDATA  #IMPLIED
                frame       CDATA  #IMPLIED
                align       CDATA  'Center'
                cellpadding CDATA  '0'
                border      CDATA  '0'
                cellspacing CDATA  '0' >

<!ELEMENT tr  (td+ )>
<!ATTLIST tr  %attrs; >

<!ELEMENT td  (cellcontent )>
<!ATTLIST td  %attrs;
                bgcolor  (Cyan|Lime|Black|White|Maroon ) 'White'
                align    CDATA  'Center'
                rowspan CDATA  #IMPLIED
                colspan CDATA  #IMPLIED >

<!ELEMENT cellcontent   (%Block; | p?)+>
<!ATTLIST cellcontent   cellname CDATA  #REQUIRED >

<!ELEMENT h1 %Inline;>
<!ATTLIST h1  align CDATA  #IMPLIED
              %attrs; >
<!ELEMENT h2 %Inline;>
<!ATTLIST h2  align CDATA  #IMPLIED
              %attrs; >
<!ELEMENT h3 %Inline;>
<!ATTLIST h3  align CDATA  #IMPLIED
              %attrs; >
<!ELEMENT h4 %Inline;>
```

```
<!ATTLIST h4   align CDATA   #IMPLIED
              %attrs; >
<!ELEMENT h5 %Inline;>
<!ATTLIST h5   align CDATA   #IMPLIED
              %attrs; >
<!ELEMENT h6 %Inline;>
<!ATTLIST h6   align CDATA   #IMPLIED
              %attrs; >
<!ELEMENT p %Inline;>
<!ATTLIST p   %attrs; >

<!-- Inline Element Declarations ==================-->

<!-- Forced line break -->
<!ELEMENT br EMPTY>
<!ATTLIST br   %coreattrs;
               clear     CDATA  #REQUIRED >

<!-- Emphasis -->
<!ELEMENT em %Inline;>
<!ATTLIST em   %attrs; >

<!-- Strong emphasis -->
<!ELEMENT strong %Inline;>
<!ATTLIST strong   %attrs; >

<!-- Inlined quote -->
<!ELEMENT q %Inline;>
<!ATTLIST q   %attrs;
               cite  CDATA  #IMPLIED >

<!-- Subscript -->
<!ELEMENT sub %Inline;>
<!ATTLIST sub   %attrs; >

<!-- Superscript -->
<!ELEMENT sup %Inline;>
<!ATTLIST sup   %attrs; >

<!-- Fixed-pitch font -->
<!ELEMENT tt %Inline;>
<!ATTLIST tt   %attrs; >

<!-- Italic font -->
<!ELEMENT i %Inline;>
<!ATTLIST i   %attrs; >
```

(continued)

```
<!-- Bold font -->
<!ELEMENT b %Inline;>
<!ATTLIST b  %attrs; >

<!-- Bigger font -->
<!ELEMENT big %Inline;>
<!ATTLIST big  %attrs; >

<!-- Smaller font -->
<!ELEMENT small %Inline;>
<!ATTLIST small  %attrs; >

<!-- hspace, border, align, and vspace are not in the strict
     XHTML standard for img. -->
<!ELEMENT img EMPTY>
<!ATTLIST img  %attrs;
               align  CDATA  #IMPLIED
               border CDATA  #IMPLIED
               width  CDATA  #IMPLIED
               height CDATA  #IMPLIED
               hspace CDATA  #IMPLIED
               vspace CDATA  #IMPLIED
               src    CDATA  #REQUIRED >

<!ELEMENT ul  (font? , li+ )>
<!ATTLIST ul  %attrs;
              type  CDATA  'text' >

<!ELEMENT ol  (font? , li+ )>
<!ATTLIST ol  type  CDATA  'text'
              start CDATA  #IMPLIED
              %attrs; >

<!ELEMENT li  %Flow; >
<!ATTLIST li  %attrs; >

<!--================= Form Elements================-->
<!--Each label must not contain more than one field.
    Label elements shouldn't be nested.
-->
<!ELEMENT label %Inline;>
<!ATTLIST label  %attrs;
                 for    IDREF  #IMPLIED >

<!ENTITY % InputType "(text | password | checkbox |
    radio | submit | reset |
    file | hidden | image | button)">
```

```
<!-- The name attribute is required for all elements but
     the submit and reset elements. -->
<!ELEMENT input EMPTY>
<!ATTLIST input  %attrs; >


<!ELEMENT select  (optgroup | option )+>
<!ATTLIST select %attrs;>


<!-- Option selector -->
<!ATTLIST select name     CDATA   #IMPLIED>
<!ATTLIST select size     CDATA   #IMPLIED>
<!ATTLIST select multiple (multiple) #IMPLIED>
<!ATTLIST select disabled (disabled) #IMPLIED>
<!ATTLIST select tabindex CDATA   #IMPLIED>
<!ATTLIST select onfocus  CDATA   #IMPLIED>
<!ATTLIST select onblur   CDATA   #IMPLIED>
<!ATTLIST select onchange CDATA   #IMPLIED>
<!ELEMENT optgroup  (option )+>
<!ATTLIST optgroup  %attrs;
                    disabled  (disabled ) #IMPLIED
                    label     CDATA  #REQUIRED>


<!ELEMENT option  (#PCDATA )>
<!ATTLIST option  %attrs;
                    selected  (selected ) #IMPLIED
                    disabled  (disabled ) #IMPLIED
                    label     CDATA  #IMPLIED
                    value     CDATA  #IMPLIED >
<!-- Multiple-line text field -->
<!ELEMENT textarea  (#PCDATA )>
<!ATTLIST textarea  %attrs; >


<!ELEMENT legend %Inline;>
<!ATTLIST legend  %attrs; >


<!--==================== Horizontal Rule =============-->
<!ELEMENT hr EMPTY>
<!ATTLIST hr  %attrs; >
<!--==================== Block-like Quotes ==========-->
<!ELEMENT blockquote %Block;>
<!ATTLIST blockquote  %attrs;
                      cite  CDATA  #IMPLIED >
```

(continued)

```
<!-- The fieldset element is used to group form fields.
  Only one legend element should occur in the content,
  and if present it should be preceded only by white space.
-->

<!ELEMENT fieldset
   (#PCDATA | legend | %block; | form | %inline; | %misc; )*>
<!ATTLIST fieldset  %attrs; >


<!ELEMENT script  (#PCDATA )>
<!ATTLIST script   charset   CDATA   #IMPLIED
                   type      CDATA   #REQUIRED
                   src       CDATA   #IMPLIED
                   defer     CDATA   #IMPLIED
                   xml:space CDATA   #FIXED 'preserve' >

<!-- Alternative content container for non-script-based
     rendering -->

<!ELEMENT noscript %Block;>
<!ATTLIST noscript %attrs; >


<!ELEMENT button  (#PCDATA | p | %heading; | div | %lists; |
   %blocktext; | table | %special; | %fontstyle; |
   %phrase; | %misc; )*>
<!ATTLIST button   %attrs;
                   name      CDATA  #IMPLIED
                   value     CDATA  #IMPLIED
                   type      (button | submit | reset )  'submit'
                   disabled  (disabled )  #IMPLIED
                   tabindex  CDATA  #IMPLIED
                   accesskey CDATA  #IMPLIED
                   onfocus   CDATA  #IMPLIED
                   onblur    CDATA  #IMPLIED >


<!ELEMENT span %Inline;>
<!ATTLIST span   %attrs; >
<!--The font element is not included in the XHTML standard. -->
<!ELEMENT font   (b )>
<!ATTLIST font   color CDATA  #REQUIRED
                 face  CDATA  #REQUIRED
                 size  CDATA  #REQUIRED >


<!ELEMENT form %form.content;>
<!ELEMENT div %Flow;>
<!ATTLIST div %attrs; >
```

This might look like a completely different DTD, but it is essentially the same as the DTD we created in Chapter 4. Only one structural change has occurred: the block elements, such as the *h1* element, have been moved out of the *p* element and now are child elements of the *body* element. Several elements have been added, including the *form* element itself and its child elements (*button*, *label*, *select*, and so on) and the font formatting elements, including *i* and *b*. Numerous additions have been made to the attributes, including *language*, *id*, and the scripting events. This sample DTD is also available on the companion CD.

XML documents built using this new DTD will still use a table to format and contain all of the elements that will be displayed in the browser. However, in the new DTD, the declaration for the *body* element is different from that in our original DTD. In our original DTD, the *a* (anchor) element at the top of the page is a child element of the *body* element. However, this element is not a child element of the *body* element in the XHTML standard. As we have seen, the declaration for the *body* element in the XHTML standard is as follows:

```
<!ELEMENT body %Block;>
```

As we have discussed, the *Block* internal parameter entity is declared as follows:

```
<!ENTITY % Block " (%block; | form | %misc;)*">
```

Replacing *%block;* and *%misc;* results in the following code:

```
<!ENTITY % Block " (p | %heading; | div | %lists; |
    %blocktext; | fieldset | table | form | script |
    noscript)*">
```

Replacing *%heading;* and *%blocktext;* will give you the actual declaration for the *body* element, as shown here:

```
<!ENTITY % Block " (p | h1 | h2 | h3 | h4 | h5 | h6 | div | ul |
    ol | hr | blockquote | fieldset | table |
    form | script | noscript)*">
```

> **NOTE** It would be worth your time to go through the DTD and replace the entities with their actual values. You may also find it interesting to download the latest version of the XHTML standard and do all of the replacements in that document, too.

Creating this expanded declaration manually took some time, but any of the DTD tools could have done this work for you in just a few moments. For example, Figure 5-2 shows our sample XHTML DTD as it appears in XML Authority.

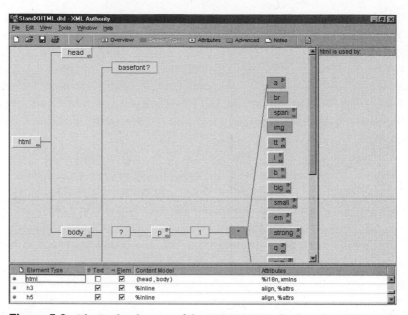

Figure 5-2. *The* Body *element of the XHTML DTD displayed in XML Authority.*

The child elements of the *Body* element are readily visible. (You can scroll down to see the complete list.)

NOTE   You do not have to include all of these child elements in your DTD to be compatible with the XHTML standard; instead, you can include only those elements that you need for your projects. If you want to be compliant with the standard, however, you cannot add elements to the *body* element that are not included in the standard.

Notice that the *a* element is not a child element of the XHTML *body* element; it is actually a child element of the *p* element. Therefore, you cannot use the declaration included in the original DTD we discussed in Chapter 4, shown here:

```
<!ELEMENT body (basefont? , a? , table)>
```

In this declaration, the *a* element is a child element of the *body* element, which does not comply with the standard. To solve this problem, you will need to use the *p* element, as shown here:

```
<!ELEMENT body (basefont? , (p)? , table)>
```

While this declaration makes the DTD conform to the XHTML standard, it also means that any of the inline elements, not just the *a* element, can be used in the *body* element as long as they are contained within a *p* element.

Many child elements that are included in the *body* element of the XHTML standard are not included in the example DTD. This is because you are using the table to hold most of the content and do not need most of these child elements. You can think of the XML documents defined by the example DTD as a subset of the XML documents defined by the more general XHTML DTD. The example DTD includes only the structure you need for your documents.

The XHTML standard declaration for the table cell element (*td*) is shown here:

```
<!ELEMENT td %Flow;>
```

If you replace the *Flow* parameter entity and all of the parameter entities contained within *%Flow;* as you did earlier for the *body* element, your final *td* declaration will look like this:

```
<!ELEMENT td #PCDATA | p | h1|h2|h3|h4|h5|h6| div | ul | ol |
    hr | blockquote | fieldset | table | form | a | br | span |
    img | tt | i | b | big | small | em | strong | q | sub |
    sup |input | select | textarea | label | button | script |
    noscript>
```

As you can see, the *Flow* entity includes virtually everything. You can use a *td* element as a container for all of the *block* and *inline* elements, which is exactly what you want to do.

In the example DTD, the following declaration is created for the *td* element and the *cellcontent* element:

```
<!ELEMENT td (cellcontent)>
<!ELEMENT cellcontent (%Block;)+>
```

This declaration doesn't comply with the XHTML standard. The *cellcontent* element does not belong to the standard; it was created for marking up the text. When you use custom elements, such as the *cellcontent* element in this example, you will need to remove them using Extensible Stylesheet Language (XSL). Using XSL, you can transform the preceding definitions to be:

```
<!ELEMENT td (%Block;)+>
```

This declaration will be compliant with the XHTML standard. We'll have a detailed discussion about XSL in Chapter 12.

The New HelpHTM.htm Document

Because of the changes in the DTD, you will have to make some minor changes to the sample HelpHTM.htm document we created in Chapter 4. You will now have to delete all the *p* elements because the *block* elements are no longer child elements of the *p* elements. You will also have to add several *p* elements to wrap the *a* elements. Change the *a* element at the beginning of the document as shown here:

```
<p><a name="Top"><!--Top tag--></a></p>
```

Then wrap all the links in the lists using the *p* element. For example, you can wrap the first link in the HelpHTM.htm document as follows:

```
<p>
    <a href="FirstTimeVisitorInfo.html" target="">
        First-Time Visitor Information</a>
</p>
```

If you do this and then reference the new DTD, the document is valid.

> **NOTE** The new version of the HelpHTM.htm file is included on the companion CD.

Possible Problems with Parameter Entities

The parameter entities have made the overall DTD more compact, but have they made it more readable? In general, grouping items into parameter entities can make the document more readable, but keep in mind that if you go too far and create too many parameter entities, it might be nearly impossible for a human to read your DTD. For example, most developers would consider the basic form objects (*button*, *label*, *textArea*, and so on) to be the primary child elements of a *form* element. However, you will need to dig through many layers of the XHTML DTD to discover that these elements are actually child elements of the *form* element.

In the XHTML DTD, the form objects are defined in an internal parameter entity named *inline.forms*, which is included in the *inline* parameter entity. The *inline* entity is used in the *Inline* parameter entity, which in turn is used in the *p* element's declaration. The *p* element is included in the *block* parameter entity's declaration, and the *block* entity is included in the *form.content* parameter entity. Finally, the *form.content* entity is included in the *form* element's declaration, as shown here:

```
<!ENTITY % inline.forms "input | select | textarea | label
    | button">
<!ENTITY % inline
        "a | %special; | %fontstyle; | %phrase; | %inline.forms;">
<!ENTITY % Inline "(%inline;| %misc;)*">

<!ELEMENT p %Inline;>
<!ENTITY % block
    "p | %heading; | div | %lists; | %blocktext; | fieldset |
    table">
```

```
<!ENTITY % form.content "(%block; | % inline; | %misc;)*">
<!ELEMENT form %form.content;>
```

To use a form object such as *select*, you will need to include the following statement in your XML document:

```
<form><p><select/></p></form>
```

There is another path to the form objects. Notice that the *block* entity declaration includes a *fieldset* element. The *fieldset* element also contains the *inline* element, just as the *p* element did, as shown here:

```
<!ENTITY % inline.forms "input | select | textarea | label |
    button">
<!ENTITY % inline
    "a | %special; | %fontstyle; | %phrase; |
    %inline.forms;">
<!ELEMENT fieldset (#PCDATA | legend | %block; | form |
    %inline; | %misc;)*>
<!ENTITY % block
    "p | %heading; | div | %lists; | %blocktext; | fieldset |
    table">
<!ENTITY % form.content "(%block; | %misc;)*">
<!ELEMENT form %form.content;>
```

To use a form object such as *select* in this case, you would include the following statement in your XML document:

```
<form><fieldset><select/></fieldset></form>
```

You can use an XML tool to view this relationship. An excellent tool for viewing the structure of an XML DTD is Near and Far, available at *http://www.microstar.com*. Without an XML tool, the parameter entities make the DTD nearly impossible to read. Try to strike a balance by using enough parameter entities to create reusable groups that make your DTD neater but not so many parameter entities that your DTD is unreadable.

You must also be careful that the document is still valid and well formed once the parameter entity has been substituted. For example, consider the following declaration:

```
<!ENTITY % Inline " (#PCDATA
                | %inline;
                | %misc;)*">
```

As you can see, this declaration is missing the closing parenthesis. When the *Inline* parameter entity is substituted, it will create an invalid declaration. Be sure that all your components are properly nested, opened, and closed after the entities are substituted.

A common problem when working with XML is finding errors in your XML documents and your DTDs. Often XML tools display cryptic error messages that leave you with no idea as to the real source of a problem. XML Notepad, which was used to write the code in this book, can be used for writing and debugging XML documents that have no external DTDs. XML Authority works well with DTDs and usually provides clear error messages that help you locate errors in your DTD. If you are working with an XML document that references an external DTD, Web Writer usually provides helpful error messages. All of these products provide trial versions. Try them all, and then choose the tools that best meet your needs. Be aware that sometimes a small error in a DTD could take a long time to track down (for example, using *Block* instead of *block* in the preceding DTD will cause an error that might take several hours to track down).

EXTERNAL ENTITIES

In this section, we'll look at the three categories of external entities: external parsed general entities, external unparsed general entities, and external parameter entities. External entities can be used when more than one DTD uses the same entities. You can reduce the amount of time it takes to produce new DTDs by creating a repository of documents containing entity declarations.

External Parsed General Entities

External parsed general entities enable you to store a piece of your XML document in a separate file. An external parsed general entity can be set equal to this external XML document. Using the external general entity, the external XML file can be referenced anywhere in your XML document.

Declaring an external parsed general entity

The syntax for declaring an external general entity is shown here:

```
<!ENTITY name SYSTEM URI>
```

Notice that the external general entity declaration uses a keyword following the entity name. This keyword can be SYSTEM or PUBLIC. The PUBLIC identifier is used when the document is officially registered. The SYSTEM identifier is used with unregistered documents that are located using a *URI*, which stands for *Uniform Resource Identifier*, to tell the parser where to find the object referenced in the declaration. Since we are now working with unregistered documents, we will use the SYSTEM identifier in the examples below.

Using external parsed general entities

External parsed general entities can be referenced in the document instance and in the content of another general entity. Unlike internal general entities, external parsed general entities cannot be referenced in an attribute value. To reference an external parsed general entity, you need to precede the entity with an ampersand and follow it with a semicolon, the same way you reference internal general entities. Let's look at how to use external parsed general entities in the XML document. Since our sample file HelpHTM.htm is a well-formed XML document, we can save it as Help.xml. To divide the Web page in this document into header, footer, left navigation bar, and body sections, add the following code to the Help.xml:

```
<?xml version="1.0" encoding="UTF-8" standalone="no" ?>
<!DOCTYPE html SYSTEM  "StandXHTML.dtd" [
<!ENTITY topheader SYSTEM "Topheader.htm">
<!ENTITY leftnav SYSTEM "Leftnav.htm">
<!ENTITY footer SYSTEM "Footer.htm">
<!ENTITY body SYSTEM "Body.htm">
]>
<html>
    <head>
        <title>Northwind Traders Help Desk</title>
    </head>
    <body text="#000000" bgcolor="#FFFFFF" link="#003399"
        alink="#FF9933"  vlink="#996633">
        &topheader;
        &leftnav;
        &body;
        &footer;
    </body>
</html>
```

Using this new DTD, the Body.htm file referenced in our sample Web help page would look like this:

```
<html>
    <p><a name="Top"><!--Top tag--></a></p>
      <table border="5" frame="" rules="" width="100%"
          cellspacing="0" cellpadding="0">
        <tr>
            <td  colspan="2" align="Center">
                <cellcontent cellname="Help Topic List ">
                    <h1 align="Center">Help Desk</h1>
                </cellcontent>
            </td>
        </tr>
```

(continued)

```
<tr  valign="Top" >
    <td align="Left" >
        <cellcontent cellname="First-Time Visitor">
            <ul >
            <font  size="3">
               <b>For First-Time Visitors</b>
            </font>
            <li>
            <p>
            <a href="FirstTimeVisitorInfo.html"
               target=""> First-Time Visitor Information</a>
            </p>
            </li>
            <li>
            <p>
            <a href="SecureShopping.html" target="">
               Secure Shopping at Northwind Traders</a>
            </p>
            </li>
            <li>
            <p>
            <a href="FreqaskedQ.htm" target="">
               Frequently Asked Questions</a>
            </p>
            </li>
            <li>
            <p>
            <a href="NavWeb.html" target="">
               Navigating the Web</a>
            </p>
            </li>
            </ul>
        </cellcontent>
    </td>
    <td align="Left">
        <cellcontent cellname="Shipping links">
            <ul type="">
                <font size="3">
                    <b>Shipping</b>
                </font>
                <li>
                <p>
                    <a href="Rates.htm" target="">Rates</a>
                </p>
                </li>
                <li>
                    <p>
                    <a href="OrderCheck.htm" target="">
                        Checking on Your Order</a>
                    </p>
                </li>
```

```
                    <li>
                    <p>
                        <a href="Returns.htm" target="">
                            Returns</a>
                    </p>
                    </li>
                </ul>
            </cellcontent>
        </td>
    </tr>
</table>
</html>
```

The Help.xml file and the Body.htm file are included on the companion CD. Similarly you can create three other external files: Topheader.htm, Leftnav.htm, and Footer.htm. All of the rules that apply to internal general entities also apply to the external parsed general entities. Only the declaration and the source of the replaced text are different.

External Unparsed General Entities

External unparsed general entities are similar to other entities, except that the XML parser will not try to parse the information within them. Essentially, the data within an external unparsed general entity is ignored by the XML parser and passed on to the application that is using the document in its original format. This is exactly what we want done for non-XML files such as images.

Notations

External unparsed general entities contain one additional component: *notations*. Notations are used by the application to identify the data in the external unparsed general entity or to identify what application needs to be used to interpret the data. For example, if the data contained in the entity is a GIF image file, the following notation would identify it:

```
<!NOTATION GIF89a SYSTEM
    "-//Compuserve//NOTATION Graphic Interchange Format 89a//EN">
```

It would be up to the application to determine how to interpret this information and present the image properly.

Notations can be declared in two different ways. The first method is used when the notation is not public and is located at some URI. It uses the syntax shown here:

<!NOTATION *notation_name* SYSTEM *resource_URI* >

The second method is used for a notation that has been registered as public and given a unique ID. It uses the following syntax:

<!NOTATION *notation_name* PUBLIC *public_ID resource_URI*>

Examples of the two types of declarations are shown here:

```
<!NOTATION GIF89a SYSTEM
    "-//Compuserver//NOTATION Graphic Interchange Format 89a//EN">
<!NOTATION GIF SYSTEM "GIF">
<!NOTATION BMP SYSTEM "MSPAINT.EXE">
<!NOTATION GIF89a PUBLIC "-//Compuserve//NOTATION Graphic
    Interchange Format 89a//EN" "ps4prp.exe">
```

Declaring an external unparsed general entity

Once you have created a notation, you can use the notation to declare external unparsed general entities. The format for these declarations is similar to the declarations for external parsed general entities, except that in this case a notation appears at the end of the declaration. The NDATA keyword is used to associate the external unparsed general entity with a particular notation. The syntax for the declaration is shown here:

<!ENTITY *entity_name* SYSTEM *URI* NDATA *notation_name*>

Using our second notation definition, you could create the following declaration:

```
<!ENTITY image.topnav SYSTEM "topnav.gif" NDATA GIF>
```

Now that you have defined the notation and then defined an external unparsed general entity that uses this notation, you will want to use this external unparsed general entity in your XML document body. For example, you might want to insert this GIF image at the top of a Web page.

Using external unparsed general entities

When you are using an external unparsed general entity as a value for an attribute in your XML document, you will want the XML parser to ignore the data returned by the entity. To accomplish this, you must tell the XML parser that you are referencing an external unparsed general entity in the declaration of the attribute. The ENTITY or ENTITIES keyword will be used in the attribute declaration to mark an attribute as containing an external unparsed general entity reference, as shown here:

```
<!--Part of the DTD-->
<!NOTATION gif SYSTEM "gif">
<!NOTATION jpeg SYSTEM "jpg">
<!NOTATION bmp SYSTEM "bmp">
```

```
<!ENTITY image.topimage SYSTEM "topimage.gif" NDATA gif>
<!ENTITY image.topnav1 SYSTEM "topnav1.gif" NDATA gif>
<!ENTITY image.topnav2 SYSTEM "topnav2.gif" NDATA gif>
<!ENTITY Welcome SYSTEM "Welcome.jpg" NDATA jpg>
<!ELEMENT topimages EMPTY>
<!ATTLIST topimages
    topimage ENTITY #FIXED "image.topimage"
    topnav ENTITIES "image.topnav1 image.topnav2">
<!ELEMENT img EMPTY>
<!ATTLIST img  %attrs;
             align  CDATA  #IMPLIED
             border CDATA  #IMPLIED
             width  CDATA  #IMPLIED
             height CDATA  #IMPLIED
             hspace CDATA  #IMPLIED
             vspace CDATA  #IMPLIED
             src    ENTITY #REQUIRED
             type   NOTATION (gif|jpg|bmp) "jpg">
<!--XML Body-->
<topimages topimage="image.topimage" topnav="image.topnav1
    image.topnav2"></topimages>
<img src = "Welcome"></img>
```

This code declares two elements: *topimages* and *img*. The *topimages* element has two attributes associated with it: *topimage* and *topnav*. The *img* element is the one used in the DTD example discussed in the "Rewriting the sample DTD using parameter entities" section, except that here it contains the *type* attribute. The *type* attribute is a *notation attribute*, as it contains the keyword NOTATION. The items listed in the enumerated type must be defined in the DTD as notations, as is done in the above declaration.

External Parameter Entities

External parameter entities are just like internal parameter entities except that they retrieve the replacement text from external files.

Declaring an external parameter entity

The syntax for declaring an external parameter entity is similar to the declarations for internal parameter entities, except that the SYSTEM keyword or the PUBLIC keyword is used. The syntax for the declaration is shown here:

<!ENTITY % *name* SYSTEM *"string_of_characters"*>

To use the external parameter entity, you could place all of the parameter entities that were defined in the example DTD in a file named Parameter.dtd. To do so, you would add the following code to the XML document:

```
<!ENTITY % parameterentities SYSTEM "Parameter.dtd">
%parameterentities;
<!--================ Document Structure=========================-->
<!ELEMENT html   (head , body)>
<!ATTLIST html   %i18n;
                 xmlns CDATA #FIXED 'http://www.w3.org/1999/xhtml'>

<!--Rest of DTD here-->
```

First we declare the *parameterentities* entity, which links to the external Parameter.dtd, and then we use *parameterentities* to insert this document into the XML document. This external parameter entity could be used to create several DTDs. External parameter entities are useful when parts of your DTD will be used by several other DTDs.

PROCESSING ORDER

It is important to understand exactly how the DTD will be processed, especially if it includes internal and external entities. We are most interested in the processing order of the different types of entities because the processing order will affect the final result of the DTD and the XML document if the DTD and the XML document include entities and the entities are substituted. Before we examine processing order, let's look at the rules for processing a document:

- If a document contains more than one entity declaration using the same entity name, the first entity declaration that is encountered will be used. All subsequent declarations with the same name will be ignored.

- If a document contains more than one attribute declaration using the same attribute name, the first attribute declaration that is encountered will be used. All subsequent declarations with the same name will be ignored.

- If more than one element declaration has the same element name, a fatal error will be raised by the processor.

Now that you know the rules for processing an XML document, let's look at the processing order that the processor follows:

1. The internal subset of the DTD is read before everything else. This guarantees that any attribute or entity definitions listed in the internal subset will override any definitions in an externally referenced DTD. Developers can still use external DTDs, but they can override the declarations in the external DTDs.

2. If the internal DTD contains external parameter entities, these entities will be replaced when the processor reaches them in the DTD. The internal DTD will be expanded to include the replacement text, and the replacement text will be processed. Once this is done, the rest of the internal DTD is processed. If the internal DTD contains additional external parameter entities, they will be replaced in the same manner when the processor reaches them. All general entities will be ignored at this step.

3. Once the entire internal DTD is processed, any external DTDs referenced in the DOCTYPE declaration using the PUBLIC or SYSTEM keyword will be processed.

4. Once the internal and external DTDs are processed and validated, the processor will replace general entities in the document body when they are referenced in the document.

Thus, you can create general external DTD documents containing declarations that apply to a large set of applications. You can override entities and attributes in these external DTDs in an internal DTD because the internal DTD will be processed first. Notice that the DTD is validated before the general entities are replaced. This order explains why general entities can never be used in any part of your declarations that are being validated, such as the enumerated values for an attribute.

CONDITIONAL SECTIONS

The XML specification defines conditional sections of your DTD so that you can decide to include or exclude portions of your DTD. The conditional sections can occur only in the external subset of the DTD and in those external entities referenced from the internal subset. The syntax is shown here:

```
<![ INCLUDE [
    <!--The declarations you want to include-->
⋮
]]>
```

(continued)

```
<![ IGNORE [
    <!--The declarations you want to ignore-->
    :
]]>
```

If you combine these conditional sections with parameter entities, you will have a way to include and exclude blocks of text by changing the values of the parameter entities. For example, if you wanted to include declarations that could be used for debugging your application, you could add the following declaration:

```
<!ENTITY % debug "INCLUDE">
<![ %debug; [
    <!--Debugging code here -->
]]>
```

You could turn debugging off by changing the entity declaration as follows:

```
<!ENTITY % debug "IGNORE">
```

SUMMARY

Entities provide a useful shorthand notation that allows you to assign strings (binary data) to a particular name. This name can then be inserted into either the DTD (parameter entities) or the XML document body (general entities).

Using XML tools such as XML Authority or Near and Far, you can build DTDs from these entities. The tools will also help you view the structure of complicated documents. Entities used carefully can make DTDs more readable; too many entities can make your DTD readable only by using one of the XML tools.

External entities enable you to include external files in your document. These files can be reusable declarations for your DTDs, reusable XML code for your XML document, and non-text information in your document body. By carefully planning the structure of your documents, how you are going to build them, and what information they will contain, you can create a set of reusable documents using entities and external DTDs.

In Chapter 6, we will discuss four additional XML specifications: XLink, XPath, XPointer, and Namespaces. The first three specifications are used for placing links in your documents. Namespaces are used to prevent names from clashing when a DTD is imported.

Chapter 6

XML Namespace, XPath, XPointer, and XLink

As we've seen in Chapter 2, the XML language is defined in several specifications. In this chapter, we will look at four of the XML specifications: XML Namespaces, XML Path Language (XPath), XML Pointer Language (XPointer), and XML Linking Language (XLink). You can view these four specifications at the W3C Web site (*http://www.w3c.org.*)

XLink is part of the XML standard that currently defines the linking components of XML. XLink is similar to the functionality of the <a> tag in HTML in that XLink allows elements to be inserted into XML documents to create links between resources. XLink also has additional features. *XPath* is a language that views the XML document as a tree with nodes. Using XPath, you can locate any node in the XML document tree. *XPointer* provides a way to address the internal structure of an XML document. XPointer extends XPath by allowing you to address points and ranges in addition to nodes, locate information by string matching, and use addressing expressions in URI-references as fragment identifiers. XLink works with either

XPath or XPointer. The XPath or XPointer language is used to define where you want to link in an XML document, and XLink will provide the actual link to that point in the document.

Namespaces are also an important part of the XML specification. When creating DTDs or schemas from multiple documents, you need a way to define where each definition originated. This is especially important if two external documents use the same name for an element, but each is defining a different element. For example, *title* could refer to Mr., Mrs., and Miss in one DTD and to the title of the document in another DTD. If you merged these two DTDs, you would have a name conflict. Namespaces prevent this conflict from happening.

In this chapter, we'll begin by looking at namespaces and then move on to the XPath, XPointer, and XLink languages.

> **NOTE**   At the time of this writing, the specifications for XLink and XPointer are still being reviewed, and it's possible that some of the syntax will change. The overall structure of XPointer, XPath, and XLink should not change.

NAMESPACES

XML namespaces offer a way to create names in an XML document that are identified by a Uniform Resource Identifier (URI). By using namespaces in your XML document, you can uniquely identify elements or attributes in the document. For example, consider the following XML document fragment:

```
<order>
   <type ordertype="New"/>
   <customer>
      <type customertype="Rich"/>
   </customer>
</order>
```

This is a valid XML document, yet it would be difficult for an application reading this document to differentiate between the *type* element associated with the *order* element and the *type* element associated with the *customer* element. Although in this instance you could change the names of the elements in the DTD and XML document, this solution is not always possible.

Let's look more closely at how these element name problems can occur. For the most part, you want the DTDs you create to be *modular,* meaning that they contain definitions for only one type of information. These modular DTDs can then be combined to create more complex DTDs.

NOTE Schemas are like DTDs, except they use a different syntax than DTDs and use XML to define the structure of a set of XML documents. For a detailed discussion of schemas, see Chapter 7.

For example, you could have DTDs that define the structure of the following XML documents: Customer, Order, Order Details, Product, and Category. These DTDs can be used to create Customer, Order, Order Details, Product, and Category XML documents. You can also combine these DTDs to create a single, complete order XML DTD that contains all the detailed information about an order, including the customer, order, order details, product, and category information. The most common problem that occurs when you combine DTDs is naming conflicts between elements.

If we defined the *order* entity in an external file named Order.dtd and the *customer* entity in an external file named Customer.dtd, our example order DTD might look like this:

```
<?xml version="1.0"?>
<!--Order -->
<!ENTITY order SYSTEM "Order.dtd">
<!--Customer -->
<!ENTITY customer SYSTEM "Customer.dtd">
⋮
```

When the *Order* and *Customer* entities are replaced, the DTD might look like this:

```
<?xml version="1.0"?>
<!--Order -->
<!ELEMENT order (id, customer)>
<!ELEMENT type()>
<!ATTRIBUTE type ordertype CDATA "Old">
<!--Customer -->
<!ELEMENT customer>

<!ELEMENT type()>
<!ATTRIBUTE type customertype CDATA "Rich">
```

This DTD is invalid because the *type* element is declared twice with two different types of attributes. This repetition is one of the potential problems of using external entities.

Namespaces enable you to solve this problem. Namespaces are defined within the elements in your XML document. If an element has child elements, the child elements can either inherit the parent's namespace or override the parent's namespace.

Namespace Prefixes

Let's begin our examination of namespaces by looking at *prefixes*. Each namespace has a prefix that is used as a reference to the namespace. This prefix must follow all the usual naming conventions for XML names as we discussed in Chapter 3. In addition, prefixes must not begin with *xmlns* or *xml*. You can't use *xmlns* because it's the keyword that's used to define a namespace, and *xml* can't be used because it's the processing instruction used to define attributes of an XML document.

Namespaces are declared within an element's begin tag. The syntax for declaring a namespace looks like this:

<namespacePrefix:elementName xmlns:*namespacePrefix* = '*URL*'>

This particular URL does not refer to a DTD or a schema. The URL doesn't even have to point to an existing file. Its purpose is to provide a unique name to associate with the elements and attributes in the XML document. The namespace can also be identified by a URI or a URN.

Because each URL, URI, or URN is unique, using a company's URL followed by additional text should create unique identifiers for each namespace. Here is an example of this format:

```
<?xml version="1.0"?>
<bill:message xmlns:bill='http://www.northwindtraders.com/bill'>
    <bill:date>1/1/2002</bill:date>
    <bill:body>Your current balance is $1,999,999.00. Please pay
        immediately. Thank you.</bill:body>
</bill:message>
```

You can also declare more than one namespace in an element's begin tag, as shown here:

```
<?xml version="1.0"?>
<bill:message xmlns:bill='http://www.northwindtraders.com/bill'
    xmlns:body='http://www.northwindtraders.com/message'>
    <bill:date>1/1/2002</bill:date>
    <body:body>Your current balance is $1,999,999.00. Please pay
        immediately. Thank you. </body:body>
</bill:message>
```

In this example, the *message* element contains two namespace declarations: *bill* and *body*. The *bill* namespace is used to define the *message* element and the *date* child element. The *body* namespace is used to define the *body* child element.

Default Namespaces

A *default namespace* is used by an element if the element does not have a namespace prefix; this default is also used by all child elements of that element if they do not have a namespace prefix. The declaration for a default namespace looks like this:

> *<elementName* xmlns=*'URL'>*

Our earlier example could be rewritten using default namespaces as follows:

```
<?xml version="1.0"?>
<message xmlns='http://www.northwindtraders.com/bill'
   xmlns:body='http://www.northwindtraders.com/message'>
   <date>1/1/2002</date>
   <body:body>Your current balance is $1,999,999.00. Please pay
      immediately. Thank you. </body:body>
</message>
```

The first namespace is the default namespace. The default namespace is used by the *message* element and the *date* child element. The *body* child element still uses the *body* namespace.

You can also declare namespaces in the begin tag of child elements, as shown here:

```
<?xml version="1.0"?>
<message xmlns='http://www.northwindtraders.com/bill'
   xmlns:body='http://www.northwindtraders.com/message'>
   <date>1/1/2002</date>
   <body:body>
      <customerName xmlns='http://www.northwindtraders.com/name'>
         Fred Smith
      </customerName>
      Your current balance is $1,999,999.00. Please pay
      immediately. Thank you.
   </body:body>
</message>
```

Here the *customerName* child element is defined by a default namespace.

You can set the default namespace equal to an empty string (""), as shown here:

```
<?xml version="1.0"?>
<message xmlns=""
   xmlns:body='http://www.northwindtraders.com/message'>
   <date>1/1/2002</date>
   <body:body>Your current balance is $1,999,999.00. Please pay
      immediately. Thank you. </body:body>
</message>
```

If you do this, there will be no namespace associated with elements that are not preceded by a namespace prefix.

> **NOTE** Default namespaces apply only to elements; they do not apply to attributes.

Attributes and Namespaces

An attribute name can be used only once in an element. When you combine a namespace prefix with an attribute name, the combination must be unique. The following is acceptable:

```
<?xml version="1.0"?>
<message xmlns='http://www.northwindtraders.com/bill'
   xmlns:body='http://www.northwindtraders.com/message'>
   <date>1/1/2002</date>
   <body:body body:importance='High' importance='High'>Your current
      balance is $1,999,999.00. Please pay immediately. Thank you.
   </body:body>
</message>
```

In this case, the first *importance* attribute is associated with the *body* namespace, and the second *importance* attribute is associated with the default namespace.

Remember, you can define an element name only once in your DTD. Namespaces resolve the element naming conflicts. By using namespaces, you can reference several different documents that all use the same element names.

Declaring Namespaces in DTDs

In the preceding example, we used the tag form *<body:body>*. You must declare the element using this format in your DTD if a namespace is used. For example, this *body* element would need to be declared in your DTD as follows:

```
<!ELEMENT body:body (#PCDATA)>
```

If this declaration is used in an external DTD, all documents that reference this external DTD will need to use the name specified in the DTD (in this case, *body:body*).

You can use entities to enable users to decide whether they want to use a namespace, and if they do, what prefix they want to use. To do so, make the following declarations in your DTD:

```
<!ENTITY % ns ''> <!-- Can be overridden in the internal
                       subset of a schema document to establish a
                       namespace prefix -->
<!ELEMENT %ns;body (#PCDATA)>
```

If these declarations were included in an external DTD named MessageBody.dtd, you could include the following reference in your internal DTD:

```
<?xml version="1.0"?>
<!DOCTYPE message
[
<!ENTITY % ns 'body:'>
<!ENTITY messagebody SYSTEM "MessageBody.dtd">
⋮
```

The local declaration of the *ns* entity will override the declaration in MessageBody.dtd. Using this technique, each document that uses elements defined in an external DTD can create its own names for the namespace. Let's now move on to the other three specifications related to XML: XPath, XPointer, and XLink.

XPATH

Identifying sections of XML documents is an essential part of using Extensible Stylesheet Language (XSL) and XPath. XSL is based on the idea of identifying sections of an XML document and transforming them according to a set of rules. XPath provides a means for identifying sections of an XML document.

XPath is based on the idea of repeating patterns. XML documents develop distinctive patterns in the way their elements are presented and ordered. For example, in Chapter 5 we put an *a* element within the *body* element of an XML document to create an anchor to the top of the document. This established a pattern in which the *a* element was always included within a *p* element and the *p* element was included within the *body* element. We also had a pattern in which the *a* element was included in a *p* element within a *td* element. In this instance, the *a* element was used as a hyperlink. Thus, the *body*, *p*, *a* pattern represents an anchor and the *td*, *p*, *a* pattern represents a hyperlink.

If you can identify these two patterns in the document, you can use XSL to transform the two *a* elements in different ways—for example, the hyperlinks can be underlined and displayed in a specified color, and the anchor can be made invisible in the document. Pattern identification enables XSL to find specific elements and transform them in a specified manner. We'll have a detailed discussion of XSL in Chapter 12.

You can also use patterns to select and link to specific sections of a document. For example, you could create a link that finds all of the *item_name* elements in a purchase order document and returns a reference to these elements. In both XLink and XSL, XPath is used to identify portions of an XML document. Let's begin with location paths.

Location Paths

The XPath specification is designed to address different parts of the XML document through the use of *location paths*. The location path provides instructions for navigating to any location in an XML document. You can use XPointer to specify an *absolute location* or a *relative location*. An absolute location points to a specific place in the document structure. A relative location points to a place that is dependent upon a starting location. If you were giving directions, an absolute location would be 12 Main Street, whereas a relative location would be drive 1 mile up Main Street from the intersection of Oak Street and Main Street. In the case of an XML document, an absolute location would be the root or the second *customer* element. A relative path would be the fourth child node of the root.

The entire XML document is called the *document* element. The document is represented as a treelike structure where location paths return sets of nodes on node axes. Movement will occur up and down these node axes.

Types of Nodes

The XPath data model includes seven possible node types: *root*, *element*, *attribute*, *namespace*, *processing instruction*, *comment*, and *text*. Let's look at each of these node types in detail.

root nodes

The *root* node is at the root of the tree. It is the parent of the *document* element. As mentioned, in XPath the *document* element contains the entire document. The *root* node contains *element* nodes. It also contains all of the processing instructions and comments that occur in the *prolog* and end of the document. The prolog consists of two optional parts: the XML declaration and a DTD.

element nodes

Every element in the document has a corresponding *element* node. The children of an *element* node include other *element* nodes, *comment* nodes, *processing instruction* nodes, and *text* nodes for their content. When you view an *element* node, all internal and external entity references are expanded. All character references are resolved. The descendants of an *element* node are the children of the element and their descendants.

The *value* for an *element* node is the string that results from concatenating all the character content in all the element's descendants. The value for the *root* node and the *document element* node are the same. *Element* nodes are ordered according to the order of the begin tags of the elements in the document after expansion of general entities. This ordering is called *document order*.

An *element* node can have a unique identifier that is declared in the DTD as *ID*. No two elements can have the same value for an ID in the same document. If two elements have the same ID in the same document, the document is invalid.

attribute nodes

Each element has an associated set of *attribute* nodes. An attribute that is using a default value is treated the same as an attribute that has a specified value. For an optional attribute (declared as #IMPLIED) that has no default value, if there is no value specified for the attribute, there will be no node for this attribute.

Each *attribute* node has a name and a string value. The value can be a zero length string ("").

namespace nodes

Every element has an associated set of *namespace* nodes, one for each namespace prefix that is within the scope of the element and one for the default namespace if it exists. This means that there will be a *namespace* node for the following attributes:

- Every attribute of the element whose name begins with *xmlns;*

- Every attribute of an *ancestor* element whose name begins with *xmlns* (unless the *ancestor* element has been used previously);

- The *xmlns* attribute, unless its value is an empty string

Each *namespace* node has a name, which is a string giving the prefix, and a value, which is the namespace URI.

processing instruction nodes

An XML parser ignores processing instructions, but they can be used to pass instructions to an XML application. Every processing instruction in the XML document has a corresponding *processing instruction* node. Currently, processing instructions located within the DTD don't have corresponding *processing instruction* nodes. A *processing instruction* node has a name, which is a string equal to the processing instruction's target, and a value, which is a string containing the characters following the target and ending before the terminating *?>* characters.

comment nodes

Every comment in the XML document has a corresponding *comment* node. Every *comment* node has a value, which is a string containing the comment text.

text nodes

All character content is grouped into *text* nodes. *Text* nodes do not have preceding or following *text* nodes.

Node Axes

Each element in the XML document can be considered a point in the tree structure. These element points can be seen as having a set of axes, each containing nodes extending from the element point. For example, you could have the following XML fragment:

```
<message>
   <customer customerID = "c1" customerName = "John Smith"/>
   <customer customerID = "c2" customerName = "William Jones"/>
   <order orderID = "o100" customerID = "1"/>
</message>
```

As shown in Figure 6-1, this *message* element has a *child* axis that consists of three nodes: two *customer element* nodes and one *order element* node.

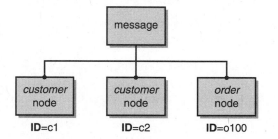

Figure 6-1. *Representation of a* child *axis consisting of three nodes.*

Thus, each axis moves through the element tree, selecting a set of nodes based on its axis type (*child* in this example), and places these elements on the axis. Using node axes, you can select a set of elements within the document. The syntax for an XPath node axis is shown here:

   context axis::name

The *name* can be the name of an element, attribute, or other node. The *context* is the starting point of the path, which is usually the root of the XML document. The *axis* is the type of the axis that you want to select. As you will see, this format is extremely flexible and will allow you to select any pattern of elements within your XML documents.

The root element can be represented by a slash (/). When the root element is used as the context, it is equivalent to the document element.

XPath defines the following types of the node axis:

- **child**   The *child* axis selects all children of the context element in document order.

- **descendant**   The *descendant* axis contains all the descendants of the context node in document order. A descendant can be a child, a child of a child, and so on. The *descendant* axis does not contain *attribute* or *namespace* nodes.

- **parent**   The *parent* axis contains the parent of the context node.

- **following-sibling**   The *following-sibling* axis contains the following siblings of the context node in document order. A *sibling* is an element on the same level of the tree. If the context node is either an *attribute* or a *namespace* node, the *following-sibling* axis is empty.

- **preceding-sibling**   The *preceding-sibling* axis contains the preceding siblings. If the context node is either an *attribute* or a *name-space* node, the *preceding-sibling* axis is empty.

- **following**   The *following* axis contains the nodes in the same document as the context node that are immediately after the context node. *Attribute*, *namespace*, and *descendant* nodes are not included on the *following* axis.

- **preceding**   The *preceding* axis contains all the nodes in the same document as the context node that are immediately before the context node. *Attribute*, *namespace*, and *ancestor* nodes are not included on the *preceding* axis.

- **ancestor**   The *ancestor* axis contains all the context node ancestors, including the context node's parent, the parent's parent, and so on. The *ancestor* axis will store the nodes in reverse document order.

- **attribute**   The *attribute* axis contains the attributes of the context node. There are three possible *attribute* axes. If you use the following syntax, the *attribute* axis will contain the value of the attribute with *attributeName*:

attribute::attributeName

In the following syntax, the *attribute* axis contains all the *elementName* elements that have an attribute with the value of *attributeName*:

elementName[attribute::attributeName]

Finally, in the following syntax, the axis contains all the *element-Name* elements that have an attribute with the *attribute-Name* equal to the *attributeValue*:

elementName[attribute::attributeName=attributeValue]

All of these axes will be empty unless the context node is an element node.

- **namespace** The *namespace* axis contains the *namespace* nodes of the context nodes; the order will be defined by the implementation. This axis will be empty unless the context node is an *element* node.

- **self** The *self* axis contains only the context node.

- **ancestor-or-self** The *ancestor-or-self* axis contains the context node and all the context node's ancestors, in reverse document order.

- **descendant-or-self** The *descendant-or-self* axis contains the context node and all the context node's descendants.

When an axis contains more than one element, you can select an element by using *[position()=positionNumber]*. The first element is assigned a *positionNumber* value of *1*.

The following XML document fragment will be used to demonstrate how these axes can be used:

```
<message>
   <date>01-01-2001</date>
   <customer customerID = "c1" customerName = "John Smith"/>
     <order orderID = "o100"/>
   <customer customerID = "c2" customerName = "William Jones" >
     <order orderID = "o101"/>
   </customer>
</message>
```

As you can see, this document has a *message* root element, one *date* child element, and two *customer* child elements; each *customer* element has one *order* child element. Let's take a look at how an axis selects a set of nodes when it navigates through the element tree according to the instruction provided by the location path. The following table lists the example location paths and the *element* nodes selected based on these location paths.

Example Location Paths

Location Path	Description
/child::customer	/child selects all the children of the root (the date and two customer elements). /child::customer selects all the customer elements that are children of the root—in this case, there are two customer elements.
/descendant::order	/descendant selects all the descendants of the root (the date element, the two customer elements, and the order elements). /descendant::order selects the two order elements.
/descendant-or-self::message	/descendant-or-self selects all the descendants of the root (the date element, the two customer elements, the two order elements, and the message root element). /descendant-or-self::message selects the message element.
/child::customer [attribute::customerID= c1]	Selects the customer element that has an attribute with a value of c1.
/child::customer [attribute:: customerID= c1] [position() = 1]	Selects the first customer element having an attribute with a value of c1 (the first customer element—which is actually the only customer element with an attribute value equal to c1).
/child::customer [attribute:: customerID= c1] [position() = 1]/ following-sibling::customer	Selects all the customer elements that are following siblings to the customer element having an attribute with a value of c1—in this case, the second customer element (customerID = c2).
/child::customer [attribute:: customerID= c2] [position() = 2]/ preceding-sibling::customer	Selects all of the customer elements that are preceding siblings to the customer element having an attribute with a value of c2—in this case, the first customer element (customerID = c1).
/following::customer	Selects the two customer elements.
/child::customer [attribute:: customerID= c1] [position() = 1]/ preceding::date	Selects the date elements preceding the first customer element that has an attribute with a value of c1. Our example document has only one.
/self	Selects the message element.

Basic XPath Patterns

XPath includes a set of terms that can be used to find patterns within an XML document. These patterns are described here:

- **node**   Selects all child elements with a given node name
- *   Selects all child elements
- **@attr**   Selects an attribute
- **@***   Selects all attributes
- **ns:***   Selects elements in a given namespace
- **node()**   Matches an element node
- **text()**   Matches a text node
- **comment()**   Matches a comment node
- **processing-instruction()**   Matches a processing instruction node
- **. (dot)**   Selects the current node
- **.. (double dots)**   Selects the parent of the current node
- **/ (slash)**   Selects the document node
- **// (double slash)**   Selects descendants and self—which is equivalent to *descendant-or-self*

Note that because the default axis is *child*, when an axis is omitted, the *child* axis is used. The XML document fragment mentioned in the previous section is used to demonstrate how to use these basic patterns. The following table lists a set of example XPath patterns and the *element* nodes selected based on these shortcuts.

Example XPath Patterns

Location Path	Description
/customer	/ is equal to /*child* and selects all the children of the root (the *date* element and the two *customer* elements in our sample document). /*customer* selects all the *customer* elements that are children of the root—in this case, there are two *customer* elements.
//order	Selects all the *order* elements that are descendants of the root (document) node—in this case, there are two *order* elements.

Location Path	Description
/.//order	*/.//order* is equivalent to */self::node()/descendant-or-self/child/order*. */self::node()* is the *root* node, */self:: node()/descendant-or-self* selects all of the *descendant* elements of the root and the root itself, and */self::node()/ descendant-or-self/child/order* selects the *order* elements that are descendants of the root.
/.//order[@orderID =o100]../customer	*/.//order* selects the two *order* elements. *[@orderID =o100]* selects the order element with an attribute named *orderID* that has a value equal to *o100* (the first *order* element in the document). .. selects the *parent* element, */.//order[@orderID =o100]../customer* selects the *customer* element containing the *order* element with an *orderID* attribute equal to *o100*.
/descendants[@customerID]	Selects all the elements that are descendants of the root element and that have a *customerID* attribute (the two *customer* elements).
/*	Selects all the children of the root element (the two *customer* elements and the *date* element).
/*/order	Selects all the *order* elements that are grandchildren of the root element (in this case, the two *order* elements).
//order[2]/@orderID	*//order[2]/* selects the second *order* element, *//order[2]/@orderID* retrieves the value of the *orderID* attribute for the second *order* element.

XPath also contains functions. These functions will be discussed when we discuss XSL in Chapter 12.

XPOINTER

XPointer provides access to the values of attributes or the content of elements anywhere in an XML document. Using XPointer, you can link to sections of text, select particular attributes or elements, navigate through elements, and so on. The specification does not dictate what an application will do with the information returned by the XPointer.

Unlike XPath, XPointer enables you to select information that is contained within more than one set of nodes. For example, if you are presenting a document that contains several sections of text, where each section is contained within a *paragraph* element, it's possible that a user may highlight text that begins in the middle of one *paragraph* element and ends in the middle of another *paragraph* element. XPath allows you to define only complete sets of nodes, and because this example includes parts of nodes, XPath can't be used to represent the section. XPointer has extensions to XPath that allow you to get a reference to the text that was selected. Any XPath expression that returns a node-set may be used with XPointer. Thus, the following XPointer expression will select all the *order* elements that are grandchildren of the root element (in this case, the two *order* elements in our example XML document):

xpointer(/*/order)

In addition to defining nodes, XPointer also defines points and ranges. The combination of nodes, points, and ranges creates *locations*. A *point* is a position in an XML document. A *point location* is the combination of a node, called the container node, and an index. When the container node of a point is a *root* node or an *element* node, the point is called a *node point*. The index must be equal to or greater than 0 and less than or equal to the number of children nodes of the container node. The index zero represents the point before any child nodes, and a non-zero index n represents the point directly after the nth child node.

If the container node is not a *root* node or an *element* node, the point is called a *character point*. The index must be either zero or less than or equal to the number of characters associated with the node. The index zero represents the point immediately before the first character. A non-zero index represents a point immediately after the nth character.

A range represents all the XML structure and content between a start point and an end point. The start and end points must be in the same document, and the start point must occur before the end point in document order. The start and end points can be located in the middle of a node. If the start and end points are at the same point, it is called a *collapsed range*. If the container node of the start point is a node other than an *element* node, a *text* node, or a *root* node, the end point must be in the same container node. The string value of a range is all of the *text* nodes within the range.

We can now use the XPointer to define a range as follows:

Xpointer (/child::customer [attribute::customerID= c1 to /child::customer [attribute::customerID= c2]

This XPointer selects a range starting at the beginning of the child *customer* element that has an attribute with a value of *c1* and ending at the end of the child *customer* element that has an attribute with a value of *c2*. For our example XML fragment, the two *customer* child nodes are selected.

XLINK

XLink provides links similar to hyperlinks. XLink enables you to define *link* elements in your DTD. XLink elements can have the following attributes: *type, href, role, title, show*, and *actuate*. There are two types of XLinks, *simple* and *extended*. A simple link connects two resources: a source and a destination. An extended link connects any number of resources. In this section, let's take a look at these two types and the attributes defined in XLink in detail.

Simple Links

A declaration for a simple XLink element might look like this:

```
<!ELEMENT Mylink ANY>
<!ATTLIST Mylink
  xlink:type     (simple)              #FIXED "simple"
  xlink:href     CDATA                 #REQUIRED
  xlink:role     NMTOKEN               #FIXED "roleName"
  xlink:title    CDATA                 #IMPLIED
  xlink:show     (new
                 |replace
                 |embed
                 |undefined)           #FIXED "replace"
  xlink:actuate (onLoad
                 |onRequest
                 |undefined)           #FIXED "onRequest"
>
```

The attributes are defined as follows:

- **type** Specifies whether the link is *simple* or *extended*.

- **href** Refers to the URI of the other end of the link. This can be an entire document, or it can be a point or an element in a document. An XPointer can be used to identify a point in the document.

- **role** Describes the function of the other end of the link. There are no predefined *role* values. You can create your own roles that will be interpreted by your applications to define different types of XLink. For more information on roles, see the W3C specification at *http://www.w3c.org/TR/2000/WD-xlink-20000221/*.

- **title** The *title* attribute is the same as the HTML link title. It can be used to display floating tips or a default value when the link cannot be displayed.

- **show** If no style sheet is used, the *show* attribute will tell the application what to do with the link. The *embed* value causes the content of the link target to be embedded in the content of the link source. The *replace* value causes the content of the link source to be replaced by the content of the link target. The *new* value creates a new instance of the application containing the linked document. An *undefined* value means there is no defined behavior for this link.

- **actuate** Specifies when the link should be activated. The *onRequest* value indicates that the application will wait for the user to request that the link be followed. The *onLoad* value causes the link to be followed immediately. The *onRequest* value behaves like the HTML *a* element; *onLoad* behaves like the *img* element.

Extended Links

Extended links are similar to simple links, except they allow you to link to multiple links instead of just one link. An extended link consists of a set of linking resources and a set of connections between these resources. The linking resources may be local or remote. If all the resources are remote, the link is an out-of-line link. If all the resources are local, the link is an inline link. A local resource is contained in the extended link element and a remote resource is outside of the extended link element.

For more information about extended links, visit the specification Web site, at *http://www.w3.org/TR/xlink/*.

SUMMARY

XML namespaces allow you to avoid naming collisions when you define elements and attributes using different DTDs or schemas. Namespaces can be defined with prefixes, or you can use default namespaces.

XPointer and XPath enable you to link to specific parts of an XML document. XPath can use patterns to identify sections of an XML document. XPointer allows you to do everything XPath can do, but also extends XPath to allow you to address points in the document and ranges between points. The range may not correspond to any one node. XLink enables you to create links within XML documents. In Chapter 7, we'll discuss an XML schema that enables you to validate data types, use namespaces, and check ranges of values.

Chapter 7

XML Schemas

Up to now, we've been looking almost exclusively at document type definitions (DTDs) as a way of defining rules for an XML document. Although this is an excellent method, there are a few problems with DTDs. The most obvious problem is the fact that DTDs are written in their own special text format, not in XML. It would make a great deal of sense to create a document written in XML to define the rules of an XML document.

In the XHTML sample we discussed in Chapter 5, data types were not that important—all the document content was of the string data type. Often, however, you will have documents that contain several different data types, and you will want to be able to validate these data types. Unfortunately, DTDs are not designed for validating data types or checking ranges of values. DTDs also do not understand namespaces.

To solve these problems, *schemas* were invented. Unlike DTDs, which have their own peculiar syntax, XML schemas are written in XML. In addition to providing the information that DTDs offer, schemas allow you to specify data types, use namespaces, and define ranges of values for attributes and elements. In this chapter, you'll learn about XML schemas and how to use them in your XML documents. We'll look at the XML schema data types and their categories and then explore how to create simple and complex data types. Finally, we'll examine namespaces used in XML schemas.

SIMPLE SCHEMA DATA TYPES

For the most part, XML documents fall into two categories: *document-oriented* and *data-oriented*. The document-oriented XML document contains text sections mixed with field data, whereas the data-oriented XML document contains only field data.

The XHTML document we created in Chapter 5 is an example of a document-oriented XML document. Another example of a document-oriented XML document is a message such as the one shown here:

```
<message priority="high"
    date="2000-01-11">
    <from>Jake Sturm</from>
    <to>Gwen Sturm</to>
    <subject>DNA Course</subject>
    <body>
        The new DNA course that we are offering is now complete.
        It will provide a complete overview discussion of
        designing and building DNA systems, including DNS, DNA,
        COM, and COM+. The course is also listed on the Web site, at
        http://ies.gti.net.
    </body>
</message>
```

This message has a large text body, but it also contains attributes—in this case, *date* and *priority*. The *date* attribute has a *date* data type, and the *priority* attribute has an *enumerated* data type. It will be useful to be able to validate that these attributes are correctly formatted for these two data types. Schemas will allow you do this.

A data-oriented document looks like this:

```
<bill>
    <OrderDate>2001-02-11</OrderDate>
    <ShipDate>2001-02-12</ShipDate>
    <BillingAddress>
        <name>John Doe</name>
        <street>123 Main St.</street>
        <city>Anytown</city>
        <state>NY</state>
        <zip>12345-0000</zip>
    </BillingAddress>
    <voice>555-1234</voice>
    <fax>555-5678</fax>
</bill>
```

This entire document contains data fields that will need to be validated. Validating data fields is an essential aspect of this type of XML document. We'll look at an example schema for a data-oriented document in the section "A Schema for a Data-Oriented XML Document" later in this chapter.

Up to this point, we've been looking only at document-oriented XML documents that contain only one data type (the *string* data type) because DTDs work best with document-oriented XML documents that contain only *string* data types.

Because schemas allow you to validate datatype information, it's time now to take a look at data types as they are defined in the schema specification.

The term *data type* is defined in the second schema standard, which can be found at *http://www.w3.org/TR/xmlschema-2/*. A data type represents a type of data, such as a string, an integer, and so on. The second schema standard defines *simple data types* in detail, and that's what we'll look at in this section.

The Components of a Schema Data Type

In a schema, a data type has three parts: a *value space*, a *lexical space*, and a *facet*. The value space is the range of acceptable values for a data type. The lexical space is the set of valid *literals* that represent the ways in which a data type can be displayed—for example, *100* and *1.0E2* are two different literals, but both denote the same floating point value. A facet is some characteristic of the data type. A data type can have many facets, each defining one or more characteristics. Facets specify how one data type is different from other data types. Facets define the value space for the data type.

There are two kinds of facets: *fundamental* and *constraining*. Fundamental facets define the data type, and constraining facets place constraints on the data type. Examples of fundamental facets are rules specifying an order for the elements, a maximum or minimum allowable value, the finite or infinite nature of the data type, whether the instances of the data type are exact or approximate, and whether the data type is numeric. Constraining facets can include the limit on the length of a data type (number of characters for a string or number of bits for a binary data type), minimum and maximum lengths, enumerations, and patterns.

We can categorize the data types along several dimensions. First, data types can be *atomic* or *aggregate*. An atomic data type cannot be divided. An integer value or a date that is represented as a single character string is an atomic data type. If a date is presented as day, month, and year values, the date is an aggregate data type.

Data types can also be distinguished as primitive or generated. *Primitive data types* are not derived from any other data type; they are predefined. *Generated data types* are built from existing data types, called *basetypes*. Basetypes can be primitive or generated data types. Generated types, which will be discussed later in the chapter, can be either simple or complex data types.

Primitive data types include the following: *string, Boolean, float, decimal, double, timeDuration, recurringDuration, binary,* and *uri*. In addition, there is also the *timeInstant* data type that is derived from the *recurringDuration* data type.

Among these primitive data types, two of them are specific to XML schemas: *time-Duration*, and *recurringDuration*. The *timeInstant* data type is also specific to XML. Let's have a look at them here.

The *timeInstant* data type represents a combination of date and time values that represent a specific instance of time. The pattern is shown here:

CCYY-MM-DDThh:mm:ss.sss

CC represents the century, *YY* is the year, *MM* is the month, and *DD* is the day, preceded by an optional leading sign to indicate a negative number. If the sign is omitted, a plus sign (+) is assumed. The letter *T* is the date/time separator, and *hh*, *mm*, and *ss.sss* represent the hour, minute, and second values. Additional digits can be used to increase the precision of fractional seconds if desired. To accommodate year values greater than 9999, digits can be added to the left of this representation.

The *timeInstant* representation can be immediately followed by a Z to indicate the Universal Time Coordinate (UTC). The time zone information is represented by the difference between the local time and UTC and is specified immediately following the time and consists of a plus or minus sign (+ or −) followed by *hh:mm*.

The *timeDuration* data type represents some duration of time. The pattern for *timeDuration* is shown here:

PyYmMdDThHmMsS

Y represents the number of years, *M* is the number of months, *D* is the number of days, *T* is the date/time separator, *H* is the number of hours, *M* is the number of minutes, and *S* is the number of seconds. The P at the beginning indicates that this pattern represents a time period. The number of seconds can include decimal digits to arbitrary precision. An optional preceding minus sign is allowed to indicate a negative duration. If the sign is omitted, a positive duration is assumed.

The *recurringDuration* data type represents a moment in time that recurs. The pattern for *recurringDuration* is the left-truncated representation for *timeInstant*. For example, if the *CC* century value is omitted from the *timeInstant* representation, that *timeInstant* recurs every hundred years. Similarly, if *CCYY* is omitted, the *timeInstant* recurs every year.

Every two-character unit of the representation that is omitted is indicated by a single hyphen (-). For example, to indicate 1:20 P.M. on May 31 of every year for Eastern Standard Time that is 5 hours behind UTC, you would write the following code:

```
--05-31T13:20:00-05:00
```

Creating Simple Data Types

New simple data types can be created by using *simpleType* elements. A simplified version of a DTD declaration required for the *simpleType* element is shown below. (For a complete declaration, see the schema specification at http://www.w3.org/IR/xmlschema-2/.)

```
<!ENTITY % ordered ' (minInclusive | minExclusive) | (maxInclusive |
    maxExclusive) | precision | scale '>
<!ENTITY % unordered 'pattern | enumeration | length | maxlength |
    minlength | encoding | period'>
<!ENTITY % facet '%ordered; | %unordered;'>
<!ELEMENT simpleType ((annotation)?, (%facet;)*)>
<!ATTLIST simpleType
    name       NMTOKEN         #IMPLIED
    base       CDATA           #REQUIRED
    final      CDATA           ''
    abstract (true | false) 'false'
    derivedBy (list | restriction | reproduction) 'restriction'>
<!ELEMENT annotation (documentation)>

<!ENTITY % facetAttr 'value CDATA #REQUIRED'>
<!ENTITY % facetModel '(annotation)?'>
<!ELEMENT maxExclusive %facetModel;>
<!ATTLIST maxExclusive %facetAttr;>
<!ELEMENT minExclusive %facetModel;>
<!ATTLIST minExclusive %facetAttr;>

<!ELEMENT maxInclusive %facetModel;>
<!ATTLIST maxInclusive %facetAttr;>
<!ELEMENT minInclusive %facetModel;>
<!ATTLIST minInclusive %facetAttr;>

<!ELEMENT precision %facetModel;>
<!ATTLIST precision %facetAttr;>
<!ELEMENT scale %facetModel;>
<!ATTLIST scale %facetAttr;>

<!ELEMENT length %facetModel;>
<!ATTLIST length %facetAttr;>
<!ELEMENT minlength %facetModel;>
<!ATTLIST minlength %facetAttr;>
<!ELEMENT maxlength %facetModel;>
<!ATTLIST maxlength %facetAttr;>

<!-- This one can be repeated. -->
<!ELEMENT enumeration %facetModel;>
```

(continued)

```
<!ATTLIST enumeration %facetAttr;>
<!ELEMENT pattern %facetModel;>
<!ATTLIST pattern %facetAttr;>
<!ELEMENT encoding %facetModel;>
<!ATTLIST encoding %facetAttr;>
<!ELEMENT period %facetModel;>
<!ATTLIST period %facetAttr;>
<!ELEMENT documentation ANY>
<!ATTLIST documentation source CDATA #IMPLIED>
<!ELEMENT documentation ANY>
<!ATTLIST documentation
        source   CDATA #IMPLIED
        xml:lang CDATA #IMPLIED>
```

As you can see, the *simpleType* element, which represents a simple data type, can be either *ordered* or *unordered*. An ordered type can be placed in a specific sequence. Positive integers are ordered—that is, you can start at 0 and continue to the maximum integer value. Unordered data types do not have any order, and would include data types such as a Boolean that cannot be placed in a sequence. Using the preceding DTD, you can create your own simple data types. These simple data types can then be used in your schemas to define elements and attributes.

Unordered data types include *Boolean* and *binary* data types. All of the numeric data types are ordered. Strings are ordered, but when you are defining your own string data types, they will be defined with the unordered elements.

For each data type, numerous possible child elements can be used to define the *simpleType* element. Each child element will contain an attribute with the value for the child element and an optional comment. The child elements define facets for the data types you create.

Let's look now at how to create simple data types using ordered and unordered facets.

Using ordered facets

Notice that in the previous code listing, *ordered* facets consist of the following facets: *maxExclusive*, *minExclusive*, *maxInclusive*, *minInclusive*, *precision*, and *scale*. The value of *maxExclusive* is the smallest value for the data type outside the upper bound of the value space for the data type. The value of *minExclusive* is the largest value for the data type outside the lower bound of the value space for the data type. Thus, if you wanted to have an integer data type with a range of 100 to 1000, the value of *minExclusive* would be 99 and the value of *maxExclusive* would be 1001. The simple data type could be declared as follows:

```
<simpleType name="limitedInteger" base="integer">
    <minExclusive = "99"/>
```

```
    <maxExclusive = "1001"/>
</simpleType>
```

The *minInclusive* and *maxInclusive* facets work in the same way as *minExclusive* and *maxExclusive*, except that the *minInclusive* value is the lower bound of the value space for a data type, and the *maxInclusive* is the upper bound of the value space for a data type. Our simple data type could be rewritten as follows:

```
<simpleType name="limitedInteger" base="integer">
    <minInclusive = "100"/>
    <maxInclusive = "1000"/>
</simpleType>
```

Precision is the number of digits that will be used to represent a number. The *scale*, which must always be less than the precision, represents the number of digits that will appear to the right of the decimal place. For example, a data type that does not go above but includes 1,000,000 and that has two digits to the right of the decimal place (1,000,000.00) has a precision of 9 (ignore commas and decimals) and a scale of 2. The declaration would look as follows:

```
<simpleType name="TotalSales" base="integer">
    <minInclusive = "0"/>
    <maxInclusive = "1000000"/>
    <precision = "9"/>
    <scale = "2"/>
</simpleType>
```

If you had left out the *maxInclusive* facet, numbers up to 9,999,999 would have been valid. If you had needed a value less than 1,000,000, the following declaration would have been sufficient:

```
<simpleType name="TotalSales" base="integer">
    <precision = "8"/>
    <scale = "2"/>
</simpleType>
```

Now that you have learned how to use ordered facets to create simple data types, let's look at how to use unordered facets to create simple data types.

Using unordered facets

In the code on pages 127 and 128, you can see that unordered facets are made up of the following facets: *period*, *length*, *maxLength*, *minLength*, *pattern*, *enumeration*, and *encoding*.

For time data types, you can use the *period* facet to define the frequency of recurrence of the data type. The *period* facet is used in a *timeDuration* data type. For example, if you wanted to create a special holiday data type that includes recognized U.S. holidays, you could use the following declaration:

```
<simpleType name="holidays" base="date">
   <annotation>
      <documentation>Some U.S. holidays</documentation>
   </annotation>
   <enumeration value='--01-01'>
      <annotation>
         <documentation>New Year's Day</documentation>
      </annotation>
   </enumeration>
   <enumeration value='--07-04'>
      <annotation>
         <documentation>Fourth of July</documentation>
      </annotation>
   </enumeration>
   <enumeration value='--12-25'>
      <annotation>
         <documentation>Christmas</documentation>
      </annotation>
   </enumeration>
</simpleType>
```

When you use the *length* facet, the data type must be a certain fixed length. Using *length*, you can create fixed-length strings. The *maxLength* facet represents the maximum length a data type can have. The *minLength* facet represents the smallest length a data type can have. Using *minLength* and *maxLength,* you can define a variable-length string that can be as small as *minLength* and as large as *maxLength*.

The pattern facet is a constraint on the value space of the data type achieved by constraining the lexical space (the valid values). The enumeration facet limits the value space to a set of values. The encoding facet is used for binary types, which can be encoded as either hex or base64. In addition to containing a facet, simple data types also contain a set of attributes that can be used to define the data type. Let's now take a look at these attributes.

Attributes for simple data types

Notice in the code on this page that the *simpleType* element has the following attributes: *name*, *base*, *abstract*, *final*, and *derivedBy*. The *name* attribute can be either a built-in type or a user-defined type. The *base* attribute is the basetype that is being used to define the new type. The *final* attribute is discussed in detail later in this chapter. The *abstract* attribute of a data type is beyond the scope of this book. For more information about this attribute, refer to the schema specification.

The *derivedBy* attribute can be set to *list*, *restriction*, or *reproduction*. The *list* value allows you to create a data type that consists of a list of items separated by space. For example, you can use the following declaration to create a list data type:

```
<simpleType name='StringList' base='string' derivedBy='list'/>
```

This data type can then be used in an XML document to create a new list type, as shown here:

```
<myListElement xsi:type='StringList'>
    This is not list item 1.
    This is not list item 2.
    This is not list item 3.
</myListElement>
```

By using *xsi*, you overrode the default declaration of the *myListElement* and made it a *StringList* data type. Since a *StringList* data type contains a list of strings, you can now use a list of strings as content for the *myListElement*. The *xsi* namespace will be discussed in more detail later in the chapter.

Up to this point, we have been discussing the XML schema 2 specification, which covers simple data types. The XML schema 1 specification covers all the general issues involving schemas and also covers complex data types. Let's now take a look at the complex data types described in the first schema specification.

COMPLEX DATA TYPES

A data type can either be simple or complex. Simple data types include the data types discussed in the previous section. Complex data types contain the child elements that belong to an element, as well as all the attributes that are associated with the element. If you visit *http://www.w3.org/TR/xmlschema-1/*, you'll find the first schema specification. Combining this specification with that for simple data types, you will have the complete schema specification. Our discussion of complex data types in this section will include an explanation of all of the elements of a schema, a sample DTD for a schema, and numerous examples showing how to create a schema and complex data types.

Viewing Schemas in XML Tools

On the companion CD, you'll find a file named XHTMLschema.xsd, which is a schema document based on a schema generated by XML Authority. The schema was generated based on the XHTML DTD we created in Chapter 5. You can open XHTML-schema.xsd in XML Authority version 1.2 or higher.

Because schemas are written as well-formed XML documents, you can also view the schema in any other XML tools, such as XML Spy or Microsoft XML Notepad. For example, Figure 7-1 shows the schema as it would appear in XML Spy.

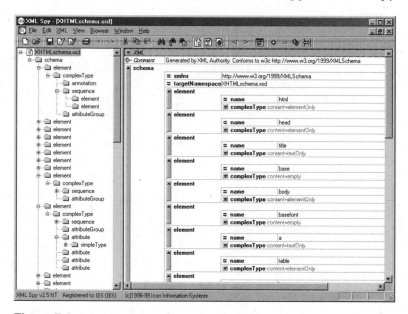

Figure 7-1. *The schema in XML Spy.*

As you can see in Figure 7-1, a schema has a well-defined structure. This structure includes a root element named *schema*, with one or more *element* child elements. These *element* elements can have *complexType* child elements; the *complexType* elements can in turn have *annotation*, *group*, *attributeGroup*, and *attribute* child elements. Clearly, this schema is a well-formed XML document.

Important Elements in XHTMLschema.xsd

In Figure 7-1, you can also see that the essential components of a schema are *element*, *complexType*, and *simpleType* elements. Essentially, a schema is all about associating data types with *element* elements. A portion of the source code from XHTMLschema.xsd is shown below.

```
<schema targetNamespace = "XHTMLschema.xsd"
    xmlns = "http://www.w3.org/XMLSchema">
    <element name = "html">
        <complexType content = "elementOnly">
            <annotation>
<documentation>
a Uniform Resource Identifier, see [RFC2396]
</documentation>
            </annotation>
        <group>
            <sequence>
                <element ref = "head"/>
                <element ref = "body"/>
            </sequence>
        </group>
        <attributeGroup ref = "i18n"/>
        </complexType>
    </element>
    <element name = "head">
        <complexType content = "elementOnly">
        <group>
            <sequence>
                <element ref = "title"/>
                <element ref = "base" minOccurs = "0"
                    maxOccurs = "1"/>
            </sequence>
```

(continued)

```
            </group>
            <attributeGroup ref = "i18n"/>
            <attribute name = "profile" type = "string"/>
        </complexType>
    </element>
    <element name = "title">
        <complexType content = "textOnly">
            <attributeGroup ref = "i18n"/>
        </complexType>
    </element>
    <element name = "base">
        <complexType content = "empty">
            <attribute name = "target" use = "required"
                type = "string"/>
        </complexType>
    </element>
    <element name = "atop">
        <complexType content = "elementOnly">
            <sequence>
                <element ref = "p"/>
                <element ref = "a"/>
            </sequence>
        </complexType>
    </element>
    <element name = "body">
        <complexType content = "elementOnly">
            <group>
                <sequence>
                    <element ref = "basefont" minOccurs = "0"
                        maxOccurs = "1"/>
                    <element ref = "atop" minOccurs = "0"
                        maxOccurs = "1"/>
                    <element ref = "table"/>
                </sequence>
            </group>
            <attribute name = "alink" type = "string"/>
            <attribute name = "text" type = "string"/>
            <attribute name = "bgcolor" type = "string"/>
            <attribute name = "link" type = "string"/>
            <attribute name = "vlink" type = "string"/>
        </complexType>
    </element>
```

```
            ⋮
    <element name = "h1">
        <complexType content = "elementOnly">
            <sequence>
                <group ref = "Inline" />
            </sequence>
            <attributeGroup ref = "attrs"/>
            <attribute name = "align" type = "string"/>
        </complexType>
    </element>
            ⋮
</schema>
```

> **NOTE**   This listing shows only parts of the schema. For the full schema, refer
> to the version of the document on the companion CD.

This particular version of the schema does not use anything like the entities in a
DTD—everything is listed out here. Schemas do provide components that are similar
to parameter entities, which will be discussed later in this chapter. Comments located
within the *schema* element are contained within *documentation* elements. The
schema element is the root for the document. The *schema* element and other elements and attributes will be discussed in detail in the next section.

A DTD for Schemas

The schema specification provides a fairly complex DTD that can be used to define
every possible schema. This DTD is designed to work with a wide range of possible
schemas and to cover every possible condition. Here we'll work with a simplified DTD
that presents a subset of the schema specification DTD. Any schema that conforms
to the simplified DTD will also conform to the schema specification DTD.

A simplified DTD for schemas is shown below. (For the full DTD, visit *http://
www.w3.org/TR/xmlschema-1* to see the schema specification.)

```
<!ENTITY % xs-datatypes PUBLIC 'datatypes' 'Datatypes.dtd'>
   %xs-datatypes;
<!ELEMENT schema  ((include | import | annotation )*,
                    (element, simpleType, complexType,
                     attributeGroup, group, notation)*>
```

```
<!ATTLIST schema    targetNamespace CDATA  #IMPLIED
                    version         CDATA  #IMPLIED
                    xmlns           CDATA  #REQUIRED
                    xmlns:dt        CDATA  #REQUIRED >
<!ELEMENT element  ((annotation)?, (complexType | simpleType)?,
                   (unique | key | keyref)*)>
<!ATTLIST element  type    CDATA  #IMPLIED
                   name    CDATA  #IMPLIED
                   ref     CDATA  #IMPLIED
                   minOccurs (1 | 0 ) #IMPLIED
                   maxOccurs CDATA  #IMPLIED
                   id      ID     #IMPLIED
                   nullable (true | false ) 'false'
                   default CDATA #IMPLIED
                   fixed   CDATA #IMPLIED >
<!ELEMENT complexType  (((annotation)? , (%ordered;, %unordered;)* |
    (element | all | choice | sequence | group | any )*,
    (attribute | attributeGroup) , anyAttribute )>
<!ATTLIST complexType   content
        (mixed | empty | textOnly | elementOnly ) #REQUIRED
        name CDATA #REQUIRED
        derivedBy "(restriction|extension|reproduction)" #IMPLIED
        base CDATA #IMPLIED
        id    ID   #IMPLIED
        final
        block>
<!ELEMENT group ((annotation)?, (all | choice | sequence)*)>
<!ATTLIST group
          minOccurs   CDATA                  '1'
          maxOccurs   CDATA               #IMPLIED
          order       (choice | seq | all) 'seq'
          name        CDATA               #IMPLIED
          ref         CDATA               #IMPLIED
          id          ID                  #IMPLIED>
<!ELEMENT all ((annotation)?, (element | group | any |
          choice | sequence)*)>
<!ATTLIST all minOccurs CDATA #FIXED '1'
          maxOccurs CDATA #FIXED '1'
          id            ID   #IMPLIED>
```

```
<!ELEMENT choice ((annotation)?, (element | group | any | choice |
                  sequence)*)>
<!ATTLIST choice minOccurs CDATA '1'
            maxOccurs CDATA #IMPLIED
            id        ID    #IMPLIED>
<!ELEMENT sequence ((annotation)?, (element | group | any |
                  choice | sequence)*)>
<!ATTLIST sequence minOccurs CDATA '1'
            maxOccurs CDATA #IMPLIED
            id        ID    #IMPLIED>
<!ELEMENT attribute  ((annotation)?, (simpleType)? )>
<!ATTLIST attribute  type      CDATA  #IMPLIED
                     default   CDATA  #IMPLIED
                     fixed     CDATA  #IMPLIED
                     name      CDATA  #REQUIRED
                     minOccurs (0|1)   '0'
            maxOccurs  (0|1)    '1' >
<!ELEMENT attributeGroup ((annotation)?,
     (attribute | attributeGroup)*,
     (anyAttribute)?)>
<!ELEMENT anyAttribute EMPTY>
<!ATTLIST anyAttribute
        namespace   CDATA   '##any'>
<!ELEMENT unique ((annotation)?, selector, (field)+)>
<!ATTLIST unique name    CDATA        #REQUIRED
                 id      ID           #IMPLIED
                 uniqueAttrs>
<!ELEMENT key     ((annotation)?, selector, (field)+)>
<!ATTLIST key     name    CDATA      #REQUIRED
                  id      ID         #IMPLIED
                  keyAttrs>

<!ELEMENT keyref ((annotation)?, selector, (field)+)>
<!ATTLIST keyref  name    CDATA      #REQUIRED
                  id      ID         #IMPLIED
                  refer   CDATA      #REQUIRED>
<!ELEMENT any EMPTY>
```

(continued)

```
<!ATTLIST any
        namespace       CDATA                   '##any'
        processContents (skip|lax|strict)       'strict'
        minOccurs       CDATA                   '1'
        maxOccurs       CDATA                   #IMPLIED>
<!ELEMENT selector (#PCDATA)>
<!ELEMENT field (#PCDATA)>
<!ELEMENT include EMPTY>
<!ATTLIST include schemaLocation CDATA #REQUIRED>
<!ELEMENT import EMPTY>
<!ATTLIST import namespace       CDATA #REQUIRED
               schemaLocation CDATA #IMPLIED>
```

This DTD includes all the essential elements of a schema and also includes the data types' DTD. All the *schema* elements that will be defined in this chapter are listed. Notice that the elements you saw in XML Spy are now much more visible. The DTD uses a set of elements and attributes to define the structure of a schema document. The principal elements of a schema are *simpleType*, *datatype*, *enumeration*, *schema*, *annotation*, *complexType*, *element*, *attribute*, *attributeGroup*, and *group*. We've already looked at the first three elements; we'll examine the remaining elements next.

The *schema* Element

The *schema* element corresponds to the root element defined in a DTD. In a schema, all *element* elements are child elements of the *schema* root element. We will discuss the attributes of the *schema* element in the section on namespaces in this chapter.

> NOTE   Technically speaking, the DTD for a schema in the specification does not require that the *schema* element be the root element. The usual definition of a schema does have a *schema* element as the root, however.

The *annotation* Element

The *annotation* element is used to create comments within the *complexType* element. Comments are contained within one of two possible child elements of the *annotation* element: *appinfo* and *documentation*. The *documentation* element is used for human-readable comments. The *appinfo* elements are used for application-readable comments, as shown here:

```
<annotation>
    <appinfo>
        The machine-readable comment goes here.
    </appinfo>
</annotation>
```

Notice that the comment is content of the *annotation* element, which means that it is not enclosed in the usual comment symbols (<!--... -->). When the *annotation* element is an allowable child element for an element, it will always be the first child element.

The *complexType* Element

You can think of the *complexType* element as equivalent to a combination of the attributes and the child element list enclosed in parentheses in the *element* element declaration used in a DTD—essentially, it defines the child elements and attributes for an *element* element. The *complexType* element will define the *element* elements, attributes, or a combination that will be associated with an *element* element that has attributes or child elements. The simplified DTD on page 136 declared the *complexType* element as follows:

```
<!ELEMENT complexType  ( ((annotation)?, (%ordered;, %unordered;)*|
    (element | all | choice | sequence | group | any )*,
    (attribute | attributeGroup), anyAttribute)>
<!ATTLIST complexType   content
        (mixed | empty | textOnly | elementOnly)  #REQUIRED
        name CDATA #REQUIRED
        derivedBy "(restriction|extension|reproduction)"> #IMPLIED
        base CDATA #IMPLIED
        id    ID   #IMPLIED >
```

The *complexType* element can contain three types of elements in the following order: *comment*, *element*, and *attribute*. The comment is located in the *annotation* element. Element information is usually defined using *element* or *group* elements. You can also use *choice*, *sequence*, *any*, or *all* elements to define the attributes within a *complexType*, as described later in this section. Attributes can be defined using the *attribute*, *attributeGroup*, or *group* elements.

The schema on page 136 uses what is called an embedded *complexType* declaration—the declaration is embedded in the *element* declaration. The following fragment shows the *complexType* element embedded within the *element* element:

```
<element name = "title">
    <complexType content = "textOnly">
      <attributeGroup ref = "i18n"/>
    </complexType>
</element>
```

The *complexType* declarations have a scope, specifying where the data type can be seen in the document. Embedded datatype declarations can be seen only within the element in which they are embedded—that is, they have local scope.

Thus, the *title* element can see the *complexType* element declared inside of it, but this *complexType* declaration is not visible from anywhere else in the document. You can also declare *complexType* elements outside of an *element* element. The *complexType* elements declared outside the *element* element are visible to the entire document and have document scope. You can reference a document scope element using the *ref* attribute. The document scope *complexType* elements will be discussed in detail later in this chapter.

> **NOTE**   As we have mentioned, the *schema* element can contain *element*, *simpleType*, *complexType*, *atttributeGroup*, and *group* elements as child elements. When any of these elements are child elements of the *schema* element, they also have document scope.

The *content* attribute can be *textOnly*, *mixed*, *elementOnly*, or *empty*. If the content consists of only text and no elements, you can use *textOnly*. For both text and elements, you would use *mixed*. If the content is only elements, you would use *elementOnly*. When there is no content, you can use *empty*.

The *ref* attribute is used to reference document scope elements. The *ref* attribute can be used with *attributeGroup*, *element*, and *group* elements. When used with the *attributeGroup* element, it can reference only *simpleType* elements.

When an *element* element is included as the content of the *complexType* element, it represents a child element. Thus, the following code declares a child element of *h1*:

```
<element name = "h1">
    <complexType content = "mixed">
        <element ref = "a"/>
        ⋮
```

Notice that the *ref* attribute is used to reference the name of the child element, in this case, *a*.

You can also use the *minOccurs* and *maxOccurs* attributes with the child element to specify its occurrence, as shown here:

```
<element name = "h1">
    <complexType content = "mixed">
        <element ref = "a" minOccurs = "0" maxOccurs = "1"/>
⋮
```

We'll discuss the *minOccurs* and *maxOccurs* attributes in the next section. When you use an element that uses the *ref* attribute, it's as if the element that is being referenced is substituting the element that contains the *ref* attribute.

The *element* Element

As shown in the code on page 136, the simplified DTD declaration for an *element* element is as follows:

```
<!ELEMENT element  ((annotation)?, (complexType | simpleType)?,
                    (unique | key | keyref)*)>
<!ATTLIST element  type      CDATA   #IMPLIED
                   name      CDATA   #IMPLIED
                   ref       CDATA   #IMPLIED
                   minOccurs (1 | 0 )  #IMPLIED
                   maxOccurs CDATA   #IMPLIED
                   id        ID      #IMPLIED
                   nullable (true | false ) 'false'
                   default CDATA #IMPLIED
                   fixed CDATA #IMPLIED >
```

The *name* attribute is the name of the element. The *name* attribute must follow all the rules defined for DTD element names. You can define your element using a *complexType* element, a *simpleType* element, or a *type* attribute. The *type* attribute and either the *simpleType* element or the *complexType* element are mutually exclusive. If you are declaring a data type, then one and only one of these must be used for the datatype declaration to be valid.

The *type* attribute

The *type* attribute associates either a simple or complex data type with an element. As we've seen, simple data types are either the predefined simple data types or simple data types you define based on these predefined simple data types. Complex data types can be used to associate attributes, elements, or a combination of both to an element. For example, you can declare the simple data type *String24* and associate it with the *customerName* element, as shown here:

```
<simpleType name="String24" base="string">
    <maxLength= "24"/ >
    <minLength = "0"/>
</simpleType>
<element name = "customerName" type = "String24"/>
```

In this case, you have created a data type named *String24* that has a length between 0 and 24 characters. This data type is then used in the element declaration, which means that the *customerName* element will be a string that is between 0 and 24 characters.

The *customerName* declaration uses document scope, meaning that all elements in the document can see the *String24* data type. The *type* attribute can be used to assign either a complex or a simple data type with document scope to an element.

The *minOccurs* and *maxOccurs* attributes

Notice that the *minOccurs* and *maxOccurs* attributes are also used in the DTD declaration for an *element* element to specify the number of occurrences of an element. When working with DTDs, we used the markers *, ?, and + to indicate the number of times a particular child element could be used as content for an element. For attributes, we used #IMPLIED for optional attributes, #REQUIRED for required attributes, #FIXED for attributes that had a fixed default value, and a default value when the attribute was optional. In schemas, both elements and attributes use the *minOccurs* and *maxOccurs* attributes. The *minOccurs* and the *maxOccurs* attributes are also used with the *group* element; the *choice*, *sequence*, and *all* elements that are contained within the *group* element; and the *any* element.

When used with elements, the *minOccurs* and *maxOccurs* attributes specify the number of occurrences of the element. For example, if an element has a *minOccurs* value of *0*, the element is optional. You can also declare an element to occur one or more times by setting a *maxOccurs* attribute to *1* or * respectively. The default value for *minOccurs* is 1, and *maxOccurs* has no default value.

When used with attributes, *minOccurs* and *maxOccurs* indicate whether the attribute is required. The *maxOccurs* attribute defaults to 1 unless it is specified or *minOccurs* is greater than 1. If *minOccurs* is set to *0* for an attribute and the default *maxOccurs* is equal to 1, you can have between 0 and 1 occurrences of this attribute. Thus, an attribute with *minOccurs* set to *0* is optional. If *minOccurs* is set to *1*, the attribute is required. The default for *minOccurs* is 0, but it's better to specify a value for it in your schema. The *minOccurs* and *maxOccurs* attributes can be set only to 0 or 1. For example, the following declaration makes the *target* attribute required:

```
<attribute name = "target" minOccurs = "1" maxOccurs = "1"
    type = "string"/>
```

Notice that the attributes we have discussed in this section can also be used to define other elements such as the *attribute* element.

The *attribute* Element

Attributes were declared in the simplified DTD on page 137 as follows:

```
<!ELEMENT attribute  ((annotation)?, (simpleType)?)>
<!ATTLIST attribute  type      CDATA   #IMPLIED
                     default   CDATA   #IMPLIED
                     fixed     CDATA   #IMPLIED
                     name      CDATA   #REQUIRED
                     minOccurs (0|1)     '0'
                     maxOccurs (0|1)     '1' >
```

In schemas, attributes are the association of a name with a particular simple data type. The *attribute* element is not included in the *schema* element, and therefore can only be used as a child element of the *complexType* or *attributeGroup* element. This means that all *attribute* elements will have local scope.

You can use the *attribute* element within a *complexType* element that has either local or document scope. As we'll see in the next section, you can group *attribute* elements together in an *attributeGroup* element. The *name* attribute must follow the same naming conventions as attribute names for DTDs.

You can use either a *default* attribute or a *fixed* attribute with *attribute* elements, but not both for the same *attribute* element. Unlike in DTDs, the *fixed* and *default* values are not linked to an attribute as optional or required—you can choose to make any attribute have a fixed value or a default value. A *fixed* value cannot be changed. The value of the *default* attribute will be the *default* value if one is not supplied for the attribute. The following declarations show the usage of *default* and *fixed* attributes:

```
<attribute name = "myAttribute" minOccurs = "1" fixed = "preserve"
    type = string"/>
<attribute name = "align" minOccurs = "0" default = "Center"
    type = "string"/>
```

The *attributeGroup* Element

As you can see in the simplified DTD for schemas on page 136, there is nothing equivalent to the DTD parameter entity used for attributes in schemas. Schemas do, however, allow you to create something similar to a parameter entity for attributes by using the *attributeGroup* element. Attribute groups declared using the *attributeGroup* element can have either document-level scope or local scope. (The element can be included in the declaration of the *schema* element or in the declaration of the *complexType* element.) In the original version of the schema, all attributes were defined without using the *attributeGroup* element.

The sample DTD we created in Chapter 5 included a parameter entity named *attrs*. You can define an attribute group named *attrs* in your schema as follows:

```
<schema>
    <attributeGroup name="attrs">
        <attribute name = "id" type = "ID"/>
        <attribute name = "class" type = "string"/>
        <attribute name = "style" type = "string"/>
        <attribute name = "lang" type = "NMTOKEN"/>
        <attribute name = "xml:lang" type = "NMTOKEN"/>
        <attribute name = "dir">
            <simpleType source = "ENUMERATION">
                <enumeration value = "ltr"/>
                <enumeration value = "rtl"/>
            </simpleType>
        </attribute>
        <attribute name = "onclick" type = "string"/>
        <attribute name = "ondblclick" type = "string"/>
        <attribute name = "onmousedown" type = "string"/>
        <attribute name = "onmouseup" type = "string"/>
        <attribute name = "onmouseover" type = "string"/>
        <attribute name = "onmousemove" type = "string"/>
        <attribute name = "onmouseout" type = "string"/>
        <attribute name = "onkeypress" type = "string"/>
        <attribute name = "onkeydown" type = "string"/>
        <attribute name = "onkeyup" type = "string"/>
        <attribute name = "href" type = "string"/>
        <attribute name = "name" type = "string"/>
        <attribute name = "target" type = "string"/>
    </attributeGroup>
    ⋮
</schema>
```

You can use *attrs* as follows:

```
<element name = "option">
    <type content = "textOnly">
        <attributeGroup ref = "attrs"/>
        <attribute name = "selected"/>
        ⋮
```

Thus, you declare the *attributeGroup* element as a child element of the *schema* element to create a document scope group of attributes. You can then reference the document scope *attributeGroup* element in a *type* element by including an *attributeGroup* element in the *type* element with the *ref* attribute set equal to the name of the document scope group. As you can see, this greatly simplifies the schema.

NOTE Attribute groups can contain only simple data types.

The *group* Element

The *group* element enables you to group elements in the same way you use parentheses when declaring elements in a DTD. The *group* element also enables you to create something similar to DTD parameter entities. The order of the elements in the *group* element can vary as defined by the *order* attribute.

The declaration for a *group* element looks like this:

```
<!ELEMENT group ((annotation)?, (all | choice | sequence)*)>
<!ATTLIST group
        minOccurs    CDATA                    '1'
        maxOccurs    CDATA                 #IMPLIED
        order       (choice | seq | all)   'seq'
        name         CDATA                 #IMPLIED
        ref          CDATA                 #IMPLIED
        id           ID                    #IMPLIED>
```

A *group* element can optionally contain an *annotation* element (comments) and must contain an *all*, a *choice,* or a *sequence* element. These elements define the order and usage of the elements in the group, and are examined in detail in the next section. Notice that *group* elements do not include attributes—they are used only for grouping elements.

The *minOccurs* and *maxOccurs* attributes indicate how many times the *group* element can occur. They replace the markers (*, ?, and +) in the DTD.

The *choice, sequence,* and *all* elements

The *choice* element indicates a choice of elements in the *group* element—its function is the same as the bar (|) in the DTD. The DTD declaration <!*ELEMENT select (optGroup | option)+>* would thus become the following schema declaration:

```
<group minOccurs = "1" maxOccurs = "*">
    <choice>
        <element ref = "optGroup"/>
        <element ref = "option"/>
    </choice>
</group>
```

The *sequence* element indicates that the elements must appear in the sequence listed and that each element can occur 0 or more times. When using *sequence,* you can use *minOccurs* and *maxOccurs* as attributes for the elements to specify the number of allowable occurrences of an *element* element in the group. Using *sequence* is the same as using the comma separator in the DTD with subgroups that are enclosed in parentheses with occurrence operators. In its simplest form, a *sequence* element can consist of only one element. For example, the DTD declaration <*!ELE-MENT optGroup (option)+*> would look like this in a schema declaration:

```
<group minOccurs = "1" maxOccurs = "*">
    <sequence>
        <element ref = "option"/>
    </sequence>
</group>
```

The DTD declaration <*!ELEMENT ol (font? , li+)*> would look like this as a schema declaration:

```
<group >
    <sequence>
        <element ref = "font" minOccurs = "0"
                maxOccurs = "1"/>
        <element ref = "li" minOccurs = "1" maxOccurs = "*"/>
    </sequence>
</group>
```

The *all* element indicates that all the *element* and *group* elements listed in the schema must be used, in any order. Each *element* element in an *all group* element must have *minOccurs* and *maxOccurs* attributes set to 1. The *minOccurs* and *maxOccurs* attributes cannot be used for the *group* element when you are using *all*; they can be used only for the *element* elements in the group. A *group* element declared with *order* equal to *all* must not be a subgroup of another *group* element. For example, because every HTML document must have one and only one *head* and *body*, you could declare them in your schema as follows:

```
<group >
    <all>
        <element ref = "head" minOccurs= "1" maxOccurs= "1"/>
        <element ref = "body" minOccurs= "1" maxOccurs= "1"/>
    </all>
</group>
```

Local embedded groups

When you include the *group* element declaration within a *complexType* element, you are embedding the *group* element declaration inside the *complexType* element. If you define the *group* element within the *complexType* element, that *group* element is not visible from anywhere else within the schema document—it has local scope. If you are going to use a *group* element to contain only one element, it makes sense to use a local group.

Wildcards, particles, and compositors

According to the schema specification, the term *particle* refers to content of an *element* element that contains only other elements, groups, and wildcards—in other words, no text. Wildcards include several different ways to use the *any* keyword.

> **NOTE** The *any* keyword in schemas is similar to the *ANY* keyword in DTDs, except that in a schema *any* refers only to *element* and *group* elements. In a DTD, *ANY* refers to text and elements. Text content is not part of the *any* keyword in the schema specification.

One way to reference all *element* or *group* elements within the specified namespace and schema as the *complexType* element is to use the *any* keyword. If this keyword is used within a *complexType* element, it indicates that any element or group in the schema in the same namespace as the *complexType* element could be included within this *complextype* element. If the value for the namespace is *##targetNamespace*, all of the elements within the current document will be used.

Another possibility is to reference all *element* and *group* elements in a namespace other than the one the *complexType* element is in. In this case, you would use the following declaration:

```
<any namespace="##name_of_namespace"/>
```

In a schema, the *order* element and the *minOccurs* and *maxOccurs* attributes together define what is called a *compositor*. A compositor for a given *group* element will specify whether elements in the group provide the following conditions:

■ A sequence of the elements that are permitted or required by the specified particles

■ A choice between the elements permitted or required by the specified particles

■ A repeated choice among the elements permitted or required by the specified particles

■ A set of the elements required by the specified particles

A more precise definition can now be created: a group consists of two or more particles plus a compositor.

Document scope groups

Just as you can create *complexType* elements that have document scope, you can create *group* elements that have document scope. The same basic rules apply—that is, including a *name* attribute and declaring the elements as child elements of the *schema* element. Thus, you could create the following global *group* elements:

```
<schema>
    <group name = "Block" minOccurs = "1" maxOccurs = "*">
        <choice>
            <element ref = "p"/>
            <element ref = "h1"/>
            <element ref = "h2"/>
            <element ref = "h3"/>
            <element ref = "h4"/>
            <element ref = "h5"/>
            <element ref = "h6"/>
            <element ref = "div"/>
            <group >
                <choice>
                    <element ref = "ul"/>
                    <element ref = "ol"/>
                </choice>
            </group>
            <element ref = "hr"/>
            <element ref = "blockquote"/>
            <element ref = "fieldset"/>
            <element ref = "table"/>
            <element ref = "form"/>
            <element ref = "script"/>
            <element ref = "noscript"/>
        </choice>
    </group>
    ⋮
</schema>
```

This declaration states that any element that uses this group must include at least one of these elements as its content. The content of the element can also be any number of copies of the elements in any order. This declaration is identical to the DTD declaration shown here:

```
<!ENTITY % Block " (%block; | form | %misc;)*">
<!ELEMENT noscript %Block;>
```

Thus, document scope *group* elements allow you to create something similar to the parameter entities in DTDs that contained element declarations. You can now use the *group* element as follows:

```
<element name = "noscript">
    <complexType content = "elementOnly">
        <group ref = "Block"/>
        <attributeGroup ref = "attrs"/>
    </complexType>
</element>
<element name = "blockquote">
    <complexType content = "elementOnly">
        <group ref = "schemaBlock"/>
        <attributeGroup ref = "attrs"/>
        <attribute name = "cite" type = "string"/>
    </complexType>
</element>
```

complexType Elements with Document Scope

Now that we've covered *group* and *attributeGroup* elements, we can examine document scope *complexType* elements in more detail. If you have a grouping of attributes and elements that will be used by more than one *element* element, you can create a document scope *complexType* element. You declare the document scope *complexType* element exactly as you declare the embedded *complexType* element, except the declaration will include the *name* attribute and will not be within the content of an *element* element—that is, it will be outside an *element* element declaration. Thus, it will be declared as a child element of the *schema* element. For example, all the *h* elements share a common set of child elements and attributes. You could declare a global *complexType* element and use it as shown here:

```
<schema>
    <complexType name= "standardcontent" content = "mixed">
        <element ref = "a"/>
        <element ref = "br"/>
        <element ref = "span"/>
        <element ref = "img"/>
        <element ref = "tt"/>
        <element ref = "i"/>
        <element ref = "b"/>
        <element ref = "big"/>
        <element ref = "small"/>
        <element ref = "em"/>
```

(continued)

```
            <element ref = "strong"/>
            <element ref = "q"/>
            <element ref = "sub"/>
            <element ref = "sup"/>
            <element ref = "input"/>
            <element ref = "select"/>
            <element ref = "textarea"/>
            <element ref = "label"/>
            <element ref = "button"/>
            <element ref = "script"/>
            <element ref = "noscript"/>
            <attribute name = "align" type = "string"/>
            <attributeGroup ref = "attrs"/>
        </complexType>
        <element name= "h1" type ="standardcontent"/>
        <element name= "h2" type ="standardcontent"/>
        ⋮
</schema>
```

You can also extend a *complexType* element using the *base* attribute. For example, the *li* element uses all the preceding content and several other elements. You can extend the *complexType* element example as follows:

```
<complexType name = "licontent" base = "standardcontent"
    derivedby = "extension">
    <element ref = "p"/>
    <element ref = "h1"/>
    <element ref = "h2"/>
    <element ref = "h3"/>
    <element ref = "h4"/>
    <element ref = "h5"/>
    <element ref = "h6"/>
    <element ref = "div"/>
    <element ref = "ul"/>
    <element ref = "ol"/>
    <element ref = "hr"/>
    <element ref = "blockquote"/>
    <element ref = "fieldset"/>
    <element ref = "table"/>
    <element ref = "form"/>
</complexType>
<element name= "li" type ="licontent"/>
⋮
```

To extend a *complexType* element, you need to use the *base* and *derivedBy* attributes of the *complexType* element. The *base* attribute identifies the source of the element and can be either *#all*, a single element, or a space-separated list.

The *derivedBy* attribute can be set to *restriction, extension,* or *reproduction.* When you are adding elements or attributes to a *complexType* element, the *derivedBy* attribute should be set to *extension.*

The *restriction* value for the *derivedBy* attribute allows you to add restrictions to the *element* elements included within the *complexType* element. For *element* elements included in the original *complexType* element, you can restrict the number of occurrences of an element or replace a wildcard with one or more elements. For example, if you wanted to restrict the *a* element to one or more occurrences and remove the *br* element in a new *complexType* element, based on the *standardcontent* type defined in the preceding example, you could write the following code:

```
<type name = "licontent" base = "standardcontent"
    derivedby = "restriction">
    <element name = "a"  minOccurs = "1"/>
    <element name ="br" maxOccurs ="0"/>
</type>
```

For attributes, you can add or fix defaults or restrict the attribute's simple data type definition.

If you set the *derivedBy* attribute to *reproduction,* the new element is identical to the type it is derived from. Essentially, *reproduction* indicates neither *restriction* nor *extension.*

If the value for the *final* attribute for the *complexType* element is not empty, the *complexType* cannot be extended, restricted, or reproduced. A *complexType* that is derived by extension, restriction, or reproduction also cannot be extended, restricted, or reproduced. The *block* attribute allows you to block extension, restriction, or reproduction. If you set the *block* attribute to *restriction,* the *complexType* element cannot be used to create a new complex type by restriction.

A Schema for a Data-Oriented XML Document

The example that has been used up to this point has been a document-oriented XML document with no data types besides *string.* To see how the other data types work, in this section we'll create an example using the Northwind Traders database. (This database can be found in Microsoft Access, Visual Studio, and Microsoft SQL Server 7.) For the Customer and Categories tables, you could create the schema shown below.

```
<?xml version ="1.0"?>
<schema targetNamespace = "http://www.northwind.com/Category"
    xmlns = http://www.w3.org/1999/XMLSchema
    xmlns:Categories = "http://www.northwind.com/Category">
<simpleType name="String15" source="string">
        <maxLength= "15" />
```

(continued)

```
            <minLength = "0"/>
        </simpleType>
        <simpleType name="String5" base="string">
            <maxLength= "5"/ >
            <minLength = "0"/>
        </simpleType>
        <simpleType name="String30" base="string">
            <maxLength= "30" />
            <minLength = "0"/>
        </simpleType>
        <simpleType name="String60" base="string">
            <maxLength= "60" />
            <minLength = "0"/>
        </simpleType>
    <simpleType name="String10" base="string">
            <maxLength= "10" />
            <minLength = "0"/>
        </simpleType>
        <simpleType name="String24" base="string">
            <maxLength= "24" />
            <minLength = "0"/>
        </simpleType>
    <simpleType name="String40" base="string">
            <maxLength= "40" />
            <minLength = "0"/>
        </simpleType>


    <element name = "Categories">
        <complexType content = "elementOnly">
            <group>
            <sequence>
            <element ref = "Categories.CategoryID"
                        minOccurs = "1" maxOccurs = "1" />
                <element ref = "Categories.CategoryName"
                        minOccurs = "1" maxOccurs = "1" />
                <element ref = "Categories.Description"
                        minOccurs = "0" maxOccurs = "1" />
                <element ref = "Categories.Picture" minOccurs = "0"
                        maxOccurs = "1"/>
            </sequence>
            </group>
        </complexType>
    </element>

    <element name = "Categories.CategoryID" type = "integer">
        <annotation>
            <documentation>Number automatically assigned to a new
                            category
            </documentation>
```

```
        </annotation>
    </element>

    <element name = "Categories.CategoryName" type = "String15">
        <annotation>
            <documentation>Name of food category</documentation>
        </annotation>
    </element>

    <element name = "Categories.Description" type = "string"/>
    <element name = "Categories.Picture" type = "binary">
        <annotation>
            <documentation> Picture representing the food category
            </documentation>
        </annotation>
    </element>

    <element name = "Customers">
        <complexType content = "elementOnly">
            <group>
                <sequence>
                    <element ref = "Customers.CustomerID"
                            minOccurs = "1" maxOccurs = "1"/>
                    <element ref = "Customers.CompanyName"
                            minOccurs = "1" maxOccurs = "1"/>
                    <element ref = "Customers.ContactName"
                            minOccurs = "1" maxOccurs = "1"/>
                    <element ref = "Customers.ContactTitle"
                            minOccurs = "0" maxOccurs = "1"/>
                    <element ref = "Customers.Address"
                            minOccurs = "1" maxOccurs = "1"/>
                    <element ref = "Customers.City" minOccurs = "1"
                            maxOccurs = "1"/>
                    <element ref = "Customers.Region"
                            minOccurs = "1" maxOccurs = "1"/>
                    <element ref = "Customers.PostalCode"
                            minOccurs = "1" maxOccurs = "1"/>
                    <element ref = "Customers.Country"
                            minOccurs = "1" maxOccurs = "1"/>
                    <element ref = "Customers.Phone" minOccurs = "1"
                            maxOccurs = "1"/>
                    <element ref = "Customers.Fax" minOccurs = "0"
                            maxOccurs = "1"/>
                </sequence>
            </group>
        </complexType>
    </element>
```

(continued)

```
<element name = "Customers.CustomerID" type = "CustomerIDField">
    <annotation>
        <documentation>
            Unique five-character code based on customer name
        </documentation>
    </annotation>
</element>

<element name = "Customers.CompanyName" type = "String5"/>
<element name = "Customers.ContactName" type = "String40"/>
<element name = "Customers.ContactTitle" type = "String30"/>
<element name = "Customers.Address" type = "String60">
    <annotation>
        <documentation>Street or post-office box</documentation>
    </annotation>
</element>

<element name = "Customers.City" type = "String15"/>
<element name = "Customers.Region" type = "String15">
    <annotation>
        <documentation>State or province</documentation>
    </annotation>
</element>

<element name = "Customers.PostalCode" type = "String10"/>
<element name = "Customers.Country" type = "String15"/>
<element name = "Customers.Phone" type = "String24">
    <annotation>
        <documentation>
            Phone number includes country code or area code
        </documentation>
    </annotation>
</element>
<element name = "Customers.Fax" type = "String24">
    <annotation>
        <documentation>
            Fax number includes country code or area code
        </documentation>
    </annotation>
</element>
</schema>
```

Notice that *Categories* and *Customers* have been used as prefixes to identify what objects the elements belong to. If you look in the Northwind Traders database, you'll see that the *field* data types and the lengths for *character* data types match those in the database. The comments that were included in the Northwind Traders database were also used in the schema. You can see that it's fairly easy to convert a database table into a schema.

Now that we have discussed schemas, we'll need to cover namespaces and schemas. In the following section, we'll examine how to use namespaces in schemas.

NAMESPACES AND SCHEMAS

In Chapter 6, we looked at using namespaces for DTDs. Namespaces can be read and interpreted in well-formed XML documents. Unfortunately, DTDs are not well-formed XML. If you use a namespace in a DTD, the namespace cannot be resolved. Let's look at the following DTD as an example:

```
<!DOCTYPE doc [
<!ELEMENT doc (body)>
<!ELEMENT body EMPTY>
<!ATTLIST body bodyText CDATA #REQUIRED>
<!ELEMENT HTML:body EMPTY>
<!ATTLIST HTML:body HTML:bodyText CDATA #REQUIRED>
]>
```

A valid usage of this DTD is shown here:

```
<doc><body bodyText="Hello, world"/></doc>
```

The following usage would be invalid, however, because the *HTML:body* element is not defined as a child element of the *doc* element:

```
<doc><HTML:body bodyText="Hello, world"/></doc>
```

As far as the DTD is concerned, the *HTML:body* element and the *body* element are two completely different elements. A DTD cannot resolve a namespace and break it into its prefix (*HTML*) and the name (*body*). So the prefix and the name simply become one word. We want to be able to use namespaces but to be able to separate the prefix from the name. Schemas enable us to do this.

Including Schemas in the Same *targetNamespace*

We could write a similar schema with a namespace to identify *schema* elements. For example, let's create a schema named NorthwindMessage.xsd, as shown here:

```
<schema targetNamespace="http://www.northwindtraders.com/Message"
    xmlns:northwindMessage="http://www.northwindtraders.com/Message"
    xmlns ="http://www.w3.org/1999/XMLSchema">
<include schemaLocation=
    "http://www.northwindtraders.com/HTMLMessage.xsd"/>
    <element name="doc">
        <group>
```

(continued)

```
        <option>
            <element ref="northwindMessage:body"/>
            <element ref="northwindMessage:HTMLbody"/>
        </option>
    </group>
</element>
<element name="body">
    <attribute name="bodyText" type="northwindMessage:TextBody"/>
</element>
</schema>
```

> **NOTE**   The schema namespace is not assigned a prefix, so it is the default namespace. All elements without a prefix will belong to the schema namespaces. When elements that are defined in the schema are used, the schema's namespace must be used, as was done with the *body* and *HTMLbody* elements. In schemas, the *body* and *HTMLbody* elements can be separated from their namespace prefixes and properly identified.

The included file, HTMLMessage.xsd, would look like this:

```
<xsd:schema targetNamespace:xsd="http://www.northwindtraders.com/
    Message"
    xmlns:northwindMessage="http://www.northwind.com/Message"
    xmlns ="http://www.w3.org/1999/XMLSchema">
    <xsd:simpleType name="TextBody" base="string"
        minLength="0"
        maxLength="20"/>
    <xsd:element name="HTMLbody">
        <xsd:attribute name="bodyText" type="string"/>
    </xsd:element>
</xsd:schema>
```

> **NOTE**   In this case, we did assign a prefix to the schema namespace and used this prefix throughout the document. You can use either method, but keep in mind that defaults can sometimes be harder for people to interpret.

As you can see, namespaces play a major role in schemas. Let's look at the different elements included in this example. Both documents include a *targetNamespace*. A *targetNamespace* defines the namespace that this schema belongs to (http://www.northwindtraders.com/Message). Remember, a namespace uses a URI as a unique identifier, not for document retrieval (although an application could use the namespace to identify the associated schema). It will be up to the application to determine how the namespace is used. The *include* element has a *schemaLocation* attribute that can be used by an application or a person to identify where the schema is located.

The HTMLMessage.xsd file is included in the NorthwindMessage.xsd by using the *include* element. For one schema to be included in another, both must belong to the same namespace. Using the *include* element will result in the included document being inserted into the schema in place of the *include* element. Once the insertion is complete, the schema should still be a well-formed XML document. A top-level schema can be built that includes many other schemas.

Notice that the *simpleType TextBody* is declared in the included document but used in the top-level documents. This separation makes no difference, as both documents will be combined into one document by the processing application.

The XML document that is based on the schema is referred to as an *instance document*. This instance document will have only a reference to the top-level schema. The instance document will need to use only the namespace of the top-level schema. Thus, the instance document for our example schema would look like this:

```
<?xml version="1.0"?>
<northwindMessage:doc xmlns: northwindMessage=
    "http://www.northwindtraders.com/Message" >
    <body bodyText="Hello, world"/>
</northwindMessage:doc>
```

You could also have the following instance document:

```
<?xml version="1.0"?>
<northwindMessage:doc xmlns:northwindMessage=
    "http://www.northwindtraders.com/Message">
    <HTMLbody bodyText="<h1>Hello, world</h1>"/>
</northwindMessage:doc>
```

As far as the instance document is concerned, all the elements come from the top-level schema. The instance document is unaware of the fact that *HTMLbody* element actually comes from a different schema because the schema resolves all the different namespaces.

Including Schemas from a Different *targetNamespace*

When you use the *include* element, you insert the entire referenced schema into the top-level schema and both documents must have the same *targetNamespace* attribute. You might also want to create schema documents that contain *simpleType* and *complexType* declarations that you can use in multiple schemas. If the multiple schemas have a different *targetNamespace*, you cannot use the *include* element for a document shared between them. Instead of using the *include* element, you can use the *import* element. If you use the *import* element, you can reference any data type created in the imported document and use, extend, or restrict the data type, as shown here:

```
<schema targetNamespace="http://www.northwindtraders.com/Message"
    xmlns:northwindMessage="http://www.northwindtraders.com/Message"
    xmlns:northwindType="http://www.northwindtraders.com/Types"
    xmlns ="http://www.w3.org/1999/XMLSchema">
    <import schemaLocation="http://www.northwindtraders.com/
        HTMLTypes.xsd"/>
    <element name="doc">
        <element ref="northwindMessage:body"/>
    </element>
    <element name="body">
        <attribute name="bodyText" type="northwindType:TextBody"/>
    </element>
</schema>
```

The HTMLTypes.xsd file might look like this:

```
<xsd:schema targetNamespace:xsd="http://www.northwindtraders.com/    Types"
    xmlns:northwindMessage="http://www.northwindtraders.com/Types"
    xmlns ="http://www.w3.org/1999/XMLSchema">
    <xsd:simpleType name="TextBody" base="string"
        minLength="0"
        maxLength="20"/>
</xsd:schema>
```

In the top-level schema, we associated a namespace called *http://www. northwindtraders.com/Types* with the prefix *northwindType*. Using the *import* element, we can associate that namespace with a schema location. The application will determine how to use the *schemaLocation* attribute. Once you have done this, you can use the data type. An instance document for this schema is shown here:

```
<?xml version="1.0"?>
<northwindMessage:doc xmlns:northwindMessage=
    "http://www.northwindtraders.com/Message" >
    <body bodyText="Hello, world"/>
</northwindMessage:doc>
```

Once again, as far as the instance document is concerned, it does not matter where the data types are defined—everything comes from the top-level document.

Overriding Data Types

Using namespaces, we have managed to build a schema from other schemas and include data types from other schemas. In both of these cases, the instance document uses only the top-level schema. You can also declare an element as being one particular data type and then override that data type in the instance document. Consider the following top-level schema:

```
<schema targetNamespace="http://www.northwindtraders.com/Message"
    xmlns:northwindMessage="http://www.northwindtraders.com/Message"
    xmlns="http://www.w3.org/1999/XMLSchema">
<include schemaLocation=
    "http://www.northwindtraders.com/HTMLMessage.xsd"/>
    <element name="doc" type="Body"/>
    <complexType name="Body">
        <element name="body">
            <attribute name="bodyText" type="string"/>
        </element>
    </complexType>
    <complexType name="HTMLBodyCT">
        <element name="HTMLBody">
            <complexType>
                <element name="h1" type="string" content="text"/>
            </complexType>
        </element>
    </complexType>
</schema>
```

This schema has defined the *doc* element as being a *Body* data type, and the *doc* element will contain a *body* child element that has a *bodyText* attribute. Now suppose you also want to be able to create messages from other body data types, such as the *HTMLBodyCT* data type defined in the schema. You could do this by creating a *group* element with *choices*.

Another option is to declare the schema as above and then substitute the *HTMLBodyCT* data type for the *Body* data type in the instance document. To do this, you will need to reference the schema instance namespace in the instance document. To use the *HTMLBodyCT* data type, you would need to create an instance document such as this:

```
<?xml version="1.0"?>
<northwindMessage:doc xmlns:northwindMessage=
    "http://www.northwindtraders.com/Message"
```

(continued)

```
xmlns:xsi="http://www.w3.org/1999/XMLSchema/instance"
xsi:type="HTMLBodyCT" >
<HTMLBody>
    <h1>"Hello, world"</h1>
</HTMLBody>
</northwindMessage:doc>
```

In this example, you have used the *xsi:type* attribute to reference a type defined in the schema (*HTMLBodyCT*). The *xsi:type* is part of the schema instance namespace and is used to override an element's type with another type that is defined in the schema. In this example, you have now redefined the *doc* element as being of *HTMLBodyCT* data type instead of a *Body* data type. You could also have defined the *HTMLBodyCT* data type in a separate schema and used the *include* element in the top-level schema.

SUMMARY

Schemas enable you to associate data types with attributes, create your own data types, and define the structure of your document using well-formed XML. Schemas are used to define elements that are associated with a name and a type. The type is either a data type or one or more attributes or elements. Elements can be grouped together in *group* elements, and attributes can be grouped together in *attributeGroup* elements. The *group* and *attributeGroup* elements can either be used locally or they can have document level scope.

Schemas provide many advantages over DTDs; namely, they use namespaces, they utilize a wide range of data types, and they are written in XML. It's likely that schemas will gradually replace DTDs over the next few years. Schemas will be discussed in more detail when we look at BizTalk in Chapter 8 and the Document Object Model in Chapter 11.

Chapter 8

SOAP

Simple Object Access Protocol (SOAP) version 1.1 is an industry standard designed to improve cross-platform interoperability using the Web and XML. The Web has evolved from simply pushing out static pages to creating customized content that performs services for users. A user can be a customer retrieving specialized Web pages for placing orders or a business partner using a customized form for reviewing stock and sales figures. A wide range of components located on various computers are involved in performing these Web-based services. Because these systems consist of many computers, including the client computer, middle-tier servers, and usually a database server, these systems are called *distributed systems*. To understand how SOAP works, let's take a look at the distributed system first.

COMMUNICATION OVER DISTRIBUTED SYSTEMS

Distributed systems commonly use two models for communication: *message passing* (which can be combined with message queuing) and *request/response messaging system*. A message passing system allows messages to be sent at any time. Once a message has been sent, the application that sent the message usually moves on. This type of system is called asynchronous. An asynchronous system typically uses messages, but it can also be based on other models. With the request/response model, the request and the response are paired together and can be thought of as a synchronous system. The request is sent by an application, and the application usually waits until a response is received before continuing. When one application calls an object on another computer by making a Remote Procedure Call (RPC), we can think of this call as synchronous request/response message passing.

The request/response model is commonly used to allow components on different computers to communicate with each other using RPCs. Over the last several years, many attempts have been made to develop a standard that would allow this communication between components on different computers. Currently, the two most commonly used standards are Distributed Component Object Model (DCOM) and the Object Management Group's Internet Inter-Orb Protocol (IIOP). Both of these standards work well; their greatest shortcoming is that they do not natively interoperate with each other. Therefore, you cannot arbitrarily make a call to a component on a server from a client without first knowing what standard that server is using. Usually, you will also have to configure the client so that it can communicate with the server, especially when there are security issues. DCOM works best when all the computers in the system are using Microsoft operating systems. An IIOP system works best when all the computers in the system use the same *CORBA Object Request Broker* (ORB).[1]

> **NOTE** IIOP is only a specification: it will be up to individual vendors to create an implementation of the specification in the form of an ORB. There are currently many different ORBs.

When you are working on an internal system, it might be possible to limit the system to one platform or the other. Once you start working with the Internet or expanding the intranet out to extranets (for example, networks that include the corporation and its partners), it will usually be impossible to have a uniform platform across the entire system. At this point, DCOM and IIOP will no longer allow communication between any two components within the system, and neither of these two standards allows users to cross trust domains easily. Thus, for larger systems expanding across computers with multiple platforms, we need a way to enable objects to communicate with each other. The solution to this problem is SOAP.

---

1. CORBA stands for Common Object Request Broker Architecture, a specification developed by the Object Management Group. This specification provides the standard interface definition between objects in different programs, even if these programs are written in different programming languages and are on different platforms. In CORBA, ORB acts as a "broker" between a client request for an object from a distributed object and the completion of that request.

SOAP AND THE REQUEST/RESPONSE MODEL

The SOAP standard introduces no new concepts—it's built completely from existing technology. It currently uses HTTP as its request/response messaging transport and is completely platform independent. As you know, HTTP connects computers across the entire world. HTTP can go through firewalls and is the easiest means to transport messages to any computer in the world. It's likely that SOAP will evolve to use other protocols in the future.

A SOAP *package* contains information that can be used to invoke a method. How that method is called is not defined in the SOAP specification. SOAP also does not handle distributed garbage collection, *message boxcarring,*[2] type safety, or bidirectional HTTP. What SOAP does allow you to do is pass parameters and commands between HTTP clients and servers, regardless of the platforms and applications on the client and server. The parameters and commands are encoded using XML. Let's take a look at how SOAP uses the standard HTTP headers.

HTTP HEADERS AND SOAP

Two types of headers are available in HTTP: request headers and response headers. When you are using your Web browser to surf the Internet, each time you navigate to a new URL the Web browser will create a request and send it to the Web server. These requests are written in plain text; each has headers in a standard format. When creating SOAP messages, you will be adding additional information to these standard formats. HTTP servers generate a response message upon receiving the client request. This message contains a status line and response headers. Let's look at the two headers in more detail.

Request Headers

A typical HTTP message in a SOAP request being passed to a Web server looks like this:

```
POST /Order HTTP/1.1
Host: www.northwindtraders.com
Content-Type: text/xml
Content-Length: nnnn
SOAPAction: "urn:northwindtraders.com:PO#UpdatePO"

Information being sent would be located here.
```

---

2. A boxcar message is a type of message that contains more than one business document.

The first line of the message contains three separate components: the request method, the request URI, and the protocol version. In this case, the request method is *POST*; the request URI is */Order*; and the version number is *HTTP/1.1*. The Internet Engineering Task Force (IETF) has standardized the request methods. The GET method is commonly used to retrieve information on the Web. The POST method is used to pass information from the client to the server. The information passed by the POST method is then used by applications on the server. Only certain types of information can be sent using GET; any type of data can be sent using POST. SOAP also supports sending messages using M-POST. We'll discuss this method in detail later in this chapter. When working with the POST method in a SOAP package, the request URI actually contains the name of the method to be invoked.

The second line is the URL of the server that the request is being sent to. The request URL is implementation specific—that is, each server defines how it will interpret the request URL. In the case of a SOAP package, the request URL usually represents the name of the object that contains the method being called.

The third line contains the content type, *text/xml*, which indicates that the *payload* is XML in plain text format. The payload refers to the essential data being carried to the destination. The payload information could be used by a server or a firewall to validate the incoming message. A SOAP request must use the *text/xml* as its content type. The fourth line specifies the size of the payload in bytes. The content type and content length are required with a payload.

The *SOAPAction* header field must be used in a SOAP request to specify the intent of the SOAP HTTP request. The fifth line of the message, *SOAPAction: "urn: northwindtraders.com:PO#UpdatePO"*, is a namespace followed by the method name. By combining this namespace with the request URL, our example calls the *UpdatePO* method of the *Order* object and is scoped by the *urn:northwindtraders.com:PO* namespace URI. The following are also valid SOAPAction header field values:

```
SOAPAction: "UpdatePO"
SOAPAction: ""
SOAPAction:
```

The header field value of the empty string means that the HTTP request URI provides the intent of the SOAP message. A header field without a specified value indicates that the intent of the SOAP message isn't available.

Notice that there is a single blank line between the fifth line and the payload request. When you are working with message headers, the carriage-return/line-feed sequence delimits the headers and an extra carriage-return/line-feed sequence is used to signify that the header information is complete and that what follows is the payload.

Response Headers

A typical response message that contains the response headers is shown here:

```
200 OK
Content-Type: text/plain
Content-Length: nnnn

Content goes here.
```

The first line of this message contains a status code and a message associated with that status code. In this case, the status code is *200* and the message is *OK*, meaning that the request was successfully decoded and that an appropriate response was returned. If an error had occurred, the following headers might have been returned:

```
400 Bad Request
Content-Type: text/plain
Content-Length: 0
```

In this case, the status code is *400* and the message is *Bad Request*, meaning that the request cannot be decoded by the server because of incorrect syntax. You can find other standard status codes in RFC 2616.

SIMPLE SOAP PAYLOADS

As you can see, SOAP uses HTTP as the request/response messaging transport. We can add a SOAP request payload in the request message and a response payload in the response message. In this way, we can issue an RPC to any component using HTTP.

The Payload for a Request Message

The SOAP specification defines several SOAP elements that can be used with a SOAP request: *envelope*, *head*, and *body*. The envelope is a container for the head and body. The head contains information about the SOAP message, and the body contains the actual message. Namespaces are used to distinguish the SOAP elements from the other elements of the payload. For example, *SOAP-ENV:Envelope*, *SOAP-ENV:Head*, and *SOAP-ENV:Body* are used in a SOAP document.

The SOAP schema for the envelope will look as follows:

```
<?xml version="1.0" ?>
<!-- XML Schema for SOAP v 1.1 Envelope -->
<!-- Copyright 2000 DevelopMentor, International Business
```

(continued)

```
Machines Corporation, Lotus Development Corporation,
Microsoft, UserLand Software -->
<schema xmlns="http://www.w3.org/1999/XMLSchema"
    xmlns:tns="http://schemas.xmlsoap.org/soap/envelope/"
    targetNamespace="http://schemas.xmlsoap.org/soap/envelope/">
    <!-- SOAP envelope, header, and body -->
    <element name="Envelope" type="tns:Envelope"/>
    <complexType name="Envelope">
        <element ref="tns:Header" minOccurs="0"/>
        <element ref="tns:Body" minOccurs="1"/>
        <any minOccurs="0" maxOccurs="*"/>
        <anyAttribute/>
    </complexType>
    <element name="Header" type="tns:Header"/>
    <complexType name="Header">
        <any minOccurs="0" maxOccurs="*"/>
        <anyAttribute/>
    </complexType>
    <element name="Body" type="tns:Body"/>
    <complexType name="Body">
        <any minOccurs="0" maxOccurs="*"/>
        <anyAttribute/>
    </complexType>
    <!-- Global Attributes.  The following attributes are
         intended to be usable via qualified attribute names on
         any complex type referencing them.
    -->
    <attribute name="mustUnderstand" default="0">
        <simpleType base="boolean">
            <pattern value="0|1"/>
        </simpleType>
    </attribute>
    <attribute name="actor" type="uri-reference"/>
    <!-- 'encodingStyle' indicates any canonicalization
     conventions followed in the contents of the containing
     element.  For example, the value
     'http://schemas.xmlsoap.org/soap/encoding/' indicates
     the pattern described in SOAP specification.
    -->
<simpleType name="encodingStyle" base="uri-reference"
    derivedBy="list"/>
    <attributeGroup name="encodingStyle">
        <attribute name="encodingStyle"
            type="tns:encodingStyle"/>
    </attributeGroup>
```

```
<!-- SOAP fault reporting structure -->
<complexType name="Fault" final="extension">
    <element name="faultcode" type="qname"/>
    <element name="faultstring" type="string"/>
    <element name="faultactor" type="uri-reference"
        minOccurs="0"/>
    <element name="detail" type="tns:detail" minOccurs="0"/>
</complexType>
<complexType name="detail">
    <any minOccurs="0" maxOccurs="*"/>
    <anyAttribute/>
</complexType>
</schema>
```

A SOAP request including the payload defined in the schema would look like this:

```
POST /Order HTTP/1.1
Host: www.northwindtraders.com
Content-Type: text/xml
Content-Length: nnnn
SOAPAction: "urn:northwindtraders.com:PO#UpdatePO"

<SOAP-ENV:Envelope
xmlns:xsi="http://www.w3.org/1999/XMLSchema/instance"
    xmlns:SOAP-ENV="http://schemas.xmlsoap.org/soap/envelope"
    xsi:schemaLocation=
        "http://www.northwindtraders.com/schemas/NPOSchema.xsd">
    <SOAP-ENV:Body xsi:type="NorthwindBody">
        <UpdatePO>
            <orderID>0</orderID>
            <customerNumber>999</customerNumber>
            <item>89</item>
            <quantity>3000</quantity>
            <return>0</return>
        </UpdatePO>
    </SOAP-ENV:Body>
</SOAP-ENV:Envelope>
```

> **NOTE** Notice that the default *Body* declaration is overridden by using an *xsi:type* attribute associating *NorthwindBody* with the *Body* element. A schema that defines *NorthwindBody* and the additional elements, such as *UpdatePO*, will be shown in the section "A Schema for the Body Content of the SOAP Message" later in this chapter.

Because the *Body* element contains the *any* element in the SOAP schema, you could also have written SOAP body as follows:

```
<SOAP-ENV:Envelope
    xmlns:xsi="http://www.w3.org/1999/XMLSchema/instance"
    xmlns:SOAP-ENV="http://schemas.xmlsoap.org/soap/envelope">
    <SOAP-ENV:Body xsi:type="NorthwindBody">
        <m:UpdatePO xmlns:m=
            "http://www.northwindtraders.com/schemas/NPOSchema.xsd">
            <orderID>0</orderID>
            <customerNumber>999</customerNumber>
            <item>89</item>
            <quantity>3000</quantity>
            <return>0</return>
        </m:UpdatePO>
    </SOAP-ENV:Body>
</SOAP-ENV:Envelope>
```

As you can see, the payload of a SOAP request is an XML document that contains the parameter values of the method. The HTTP header of this package has identified the *UpdatePO* method of the *Order* object as the recipient of this method call. The top-level element of the method call must have the same name as the method identified in *SOAPAction*.

The elements contained within the top element are the parameters for the method. The preceding example contains four parameters: *orderID*, *customerNumber*, *item*, and *quantity*. In Microsoft Visual Basic, this method could be written as follows:

```
Public Sub UpdatePO(byval orderID as Integer, _
    byval customerNumber as Integer, _
    byval item as Integer, _
    byval quantity as Integer, _
    byref return as Integer)
```

In Java, this method would look like this:

```
public class UpdatePO {public int orderID;
    public int customerNumber;
    public int item;
    public int quantity;
    public int return;}
```

When you are building the request, you will include one element for each *in* or *in/out* parameter. This technique of associating one element with each parameter is also known as the *element-normal form (ENF)*. The name of each element is the name of the parameter the element is associated with.

The request can also contain a *header* element that includes additional information. There are no predefined elements in the *header* element—you can include any element you want, as long as it is either prefixed by a namespace or the header type is overridden using *xsi:type* and a type defined in a schema.

We can add a *header* element to our payload example as shown here:

```
<SOAP-ENV:Envelope
   xmlns:xsi="http://www.w3.org/1999/XMLSchema/instance"
   xmlns:SOAP-ENV="http://schemas.xmlsoap.org/soap/envelope"
   xsi:schemaLocation=
      "http://www.northwindtraders.com/schemas/NPOSchema.xsd">
   <SOAP-ENV:Header xsi:type="NorthwindHeader">
      <GUID>
      10000000-0000-abcd-0000-000000000001
      </GUID>
   </SOAP-ENV:Header>
   <SOAP-ENV:Body xsi:type="NorthwindBody">
      <UpdatePO>
         <orderID>0</orderID>
         <customerNumber>999</customerNumber>
         <item>89</item>
         <quantity>3000</quantity>
         <return>0</return>
      </UpdatePO>
   </SOAP-ENV:Body>
</SOAP-ENV:Envelope>
```

Because the *any* element is used in the *header* element in the SOAP schema, we could also rewrite the SOAP header as follows:

```
<SOAP-ENV:Header>
      <COM:GUID xmlns:COM="http://comobject.Northwindtraders.com">
         10000000-0000-abcd-0000-000000000001
      </COM:GUID>
</SOAP-ENV:Header>
```

In this case, we have created an element named *GUID*. It will be up to the receiving application to interpret this header, but it's likely that it will be used to instantiate the correct COM object. These additional elements can be considered processing instructions.

You can include a predefined attribute named *mustUnderstand* as an attribute of a header element. The *mustUnderstand* attribute can be used to indicate whether the header information is essential for processing of the information. If the header information is essential, *mustUnderstand* should be set to *true*. If the receiving element cannot recognize the processing instruction and *mustUnderstand* is set to *1*, the message must be rejected. Thus, we could have the following *header* element:

```
<SOAP-ENV:Header xsi:type="Transaction">
    <transactionID mustUnderstand="1">
        10000000
    </transactionID >
</SOAP-ENV:Header>
```

In this case, we are creating an element named *TransactionID*. This element must be understood by the receiving application, or the message will be rejected.

Sending Messages Using M-POST

You can restrict messages coming through a firewall or a proxy server by using the M-POST method instead of POST. M-POST is a new HTTP method defined using the HTTP Extension Framework located at *http://www.w3.org/Protocols/HTTP/ietf-ext-wg*. This method is used when you are including mandatory information in the HTTP header, just as you used the *mustUnderstand* attribute in the SOAP *header* element.

As we mentioned, SOAP supports both POST and M-POST requests. A client first makes a SOAP request using M-POST. If the request fails and either a 501 status code (*Not Implemented* status message) or a 510 status code (*Not Extended* status message) returns, the client should retry the request using the POST method. If the client fails the request again and a 405 status code (*Method Not Allowed* status message) returns, the client should fail the request. If the returning status code is 200, the message has been received successfully. Firewalls can force a client to use the M-POST method to submit SOAP requests by blocking regular POSTs of the *text/xml-SOAP* content type.

If you use M-POST, you must use a mandatory extension declaration that refers to a namespace in the *Envelope* element declaration. The namespace prefix must precede the mandatory headers. The following example illustrates how to use M-POST and the mandatory headers:

```
M-POST /Order HTTP/1.1
Host: www.northwindtraders.com
Content-Type: text/xml
Content-Length: nnnn
Man: "http://schemas.xmlsoap.org/soap/envelope; ns=49"
49-SOAPAction: "urn:northwindtraders.com:PO#UpdatePO"
```

The *Man* header maps the URI *http://schemas.xmlsoap.org/soap/envelope* to the header prefix *49*. Any header that has a prefix of *49* will be associated with this URI and will therefore be a mandatory header. In this case, the *SOAPAction* will be associated with the URI and is a mandatory header.

NOTE If you use M-POST and do not have any mandatory header elements, an error will occur, resulting in either a 501 or 510 status code.

The Payload for a SOAP Response

Just as our sample SOAP request message contained child elements for all the *in* and *in/out* parameters of the method, the SOAP response will contain child elements for each *out* and *in/out* parameter. Let's say you have the following Visual Basic function:

```
Public Function UpdatePO(byref OrderID as Integer, _
    byval CustomerNumber as Integer, _
    byval Item as Integer, _
    byval Quantity as Integer) as Integer
```

In this case, the server would set the *orderID* variable to some value and return the value to the client. Because the *orderID* parameter is *byref*, it is an *in/out* parameter. *UpdatePO* is now a function, and it will return a value (a Boolean value, in this case). The return value of the function can be considered an *out only* parameter.

For this *UpdatePO* function, the request payload containing all the *in* and *in/out* parameters might look like this:

```
<SOAP-ENV:Envelope
    xmlns:xsi="http://www.w3.org/1999/XMLSchema/instance"
    xmlns:SOAP-ENV="http://schemas.xmlsoap.org/soap/envelope"
    xsi:schemaLocation=
      "http://www.northwindtraders.com/schemas/NPOSchema.xsd">
    <SOAP-ENV:Body xsi:type="NorthwindBody">
      <UpdatePO>
      <orderID>0</orderID>
      <customerNumber>999</customerNumber>
      <item>89</item>
      <quantity>3000</quantity>
      </UpdatePO>
    </SOAP-ENV:Body>
</SOAP-ENV:Envelope>
```

The response package including the payload that contains all the *out* and *in/out* parameters would look like this:

```
HTTP/1.1 200 OK
Content-Type: text/xml
Content-Length: nnnn

<SOAP-ENV:Envelope
   xmlns:xsi="http://www.w3.org/1999/XMLSchema/instance"
   xmlns:SOAP-ENV="http://schemas.xmlsoap.org/soap/envelope"
   xsi:schemaLocation=
      "http://www.northwindtraders.com/schemas/NPOSchema.xsd">
   <SOAP-ENV:Body xsi:type="NorthwindBody">
      <UpdatePO>
         <orderID>09877</orderID>
         <return>0</return>
      </UpdatePO>
   </SOAP-ENV:Body>
</SOAP-ENV:Envelope>
```

Notice that the SOAP response message doesn't have the *SOAPAction* header field. This header field is required only in the SOAP request message. During request processing, a SOAP package will be passed to a SOAP application on the server that handles SOAP requests. This SOAP application will in turn pass on the request to the appropriate method.

Sometimes a request cannot be processed properly and errors might occur. Errors can be handled in several ways, depending on where the error occurs. If an error occurs during the transport of the package to the method, the error is usually handled by returning status codes other than 200. An example of this situation is when there is a problem getting the package through a firewall or the specified host does not exist or is down.

Once the information has been passed to the method, it is possible that the application handling the request will experience an error. In this case, you can return a custom HTTP code, use one of the predefined HTTP codes, use an element, such as the *return* element in the preceding example, or return a SOAP package that contains a *Fault* element to pass back the error information. Let's look at how to use the *Fault* element to report errors.

The *Fault* Element

A *Fault* element can contain four child elements: *faultcode, faultstring, faultactor,* and *detail.* The fault codes are identified at the URL *http://schemas.xmlsoap.org/ soap/envelope.* The currently available code values are shown in the following table.

CURRENTLY AVAILABLE FAULT CODE VALUES

Name	*Meaning*
VersionMismatch	The call used an invalid namespace.
MustUnderstand	The receiver did not understand an XML element that was received containing an element tagged with *mustUnderstand="true"*.
Client	These are a class of errors that were caused by improper information in the actual SOAP message. For example, a new order could be missing a required value such as the item number or amount. These errors represent a problem with the actual message content and indicate that the message should not be resent without change. A class of client errors can be created using the dot (.) operator. For example, you could have *Client.InvalidPartNumber*, *Client.InvalidQuantity*, and so on.
Server	These errors are related to problems with the server and usually do not represent problems with the actual SOAP message. These messages might be resent at a later time to the server. A class of server errors can be created using the dot (.) operator.

The *faultstring* element is a string. It is not used by applications; it is used only as a message to users. This element is required. The *faultactor* element can provide information about which element in the message path caused the fault to occur. The *faultactor* will be a URI that identifies the source. If the fault occurs in an application that is not the ultimate destination of the message, the *faultactor* element must be included. If the fault occurs in the ultimate destination, the *faultactor* is not required but may be included. The *detail* element is required if the contents of the SOAP *Body* element couldn't be processed. It provides application-specific error information related to the *Body* element. You cannot include error information related to the header in the *detail* element. Any child elements of the *detail* element must be associated with a namespace.

A return package with a *Fault* element will look like this:

```
HTTP/1.1 200 OK
Content-Type: text/xml
Content-Length: nnnn

<SOAP-ENV:Envelope
    xmlns:xsi="http://www.w3.org/1999/XMLSchema/instance"
    xmlns:SOAP-ENV="http://schemas.xmlsoap.org/soap/envelope"
```

(continued)

```
      xsi:schemaLocation=
        "http://www.northwindtraders.com/schemas/NPOSchema.xsd">
        <SOAP-ENV:Fault>
          <SOAP-ENV:faultcode>200</SOAP-ENV:faultcode>
          <SOAP-ENV:faultstring>Must Understand Error
          </SOAP-ENV:faultstring>
          <SOAP-ENV:detail xsi:type="Fault">
            <errorMessage>
                Object not installed on server.
            </errorMessage>
          </SOAP-ENV:detail>
        </SOAP-ENV:Fault >
      </SOAP-ENV:Body>
  </SOAP-ENV:Envelope>
```

Using the *faultstring* element, you can pass information back to the client that describes the exact error. The *faultstring* element can handle a wide range of errors.

A Schema for the Body Content of the SOAP Message

As you can see, we have not yet defined the NPO schema located at *http://www.northwindtraders.com/schemas/NPOSchema.xsd*. This schema can be defined as follows:

```
<xsd:schema xmlns:xsd="http://www.w3.org/1999/XMLSchema"
    targetNamespace="http://schemas.xmlsoap.org/soap/envelope"
    xmlns:SOAP="http://schemas.xmlsoap.org/soap/envelope">
    <xsd:complexType name="NorthwindHeader">
       <xsd:element name="GUID" type="string"/>
    </xsd:complexType>

    <xsd:complexType name="NorthwindBody">
       <xsd:element name="UpdatePO">
          <xsd:complexType>
             <element name="orderID" type="integer"/>
             <element name="customerNumber" type="integer"/>
             <element name="item" type="double"/>
             <element name="quantity" type="double"/>
          </xsd:complexType>
       </xsd:element>
    </xsd:complexType>
</xsd:schema>
```

This schema creates two elements: *NorthwindBody* and *NorthwindHeader*. Using the *xsi:type* attribute, we can extend the SOAP *body* element with the *NorthwindBody* complex type and extend the *Header* element with *NorthwindHeader* complex type. You can then create the following SOAP document:

```
<SOAP-ENV:Envelope
   xmlns:xsi="http://www.w3.org/1999/XMLSchema/instance"
   xmlns:SOAP-ENV="http://schemas.xmlsoap.org/soap/envelope"
   xsi:schemaLocation=
      "http://www.northwindtraders.com/schemas/NPOSchema.xsd">
<SOAP-ENV:Header xsi:type="NorthwindHeader">
      <COM:GUID xmlns:COM="http://comobject.northwindtraders.com">
         10000000-0000-abcd-0000-000000000001
      </COM:GUID>
   </SOAP-ENV:Header>

   <SOAP-ENV:Body xsi:type="NorthwindBody">
      <UpdatePO>
         <orderID>0</orderID>
         <customerNumber>999</customerNumber>
         <item>89</item>
         <quantity>3000</quantity>
      </UpdatePO>
   </SOAP-ENV:Body>
</SOAP-ENV:Envelope>
```

SOAP ENCODING

The SOAP encoding style provides a means to define data types similar to what is found in most programming languages, including types and arrays. The specification for encoding can be found at *http://schemas.xmlsoap.org/soap/encoding/*. SOAP defines simple and complex data types just as the schema standard does. The simple type elements are the same as those defined in the second schema standard. The complex type elements include those defined in the first SOAP standard and a special way of defining arrays. Structures follow the definitions of the complex type. For example, we could have the following structure:

```
<e:Customer>
   <CName>John Jones</CName>
   <Address>100 Main Street</Address>
   <ID>4</ID>
</e:Customer>
```

This structure would be defined as follows:

```
<element name=Customer>
   <element name="CName" type="xsd:string"/>
   <element name="Address" type="xsd:string"/>
   <element name="ID" type="xsd:string"/>
</element>
```

Arrays will have an additional attribute, *type="SOAP-ENC:Array"*, to define an element as an array. The *SOAP-ENC* namespace is defined as *http://schemas.xmlsoap. org/soap/encoding*. An array could look as follows:

```
<CustomerIDs SOAP-ENC:arrayType="xsd:int[3]">
   <number>345</number>
   <number>354</number>
   <number>399</number>
</CustomerIDs>
```

The schema would look as follows:

```
<element name="CustomerIDs" type="SOAP-ENC:Array"/>
```

In this example, the array *CustomerIDs* contains three members; each member has a value of type *xsd:int*.

SUMMARY

This chapter has introduced the basic principles of SOAP. Using these basic principles, you can pass the values for parameters of methods to and from a server using XML and HTTP. As the SOAP specification evolves, it's likely that SOAP will allow tightly bound messages to be sent to and from components on virtually any operating system.

In Chapter 9, we will discuss the BizTalk framework. The BizTalk framework builds on the concepts in SOAP, and allows companies to exchange business documents using XML schemas and industry standards for sharing information.

Chapter 9

BizTalk

In Chapter 8, we examined how to use SOAP to improve cross-platform interoperability using the Web and XML. In this chapter, we will look at BizTalk Framework 2.0, which is an extension of the SOAP 1.1 specification. BizTalk Framework 2.0 provides a structure for building solutions that move data contained in a SOAP document across boundaries. A *boundary* is a point at which information passes between two different systems. For example, a corporation and its partner may both have their own systems for processing orders. When an order is passed from the corporate system to the partner's system, the order is moved across a boundary. Often, the movement of information across boundaries is also a movement across different operating system platforms. Thus, BizTalk is also a framework for moving information across different platforms.

BizTalk Framework 2.0 addresses the following problems associated with moving information across boundaries and platforms using XML:

- The need for an easy-to-use, flexible standard to specify, package, publish, and exchange structured and unstructured information across system boundaries using XML

- The need for an easy-to-use, flexible standard to specify, package, publish, and exchange business rules for transforming information from one system's format to another system's format using XML

- The need for middleware applications that allow communication across a system boundary

- The need for a standard that provides error detection and document receipts when moving information across system boundaries

BizTalk Framework 2.0 is not one of the W3C standards; XML is the standard. BizTalk's purpose is to facilitate the implementation of the XML standard using a standardized framework. Because BizTalk addresses these problems using XML, BizTalk's solutions should be platform and technology independent.

BizTalk Message Structure

A BizTalk message can be thought of as a SOAP document that contains special BizTalk tags in the SOAP *Header* element and one or more business documents in the SOAP *Body* element. These BizTags are a set of XML tags predefined by the BizTalk Framework 2.0 specification and used to specify how the document will be handled. The BizTags provide a loosely bound method for routing the SOAP message. The SOAP body contains the information being passed in the message. This structure is illustrated in Figure 9-1.

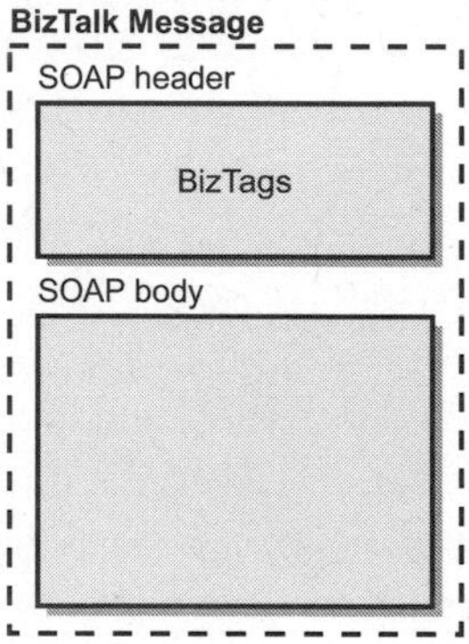

Figure 9-1. *A BizTalk message.*

The business document is a well-formed XML document that consists of business transaction data. A schema will be used to validate the business document. BizTalk schemas can be published at the Web site *http://www.biztalk.org* and can be shared among corporations.

NOTE At the time of this printing, BizTalk uses an XML Data Reduced (XDR) schema, which is slightly different from the schema defined by the current Worldwide Web Consortium (W3C) standard. The XDR schema is expected to be used until the W3C releases the final schema standard, at which time BizTalk will implement the standard schema. The differences between the two schemas will be discussed in the section "XML Data Reduced Schemas" later in this chapter.

BizTalk messages are used to pass BizTalk documents from one BizTalk Framework 2.0 Compliant (BFC) server to another. The creation and routing of a BizTalk message is illustrated in Figure 9-2.

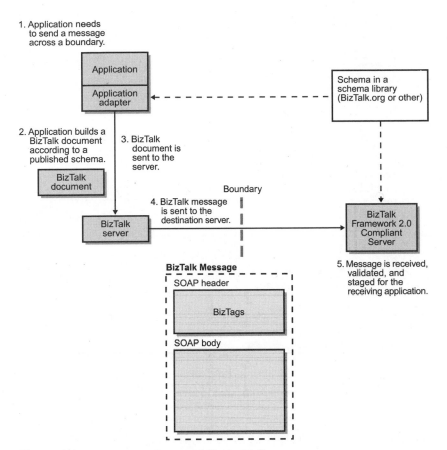

Figure 9-2. *Creation and routing of a BizTalk message.*

As you can see, an application generates a BizTalk document according to the rules of a published BizTalk schema. This document is passed to a BizTalk server to create a BizTalk message. The BizTalk message is sent across a business boundary to a BizTalk Framework Compliant (BFC) server, which will then determine the destination based on the information in the BizTalk document.

BIZTALK DOCUMENTS

The BizTalk document is a SOAP 1.1 message that consists of two primary sections: the SOAP *Header* section, which contains the *BizTalk document header* that has information about the document, and the *SOAP Body*, which contains the actual business transaction information. The SOAP Header section in a BizTalk document must contain the BizTalk-specific <properties> and <delivery> BizTags. The <manifest> and <process> BizTags can also be included in the BizTalk document header. The structure of the BizTalk document within a BizTalk message is illustrated in Figure 9-3.

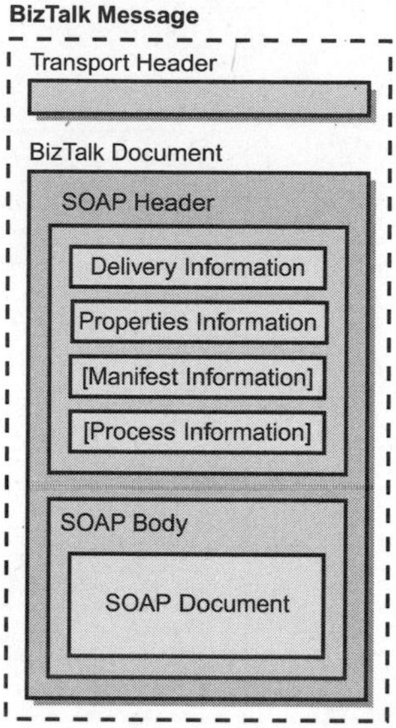

Figure 9-3. *The structure of a BizTalk document.*

BizTalk Document Header

A BizTalk document is a well-formed XML document, so the BizTalk document header contains standard XML header information, such as the XML version and the language. A typical BizTalk document that does not contain any content would look as follows:

```
<SOAP-ENV:Envelope
   xmlns:xsi= "http://www.w3.org/1999/XMLSchema/instance"
   xmlns:SOAP-ENV="http://schemas.xmlsoap.org/soap/envelope"
   xsi:schemaLocation=
   "http://www.northwindtraders.com/schemas/NPOSchema.xsd">
   <SOAP-ENV:Header xsi:type="NorthwindHeader">
   <!--BizTags begin here -->
      <dlv:delivery SOAP-ENV:mustUnderstand="1"
         xmlns:dlv="http://schema.biztalk.org/btf-2-0/delivery"
         xmlns:agr="uri/of/agreement">
         <dlv:to>
            <dlv:address xsi:type="agr:type/of/agreement">
            </dlv:address>
         </dlv:to>
         <dlv:from>
            <dlv:address xsi:type="agr:type/of/agreement">
            </dlv:address>
         </dlv:from>
         <dlv:reliability>
            <dlv:confirmTo>www.uri.where.to.send.confirmation
            </dlv:confirmTo>
            <dlv:receiptRequiredBy>
               2300-05-44T03:00:00+09:00
```

```
                    </dlv:receiptRequiredBy>
                </dlv:reliability>
            </dlv:delivery>
            <prop:properties SOAP-ENV:mustUnderstand="1"
            xmlns:prop="http://schema.biztalk.org/btf-2-0/properties">
                <prop:identity>uuid:00000000-0000-0000-0000-00000000001
                </prop:identity>
                <prop:sentAt>2300-05-14T03:00:00+09:00</prop:sentAt>
                <prop:expiresAt>2300-05-44T03:00:00+09:00
                </prop:expiresAt>
                <prop:topic>uri/topic</prop:topic>
            </prop:properties>
            <fst:manifest xmlns:fst=
                "http://schema.biztalk.org/btf-2-0/manifest">
            <fst:reference fst:uri="uri/to/reference">
                <fst:description>text description of document element
                </fst:description>
            </fst:reference>
            </fst:manifest>
            <prc:process SOAP-ENV:mustUnderstand="1"
                xmlns:prc="http://schema.biztalk.org/btf-2-0/process/">
                <prc:type>uri/type/of/business/process</prc:type>
                <prc:instance>uri/unique/identifier/of/process
                </prc:instance>
                <prc:handle>uri/with/additional/information</prc:handle>
            </prc:process>
        <!--BizTags end here -->
        </SOAP-ENV:Header>
        <SOAP-ENV:Body xsi:type="NorthwindBody">
            <!--SOAP document enclosed ends here -->
        </SOAP-ENV:Body>
</SOAP-ENV:Envelope>
```

Because *delivery* and *properties* are mandatory header elements and the *process* element must be interpreted when included, the *SOAP-ENV:mustunderstand* property for these elements must be set equal to 1 so that the receiving BFC server knows the sections contained within these elements must be understood to process the document.

The following code shows an example DTD for a BizTalk document.

```
<!ELEMENT SOAP-ENV:Envelope  (SOAP-ENV:Header )>
<!ATTLIST SOAP-ENV:Envelope  xmlns:xsi       CDATA #REQUIRED
                             xmlns:SOAP-ENV CDATA #REQUIRED >
<!ELEMENT SOAP-ENV:Header  (dlv:delivery , prop:properties ,
                            fst:manifest , prc:process )>
<!ATTLIST SOAP-ENV:Header  xsi:type CDATA  #REQUIRED >
<!ELEMENT dlv:delivery  (dlv:to , dlv:from , dlv:reliability )>
<!ATTLIST dlv:delivery  xmlns:dlv                 CDATA  #REQUIRED
                        xmlns:agr                 CDATA  #REQUIRED
                        SOAP-ENV:mustUnderstand CDATA  #REQUIRED>
<!ELEMENT dlv:to  (dlv:address )>
```

(continued)

```
<!ELEMENT dlv:address EMPTY>
<!ATTLIST dlv:address  xsi:type CDATA  #IMPLIED >
<!ELEMENT dlv:from  (dlv:address )>
<!ELEMENT dlv:reliability  (dlv:confirmTo ,
                            dlv:receiptRequiredBy )>
<!ELEMENT dlv:confirmTo  (#PCDATA )>
<!ELEMENT dlv:receiptRequiredBy  (#PCDATA )>
<!ELEMENT prop:properties  (prop:identity , prop:sentAt ,
                            prop:expiresAt , prop:topic )>
<!ATTLIST prop:properties xmlns:prop              CDATA #REQUIRED
                          SOAP-ENV:mustUnderstand CDATA #REQUIRED>
<!ELEMENT prop:identity  (#PCDATA )>
<!ELEMENT prop:sentAt  (#PCDATA )>
<!ELEMENT prop:expiresAt  (#PCDATA )>
<!ELEMENT prop:topic  (#PCDATA )>
<!ELEMENT fst:manifest  (fst:reference )>
<!ATTLIST fst:manifest  xmlns:fst CDATA  #REQUIRED >
<!ELEMENT fst:reference  (fst:description )>
<!ATTLIST fst:reference  fst:uri CDATA  #REQUIRED >
<!ELEMENT fst:description  (#PCDATA )>
<!ELEMENT prc:process  (prc:type , prc:instance , prc:handle )>
<!ATTLIST prc:process  xmlns:prc              CDATA  #REQUIRED
                       SOAP-ENV:mustUnderstand CDATA  #REQUIRED >
<!ELEMENT prc:type  (#PCDATA )>
<!ELEMENT prc:instance  (#PCDATA )>
<!ELEMENT prc:handle  (#PCDATA )>
```

As you can see in the previous two code samples, a BizTalk document consists of four major sections designated by the *delivery*, *properties*, *manifest*, and *process* elements. Let's look at these elements in the following sections in detail.

LOOSELY COUPLED MESSAGES

As mentioned, the BizTalk header contains only information about the destination and source BizTalk servers. There is no information within the BizTalk document header that identifies what method or object will use this information. In other words, the BizTalk document header has no real information about the application that will process it.

It's up to the receiving BizTalk server to identify the incoming message and route it to the correct application. For example, a BizTalk server can be set up so that all messages coming from *http://www.northwindtraders.com* with an *identity* that begins with *PO00123* will be passed to the new order processing object. (*Identity* is a child element of the *properties* element that will be discussed in detail later in this chapter.) The same message sent to a different company may be sent to a completely different component. These messages are called *loosely coupled*, meaning that they are not coupled with specific processing applications.

The *delivery* Element

The *delivery* element is a child element of the *SOAP Header* element. This element includes information about the message such as the source and destination systems. The *delivery* element identifies where the message has come from and where it is going and gives routing and other supporting information. This element is required and can appear only once. The *delivery* element contains three child elements: *to*, *from*, and *reliability*. The *to* and *from* elements are required. All three elements can appear only once.

The *to* and *from* elements

As mentioned previously, both the *to* and *from* elements are child elements of the *delivery* element. Both of these elements contain one child element: *address*. The *address* child element is required and can occur only once. The *address* child element can specify any business entity, such as a URI or a department or organization name. For the *to* element, the *address* element contains the business entity for the receiving BizTalk server. For the *from* element, the *address* element contains the business entity for the sending BizTalk server. URIs can include prefixes such as *http://* that specify the means of transport for a message. You can include a prefix, or you can leave it out and let the BizTalk server resolve the specific address system. If you omit the prefix, the URI is called a *logical identifier*.

The *address* element also has a required *xsi:type* attribute. This attribute signifies the category of the address and determines the structure of the address content. The following code shows an example of a *to* element and a *from* element:

```
<dlv:delivery SOAP-ENV:mustUnderstand="1"
xmlns:dlv="http://schema.biztalk.org/btf-2-0/delivery"
xmlns:agr="uri/of/agreement">
   <dlv:to>
      <dlv:address xsi:type="agr:URIDestination">
         http://www.northwindtraders.com/PO.asp/Billing
      </dlv:address>
   </dlv:to>
   <dlv:from>
      <dlv:address xsi:type="agr:department">
         Orders
         </dlv:address>
   </dlv:from>
</dlv:delivery>
```

This document uses two different types of addresses: the first address is a URI and the second address is a department type. The BizTalk server can identify these two types of addresses.

The *reliability* element

The *reliability* element is optional and contains information that can help guarantee reliable delivery of the BizTalk document. When the *reliability* element is present, the BizTalk server that receives the message must send a message back to the sending BizTalk server using the URI. This process will be discussed in more detail in the section "Receipt documents" below.

The *reliability* element has two mandatory elements that can occur only once each: *confirmTo* and *receiptRequiredBy*. The *confirmTo* element contains the URL that specifies the transport address to which the receipt will be sent. The *receiptRequiredBy* element contains a time instant that specifies the absolute time by which the BizTalk message must be received. The content of this element should be formatted according to the International Standard ISO 8601; refer to *http://www.cl.cam.ac.uk/~mgk25/ iso-time.html* for more information about this standard. All times in the BizTalk header will use the ISO 8601 standard. The following code shows an example of a *reliability* element:

```
<dlv:reliability>
    <dlv:confirmTo>www.northwindtraders.com/poConfirm
    </dlv:confirmTo>
    <dlv:receiptRequiredBy>
        2300-05-44T03:00:00+09:00
    </dlv:receiptRequiredBy>
</dlv:reliability>
```

If the receipt is not received within a specified period of time, the sending BFC server can attempt to resend the message. If the recipient BFC server gets the message two or more times, the *identity* element of the *properties* element can be used to eliminate duplicates of the same BizTalk document. The sending BFC server can also create a delivery failure report after a certain number of retries or when a receipt has not been received after the first attempt.

> **NOTE**   There is always a small possibility that a recipient BFC server has actually received the message, but has either failed to generate the return receipt, or the return receipt has been lost. In these cases, a failure report might be generated by the sending BFC server when the message was actually sent.

Receipt documents

The receipt document is a SOAP 1.1 compliant message that must contain at least the *receipt* and *properties* elements and an empty body. The receipt is not a BizTalk document because it contains no information in its body. The content of the *receipt* must identify the BizTalk document being acknowledged. The *receipt* will contain a timestamp marking the time the BizTalk document was received. In addition, the receipt can contain elements copied directly from the BizTalk document being acknowledged.

The *properties* Element

The *properties* element is a child element of the SOAP *Header* element and provides information that can be used for identification of the BizTalk message. The section contained within this element must be understood by any BFC server before a message can be properly processed. The *properties* element has the following child elements: *identity*, *sentAt*, *expiresAt*, and *topic*. All of these elements are mandatory and can occur only once. An example of the *properties* element is shown in the following code:

```
<prop:properties SOAP-ENV:mustUnderstand="1"
   xmlns:prop="http://schema.biztalk.org/btf-2-0/properties">
   <prop:identity>uuid:00000000-0000-0000-0000-00000000001
   </prop:identity>
   <prop:sentAt>2300-05-14T03:00:00+09:00</prop:sentAt>
   <prop:expiresAt>2300-05-44T03:00:00+09:00</prop:expiresAt>
   <prop:topic>http://northwindtranders.com/PO</prop:topic>
</prop:properties>
```

The *identity* element

The *identity* element is a URI that will uniquely identify the BizTalk document. This identity can be used for logging, tracking, error handling, or other document handling purposes. Any unique identifier can be used.

The *sentAt* element

The *sentAt* element is a timestamp for the document. The time marks the exact time the sending BFC server first attempted to transmit the document.

The *expiresAt* element

The *expiresAt* element is the time when the BizTalk message will expire. Any time beyond the time specified in the *expiresAt* element, the BizTalk message is considered to have expired and cannot be processed. A reasonable amount of time should be created between the time the document is created and the time specified in the *expiresAt* element.

The *topic* element

The *topic* element is a URI that can be used to uniquely identify the general purpose of the BizTalk message. This information has various uses, such as interest-based routing as found in a publish/subscribe arrangement.

The *manifest* Element

The *manifest* element is a child element of the SOAP *Header* element; it is used to indicate which files are actually included in or associated with a BizTalk document. The *manifest* element is a catalog of all the documents carried in the BizTalk document. Additional files, such as images or other binary information, can be included in or with the BizTalk document. The *manifest* element has one required child element: *reference*, which can occur one or more times. An example of the *manifest* element is shown in the following code:

```
<fst:manifest xmlns:fst=
   "http://schema.biztalk.org/btf-2-0/manifest">
   <fst:reference fst:uri="#Purchase_Order">
      <fst:description>Purchase order for Northwind
      </fst:description>
   </fst:reference>
   <fst:reference fst:uri="CID:po.jpg@NorthwindTraders.com">
      <fst:description>Scanned image of the contract
      </fst:description>
   </fst:reference>
</fst:manifest>
```

The *reference* element

The *reference* child element is used to reference additional XML or non-XML files that were sent as part of the BizTalk message. These files can include content that is not carried in the BizTalk document. These files can be implemented as Multipurpose Internet Mail Extensions (MIME) parts or can be implemented through other mechanisms. MIME includes a standard set of tags that can be included within the *Header* section of the document. These tags can then be used to identify, attach, and send additional documents. BizTalk currently uses MIME.

> **NOTE** If you try to include binary information in your XML document as an element, you will receive errors because the binary information will have invalid characters. You can base-64 encode the binary file, which will convert all the binary information to text characters. Unfortunately, this will increase the size of the BizTalk message and might not be the best solution. You could also use multipart MIME, which is a standard format for referencing one or more nontext attachments. We'll discuss using multipart MIME later in this chapter.

The *reference* child element can have two child elements: *uri* and *description*. The *uri* is mandatory and the *description* is optional. Both can occur only once.

The *uri* child element contains a reference that can be resolved to the resource that is being referenced in the *reference* element. The *uri* can be:

- A relative URI reference in the form of *#id* that resolves to business documents in the SOAP *Body*

- A content-ID URL in the form of *CID:content-ID-Value* that will resolve to attachments carried as MIME parts with the BizTalk message

- A URL that will resolve to attachments that are carried as MIME parts with the BizTalk message, but outside the BizTalk document

The *description* element is a text description of the document that is referenced by the *reference* element.

The *process* Element

The *process* element provides information about the business process associated with the BizTalk message. The *process* element has two mandatory child elements, *type* and *instance*, and one optional element, *handle*. All the child elements may occur only once. A *process* element may look as shown in the following code:

```
<prc:process SOAP-ENV:mustUnderstand="1"
    xmlns:prc="http://schema.biztalk.org/btf-2-0/process/">
    <prc:type>purchase:Food_Purchase_Order</prc:type>
    <prc:instance> purchase:Food_Purchase_Order:0001
    </prc:instance>
    <prc:handle>port:po_app</prc:handle>
</prc:process>
```

The *type* element

The *type* element contains a URI that defines the type of business process the BizTalk message is associated with. The *type* element is usually defined by two or more business partners. The *type* element uses a pattern that is often used in many documents. For example, the purchase of an item would be an example of a pattern.

The *instance* element

The *instance* element contains a URI reference that uniquely identifies a particular instance of the business process that a business document is associated with. For example, the *type* element might identify the business process as a BizTalk document of type order, whereas the *instance* element might identify the business process as being order number 0001. Usually, the *instance* element's content is created by appending a unique identifier onto the end of the *type* element's content as shown above.

The *handle* element

The *handle* element is an optional element that can be used to give more information that can be used to identify a process. This information can be used to identify which step the BizTalk message might be within the overall business process.

Using MultiPart MIME

A BizTalk message can be constructed using the multipart MIME format defined in Request for Comment (RFC) 2387 (*http://www.ietf.org/rfc/rfc2387.txt*). To use the MIME format with an HTTP document, you need to take some special considerations. An example of a BizTalk Message in MIME format would look as shown in the code that follows.

```
MIME-Version: 1.0
Content-Type: Multipart/Related;
        boundary=biztalk_document_boundary;
        type=text/xml;
        start="<po.xml@Northwindtraders.com>"
Content-Description: This is the optional message description.


-- biztalk_document_boundary
Content-Type: text/xml; charset=UTF-8
Content-ID: <po.xml@Northwindtraders.com>


<?xml version='1.0' ?>
<SOAP-ENV:Envelope
   xmlns:xsi= "http://www.w3.org/1999/XMLSchema/instance"
   xmlns:SOAP-ENV="http://schemas.xmlsoap.org/soap/envelope"
   xsi:schemaLocation=
   "http://www.northwindtraders.com/schemas/NorthwindPOSchema.xsd">
   <SOAP-ENV:Header xsi:type="NorthwindHeader">
   <!--BizTags begin here -->
   <dlv:delivery SOAP-ENV:mustUnderstand="1"
      xmlns:dlv="http://schema.biztalk.org/btf-2-0/delivery"
      xmlns:agr="uri/of/agreement">
    <!-- Delivery and properties header entries omitted for
        brevity -->
 <fst:manifest xmlns:fst=
    "http://schema.biztalk.org/btf-2-0/manifest">
    <fst:reference fst:uri="#Purchase_Order">
       <fst:description>Ppurchase order for Northwind
       </fst:description>
    </fst:reference>
    <fst:reference fst:uri="CID:po.jpg@Northwindtraders.com">
       <fst:description>Scanned image of the contract
       </fst:description>
    </fst:reference>
 </fst:manifest>
   <!--BizTags end here -->
   </SOAP-ENV:Header>
   <SOAP-ENV:Body xsi:type="NorthwindBody">
      <m:UpdatePO xmlns:m=
      "http://www.northwindtraders.com/schemas/NPOSchema.xsd">
      <!--SOAP document containing PO enclosed ends here -->
   </SOAP-ENV:Body>
</SOAP-ENV:Envelope>
-- biztalk_document_boundary
Content-Type: image/jpeg
Content-ID: <CID:po.jpg@Northwindtraders.com >


    ...JPEG image...


--biztalk_document_boundary
```

The *Content-Type* tag identifies this document as a Multipart MIME document. The boundary parameter defines the boundaries between different documents in the MIME document. The *start* parameter is required for a BizTalk message and refers to the document that will be processed first. For a BizTalk message, the *start* parameter will always refer to the SOAP document. The value for the *start* parameter should always be equal to the Content-ID tag's value for the SOAP element. The Content-ID tags are used to identify the different sections of the document and are therefore required for every section. The *manifest* element's child element *reference* uses a URI to identify the non-SOAP elements of the document. The Content-ID for these non-SOAP elements must be equal to these URIs. The SOAP document must be included in the root of the MultiPart MIME document. MIME documents can have a *charset* parameter, but this parameter should not be used for BizTalk messages.

XML DATA REDUCED SCHEMAS

As mentioned earlier in this chapter, BizTalk uses an XML Data Reduced schema. This schema and the schema currently defined by the W3C differ. Microsoft needed to build and release Internet Explorer 5, and it wanted to include an XML parser with Internet Explorer 5 that would work with schemas. Unfortunately, the W3C schema standard was not completed at the time Microsoft was developing Internet Explorer 5. Therefore, Microsoft used the temporary schema XDR. The XDR schema is based on a 1998 proposal to the W3C and can be found at *http://www.w3.org/TR/1998/NOTE-XML-data-0105*. Many similarities exist in the XDR and the W3C schemas, but there are also differences. The primary difference is that the two schemas use different keywords and XDR has less functionality.

The following code shows a sample DTD for the BizTalk schema.

```
<!ENTITY % dataTypes "(bin.base64 | bin.hex | boolean | char |
   date | dateTime | dateTime.tz |fixed.14.4 | float | int |
   number | time | time.tz | i1 | i2 | i4 | r4 | r8 | ui1 | ui2 |
   ui4 |uri | uuid | entity | entities | enumeration | id | idref |
   idrefs | nmtoken | nmtokens | notation | string)">
<!ENTITY % elementNamespace "urn:schemas-microsoft-com:xml-data">
<!ENTITY % dataNamespace "urn:schemas-microsoft-com:datatypes">
<!ELEMENT Schema  (AttributeType+, ElementType+, description)>
<!ATTLIST Schema  xmlns CDATA  %elementNamespace;
                  xmlns:dt    CDATA  %dataNamespace;
                  name     CDATA  #REQUIRED >
<!ELEMENT ElementType  (AttributeType, attribute, element+,
                        datatype, description, group)>
<!ATTLIST ElementType  order    (one | seq | many)  many
        content (empty | textOnly | eltOnly | mixed)  mixed
```

(continued)

```
              dt:type    %dataTypes;  #IMPLIED
              model (open | closed) open
              name    ID #REQUIRED >
<!ELEMENT AttributeType  (datatype, description)>
<!ATTLIST AttributeType
              name           ID   #REQUIRED
              default      CDATA  #REQUIRED
              dt:type (entity | entities | enumeration | id | idref |
              idrefs | nmtoken | nmtokens | notation | string) #IMPLIED
              dt:values CDATA #IMPLIED
              required (yes | no) #IMPLIED >
<!ELEMENT attribute  (description)>
<!ATTLIST attribute  type CDATA   #REQUIRED
              default CDATA #IMPLIED
              required (yes | no) #IMPLIED>
<!ELEMENT element  (description)>
<!ATTLIST element  type CDATA   #REQUIRED
              minOccurs (0 | 1) #IMPLIED
              maxOccurs  (1 | *) #IMPLIED>
<!ELEMENT description () #PCDATA>
<!ELEMENT datatype ()>
<!ATTLIST datatype
              dt:type %dataTypes; #REQUIRED>
<!ELEMENT group(element, description)>
<!ATTLIST group
              order (one | seq | many) #REQUIRED
              minOccurs (0 | 1)  1
              maxOccurs  (1 | *)  1>
```

Let's look at each of the elements contained in BizTalk schemas and see how they are used.

The *description* Element

A *description* element can be used in an *AttributeType*, an *ElementType*, a *Schema*, a *group*, an *element*, or an *attribute* element. The *description* element contains a description of the element. A typical *description* element might look like this:

```
<description>This document is a purchase order for Northwind
   Traders.
</description>
```

The *datatype* Element

The *datatype* element is used to specify the data type of an element or an attribute. The *datatype* element uses predefined data types. The current data types are listed in the following table.

CURRENT DATA TYPES

Data Type	Description
bin.base64	A MIME-style base64-encoded binary large object (BLOB).
bin.hex	Hexadecimal digits representing octets.
boolean	0 or 1, where 0 = *"false"* and 1 = *"true"*.
char	A string, one character long.
date	A date in a subset ISO 8601 format, without the time data—for example, *"2000-11-05"*.
dateTime	A date in a subset ISO 8601 format, with an optional time and no optional zone—for example, *"2000-07-07T18:39:09"*. Fractional seconds can be as precise as nanoseconds.
dateTime.tz	A date in a subset ISO 8601 format, with an optional time and an optional zone—for example, *"2000-04-07T18:39:09-08:00"*. Fractional seconds can be as precise as nanoseconds.
fixed.14.4	The same as *number*, but no more than 14 digits to the left of the decimal point and no more than 4 digits to the right.
float	A real number that has no limit on the number of digits; it can have a leading sign, or fractional digits, or an exponent. Punctuation is in U.S. English. Values range from 1.7976931348623157E+308 through 2.2250738585072014E−308.
int	A number, with optional sign, no fractions, and no exponent.
number	A number that has no limit on digits; it can have a leading sign, fractional digits, or an exponent. Punctuation is in U.S. English. Values have same range as the most significant number, r8—that is, 1.7976931348623157E+308 through 2.2250738585072014E−308.
time	A time in a subset ISO 8601 format, with no date and no time zone—for example, *"08:15:27"*.
time.tz	A time in a subset ISO 8601 format, with no date but an optional time zone—for example, *"08:1527-05:00"*.
i1	An integer represented in one byte—that is, a number with an optional sign, no fractions, and no exponent—for example, *"1, 127, −128"*.
i2	An integer represented in one word—that is, a number with an optional sign, no fractions, and no exponent—for example, *"1, 703, −32768"*.
i4	An integer represented in four bytes—that is, a number with an optional sign, no fractions, and no exponent—for example, *"1, 703, −32768, 148343, −1000000000"*.
r4	A real number, with no limit on digits. Can potentially have a leading sign, fractional digits, and optionally an exponent. Punctuation is in U.S. English. Values range from 3.40282347E+38F through 1.17549435E−38F.
r8	The same as *float*—that is, a real number that has no limit on the number of digits. Can have a leading sign, fractional digits, or an exponent. Punctuation is in U.S. English. Values range from 1.7976931348623157E+308 through 2.2250738585072014E−308.

(continued)

Current Data Types *continued*

Data Type	Description
ui1	An unsigned integer—that is, an unsigned number with no fractions and no exponent—for example, *"1,255"*.
ui2	An unsigned integer represented in two bytes—that is, an unsigned number with no fractions and no exponent—for example, *"1,255,65535"*.
ui4	An unsigned integer represented in four bytes—that is, an unsigned number—with no fractions and no exponent—for example, *"1,703,3000000000"*.
uri	A URI—for example, *"urn:schemas-microsoft-com:Office9"*.
uuid	Hexadecimal digits representing octets, optionally embedded with hyphens that are ignored—for example, *"333C7BC4-460F-11D0-BC04-0080C7055A83"*.

The *datatype* element has one attribute: *dt:type*. The *dt:type* attribute can be set to one of the values in this table.

The *datatype* element can be used as shown here:

```
<datatype dt:type=="char"/>
```

The *AttributeType* Element

Declaring attributes in BizTalk schemas is a two-step process. First, you must define the attribute using the *AttributeType* element. Second, you associate this attribute with an element using the *attribute* element. If the *AttributeType* element is declared as a child element of the *Schema* element, the *AttributeType* element will have document-level scope. If the *AttributeType* element is a child element of an *ElementType* element, it has local scope to that element. This scenario is similar to the W3C standard.

The *AttributeType* element can have two child elements: *description* and *datatype*. The *datatype* element can be used interchangeably with the *dt:type* attribute. For attributes, the Microsoft XML parser can use only the following data types: *entity*, *entities*, *enumeration*, *id*, *idref*, *idrefs*, *nmtoken*, *nmtokens*, *notation*, and *string*. You can use the *dt:values* attribute to list the possible values for an enumerated type when *dt:type* is set to *enumeration*.

The value of the *default* attribute is the default value for the attribute. If *dt:type* is set to *enumeration*, the value of the *default* attribute must be one of the values listed in *dt:values*.

The *name* attribute specifies the name of the *AttributeType* element; it will be used to reference the *AttributeType* element. The *required* attribute indicates whether the attribute is required.

An example of an *AttributeType* declaration is shown here:

```
<AttributeType name="colors"
    dt:type="enumeration" dt:values="red green"/>
<AttributeType name="pageCount" dt:type="int"/>
```

The *element* Element

The *element* element is used to declare child elements of an element. Thus, the *element* element is always a child element of either an *ElementType* element (which defines elements) or a *group* element. Just as you could for the *element* element in the W3C schema, you can define the number of occurrences of an *element* child element.

With BizTalk schemas, you will also use the *minOccurs* and *maxOccurs* attributes. In this case, *minOccurs* can only be 0 or 1. If *minOccurs* is 0, the element is optional; if it is 1, the element must occur once. The *maxOccurs* attribute can only be 1 or an asterisk (*). If *maxOccurs* is 1, the element can appear at most once; if it is *, the element can appear an unlimited number of times. This is different from the W3C schema, which allows any value to be assigned to *minOccurs* and *maxOccurs*.

The *group* Element

The BizTalk *group* element is similar to the *group* element of the W3C schema, but unlike the *group* element defined in the W3C standard, the BizTalk *group* element cannot be a child element of the *schema* element. This means that you cannot have document scope *group* elements. A *group* element can be used only to group elements within an element declaration—for example, within an *ElementType* declaration. One of the most useful features of the *group* element is that it can be used to define a sequence for the child elements of an element.

The *group* element contains *element* child elements. The sequence of the child elements can be specified by using the *group* element's *order* attribute. If the *order* attribute is set to *one*, there can only be one instance of each element in the group. The *one* value is equivalent to the pipe (|) symbol in a DTD. When the *order* attribute is set to *seq*, the elements must appear in the order in which they are declared. Using the *seq* value is the same as using parentheses and commas in a DTD. The *many* value indicates that the child elements can appear in any order. The *minOccurs* and *maxOccurs* attributes work the same as their counterparts in the *element* element. We will look at some examples of groups in the section "The *ElementType* Element" later in this chapter.

The *Schema* Element

Because the *Schema* element will be included within the body of the BizTalk document, it cannot really be considered a root element. Therefore, instead of calling the *Schema* element the root element, we will call it the *document* element—that is, the highest level element of the BizTalk document. The *Schema* element indicates the start of a schema definition.

Two namespace attributes should be associated with the *Schema* element. The first is *urn:schemas-microsoft-com:xml-data*. This namespace is used by applications such as the Internet Explorer 5 XML parser as a processing instruction to identify the

Schema elements defined in the sample DTD on page 189. This is the default namespace, so you do not have to prefix all the *Schema* element names with a namespace name. The second namespace attribute is *urn:schemas-microsoft-com: datatypes*. This namespace is used by applications to include all the data types associated with schemas. The data types listed in the *dataTypes* entity in the sample DTD are the currently allowable data types for elements.

Our sample DTD allows the following elements to be child elements of the *Schema* element: *AttributeType*, *ElementType*, and *description*. The *description* child element can occur once and provides a text description of the business document. Because the *AttributeType* child element belongs to the *Schema* element, this element is similar to the *attributeGroup* element of the W3C schema in that it represents an element with document scope. Unlike the *attributeGroup* element, however, the *AttributeType* element allows you to define only a single type of attribute instead of a group of attributes. The *ElementType* child element is equivalent to the *element* element in the W3C schema and is used to define elements.

An example of a *Schema* element is shown here:

```
<Schema name="NorthwindSchema"
    xmlns="urn:schemas-microsoft-com:xml-data"
    xmlns:dt="urn:schemas-microsoft-com:datatypes">
    ⋮
</Schema>
```

The *ElementType* Element

The *ElementType* element is used to define an element type. The *ElementType* element can have the following child elements: *attribute*, *AttributeType*, *datatype*, *description*, *element*, and *group*. The *AttributeType* element will create local definitions for the *attribute* element, the *attribute* element will be used to define attributes associated with the element, and the *element* element will be used to define child elements of the element. The *datatype* element can define an element as being any of the data types listed in the table on pages 191–192.

You can also declare an element as a certain type by using the *dt:type* attribute as one of the attributes of the *ElementType* element. In addition to this attribute, the *ElementType* element also has the *model*, *order*, *content*, and *name* attributes. The *model* attribute is used to indicate whether an element can contain content defined only in the *content model* or can contain content not specified in the content model. A content model is a pattern that you set up to declare what child element types are allowed inside an element and the order of those child elements. If the *model* attribute is set to *open*, the default value, the element can contain content that is not specified in the content model. In this case, this attribute is similar to the *any* type in the W3C standard. If the *model* attribute is set to *closed*, the element can contain only content that is defined in the content model.

The *order* attribute functions the same as its counterpart in the *group* element. The *content* attribute can be *empty* when there is no content, *textOnly* when the content is only text, *eltOnly* when the content is only elements, and *mixed* when the content is a mixture of elements and text. The *name* attribute defines the name of the element.

> **NOTE** If the *model* attribute is *open* and the *content* attribute is *textOnly*, the content can be both text and unnamed elements.

An example of the *ElementType* element is shown here:

```
<Schema name="NorthwindSchema"
   xmlns="urn:schemas-microsoft-com:xml-data"
   xmlns:dt="urn:schemas-microsoft-com:datatypes">
   <AttributeType name="colors"
      dt:type="enumeration" dt:values="red green"/>
   <ElementType name="3Dimage" content="eltOnly" model="closed">
      <attribute type ="colors"/>
      <AttributeType name="width" dt:type="int"/>
      <attribute type = "width"/>
      <group order="seq">
         <element type="x"/>
         <element type="y"/>
         <element type="z"/>
      </group>
   </ElementType>
   ⋮
</Schema>
```

This schema declares a document scope *AttributeType* element named *colors* that is defined as an attribute in the *3Dimage* element by using the *attribute* element. A local declaration of an *AttributeType* element named *width* is also defined as an attribute in the *3Dimage* element by using the *attribute* element. This pairing of a local *AttributeType* element followed by an *attribute* element that uses the *AttributeType* element as an attribute is the most common way to use these elements. The schema also uses a *group* element to sequentially group elements.

The following example demonstrates a valid use of this schema:

```
<3Dimage color="blue" width="5">
   <x>1</x>
   <y>3</y>
   <z>6</z>
</3Dimage>
```

If you change the value of the *order* attribute in the *group* element to *one* in the schema, this example would be invalid; but the following example is valid with the changed schema:

```
<3Dimage color="blue" width="5">
   <x>1</x>
</3Dimage>
```

You can also declare an *ElementType* element as a data type. The following declaration creates an integer element named *quantity*:

```
<ElementType name= "quantity" dt:type="int"/>
```

This element could also be declared as shown here:

```
<ElementType name= "quantity" >
   <datatype dt:type="int"/>
</ElementType>
```

THE NORTHWIND TRADERS BIZTALK SCHEMA

In Chapter 7, we created a schema based on the W3C standard for the Northwind Traders database. This schema rewritten as a BizTalk schema is shown here.

```
<Schema name="NorthwindSchema"
    xmlns="urn:schemas-microsoft-com:xml-data"
    xmlns:dt="urn:schemas-microsoft-com:datatypes">
    <ElementType name="Categories"
        xmlns:Categories="urn:northwindtraders.com.Categories"
        content="eltOnly"  model="closed">
        <group order="seq">
            <element type="Categories.CategoryID" minOccurs="1"
                maxOccurs="1" />
            <element type="Categories.CategoryName" minOccurs="1"
                maxOccurs="1" />
            <element type="Categories.Description" minOccurs="0"
                maxOccurs="1" />
            <element type="Categories.Picture" minOccurs="0"
                maxOccurs="1"/>
        </group>
    </ElementType>
    <ElementType name="Categories.CategoryID"
        xmlns:Categories="urn:northwindtraders.com.Categories"
        dt:type="integer">
        <description>
            Number automatically assigned to a new category
        </description>
    </ElementType>
    <ElementType name="Categories.CategoryName"
```

```
      xmlns:Categories="urn:northwindtraders.com.Categories"
      dt:type = "string">
      <description>Name of food category</description>
</ElementType>
<ElementType name="Categories.Description"
      xmlns:Categories="urn:northwindtraders.com.Categories"
      dt:type="string"/>
<ElementType name="Categories.Picture"
      xmlns:Categories="urn:northwindtraders.com.Categories"
      dt:type = "bin.base64">
      <description>
         Picture representing the food category
       </description>
</ElementType>
<ElementType name="Customers"
      xmlns:Customers="urn:northwindtraders.com.Customers"
      content="eltOnly" model="closed">
      <group order="seq">
         <element type="Customers.CustomerID" minOccurs="1"
            maxOccurs="1"/>
         <element type="Customers.CompanyName" minOccurs="1"
            maxOccurs="1"/>
         <element type="Customers.ContactName" minOccurs="1"
            maxOccurs="1"/>
         <element type="Customers.ContactTitle" minOccurs="0"
            maxOccurs="1"/>
         <element type="Customers.Address" minOccurs="1"
            maxOccurs="1"/>
         <element type="Customers.City" minOccurs="1"
            maxOccurs="1"/>
         <element type="Customers.Region" minOccurs ="1"
            maxOccurs="1"/>
         <element type="Customers.PostalCode" minOccurs="1"
            maxOccurs="1"/>
         <element type="Customers.Country" minOccurs="1"
            maxOccurs="1"/>
         <element type="Customers.Phone" minOccurs="1"
            maxOccurs="1"/>
         <element type="Customers.Fax" minOccurs="0"
            maxOccurs="1"/>
      </group>
</ElementType>
<ElementType name="Customers.CustomerID"
      xmlns:Customers="urn:northwindtraders.com.Customers"
      dt:type="CustomerIDField">
      <description>
         Unique five-character code based on customer name
       </description>
</ElementType>
```

(continued)

```
<ElementType name="Customers.CompanyName"
    xmlns:Customers="urn:northwindtraders.com.Customers"
    dt:type="string"/>
<ElementType name="Customers.ContactName"
    xmlns:Customers="urn:northwindtraders.com.Customers"
    dt:type="string"/>
<ElementType name="Customers.ContactTitle"
    xmlns:Customers="urn:northwindtraders.com.Customers"
    dt:type="string"/>
<ElementType name="Customers.Address"
    xmlns:Customers="urn:northwindtraders.com.Customers"
    dt:type="string">
    <description>Street or post-office box</description>
</ElementType>
<ElementType name="Customers.City"
    xmlns:Customers="urn:northwindtraders.com.Customers"
    dt:type="string"/>
<ElementType name="Customers.Region"
    xmlns:Customers="urn:northwindtraders.com.Customers"
    dt:type="string">
    <description>State or province</description>
</ElementType>
<ElementType name="Customers.PostalCode"
    xmlns:Customers="urn:northwindtraders.com.Customers"
    dt:type="string"/>
<ElementType name="Customers.Country"
    xmlns:Customers="urn:northwindtraders.com.Customers"
    dt:type="string"/>
<ElementType name="Customers.Phone"
    xmlns:Customers="urn:northwindtraders.com.Customers"
    dt:type="string">
    <description>
        Phone number includes country code or area code
    </description>
</ElementType>
<ElementType name = "Customers.Fax"
    xmlns:Customers="urn:northwindtraders.com.Customers"
    dt:type="string">
    <description>
        Fax number includes country code or area code
    </description>
</ElementType>
</Schema>
```

You can also find this schema on the companion CD. As you can see, a few changes have been made between the W3C version and the BizTalk version of this schema. The *annotation* elements have been replaced by *description* elements. There is no equivalent to the W3C *datatype* element, nor can you set a continuous range of values (such as 1 through 100). Also, the data type *content* has been replaced with the *content* attribute.

SHARING BIZTALK SCHEMAS

One of the fundamental concepts of BizTalk is the creation of a central repository of schemas that can be shared by any organization. The BizTalk Web site is located at *http://www.BizTalk.org*. There you can search existing published schemas, publish your own schemas, and use schemas in the repository to validate documents. Published schemas can be accessed by referring to them in your XML documents.

DTD, W3C SCHEMA, OR BIZTALK SCHEMA?

So far, we have looked at three different ways of defining XML documents. We now need to ask ourselves which is the best one for our current systems. The W3C schema is not currently being implemented in many applications because it is not a finalized standard. At the time of this printing, the W3C standard should be in candidate status, however, and it is likely that applications will begin to use it. The W3C standard is the future, and once applications such as the Microsoft, SUN, and IBM XML parsers begin using it, others will follow.

Until the W3C schema standard is implemented, the BizTalk schema can be used. When the W3C schema standard is complete, none of the XML documents based on a BizTalk schema will need to be changed. The only thing that will have to change is the schema located in the repository. It is likely that an application will be available that will automatically convert a BizTalk schema to the W3C schema, or you could write one yourself. While we are waiting for the final W3C standard to be completed, the BizTalk schema is the ideal interim candidate. The BizTalk schema has many advantages, including ease of use, simplicity, and a set of data types.

There is little question that movement of data across boundaries is one of the greatest challenges facing large and small corporations today. As we have mentioned, XML is the best available solution for moving data across boundaries, and we can use schemas to validate XML documents. In fact, you can spend the next year writing applications that do not use schemas, or that don't even work with XML, and then upgrade all of your applications when the W3C schema specification is released. However, by rewriting your applications, you will likely incur a large expense and waste a great deal of development time over the next one or two years. So a better choice is to write your applications using BizTalk schemas now and then upgrade only your schema when the new specification is complete. Using the BizTalk schema now will result in applications that integrate with the next generation of applications and require little expense to upgrade.

Even though BizTalk does offer many advantages over DTDs, DTDs do still have a place in the current development of XML. On the minus side, however, DTDs are much more complicated than schemas, especially when entities are used. They are also not written in well-formed, valid XML. On the plus side, DTDs have been in use for some time and are widely implemented across virtually every platform.

> **NOTE** The large software corporations are currently divided on how to implement XML. As you know, Microsoft, working with other organizations such as SAP and CommerceOne, has developed BizTalk so that corporations can begin to implement XML solutions using schemas now. In response to BizTalk, IBM, SUN, and other organizations have formed a group called OASIS and created their own schema repository, which can be found at *http://www.xml.org*. They are developing ebXML, which is similar to BizTalk but works only with the XML 1.0 standard—that is, only with DTDs.

As we have mentioned, the entire purpose of schemas and DTDs is to validate documents. The easiest means of accomplishing this is to have parsers, such as the Microsoft XML parser, that can validate XML documents using schemas. If a cross-platform parser for BizTalk schemas were available, the schemas could be used to validate any XML document on any platform. Unfortunately, only the Microsoft XML parser supports BizTalk schemas. If the information is passing across a Microsoft system boundary into another Microsoft system, support is not an issue. When information is moving over a boundary and across platforms, however, you need to find a way to validate XML documents. You can use the following three options.

The first option is to extend the Java or C++ parsers provided by SUN and IBM so that they use schemas instead of DTDs to validate documents. This means that all the non-Microsoft systems must have this custom-built parser installed on their servers. This may be an acceptable solution when you are working with a corporate partner or building internal solutions.

The second option is to pass the information across a boundary to a Microsoft BizTalk server, which will then pass the information over another system boundary to the non-Microsoft systems. The BizTalk server will perform the validations and then send the appropriate information to the correct server and method. When Microsoft releases its new BizTalk server, this solution will probably be the best. This too is an acceptable solution when you are working with a corporate partner or building internal solutions.

The third option is to use DTDs. Ideally, you want to be able to build a solution that is platform independent, meaning that you don't need to know whether the person on the receiving end has a BizTalk server. In many circumstances, you will be dealing with multiple organizations and will have no idea what platform they are using. For example, if you are publishing real estate information to all the real estate brokers in a certain area, you will have no way of knowing what system each broker is using. In this case, you need a platform-independent way of moving information to the recipients. As mentioned, BizTalk won't currently work in this situation. Until schemas become a widely accepted standard across all platforms, DTDs can still be used to validate XML documents. When you are working with UNIX and mainframes, DTDs will probably be the best solution until the W3C standard is released and used by all organizations.

When all platforms have applications that work with schemas, schemas will be the better choice. This shift will probably take place within the next year or two. When possible, you should try to use BizTalk schemas when building new applications. When cross-platform issues prevent the usage of schemas, DTDs will have to be used for now.

IDENTIFYING INFORMATION FOR A SCHEMA

Once you have made the decision to use XML, you will need to decide how to build your schemas. It is likely that you will be using XML to upgrade your current systems and to build new ones. The first step in using XML for these systems is identifying the type of information that is being moved throughout the corporation and what information is being moved across system boundaries.

The best way to begin identifying information is by looking at the forms that are currently being used or that will be used to input and review information. These forms contain fields that represent all the information required to complete a task. If you use Unified modeling language (UML) *use cases* (a text description of a task that uses a predefined format) to design a system, each use case will represent a task and define the information required to complete that task in business rules. As you look through the forms that exist in the corporation, try to identify general information structures. For example, you might find that a core set of information is used to define a customer throughout the corporation. Based on this core set of information, a base customer schema is created to define customer information. If other applications require additional information, namespaces can be used to include the base customer schema in another schema with the additional information.

Most corporations have generated large quantities of documentation about workflow and batch process. This documentation can be used to identify the information that is being moved through the corporation. Be aware of the fact that processes are often extended, producing two or more similar processes. These extensions are usually the result of new requirements or new systems that perform functions similar to those of existing systems. As time goes on and more and more extensions develop, the batch processes become huge and extremely redundant. Try to find the common elements in the batch processes and build schemas that bring together common elements and simplify the *business event model*.

The business event model represents the flow of events, from the beginning to the end, for a business process. It is a tool that helps you define your system and the information flowing through the system, but remember that it is only a tool. Modeling the system should be done only to the extent that it helps you understand the system, the information in the system, and the flow of information through the system. Developing a business event model that does this should not take a great deal of time. If you find that a large quantity of resources is being dumped into modeling and nothing is being built, the model has taken on a life of its own and has gone beyond its usefulness. It's often best to start by modeling small parts of your system.

NOTE   You can get more information about building your schema by reading the chapter "So, What's a Schema?" of the online book *ABC's of Schema*, by Dan Rogers. You can find this book at *http://www.biztalk.org/News/newsRead. asp?NewsID=204705*.

SUMMARY

BizTalk Framework 2.0 provides a means to move information contained in a SOAP document across boundaries. BizTalk document elements are wrapped in BizTags. Each BizTalk document must use the appropriate BizTags in the SOAP Header section and contain the structured business transaction information in the SOAP Body section. The BizTalk message can be defined and validated using schemas. You can use the BizTalk message to create a loosely coupled message that can be sent across any boundary.

Currently, only the Microsoft XML parser can properly validate BizTalk schemas. It is likely that when the W3C schema is complete, all the major software companies will add the capability to validate XML documents with schemas. When this happens, the BizTalk format will provide the capability to move information across boundaries to and from any software platform.

Up to this point, we have discussed the basic structure of XML, DTDs and schemas that are used to define XML documents. We have also examined SOAP 1.1 and the BizTalk Framework 2.0. In the rest of the book, we will see how to actually write applications using the knowledge we have gained in the first half of the book.

Part II

XML and
Windows DNA

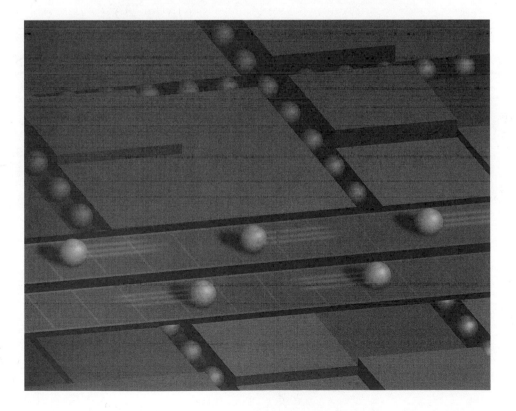

Chapter 10

Overview of Windows DNA

Microsoft Windows DNA is based on a *distributed system* architecture. Distributed systems contain components on more than one computer. An Internet-based system is a typical example of a distributed system, as it contains an application running on a client computer (usually a browser-based application) and one or more applications running on a Web server. The Web server can also communicate to other servers. In this chapter, we'll focus on building Windows DNA systems, but the discussion is equally applicable to other distributed systems.

One of the primary goals of distributed systems is to be *highly scalable*. A highly scalable system can easily expand from thousands of users to tens of thousands of users. Over the last two decades, we've witnessed a steady evolution from Windows systems that can handle a few hundred users, such as a department-size application, to systems that can handle tens of thousands of users, such as an Internet application. This chapter will demonstrate how a distributed system can be highly scalable.

Because distributed systems contain a variety of components located on several computers, these systems are usually extremely complex. Without a framework such as the one provided by Windows DNA, designing and building such a system would be impossible. The Windows DNA architecture provides two models for designing and building large, complex distributed systems: the *logical three-tier model* and the *physical three-tier model*. The logical three-tier model is used to define and design the components of the system. The physical three-tier model is used to specify the placement of these components within the distributed system. Let's begin by looking at the logical three-tier model.

LOGICAL THREE-TIER MODEL

When you build components in a Windows distributed system, you will define the components based on the services they perform. For example, the Web page running in the Web browser will perform services for the user, such as allowing the user to enter information, select information, or navigate to another Web page. Components placed on the Web server will receive requests from the Web browser to perform services such as accessing a particular Web page, searching the catalog for all occurrences of a particular word, and so on. The services that a system can perform are divided into three categories: *user services, business services,* and *data services.* Thus, you can form three tiers: the user services tier, the business services tier, and the data services tier. Each of these tiers consists of one or more components.

User Services Components

The user services components are responsible for passing information to and from the user. Specifically, they gather information from the user and then send the user information to the business services components for processing. After the information is processed, the user services components receive the processed results from the business services components and present them to the user. Typically, the user is a person and the user services components consist of user interface components such as Web pages in a browser, an .EXE application containing forms, and the like. A user could also be another system—in which case, there's no visible interface. An example of this scenario would be an application that verifies credit card information.

To design user services components, you must interview the potential users of the system. Based on these interviews, you can create a detailed description of the steps required to complete each of the tasks that the system will be asked to perform. These descriptions can then be turned into *Unified Modeling Language (UML) use cases.* UML is a set of models used to design object-oriented systems, although it can be used to design virtually any system. A use case is a text description of how a user will perform a task; each use case has a specific format such as a flowchart, a flow diagram, or a step-by-step outline in a table format. These use cases will help you organize the steps required to complete your tasks, will help you define the components your system will need to perform these tasks, and can be used as the basis of the design for your entire distributed system.

For the most part, user services components are designed to meet a specific need and are not reusable. For example, the user components specifically created for entering employee information are not likely reusable in an application that's used for obtaining order information from customers.

Besides communicating with the user, most applications must process data. For these applications, you will also need to define a set of business rules that govern how data is handled. Examples of business rules could be the requirement that every customer have a name, a customer ID, and a billing address. Business rules are similar to use cases, except that they are text descriptions of the requirements to be met to ensure a business is run correctly. In a two-tier architecture model, some or all of the business rules regarding data processing are placed in the user services components. In a three-tier architecture model, the business rules are moved from the user services components to the business services components.

Business Services Components

The business services components receive input from the user services components, interact with the data services components to retrieve or update data, and send the processed result to the user services components. The business services components ensure that the business rules are followed. For example, a user services component may ask a business services component to save a new customer record. The business services component will then verify that this new record fulfills all of the rules for a new customer record. In another example, the user services components might request that the business services components retrieve a particular Web page containing data from a database. The business services components will get the data and format it according to a set of rules and then build an HTML or XML page for the user services components.

If the business rules change, only the business services components that contain those rules will need to be changed. If the business rules are placed within the user services components, the user services components will have to be updated every time a rule changes. If such a user services component were an .EXE application installed on thousands of computers, a change in the business rules would mean reinstalling the component on all the client computers.

Separating the business rules from the user services components is only one benefit of using business services components. Business services components usually contain logic that is highly reusable. For example, if you create a business services component to retrieve product information for a Windows-based application, you don't need to rewrite this component if you want to create a Web-based application that requires the same business logic.

Using business services components also simplifies the building of your user services components. As previously mentioned, the business rules in the three-tier model are moved from the user services components to the business services components. Thus, the user services components are simplified. In addition, if you build business services components as objects that expose methods and properties, your user services components can be simplified further since the code in your user services components will consist of setting properties and calling methods of the business services objects.

For example, let's say your application requires validation of new orders. You can implement the validation logic in the user services components, but you can also separate this logic from the user services components and implement it in an *Update* method in the business services components. Thus, the validation of a new order will be done when you call the *Update* method.

Data Services Components

The business services components usually handle data processing. To get the data, they make requests to the data services components. The data services components are responsible for storing and retrieving data and maintaining data integrity. They communicate directly with a data source. A data source can be a database, a text file, an XML file, an XML document stored in memory, and so on. When a system performs the Create, Read, Update, and Delete (CRUD) operations, the business services components will validate these operations. If the operations are valid, the business services components will make a request to the data services components to actually perform the operations. If the CRUD operations are invalid, the business services components will raise an error and will not have to communicate with the data services components.

A common confusion associated with the DNA model is between the data services component and the database. A data services component can be either a component that is running on a server (usually not the database server) or a stored procedure. Often a system will have the data services tier that consists of both stored procedures and components. (Some authors refer to the database as a "fourth tier of the logical model.") Either way, the actual physical database is not the data services tier, although it may contain the data services components in the form of stored procedures.

Like business services components, data services components are highly reusable. For example, an e-commerce application, an order entry application, and a reporting program for management could use the same data services component that performs CRUD operations on customer records.

Over the past year, the view on stored procedures has been changing. Earlier it was generally believed that stored procedures were the best location for data services components. Stored procedures could use the security features of the database and be centrally controlled by the database administrators. The major problem with stored procedures, however, is scalability. Replicating databases is difficult and usually inefficient. If you build all of your data services components as stored procedures and the server you are using runs out of memory or other resources trying to run these stored procedures for thousands of users, you cannot easily build a second database server and share the load between the two database servers. Your only option is to upgrade the server. If you reach a point at which the server is already at the maximum capacity the current technology can offer, your server will no longer be able to handle the required loads.

If you build data services components that are placed on a server other than the database server, you can increase the capacity of the system by adding another server. If you use some method to balance the load between the servers, the business services components can call whichever server has the least load. Since the data services components are performing services only for the business services components, it doesn't matter on which server a data services component performs the service.

Of course, if you don't build data services components as stored procedures you will probably not be able to use the database's security mechanisms directly. Instead, you will have to implement security features within your components. This security code should go into the business services components, as they will contain the rules for validating users.

> **NOTE** Regardless of whether you use stored procedures or components for your data services tier, you should still place validation rules in your database, in the form of triggers, constraints, and so on. Although this means that you are placing the rules in two locations: one in the database and the other in the business services tier, doing so prevents users from performing invalid CRUD operations directly on the database.

Connecting the Three Tiers

So far you've learned that by using Windows DNA, you can split your application's services into three parts: user services components, business services components, and data services components. Now you will learn how you can tie the three parts together. In Windows DNA, this is done by exposing system and application services through the Component Object Model (COM).

The foundation of Windows is COM, which has become COM+ in Microsoft Windows 2000. (COM as used here refers to both COM and COM+.) COM provides a way for applications to communicate with COM objects. COM also enables one object to communicate with another object through method calling and property setting. How a COM object actually performs its services is not important. Objects hide or encapsulate the details of how they work. Because an object hides how it performs its services, you can change the way an object performs its services without breaking the application that uses the object.

If the services components in each tier are COM components, the communication between tiers will be COM method calls. To be specific, your user services components will call the methods of the business services components to request services from the business services tier, and your business services components will call the methods of the data services components to ask for services from the data services tier.

PHYSICAL THREE-TIER MODEL

The physical three-tier model includes the actual computers on which the components will be placed. There are three groups of computers: *client tier, middle tier,* and *database tier.* The client tier computers provide user services, consisting mainly of the user interfaces. The middle-tier computers provide business services, consisting of enforcement of business rules and data validations. The database tier computers provide data services, consisting of the data and the ways of accessing and maintaining the data.

Several years ago, the two-tier model, also called client server, was popular. This model consisted of a client tier that communicated with a database tier. This model required the client computer to maintain a continuous connection to the database. The database could keep track of what records were being edited and place locks on these records so that only one person could change a record at one time. Locks insured that the data would be consistent. The main drawback of this model was that the systems were not very scalable. Since developers wanted to build systems that could scale to hundreds and even thousands of users, they needed another solution.

The solution to making systems more scalable was to break the connection the client had with the database. Originally, the data was passed to the client computer where CRUD operations could be performed on the data. If the data was updated, this data could be sent back to the database. With this disconnected model, the database could no longer lock records because the client had no connection to the database. Thus, the database had no way to reconcile inconsistencies. An alternative to locking records was developed that allowed the client to communicate with an application located on the server that could make changes to the database. This application is the data services component we have been discussing in this section. Instead of running this application on the database tier, the middle tier was added to host the data services components.

The idea of a middle-tier computer had existed long before the use of a disconnected model. In non-Windows operating systems, applications were commonly placed on a central server and used by many clients. These clients often had little functionality and were called *dumb terminals*. The middle-tier computer can still be used to host components, such as the business or data services components that can be used by multiple clients, but now modern clients are usually fully functioning and have many applications running on them.

Before we look at how to place components created in the logical model onto the computers in the physical model, which we'll do in the section "Locating Logical Components" later in this chapter, we must first examine the component state.

STATEFUL VS. STATELESS COMPONENTS

One of the most important aspects of creating scalable components is the use of *stateful* and *stateless components*. A stateful component can retain information from one call to the next. For example, a Microsoft Visual Basic .EXE application can be created that keeps track of the currently logged in user from the moment the user logs in until the time the user logs off. State is stored by using properties. In our Visual Basic example, we could use a read/write property named *userName* and a write-only property named *userPassword*. A stateless component has no memory from one call to the next. For example, a data services component that retrieves customer records retrieves customer records for one client and then retrieves records for a second client without any memory of what it retrieved for the first client. A stateless component does not have any public properties.

In the physical model, components that are placed on the middle-tier server and communicate with the client computer should be stateless. If a component on the middle-tier server maintained state (that is, retained information between calls from the client), these components would need to maintain information on every client that made a request to the component. As the number of clients making requests increased, the information that would need to be stored in memory would increase until the server ran out of memory. This would not be a scalable solution.

If components on the middle-tier and database servers do not maintain state, they can quickly perform a service for one client and then perform a service for another client. This feature works even better with a technique called *just-in-time activation (JITA)*. With JITA, a component becomes active immediately before it is used. Once the component has been activated, it will quickly perform a service and then deactivate. As soon as the component has finished with one client, it is available for another client. These components can be built so that they require a minimum amount of time to perform their services. They reside in memory for only a brief time to service each client. Because these components are stateless, they will not require any memory usage between client calls. Thus, a stateless component that uses JITA will use the absolute minimum amount of server resources while still servicing a large number of clients. These types of stateless components can scale very well.

> **NOTE** It is possible to create stateful server components that communicate with the client. The most common example is stateful ASP. Using state for ASP-based systems that never have more than 100 possible users, such as a small departmental intranet application, might be appropriate. Using state in large-scale ASP-based Web applications, however, will seriously degrade performance of the system and should be avoided.

DESIGNING A DISTRIBUTED SYSTEM

As we've seen, the design of a distributed system begins with the logical three-tier model. Initially, the overall goals of the system must be defined. These goals are broken down into the series of tasks the system must perform. These tasks are defined in UML use cases that define the interaction between the user and the system, and then the use cases can be used to define the user services components. A hotel's guest registration system could have the following use case:

- **Name** Make a Reservation.

- **Overview** The purpose of this use case is to create a new reservation.

- **Primary Actor** The main actor is the Check-In Clerk.

- **Secondary Actors** None.

- **Starting Point** Request to enter a new reservation.

- **Ending Point** The Guest is either assigned a reservation or the reservation is cancelled.

- **Measurable Result** The Guest is either assigned a reservation or the guest is not assigned a reservation.

■ **Flow of Events**

❑ Actor enters First and Last Name of Guest into the system.

❑ Actor enters address of Guest into the system.

❑ Actor enters room requirements for Guest.

❑ Actor requests room reservation.

■ **Use Case Extensions** None.

■ **Business Rules**

❑ Definition Business Rule Reservation

❑ Definition Business Rule Guest

❑ Definition Business Rule Check-In Clerk

■ **Outstanding Issues** None.

You can also use the use cases to create UML diagrams, such as a *sequence diagram,* to define the system's business and data services components. Figure 10-1 shows a sequence diagram illustrating the interaction between objects in the system and the interaction between the user and the system over time.

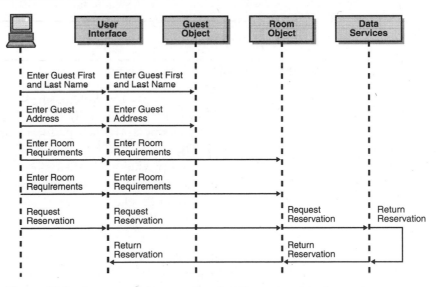

Figure 10-1. *A sequence diagram for a hotel's guest registration system.*

After the sequence diagrams have been completed, *class diagrams* are created, as shown in Figure 10-2. As you can see, class diagrams define the components of the system and the services they perform.

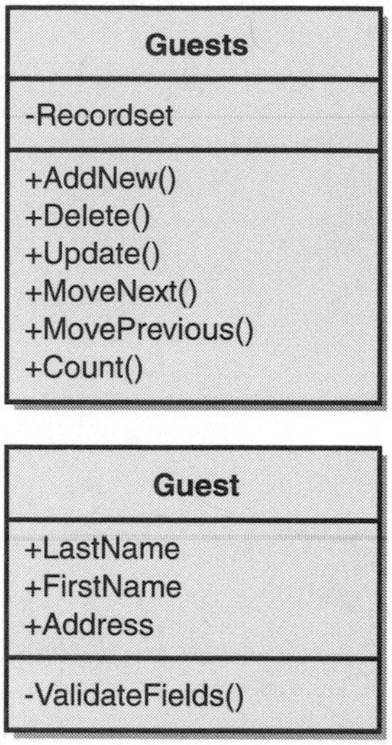

```
┌──────────────────────────────┐
│           Guests             │
├──────────────────────────────┤
│ -Recordset                   │
├──────────────────────────────┤
│ +AddNew()                    │
│ +Delete()                    │
│ +Update()                    │
│ +MoveNext()                  │
│ +MovePrevious()              │
│ +Count()                     │
└──────────────────────────────┘

┌──────────────────────────────┐
│            Guest             │
├──────────────────────────────┤
│ +LastName                    │
│ +FirstName                   │
│ +Address                     │
├──────────────────────────────┤
│ -ValidateFields()            │
└──────────────────────────────┘
```

Figure 10-2. *A class diagram for a hotel's guest registration system.*

Up to this point in the design process, there should be little discussion of how these components will actually perform these services, in keeping with the concept of encapsulation. When you have reached this point, you must decide whether to buy, reuse, or build your components.

Buying, Reusing, or Building Components

Components can be bought from third-party vendors. If a third-party component can be found that performs the services you need, it is usually the most economical solution. On the other hand, third-party components typically perform a large number of services that you do not need and may not exactly fit the needs of your project. You must also verify that the maker of the product will update the component to accommodate new operating system and development program releases.

Reusing existing components is also an excellent option. Often the best way to make your component reusable is to carefully plan your system before you build it. With planning, you can often identify components of the system that can be used in many places. Sometimes an identical component can be used in numerous places; at other times only a part of the component can be used in multiple places.

In addition to reusing components, you can also reuse a component template. During the designing phase, you may find that some components can be built from a particular pattern. If you are building an order entry application, for example, you may find that all of your business services components perform the same CRUD functionality. Thus, all of your business services components have *Create, Read, Up-*

date, and *Delete* methods. You can use this pattern of shared methods to create a template that can then be used to build all of your business services components with CRUD functionality.

Building a component is the most costly option in terms of time and resources, but with proper planning and design it will guarantee that the correct component is built. Using patterns and creating reusable components can offset the cost of designing and building components from the ground up.

The best option depends on the available resources. Finances, available personnel for development, and time allowed for development are the three most common resources that will influence your decisions. Each system should be carefully analyzed to find the best solution for that system.

Locating Logical Components

The traditional view held that user services components belong on the client computer, business services components belong on the middle-tier computer, and data services components belong in stored procedures on the database computer. This placement is usually appropriate for smaller systems with a limited number of users or large Internet-style systems, but it is not always the best configuration for all systems. There are several factors you need to take into consideration when designing your deployment plan.

Performance considerations

Business services components can perform many different functions and the middle-tier computer is not always the optimal location for these components. For example, the business services components that validate input from the user services components will provide the best performance if they are located on the client computer. When the user inputs information into the user services components, the business services components can provide immediate validation because the user and business services components are both on the same computer. On the other hand, if the business services components that validate user services components are located on the server, requests to validate input must be sent to the server. Sending the validation to the server can slow down the process, especially when network traffic is heavy, and can affect the overall performance of both the application and the user.

However, some types of business services components might have better performance even though they are placed on a server. For example, you could have a business services component called by an ASP document that builds HTML pages. The Web server is communicating with the business services component, not with the client, as in the previous example. As long as the Web server has enough resources, which is usually the case, the business services components could be placed on the Web server. The data services components and the server-side business services components could also reside on the same server. The decision would be based on the expected load and the capabilities of the server.

Component state considerations

In smaller systems, business services components located on the middle-tier computer can maintain state. These systems are typical of department-size applications with users in the tens or hundreds instead of thousands.

For example, you could build an order entry application in which all the business services objects—such as the customer, order, order details, and product objects—are located on the server. The client application could call these objects and have them maintain state from the beginning to the end of each order. This would require you to maintain state on the server, but with only a small number of clients, doing so should not adversely affect server performance. However, in a larger system, maintaining state on the server will significantly slow the server's performance.

One scenario has no performance loss caused by stateful business services components on the server: when one component on a server calls a second component on the same server, it makes no difference in performance if the second component is stateless or stateful. If the two servers share a direct network connection, you can also put the second component on a second server. A common example of this is a Web server, such as Microsoft Internet Information Server (IIS). With IIS, you can use stateless ASP documents to communicate with the client. These stateless ASP documents can use stateful or stateless business services components, such as Visual Basic objects, to build the Web pages. These Visual Basic objects will be on either the Web server or another server directly connected to the Web server. Because the ASP document is stateless and will exist only for a few milliseconds (long enough to perform a service for the client), any object it uses will also exist only for a few milliseconds. The ASP document can be considered the main business services component; the Visual Basic objects are the secondary business services components. The ASP document orchestrates the entire process of performing the service for the client.

Installation considerations

In addition to performance issues, the ease at which business services components can be installed and upgraded on the client computers must also be taken into consideration. Ideally, corporations should be using a set of client computers with a limited number of configurations. For example, let's say a corporation buys only computer models V, VII, and VIII from Northwind Traders, and each of these models has only one standard software package installed. This means that there are only three possible configurations for the client computers. If you created a new business services component, you could test the installation process on one of each of the three computer models used by the corporation. If the component installs properly and none of the software that was originally on the computers is affected by the installation, there should be no problems with installing this businesses services component on all the client computers in the corporation. If you do run into installation problems, you could find the cause of the errors and change your installation techniques to fix them. In this type of controlled client environment, installing and upgrading a component on the client should be fairly easy. In brief, for the most part, the process of installing components onto the client can be greatly simplified by performing extensive testing. The installation of a new system onto a large number of clients (hundreds to thousands) using Microsoft Systems Management Server (SMS) could require up to six months of testing.

On the other hand, if a corporation has a wide range of unknown client computers, you could not use representative test computers to make sure that the new business services components would install properly on all the clients. Upgrading a component on these unknown clients could also result in problems. There are many possible solutions to this problem. For example, Norton Antivirus will check for updates to its virus-checking program at a set interval. When that interval is reached, a component will ask users whether they want to check for any updated components over the Internet. If any updates are found, they are automatically downloaded.

Components can also be installed in typical fashion over the Internet using .CAB files or using products such as SMS that can push components onto the client. Many techniques are available for getting the components onto the client. The major drawback with any technique is the possibility of dynamic link library (DLL) conflicts and a failure of the installation process.

As you can see, there are no standard answers as to the best location for business services components. The decision depends on the system that is being built, the configuration of the clients, the servers that are available, and so forth. Each decision usually requires the balancing of many factors.

Extending the Windows DNA Model

We've now looked at several possible configurations for the logical components, and we've identified several ways of building scalable systems. This is what creating a model is all about: providing a framework that you can use to find the best way to construct your system.

It's time to get to work molding and shaping the DNA model to see just how far we can go with it. To begin, let's combine the two scenarios described earlier into an order entry application that works over the Internet. The user services components can be HTML pages in a Web browser. We can place business services components on the client computer that performs the CRUD validation. We can also place business services components on the Web server that builds the Web pages.

Now let's really extend this model. Our goal is to get the fastest performance from the user services components. If you could move some of the data into the client's memory and then use this data in memory as a data source, you could eliminate several trips to the data services components and the database. This can be accomplished in several ways. When you are working with Visual Basic, the usual way of transferring data over to the client is by using a Microsoft *ActiveX Data Objects (ADO) disconnected recordset*. The ADO disconnected recordset maintains a virtual table in memory; it does not maintain a connection to the database, which is why the name is "disconnected recordset." The full range of CRUD operations can be performed on the ADO disconnected recordset without making any connection to the database. If any changes are to be made to the database, the disconnected recordset can be sent back to the data services component. The data services component will then perform the update with the database and correct any inconsistencies. (Correcting inconsistencies during updates is another function of the data services components.) With ADO disconnected recordsets, correcting inconsistencies can be done only within a component, not in a stored procedure.

NOTE   For an example of a Visual Basic DNA system that works with disconnected recordsets and for a detailed description of UML, see *Visual Basic UML Design and Development* (published by Wrox, 1999) by Jake Sturm.

There is another way of transferring data over to the client: by using XML. You can bring data over to the client in a Web application and create islands of XML data. This XML data can then be used as a local data source. If the user services components are HTML or XML applications running in Microsoft Internet Explorer 5, this will be fairly easy to do; the process is discussed in Chapter 13. If you use an XML data source on the client, you can also have business services components that communicate with the XML data source on the client. Communication with the middle-tier computers happens only when data needs to be retrieved or updated.

SUMMARY

The Windows DNA architecture consists of a logical three-tier model and a physical three-tier model. These two models provide a framework that can be used to design and build your DNA systems. The models are extremely flexible and can be used for a wide range of systems.

In the next several chapters, we will look at how XML can be used in the three-tier model. You will learn how to create user, business, and data services components using XML. And you will learn how to use the BizTalk Server.

Chapter 11

The XML Document Object Model

The XML Document Object Model (DOM) is a platform-neutral and language-neutral interface that allows developers to create applications and scripts to access and update the content, style, and structure of XML documents. The XML DOM is based on the W3C DOM, which is a recommended specification that has been released by the DOM Working Group (WG) in several stages. The DOM Level 1 specification introduces the features that can be used to manipulate the content and structure of HTML and XML documents. The W3C is currently working on the DOM Level 2 specification. This specification extends DOM Level 1 with many new features. Microsoft Internet Explorer 5 fully supports the W3C Level 1 DOM specification.

NOTE For more information about the features included in each DOM level, visit the W3C Web site at *http://www.w3.org/dom*.

In addition to the XML DOM support included with Internet Explorer 5, Microsoft XML parser version 2.6 and version 3.0 have been released that support several extensions of the XML DOM beyond the current W3C specification, including BizTalk schemas, XPath, and XSL Transformations (XSLT). We will begin this chapter with a discussion of the implementation of the XML DOM in Internet Explorer 5 and end with a discussion of the new XML parser and the additional functionality that it adds.

INTERNET EXPLORER 5'S IMPLEMENTATION OF THE XML DOM

The implementation of the XML DOM in Internet Explorer 5 consists of a set of objects that can be used to load an XML document. Once the document is loaded, you can parse, navigate, and manipulate the information in the XML document. The DOM can also be used for retrieving information about the document.

There are four main objects included with Internet Explorer 5's implementation of the XML DOM: *XMLDOMDocument*, *XMLDOMNode*, *XMLDOMNodeList*, and *XMLDOMNamedNodeMap*. In addition, sixteen other objects are part of Internet Explorer 5's implementation of the XML DOM. All of these objects have properties and methods that you can use to gather information about the document (including its structure) and to navigate to other object *nodes* within a document tree. A node is a reference to any object that can exist in a document hierarchy. The ability to access different nodes of the document tree is a function that is also available using XPath and XPointer. Twelve different types of nodes are available in the DOM: *element*, *attribute*, *text*, *CDATA section*, *entity reference*, *entity*, *processing instruction*, *comment*, *document*, *document type*, *document fragment*, and *notation*. An interface exists for each of these node types that allows you to gather and manipulate information on the node. The most common node types are the *element*, *attribute*, and *text* nodes.

> **NOTE** Attributes are not actually child elements of any node in the tree, so they have a special programming interface called *IXMLDOMNamedNodeMap*.

The W3C DOM specification defines two types of programming interfaces: fundamental and extended. The fundamental DOM interfaces are required when writing applications that manipulate XML documents. The extended interfaces are not required, but make it easier for developers to write applications. The Internet Explorer 5 DOM implements both the fundamental and extended interfaces. In addition, it provides other interfaces to support Extensible Stylesheet Language (XSL), XSL patterns, namespaces, and data types.

For script developers, the most important object in the Internet Explorer 5's implementation of the XML DOM is the *XMLDOMDocument* object, which allows developers to navigate, query, and modify the content and structure of an XML document. This object implements the *IXMLDOMDocument* interface. We will look at this object first.

XMLDOMDocument Object

To navigate and get a reference to an XML document, you need to use the *XMLDOM-Document* object. Once you actually get a reference to the document, you can begin to work with it. The *XMLDOMDocument* object implements the *IXMLDOMDocument* interface.

Getting a reference to an XML document

Depending on the programming language you are using, you can get a reference to an XML document in several ways.

In Microsoft JScript, you can get a reference as follows:

```
var objXMLdoc = new ActiveXObject("Microsoft.XMLDOM);
objXMLdoc.load("http://www.northwindtraders.com/sales.xml");
```

In VBScript, the code for obtaining a reference appears as follows:

```
Dim objXMLdoc
Set objXMLdoc = CreateObject("Microsoft.XMLDOM")
objXMLdoc.load("http://www.northwindtraders.com/sales.xml")
```

In Microsoft Visual Basic, you should add a reference to Msxml.dll to your project by choosing References from the Project menu, and then choosing Microsoft XML version 2 from the References dialog box. The code to get a reference to an XML document appears as follows:

```
Dim objXMLdoc As DomDocument
Set objXMLdoc = New DomDocument
objXMLdoc.load("http://www.northwindtraders.com/Sales.xml")
```

You could also use the following code without setting the reference, though the above method is preferable:

```
Set objXMLdoc = CreateObject("Microsoft.XMLDOM")
objXMLdoc.load("http://www.northwindtraders.com/Sales.xml")
```

IXMLDOMDocument interface properties and methods

In the above examples, we used the *load* method to get a reference to an actual XML document. The following tables list the properties, methods, and events associated with the *IXMLDOMDocument* interface. Properties and methods that are extensions of the W3C DOM Level 1 specification will be marked with an asterisk (*) throughout this chapter.

> NOTE   Code samples illustrating how to use the *IXMLDOMDocument* interface will be presented later in this chapter.

IXMLDOMDocument Properties

Name	Description
async*	Downloads the XML document asynchronously if this property is set to *true* (the default).
attributes	Returns an *XMLDOMNamedNodeMap* object for nodes that can return attributes.
baseName*	Returns the name of the node with any namespace removed.
childNodes	Returns all children of the current node for nodes that are allowed children.
dataType*	Sets or returns the data type for an XML document node that uses a schema. For *entity references*, *elements*, and *attributes*, if a data type is specified in the schema it will return the data type as a string. If no value is specified, it returns *null*, and for all other nodes it returns *string*. Attempts to set the *dataType* property for nodes other than *attribute*, *element*, or *entity reference* are ignored.
definition*	Returns the node that contains the DTD or schema definition for the entity referenced.
doctype	Returns a reference to an *XMLDOMDocumentType* node containing a reference to the DTD or schema.
documentElement	Returns a reference to the outermost document element of an XML document.
firstChild	Returns a reference to the first child of the current node.
implementation	Returns a reference to the *XMLDOMImplementation* object for the document.
lastChild	Returns a reference to the last child node of the current node.
namespaceURI*	Returns the Uniform Resource Identifier (URI) for the namespace as a string.
nextSibling	Returns a reference to the next sibling node of the current node.
nodeName	Returns the name of the node.
nodeTypeString*	Returns the node type as a string.
nodeType	Returns the node type as a number.
nodeTypedValue*	Returns or sets the strongly typed value of the node.

Name	Description
nodeValue	Sets or returns the value of the node as text. Returns *attribute* value for *attribute* nodes. Returns the text within the *CDATA* section for *CDATASection* nodes. Returns the comment for *comment* nodes. Returns the processing instruction for *processing instruction* nodes. Returns the text for *text* nodes. For all other nodes, it returns *null* if you try to get the property and raises an error if you try to set the property.
ownerDocument	Returns the root of the document that contains this node.
parentNode	Returns the parent node of the current node for nodes that are allowed to have parents.
*parsed**	Returns *true* if the current node and all of its descendants have been parsed and instantiated.
*parseError**	Returns a reference to the *XMLDOMParseError* object that contains information about the last parsing error.
*prefix**	Returns the element namespace prefix as a string.
*preserveWhiteSpace**	Specifies if white space should be preserved. The default is *false*.
previousSibling	Returns a reference to the previous sibling node of the current node.
*readyState**	Indicates the current state of an XML document.
*resolveExternals**	Resolves the external entities, and the document is resolved against external DTDs, if this is *true*. The default is *false*.
*specified**	Returns *true* if a node value is specified. Returns *false* if a node value is derived from a default value. (This is normally used only with *attribute* nodes.)
*text**	Sets and returns the text content of the current node and all of its descendants.
*url**	Returns the URL of the last successfully loaded XML document or returns *null* if the XML document was built in memory.
*validateOnParse**	The document will validate on parsing when this property is set to *true*, but the parser will only check the document for being well formed if this property is set to *false*. Default is *true*. This property can be set or read.
*xml**	Returns the entire XML content of the current node and all of its descendant nodes.

IXMLDOMDocument Methods

Name	Description
abort( )*	Stops the asynchronous load if the *async* property is set to *true* and the document is loading. Any information that has been downloaded is discarded. If the *readyState* property is equal to *COMPLETED*, calling *abort* has no effect.
appendChild (newChild)	Appends *newChild* to the end of the child nodes list for the currently selected node.
cloneNode (deep)	Creates a *clone* node that is identical to the currently referenced node. If *deep* is set to *true*, all child nodes are also cloned.
createAttribute (name)	Creates an *attribute* node with the specified name.
createCDATASection (text)	Creates a *CDATASection* node containing *text*.
createComment (text)	Creates a *comment* node containing *text*. The comment delimiters (<!-- -->) will be inserted.
createDocumentFragment( )	Creates an empty *DocumentFragment* node that is used to build independent sections of the XML document.
createElement (name)	Creates an instance of the specified element.
createEntityReference (name)	Creates an *EntityReference* node called *name*.
createNode (type, name, namespace)*	Creates any type of node using the specified *type*, *name*, and *namespace* parameters.
createProcessingInstruction (target, data)	Creates a new processing instruction. The *target* parameter provides both the target and the node name. The *data* parameter is the actual instruction.
createTextNode (text)	Creates a *text* node containing the text specified in the *text* parameter.

Name	*Description*
getElementsByTagName (name)	Returns a collection of child elements that have the specified tag name. If the *name* parameter is *, it returns all elements.
hasChildNodes( )	Returns *true* if the node has any child nodes.
insertBefore (newNode, beforeNode)	Inserts a new node object called *newNode* into the list of child nodes for the current node to the left of the *beforeNode* or at the end if *beforeNode* is left out.
*load (url)**	Loads an XML document from the specified URL.
*loadXML (string)**	Loads a string that contains well-formed XML.
*nodeFromID (value)**	Returns the node object that has an ID attribute matching the supplied value.
removeChild (node)	Removes the child node from the current node and returns it.
replaceChild (newNode, oldNode)	Replaces the child node *oldNode* with the node *newNode*.
*save (destination)**	Saves the file to the specified destination.
*selectNodes (pattern)**	Returns a node list object containing matching nodes. The *pattern* parameter is a string containing an XSL pattern.
*selectSingleNode (pattern)**	Returns the first node object matching the pattern of a string containing XSL.
*transformNode (stylesheet)**	Processes the node and its children using XSL pattern matching. The *stylesheet* parameter must be either an *XMLDOMDocument* node object or a node object in the XSL namespace.
transformNodeToObject (stylesheet, outputobject)	Transforms the node according to the XSL document and places the transformed document into the *outputobject* parameter.

IXMLDOMDocument Events

Name	Description
*ondataavailable**	Occurs whenever data becomes available. When the *async* property is *true*, this event fires several times as data comes in. Using the *readyState* property, you can obtain information on the incoming data, including when all of the data has been downloaded.
*onreadystatechange**	Fires whenever the *readyState* property changes.
*ontransformnode**	Fires when a node is transformed using the *TransformNode* method of the node object.

XMLDOMNode Object

The *XMLDOMNode* object implements the *IXMLDOMNode* interface. This interface contains the following properties: *attributes, baseName, childNodes, dataType, definition, firstChild, lastChild, namespaceURI, nextSibling, nodeName, nodeTypeString, nodeType, nodeTypedValue, nodeValue, ownerDocument, parentNode, parsed, prefix, previousSibling, specified, text,* and *xml.* The methods associated with *IXMLDOMNode* are *appendChild, clonenode, hasChildNodes, insertBefore, removeChild, replaceChild, selectNodes, selectSingleNode, transformNode,* and *transformNodeToObject.* There are no events associated with the *IXMLDOMNode* interface.

Looking at these properties and methods, you can see that they're all included in the *IXMLDOMDocument* interface and have been defined above. The same methods exist in both interfaces because *IXMLDOMNode* is used as the base interface for building all W3C DOM objects except for *IXMLDOMImplementation, IXMLDOMNodeList,* and *IXMLDOMNamedNodeMap*, as illustrated in Figure 11-1.

Besides these interfaces, Internet Explorer 5 has three additional interfaces: *IXTLRuntime, IXMLDOMParseError,* and *IXMLHTTPRequest.* You can see all the interfaces, including those specific to Internet Explorer 5, in Figure 11-2.

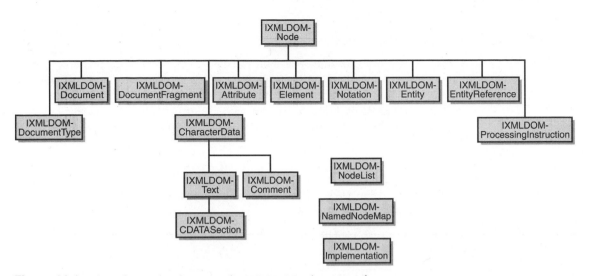

Figure 11-1. *The relationship between the W3C DOM object interfaces.*

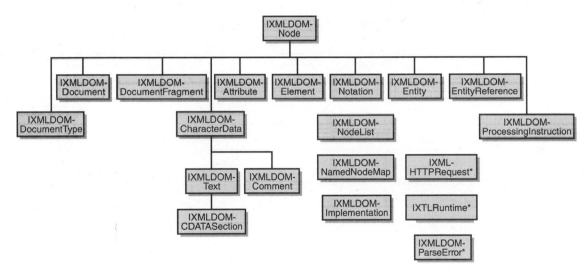

Figure 11-2. *Internet Explorer 5 DOM interfaces.*

Let's look at how to code some of the methods and properties that belong to the *IXMLDOMNode* interface.

NOTE   The following example will show you how to use some of the properties and methods of the *IXMLDOMNode* interface using Visual Basic. If you have access to Visual Basic, I highly recommend that you follow the examples. If you don't have Visual Basic, you can easily convert this example to a script sample. This example will print out the values of various properties to the Immediate Window.

To create the sample application, follow these steps:

1. Open Visual Basic, create a standard EXE project, and change the name of the default form to *frmDOMTest*.

2. Choose References from the Project menu, and add a reference to *Microsoft XML, version 2.0*.

3. Add a command button to *frmDOMTest* called *cmdNode* with a caption *Nodes*.

4. Add the following code to the click event handler of *cmdNode*:

```
Private Sub cmdNode_Click()
Dim objXMLDoc As DOMDocument
'Create a node object that is a reference to the root object.
Dim objRoot As IXMLDOMNode
'Create a node object that can be used to create a new node.
Dim objNewNode As IXMLDOMNode
Set objXMLDoc = New DOMDocument
'Turn off asynchronous load as we do not need it for this example.
objXMLDoc.async = False
'Open the file shown below.
objXMLDoc.Load ("c:\Books.xml")
'The documentElement will return the root element.
Set objRoot = objXMLDoc.documentElement
'Begin printing out properties for the root.
Debug.Print "XML for the root: " & vbCrLf & objRoot.xml
Debug.Print "BaseName for the root: " & objRoot.baseName
Debug.Print "Namespace prefix for the root: " & objRoot.prefix
Debug.Print "DataType for the root: " & objRoot.dataType
'We will begin to walk through the document starting at the first
'child.
Debug.Print "First Child XML for the root: " & vbCrLf & _
                objRoot.firstChild.xml
'We will get the next child, which is two elements down from
'the root.
```

```
Debug.Print "First Child of Child XML for the root: " & _
                objRoot.firstChild.firstChild.xml
'Nextsibling will return a node on the same level, in this case
'the same level as the second element down from the root.
Debug.Print "Second Child of Child XML for the root: " & _
                objRoot.firstChild.firstChild.nextSibling.xml
Debug.Print "Third Child of Child XML for the root: " & _
                objRoot.firstChild.firstChild.nextSibling. _
                nextSibling.xml
Debug.Print "Fourth Child of Child XML for the root: " & _
                objRoot.firstChild.firstChild.nextSibling. _
                nextSibling.nextSibling.xml
Debug.Print "Namespace URI for the root: " & _
                objRoot.namespaceURI
Debug.Print "Nodename for the root: " & objRoot.nodeName
Debug.Print "NodeType for the root: " & objRoot.nodeType
Debug.Print "NodeType String for the root: " & _
                objRoot.nodeTypeString
Debug.Print "NodeValue for the root: " & objRoot.nodeValue
Debug.Print "parentNode for the root: " & _
                objRoot.parentNode.xml
'Using XSL to get a single node
Debug.Print "XSL selecting first child node of the item node: " & _
        vbCrLf & objRoot.selectSingleNode("item/*").xml
Set objNewNode = objXMLDoc.createNode(1, "test", "")
objRoot.appendChild objNewNode
Debug.Print "Root XML after appending: " & vbCrLf & objRoot.xml
Set objNewNode = Nothing
Set objRoot = Nothing
Set objXMLDoc = Nothing

End Sub
```

Notice that we first get a reference to the document object. Using this reference, we can get a reference to the *XMLDOMNode* object. Then we start navigating the nodes in the XML document. Finally, we create a node named *test* and append it as a child node to the *root* node. To test this application, let's create an XML document called Books.xml in the C:\ directory with the following XML:

```
<?xml version="1.0" ?>
<northwind:BOOKS xmlns:northwind="www.northwindtraders.com/PO">
   <item>
      <title>Number, the Language of Science</title>
```

(continued)

```
        <author>Danzig</author>
        <price>5.95</price>
        <quantity>3</quantity>
    </item>
</northwind:BOOKS>
```

When you run the program and click the *Nodes* button, the results are as follows:

```
XML for the root:
<northwind:BOOKS xmlns:acme="www.northwindtraders.com/PO">
    <item>
        <title>Number, the Language of Science</title>
        <author>Danzig</author>
        <price>5.95</price>
        <quantity>3</quantity>
    </item>
</northwind:BOOKS>
BaseName for the root:BOOKS
Namespace prefix for the root:northwind
DataType for the root:
First Child XML for the root:
<item>
    <title>Number, the Language of Science</title>
    <author>Danzig</author>
    <price>5.95</price>
    <quantity>3</quantity>
</item>
First Child of Child XML for the root: <title>Number, the Language
    of Science</title>
Second Child of Child XML for the root: <author>Danzig</author>
Third Child of Child XML for the root: <price>5.95</price>
Fourth Child of Child XML for the root: <quantity>3</quantity>
Namespace URI for the root: www.northwindtraders.com/PO
Nodename for the root: northwind:BOOKS
NodeType for the root: 1
NodeType String for the root: element
NodeValue for the root:
parentNode for the root: <?xml version="1.0"?>
<northwind:BOOKS xmlns:northwind="www.northwindtraders.com/PO">
    <item>
        <title>Number, the Language of Science</title>
        <author>Danzig</author>
        <price>5.95</price>
        <quantity>3</quantity>
```

```
    </item>
</northwind:BOOKS>

XSL selecting first child node of ITEM:
<title>Number, the Language of Science</title>
Root XML after appending:
<northwind:BOOKS xmlns:northwind="www.northwindtraders.com/PO">
    <item>
        <title>Number, the Language of Science</title>
        <author>Danzig</author>
        <price>5.95</price>
        <quantity>3</quantity>
    </item>
    <test/></northwind:BOOKS>
```

Notice that the *test* element was inserted as the last child of the root, which is what we would have expected. Once this element is inserted, you can add text values or make other changes. All the sample programs discussed in this chapter, including the Visual Basic sample program and Books.xml, are available on the companion CD.

> **NOTE** Though we have not discussed XSL yet, we used XSL to get a single node in the previous application. XSL defines the location of elements using the XPath syntax. We'll discuss XSL in detail in Chapter 12. In this chapter, we will use the XPath syntax with the *selectSingleNode* method.

Several methods and properties belonging to the document object will return other objects in the hierarchy, such as *selectNodes* or *attributes*. We'll discuss these methods and properties while examining other object interfaces in the XML DOM.

XMLDOMNodeList Object

The *XMLDOMNodeList* object is a collection of node objects. It is primarily used to iterate through the element nodes. This object implements the *IXMLDOMNodeList* interface. The *IXMLDOMNodeList* interface reflects the current state of the nodes in the document, so a change in the nodes will be immediately reflected in the object. The property and methods of *IXMLDOMNodeList* are as follows:

IXMLDOMNODELIST PROPERTY

Name	*Description*
length	Returns the number of nodes that are contained in the node list.

IXMLDOMNODELIST METHODS

Name	Description
item (index)	Returns the node located at position *index* in the node list. The first node is indexed as 0.
nextNode()*	Returns the next node object in the node list. If there are no more nodes, it returns *null*.
reset()*	Resets the pointer so that it points before the first node element.

For an example of the *IXMLDOMNodeList* interface, you can add an attribute to the XML document and another command button to the *frmDOMTest* form. To do so, follow these steps:

1. Open the XML document Books.xml and change the *title* element to the following:

   ```
   <title language="English">Number, the Language of Science
   </title>
   ```

2. Add another command button to the *frmDOMTest* form called *cmdNodeList* with the caption *NodeList*.

3. Add the following code to the click event handler of the *cmdNodeList* button:

   ```
   Private Sub cmdNodeList_Click()
       Dim objNodeList As IXMLDOMNodeList
       Dim objXMLDoc As DOMDocument
       Set objXMLDoc = New DOMDocument
       objXMLDoc.async = False
       objXMLDoc.Load ("c:\Books.xml")
       Set objNodeList = _
           objXMLDoc.documentElement.firstChild.childNodes
       Debug.Print "The second item's basename is: " & _
           objNodeList.Item(2).baseName
       Debug.Print "The number of nodes are: " & objNodeList.length
       Debug.Print "The first node xml is: " & vbCrLf & _
           objNodeList.nextNode.xml
       Debug.Print "The second node xml is: " & _
           objNodeList.nextNode.xml
       Debug.Print "The third node xml is: " & _
   ```

```
            objNodeList.nextNode.xml
            objNodeList.Reset
        Debug.Print "After reset, the first node xml is: " & _
            vbCrLf & objNodeList.nextNode.xml
        Dim intNodeCounter As Integer
        For intNodeCounter = 0 To objNodeList.length - 1
            Debug.Print "The " & "xml of node" & _
            Str(intNodeCounter + 1) & " is: " & vbCrLf & _
            objNodeList.Item(intNodeCounter).xml
        Next
        Set objNodeList = Nothing
        Set objXMLDoc = Nothing
    End Sub
```

Notice that, once again, we first get a reference to the document object. Once we have this reference, we can get a reference to the *IXMLDOMNodeList* interface. Then we use the *item*, *nextNode*, and *reset* methods of the *IXMLDOMNodeList* interface to navigate the document. Last, we print all the nodes in the collection with a loop. When you run this updated application and click the *NodeList* button, the results are as follows:

```
The second item's basename is: price
The number of nodes are: 4
The first node xml is:
<title language="English">Number, the Language of Science</title>
The second node xml is: <author>Danzig</author>
The third node xml is: <price>5.95</price>
After reset, the first node xml is:
<title language="English">Number, the Language of Science</title>
The xml of node 1 is:
<title language="English">Number, the Language of Science</title>
The xml of node 2 is:
<author>Danzig</author>
The xml of node 3 is:
<price>5.95</price>
The xml of node 4 is:
<quantity>3</quantity>
```

Notice that the *attribute* node was not included in the results. We will need to use the *IXMLDOMNamedNodeMap* interface to get a reference to *attribute* nodes.

XMLDOMNamedNodeMap Object

The *XMLDOMNamedNodeMap* object implements the *IXMLDOMNamedNodeMap* interface. This interface is similar to the *IXMLDOMNodeList* interface except that it allows you to iterate through attributes and *namespace* nodes. The *IXMLDOMNamedNodeMap* interface has the same *length* property as the *IXMLDOMNodeList* interface. *IXMLDOMNamedNodeMap* also has the same *item*, *nextNode*, and *reset* methods as the *IXMLDOMNodeList* interface. The additional methods that are associated with the *IXMLDOMNamedNodeMap* are as follows:

ADDITIONAL *IXMLDOMNAMEDNODEMAP* METHODS

Name	Description
getNamedItem (name)	Retrieves the node object with the specified name. This method is usually used to retrieve an attribute from an element.
*getQualifiedItem (baseName, namespace)**	Returns the node object with the specified *baseName* and namespace.
removeNamedItem (name)	Removes the node object that has the specified name from the named node map. This method is usually used to remove an attribute.
*removeQualifiedItem (baseName, namespace)**	Removes the node object with the specified *baseName* and *namespace*. This method is usually used to remove attributes from the collection.
setNamedItem (newNode)	Inserts a new node into the collection. If a node with the same name as the *newNode* already exists, it's replaced.

To illustrate how to use the methods and properties of *IXMLDOMNamedNodeMap*, add another command button to the *frmDOMTest* form with the name *cmdNamedNodeMap* and the caption *NamedNodeMap*. Add the following code to the click event handler of the *cmdNamedNodeMap* button:

```
Private Sub cmdNamedNodeMap_Click()
    Dim objNamedNodeMap As IXMLDOMNamedNodeMap
    Dim objXMLDoc As DOMDocument

    Set objXMLDoc = New DOMDocument
    objXMLDoc.async = False
    objXMLDoc.Load ("c:\Books.xml")

    Set objNamedNodeMap = objXMLDoc.documentElement.Attributes
    Debug.Print _
        "The root's first attribute node's basename is: " & _
        objNamedNodeMap.Item(0).baseName
    Debug.Print "The number of root's attribute nodes is: " & _
        objNamedNodeMap.length
    Debug.Print "The first node xml is: " & _
        objNamedNodeMap.nextNode.xml

    Set objNamedNodeMap = _
        objXMLDoc.documentElement.firstChild.firstChild.Attributes
    Debug.Print _
        "The title element's attribute node's" & _
        " basename is: " & objNamedNodeMap.Item(0).baseName
    Debug.Print "The number of the title element's " & _
        "attribute nodes is: " & objNamedNodeMap.length
    Set objNamedNodeMap = Nothing
    Set objXMLDoc = Nothing

End Sub
```

Once again, to move through the XML document you will begin by getting a reference to a document object. This time, you will use the *attributes* property of the document object to get a reference to the *IXMLDOMNamedNodeMap* interface. When you run this example and click the *NamedNodeMap* button, the results are as follows:

```
The root's first attribute node's basename is: northwind
The number of the root's attribute nodes is: 1
The first node xml is:xmlns: northwind="www.northwindtraders.com/PO"
The title element's attribute node's baseName is: language
The number of the title element's attribute nodes is: 1
```

Thus, using the *IXMLDOMDocument* interface's *attributes* property and the *IXMLDOMNamedNodeMap* interface we are able to get information about the *namespace* and *attribute* nodes.

XMLDOMDocumentType Object

The *XMLDOMDocumentType* object implements *IXMLDOMDocumentType* interface. The *doctype* property of the *IXMLDOMDocument* interface identifies the document's *IXMLDOMDocumentType* interface. The *IXMLDOMDocumentType* interface gets information on the document type declaration in the XML document. This interface also extends the *IXMLDOMNode* interface, so it has all the properties and methods of the *IXMLDOMNode* interface. The *IXMLDOMDocumentType* interface also implements the following extended properties:

ADDITIONAL *IXMLDOMDOCUMENTTYPE* PROPERTIES

Name	Description
entities	Returns a node list containing references to the entity objects declared in the DTD
name	Returns the name of the document type for the document
notations	Returns a node list containing references to the notation objects in the DTD

Now that the *IXMLDOMDocumentType* interface contains information associated with the DTD, let's create a DTD named Books.dtd for the document using the following text:

```
<!ELEMENT northwind:BOOKS  (item)>
<!ATTLIST northwind:BOOKS  xmlns:northwind CDATA  #FIXED
                           "www.northwindtraders.com/PO">
<!ENTITY % ItemElements "(title, author, price, quantity)">
<!ENTITY copyright "&#xA9;">
<!ELEMENT item  %ItemElements;>
<!ELEMENT title (#PCDATA)>
<!ATTLIST title language CDATA  #REQUIRED>
<!ELEMENT author (#PCDATA)>
<!ELEMENT price (#PCDATA)>
<!ELEMENT quantity (#PCDATA)>
```

Notice that we declared a general entity called *copyright* in the above DTD, thus we need to reference this entity in the Books.xml document. We also need to add a line of code to the XML document so that it will reference the DTD:

```
<?xml version="1.0" ?>
<!DOCTYPE northwind:BOOKS SYSTEM "c:\Books.dtd">
<northwind:BOOKS xmlns:northwind="www.northwindtraders.com/PO">
   <item>
      <title language="English">Number, the Language of Science
```

```
        &copyright;
        </title>
        <author>Danzig</author>
        <price>5.95</price>
        <quantity>3</quantity>
    </item>
</northwind:BOOKS>
```

NOTE Remember that the DTD has no ability to resolve namespaces. Thus, you must declare the elements that use the namespace with the namespace prefix and define an attribute for the namespace. The XML document, though, can resolve the namespace information.

Now let's take a look at how to use the properties of the *IXMLDOMDocumentType* interface in our example application. First, add another command button to the *frmDOMTest* form with the name *cmdDocumentType* and the caption *Document Type*. Then add the following code to the click event of this button:

```
Private Sub cmdDocumentType_Click()
    Dim objDocumentType As IXMLDOMDocumentType
    Dim objXMLDoc As DOMDocument

    Set objXMLDoc = New DOMDocument
    objXMLDoc.async = False
    objXMLDoc.Load ("c:\Books.xml")

    Set objDocumentType = objXMLDoc.doctype
    Debug.Print objDocumentType.Name
    Debug.Print objDocumentType.xml
    Debug.Print objDocumentType.entities.length
    Debug.Print objDocumentType.entities.Item(0).xml
End Sub
```

When you run this example and click the *DocumentType* button, you'll see the following output:

```
northwind:BOOKS
<!DOCTYPE northwind:BOOKS SYSTEM "c:\Books.dtd">
1
<!ENTITY copyright "©">
```

Once again, you have created a reference to an *IXMLDOMDocument* interface. With this reference, you can use the *doctype* property to get a reference to an *IXMLDOMDocumentType* interface. Then you use the *name* and *xml* properties of the *IXMLDOMDocumentType* interface to get a node's name and its XML content. Notice that the *parameter* entity was not included in the entities collection.

XMLDOMDocumentFragment Object

The *XMLDOMDocumentFragment* object will be used to create fragments of documents that can be appended to another document. When the *XMLDOMDocumentFragment* object is inserted into a document object, the root node of the *XMLDOMDocument-Fragment* is not inserted, only its children. Thus, *XMLDOMDocumentFragment* objects are useful for inserting child elements into a document.

The *XMLDOMDocumentFragment* object implements the *IXMLDOMDocument-Fragment* interface. This interface inherits all the *IXMLDOMNode* interface's methods and properties, but it doesn't extend the interface, so this interface has no additional methods or properties of its own.

XMLDOMElement Object

The *XMLDOMElement* object contains the elements in the document and is the most common node. The text nodes belonging to an element object contain the content of the element. If there is no text content, the *XMLDOMText* object will be *null*. This object implements the *IXMLDOMElement* interface. When working with the *IXMLDOMElement* interface, you must know beforehand what the names of the elements and attributes are that you want to retrieve and place them in the code. This is because the *IXMLDOMElement* interface sets and retrieves attributes and elements by their names.

In addition to the methods and properties of the *IXMLDOMNode* interface, the *IXMLDOMElement* interface has the following extended property and methods:

EXTENDED *IXMLDOMELEMENT* PROPERTY

Name	Description
tagName	Sets or returns the name of the element

EXTENDED *IXMLDOMELEMENT* METHODS

Name	Description
getAttribute (attributeName)	Returns the value of the attribute with the specified *attributeName*.
getAttributeNode (attributeName)	Returns the attribute node object with the specified *attributeName*.
getElementsByTagName (elementName)	Returns an *XMLDOMNodeList* object that contains all the descendant elements named *elementName*.
normalize()	Combines the adjacent text nodes into one unified *text* node. Normalizes all descendant *text* nodes of the element.

Name	*Description*
removeAttribute (attributeName)	Removes the value of the attribute named *attributeName*.
removeAttributeNode (attributeNode)	Removes the *attribute* node named *attributeNode* and returns the node. If there is a default value in the schema or DTD, a new *attribute* node will be created with the default value.
setAttribute (attributeName, newValue)	Sets the *attribute* node named *attributeName* to the value *newValue*.
setAttributeNode (attributeName)	Adds a new *attribute* node to the element. An existing *attribute* node by the same name will be replaced.

You can get a reference to an *IXMLDOMElement* interface by using the *selectNodes* method and XSL. You will now create an example to select a single *element* node. To do so, follow these steps:

1. Add another command button to the *frmDOMTest* form with the name *cmdElement* and the caption *Element*.

2. Insert the following code into the click event handler of this button:

```
Private Sub cmdElement_Click()
Dim objXMLDoc As DOMDocument

Dim objElement As IXMLDOMElement

Set objXMLDoc = New DOMDocument
objXMLDoc.async = False
objXMLDoc.Load ("c:\Books.xml")

Set objElement = objXMLDoc.selectNodes("//item/*").Item(1)
Debug.Print objElement.xml

Set objElement = Nothing
Set objXMLDoc = Nothing
End Sub
```

This example application selects the second child node of the *item* element. Then it retrieves the entire XML content of this node by using the *xml* property. When you run this example and click the *Element* button, the result is as follows:

```
<author>Danzig</author>
```

You can get a reference to the *XMLDOMAttribute*, *XMLDOMEntity*, *XMLDOMEntityReference*, *XMLDOMNotation*, *XMLDOMCharacterData*, *XMLDOMText*, *XMLDOMCDATASection*, *XMLDOMComment*, and *XMLDOMProcessingInstruction* by using XSL. You can get references to these node objects just as we used the XSL statement "*//item/**" to get references to the node *item* in the previous application. (We will discuss the XSL syntax in detail in Chapter 12.) So in the following sections, we'll examine these interfaces without demonstrating how to use them in the applications.

XMLDOMAttribute Object

The *XMLDOMAttribute* object represents an *attribute* node of the *XMLDOMElement* object. This object implements the *IXMLDOMAttribute* interface. In addition to the properties and methods it inherits from the *IXMLDOMNode* interface, the *IXMLDOMAttribute* interface has the following additional properties:

EXTENDED *IXMLDOMATTRIBUTE* PROPERTIES

Name	Description
name	Sets or returns the name of the attribute
value	Sets or returns the value of the attribute

NOTE   The W3C specification lists this object as the *attr* object, instead of the *XMLDOMAttribute* object.

XMLDOMEntity Object

The *XMLDOMEntity* object represents a parsed or unparsed entity declared in a DTD. The *XMLDOMEntity* object is not the entity declaration. This object implements the *IXMLDOMEntity* interface. The properties of this interface are read-only. Like most of the other DOM interfaces, this interface inherits the *IXMLDOMNode* interface too. In addition to the *IXMLDOMNode* properties and methods, the *IXMLDOMEntity* object extends the *IXMLDOMNNode* object with the following properties:

EXTENDED *IXMLDOMENTITY* PROPERTIES

Name	Description
publicID	Returns the value of the PUBLIC identifier for the entity node
systemID	Returns the value of the SYSTEM identifier for the entity node
notationName	Returns the notation name

XMLDOMEntityReference Object

The *XMLDOMEntityReference* object represents an *entity reference* node contained in the XML document. Remember that an XML processor doesn't expand the entities until they are needed. Thus, if the XML processor doesn't expand the entities, there will be no *XMLDOMEntityReference* objects. The replacement text will be located in the *text* property. The *IXMLDOMEntityReference* interface implemented by the *XMLDOMEntityReference* object inherits all the methods and properties of, but does not extend, the *IXMLDOMNode* interface.

XMLDOMNotation Object

The *XMLDOMNotation* object represents a notation declared in the DTD with the declaration <!NOTATION>. The *XMLDOMNotation* object implements the *IXMLDOMNotation* interface that inherits all the methods and properties of the *IXMLDOMNode* interface and extends the *IXMLDOMNode* interface with the following properties:

ADDITIONAL *IXMLDOMNOTATION* PROPERTIES

Name	Description
publicID	Returns the value of the PUBLIC identifier for the *notation* node
systemID	Returns the value of the SYSTEM identifier for the *notation* node

XMLDOMCharacterData Object

The *XMLDOMCharacterData* object makes it easier to work with the text content in an XML document. The *IXMLDOMCharacterData* interface implemented by the *XMLDOMCharacterData* object also inherits the *IXMLDOMNode* interface, so it includes all the properties and methods of the *IXMLDOMNode* interface. Moreover, it extends the *IXMLDOMNode* interface with the following properties and methods:

EXTENDED *IXMLDOMCHARACTERDATA* PROPERTIES

Name	Description
data	Contains the node's data. The actual data will depend on the type of node.
length	Returns the number of characters in the data string.

EXTENDED *IXMLDOMCHARACTERDATA* METHODS

Name	Description
appendData (text)	Appends the *text* argument onto the existing data string
deleteData (charOffset, numChars)	Deletes *numChars* characters off the data string starting at *charOffset*
insertData (charOffset, text)	Inserts the supplied text into the data string at the *charOffset*
replaceData (charOffset, numChars, text)	Replaces *numChars* characters with the supplied text starting at *charOffset*
substringData (charOffset, numChars)	Returns the *numChars* characters as a string, starting at *charOffset*, in the data string

XMLDOMText Object

The *XMLDOMText* object represents the *text* node of an element or an attribute. You can use the *XMLDOMText* object to build *text* nodes and append them into an XML document. The *IXMLDOMText* interface implemented by the *XMLDOMText* object inherits the *IXMLDOMCharacterData* interface and extends it with the following method:

EXTENDED *IXMLDOMTEXT* METHOD

Name	Description
splitText (charOffset)	Splits the node into two nodes at the specified character offset and then inserts the new node into the XML document immediately following the node

XMLDOMCDATASection Object

An *XMLDOMCDATASection* object is used for sections of text that are not to be interpreted by the processor as markup. The *XMLDOMCDATASection* object implements the *IXMLDOMCDATASection* interface. This interface inherits the *IXMLDOMText* interface and has the same methods and properties as the *IXMLDOMText* interface.

XMLDOMComment **Object**

The *XMLDOMComment* object contains comments that are in the XML document. The *IXMLDOMComment* interface implemented by this object inherits the *IXMLDOM-CharacterData* interface and also possesses the same methods and properties as *IXMLDOMCharacterData*. The *IXMLDOMComment* interface does not extend the *IXML-DOMCharacterData* interface.

XMLDOMProcessingInstruction **Object**

The *XMLDOMProcessingInstruction* object contains the processing instructions in the document between the <? tag and the ?> tag. The content enclosed in these two tags is divided into the target and data content. The *IXMLDOMProcessingInstruction* interface implemented by the *XMLDOMProcessingInstruction* object inherits the *IXML-DOMNode* interface and has the same methods as the *IXMLDOMNode* interface. It extends the *IXMLDOMNode* interface with the following properties:

EXTENDED *IXMLDOMPROCESSINGINSTRUCTION* PROPERTIES

Name	Description
data	Sets or returns the content of the processing instruction, which doesn't contain the target
target	Sets or returns the target application to which the processing instruction is directed

XMLDOMImplementation **Object**

Because different applications that support XML can support different features of XML, the W3C included the *XMLDOMImplementation* object, which can be used to determine whether certain features are supported in a particular application. The *XMLDOMImplementation* object implements the *IXMLDOMImplementation* interface. This interface has one method called *hasFeature* that returns *true* if the specified feature is implemented by the specified version of the XML DOM implementation. To see how this object works, add another command button to the *frmDOMTest* form with the name *cmdImplementation* and the caption *Implementation*. Add the following code to the click event of this button:

```
Private Sub cmdImplementation _Click()
    Dim objImplementation As IXMLDOMImplementation
    Dim objXMLDoc As DOMDocument
```

(continued)

```
Set objXMLDoc = New DOMDocument
objXMLDoc.async = False
objXMLDoc.Load ("c:\Books.xml")
Set objImplementation = objXMLDoc.implementation
'Currently accepted values for feature: XML, DOM, and MS-DOM
Debug.Print "MS-DOM: " & _
     objImplementation.hasFeature("MS-DOM", "1.0")
Debug.Print "XML: " & _
     objImplementation.hasFeature("XML", "1.0")
Debug.Print "DOM: " & _
     objImplementation.hasFeature("DOM", "1.0")
End Sub
```

If you have Internet Explorer 5 installed on your computer, running this application and clicking the *Implementation* button will give you the following results:

```
MS-DOM: True
XML: True
DOM: True
```

HasFeature returning true shows that Internet Explorer 5 supports XML, DOM, and the MS-DOM.

XMLDOMParseError Object

The *XMLDOMParseError* object is an extension to the W3C specification. It can be used to get detailed information on the last error that occurred while either loading or parsing a document. The *XMLDOMParseError* object implements the *IXMLDOMParseError* interface that has the following properties:

I X M L D O M P A R S E E R R O R PROPERTIES

Name	Description
errorCode	Returns the error number or error code as a decimal integer.
filepos	Returns the absolute character position in the document where the error occurred.
line	Returns the number of the line where the error occurred.
linepos	Returns the absolute character position in the line where the error occurred.
reason	Returns a description of the source and reason for the error. If the error is in a schema or DTD, it can include the URL for the DTD or schema and the node in the schema or DTD where the error occurred.
srcText	Returns the full text of the line that contains the error. If the error cannot be assigned to a specific line, an empty line is returned.
url	Returns the URL for the most recent XML document that contained an error.

To see how the *IXMLDOMParseError* interface is used, we will make a change to the first line of code in the Books.dtd: *<!ELEMENT northwind:BOOKS (item)>* by removing the *northwind:* from the line, as shown here:

```
<!ELEMENT BOOKS  (item )>
```

Add another command button to the *frmDOCTest* form with the name *cmdParseError* and the caption *ParseError*. In the click event handler of this button, place the following code:

```
Private Sub cmdParseError _Click()
    Dim objXMLDoc As DOMDocument
    Dim objXMLParseError As IXMLDOMParseError
    On Error GoTo cmdParseErrorError
    Set objXMLDoc = New DOMDocument
    objXMLDoc.async = False
    objXMLDoc.Load ("c:\Books.xml")
    'Check whether there was an error parsing the file using the
    'parseError object.
    If objXMLDoc.parseError.errorCode <> 0 Then
        'If there was an error, raise it to jump into error trap.
        Err.Raise objXMLDoc.parseError.errorCode
    End If
    Exit Sub
'Error Trap
cmdParseErrorError:
    Set objXMLParseError = objXMLDoc.parseError
    With objXMLParseError
        'Because of the With objXMLParseError, .errorCode is the
        'same as objXMLParseError.errorCode.
        'First check whether the error was caused by a parse error.
        If .errorCode <> 0 Then
            Debug.Print "The following error occurred:" & vbCrLf & _
                "error code: " & .errorCode & vbCrLf & _
                "error file position: " & .filepos & vbCrLf & _
                "error line: " & .Line & vbCrLf & _
                "error line position: " & .linepos & vbCrLf & _
                "error reason: " & vbCrLf & .reason & vbCrLf & _
                "error source text: " & vbCrLf & .srcText & _
                        " Test:cmdParseError"
        Else
            'If the error was not caused by a parse error, use
            'regular Visual Basic error object.
            MsgBox "The following error has occurred:" & vbCrLf & _
                "Error Description: " & Err.Description & _
                                    vbCrLf & _
```

(continued)

```
                      "Error Source: " & vbCrLf & Err.Source &  _
                              " Test:cmdParseError" & vbCrLf & _
                      "Error Number: " & Err.Number
        End If
     End With

     Set objXMLParseError = Nothing
     Set objXMLDoc = Nothing
End Sub
```

Before you actually run this code, take a look at it to see what an error handler in production code should look like. A parse error does not raise its error. After the parse error occurs, the Visual Basic error number (*Err.Number*) is still 0. Thus, you must use the *ParseError* object to check for an error after you load an XML document. If there is a parse error, you can raise an error, as was done above, to bring you into the error trap.

The error trap provides a message if the error occurred in parsing the file. If the error was caused for some other reason, the standard Visual Basic *Err* error object is used. Also notice that the name of the application and the method are included in the source, making it easier to find and fix bugs.

Now you can run the updated application and click the *ParseError* button. With the change in the DTD, you will receive the following message:

```
The following error occurred:
error code: -1072898035
error file position: 137
error line: 3
error line position: 64
error reason:
The element 'northwind:BOOKS' is used but not declared in the
DTD/Schema.

error source text:
<northwind:BOOKS xmlns:northwind="www.northwindtraders.com/PO">
Test:cmdParseError
```

In this case, because the DTD has no awareness of namespaces, the namespace qualified northwind:BOOKS in the XML document no longer matches the DTD declaration.

To create a different error, change the DTD back to its original form by adding back the *northwind:*. Remove *#FIXED "www.northwindtraders.com/PO"* from the second line in the DTD, and the second line will look as follows:

```
<!ATTLIST northwind:BOOKS  xmlns:northwindCDATA>
```

Now run the application and click the *ParseError* button; the error message will look as follows:

```
The following error occurred:
error code: -1072896766
error file position: 86
error line: 2
error line position: 51
error reason:
A string literal was expected, but no opening quote character
  was found.

error source text:
<!ATTLIST northwind:BOOKS  xmlns:northwind CDATA>
Test:cmdParseError
```

Notice that the error source text is now the information from the DTD. The reason might not be that obvious, but by looking at the error reason you will see that you need to include #REQUIRED, #FIXED, or #IMPLIED in the DTD. You must use #FIXED because this is a namespace attribute.

XTLRuntime Object

The *XTLRuntime* object works with XSL style sheets. It implements the *IXTLRuntime* interface that has nine methods: *absoluteChildNumber*, *ancestorChildNumber*, *child-Number*, *depth*, *formatDate*, *formatIndex*, *formatNumber*, *formatTime,* and *uniqueID*. We will cover XSL style sheets and these methods in Chapter 12.

XMLHTTPRequest Object

The *XMLHTTPRequest* object, which is an extension of the W3C specification, can be used to send and receive HTTP messages to and from a Web server. Once a message is received, it can be parsed by XML DOM objects. You could use the *XMLHTTPRequest* object to create applications that build and send SOAP messages to the server. This object implements the *IXMLHTTPRequest* interface, which has the following properties and methods:

IXMLHTTPREQUEST PROPERTIES

Name	Description
readyState	Indicates the current state of the document being loaded. The value changes as the XML document loads.
responseBody	Returns the response as an array of unsigned bytes.
responseStream	Returns the response object as an *IStream* object.
responseText	Returns the response object as a text string.
responseXML	Returns the response as an XML document. When this property is used, validation is turned off to prevent the parser from attempting to download a linked DTD or schema.
status	Returns a status code as a long integer.
statusText	Returns the status as a string.

IXMLHTTPREQUEST METHODS

Name	Description
abort()*	Cancels the current HTTP request
getAllResponseHeaders()*	Returns all the HTTP headers as name value pairs separated by carriage return-linefeeds
getResponseHeader (headerName)*	Gets the response header with the name *headerName*
open (method, url, async, userID, password)*	Initializes a request and specifies the HTTP method, the URL, and if the response is asynchronous, the user information
send()*	Sends an HTTP request to the server and waits to receive a response
setRequestHeader (headerName, value)	Sets HTTP headers that are sent to the server

This chapter has described a complete set of objects that can allow you to manipulate XML information and send HTTP streams to and from a Web server. It's time we look at a more complete example of using some of these objects, including the *XMLHTTPRequest* object. To do this, we will write the code to create a SOAP client and server application.

SOAP APPLICATION USING XML DOM

The SOAP application you are about to create will use Visual Basic on the client side and Active Server Pages (ASP) on the server side. The XML DOM will be used on both the client and the server.

Instead of loading XML data from a file or a string, this application will build an XML file using the XML DOM objects and show you how to write code to build XML documents dynamically.

In a real application, you could build the XML document using a Visual Basic application that processes SOAP requests or use JScript or VBScript in a browser application with the values that the user has inputted into the browser form. For this example, we will provide values for the XML elements.

We will start by creating a new Visual Basic EXE project. For this example, you will need a copy of the XML parser, which at the time of this printing is version 3. Thus, you should add a reference to the Microsoft XML 3.0 by choosing References from the Project menu, and then choosing Microsoft XML version 3 from the References dialog box.

> NOTE   This book will use both the 3.0 and 2.6 versions of the XML parser. When you are working with these examples, you can use the most current version by changing the declarations of the *DOMDocument* objects.

Add a button to the *frmDOMTest* form with the name *cmdSoap* and the caption *Soap*. Enter the following code into the click event handler of this button:

```
Dim objXMLDoc As DOMDocument30
Dim objHTTPRequest As XMLHTTP30
Dim objXMLDocResponse As DOMDocument30
Set objHTTPRequest = New XMLHTTP30
Set objXMLDoc = New DOMDocument
Set objXMLDocResponse = New DOMDocument30
Set objXMLDocNode = New DOMDocument30
Dim lngResponse As Long
Dim lngOrderID As Long
Dim strResponse As String

objXMLDoc.async = False
'We will begin by using the loadXML string to load in the root
'node.
```

(continued)

```
objXMLDoc.loadXML _
    "<SOAP-ENV:Envelope xmlns:SOAP-ENV = " & _
    "'http://schemas.xmlsoap.org/soap/envelope'" & _
    " xmlns:xsi='http://www.w3.org/1999/XMLSchema/instance' " & _
    " xsi:schemaLocation=" & _
    "'http://www.northwindtraders.com/schemas/NPOSchema.xsd'>" & _
    "<SOAP-ENV:Body xsi:type='northwindBody'><UpdatePO>" & _
    "<OrderID>" & "</OrderID>" & _
    "<return>" & strReturn & _
    "</return></UpdatePO></SOAP-ENV:Body>" & _
    "</SOAP-ENV:Envelope>"

'The createNode method returns a node object.
'If the element has a namespace prefix, it must be included.
'The appendChild method will take the node object created with
'createNode and add it to XML document node collection.
objXMLDoc.documentElement.appendChild _
    objXMLDoc.createNode(NODE_ELEMENT, "SOAP-ENV:Body", _
    "'http://schemas.xmlsoap.org/soap'")
'For an attribute, you must use the attributes property.
objXMLDoc.documentElement.firstChild.Attributes.setNamedItem _
    objXMLDoc.createNode(NODE_ATTRIBUTE, "xsi:type", _
    "xmlns:xsi='http://www.w3.org/1999/XMLSchema/instance'")
objXMLDoc.selectSingleNode _
    ("SOAP-ENV:Envelope/SOAP-ENV:Body").appendChild _
    objXMLDoc.createNode(NODE_ELEMENT, "UpdatePO", "")
objXMLDoc.selectSingleNode _
    ("SOAP-ENV:Envelope/SOAP-ENV:Body/UpdatePO"). _
    appendChild objXMLDoc.createNode(NODE_ELEMENT, "OrderID", "")
objXMLDoc.selectSingleNode _
    ("SOAP-ENV:Envelope/SOAP-ENV:Body/UpdatePO"). _
    appendChild objXMLDoc.createNode _
    (NODE_ELEMENT, "CustomerNumber", "")
objXMLDoc.selectSingleNode _
    ("SOAP-ENV:Envelope/SOAP-ENV:Body/UpdatePO"). _
    appendChild objXMLDoc.createNode(NODE_ELEMENT, "Item", "")
objXMLDoc.selectSingleNode _
    ("SOAP-ENV:Envelope/SOAP-ENV:Body/UpdatePO"). _
    appendChild objXMLDoc.createNode(NODE_ELEMENT, "Quantity", "")
objXMLDoc.selectSingleNode _
    ("SOAP-ENV:Envelope/SOAP-ENV:Body/UpdatePO"). _
    appendChild objXMLDoc.createNode(NODE_ELEMENT, "return", "")

'We must now set the values for each node.
'We will use XSL in selectSingleNode to get the node.
'For the attribute, we must use getNamedItem to get the attribute.
objXMLDoc.selectSingleNode("SOAP-ENV:Envelope/SOAP-ENV:Body"). _
    Attributes.getNamedItem("xsi:type").nodeValue = "NorthwindBody"
```

```
objXMLDoc.selectSingleNode _
    ("SOAP-ENV:Envelope/SOAP-ENV:Body/UpdatePO/OrderID").Text = "0"
objXMLDoc.selectSingleNode _
    ("SOAP-ENV:Envelope/SOAP-ENV:Body/UpdatePO/CustomerNumber"). _
    Text = "999"
objXMLDoc.selectSingleNode _
    ("SOAP-ENV:Envelope/SOAP-ENV:Body/UpdatePO/Item").Text = "89"
objXMLDoc.selectSingleNode _
    ("SOAP-ENV:Envelope/SOAP-ENV:Body/UpdatePO/return").Text = "0"
objXMLDoc.selectSingleNode _
    ("SOAP-ENV:Envelope/SOAP-ENV:Body/UpdatePO/Quantity"). _
    Text = "35"
'Initialize HTTP request with Post.
objHTTPRequest.open "POST", "http://localhost/XMLSample/SOAP.asp"
'Set the SOAP headers.
objHTTPRequest.setRequestHeader "POST", "/Northwind.Order HTTP/1.1"
objHTTPRequest.setRequestHeader "Host", "www.northwindtraders.com"
objHTTPRequest.setRequestHeader "Content-Type", "text/xml"
objHTTPRequest.setRequestHeader "content-length", _
    Len(objXMLDoc.xml)
objHTTPRequest.setRequestHeader _
    "SOAPAction", "urn: northwindtraders.com:PO#UpdatePO"
'Send the message.
objHTTPRequest.send objXMLDoc.xml
'Set the response document object equal to the responseXML object.
Set objXMLDocResponse = objHTTPRequest.responseXML

'Wait to get result.
Dim lLoopNum As Long
Do While objXMLDocResponse.selectSingleNode _
("SOAP-ENV:Envelope/SOAP-ENV:Body/UpdatePO/return") Is Nothing _
    And lLoopNum < 10000
    DoEvents
    lLoopNum = lLoopNum + 1
Loop
'Get the return values.
strResponse = objXMLDocResponse.selectSingleNode _
    ("SOAP-ENV:Envelope/SOAP-ENV:Body/UpdatePO/return").Text
If strResponse = "" Then
    'Raise an error here.
Else
    MsgBox "Response = " & strResponse
End If

lngOrderID = CLng(objXMLDocResponse.selectSingleNode _
    ("SOAP-ENV:Envelope/SOAP-ENV:Body/UpdatePO/OrderID").Text)

Set objXMLDocResponse = Nothing
Set objXMLDoc = Nothing
Set objHTTPRequest = Nothing
```

To be able to run the application, you need to create an object named *objOrderPO* that contains the *UpdatePO* method. Since we will not actually create this object, we will comment out the code where the method will be created and create dummy variables so you can run the example. You also need to create an ASP page named SOAP.asp and put it on the local server in a folder called *XMLSample* under the default Web site. Now let's take a look at how to create an ASP page.

The ASP page uses two document objects, one called *objXMLDocRequest*, which holds the XML document sent from the server, and the other called *objXMLDocResponse*, which contains the XML document that is returned to the server. The names of the object and the method that need to be called are retrieved from the header first. Next you retrieve the XML document from the request object, retrieve the parameter values located in the XML body, and finally create the object and call the method. Once the method has been called, the return XML string is built and placed in the response object.

Create an ASP page and add the following code:

```
<%@ Language=VBScript %>
<SCRIPT LANGUAGE=vbscript RUNAT=Server>
Dim objXMLDocRequest
Dim objXMLDocResponse
Dim result, strObject, strMethod
Dim strCustomerNumber, strItem, strReturn
Dim strOrderID, strQuantity

Set objXMLDocRequest= Server.CreateObject ("Microsoft.XMLDOM")
Set objXMLDocResponse= Server.CreateObject ("Microsoft.XMLDOM")
'You must set the content type so that the returning document will
'be identified as XML.
Response.ContentType = "text/xml"
'Load the posted XML document.
strObject= Request.ServerVariables.Item ("HTTP_POST")
'Remove /
strObject= Right(strObject, len(strObject)-1)
'Remove HTTP...
strObject= Left(strObject, instr(1, strObject, " ") )
strMethod= Request.ServerVariables.Item ("HTTP_SOAPAction")
'Strip off URL.
strMethod=Right(strMethod, len(strMethod)-instr(1, strMethod,"#"))
'Use the load method to get the XML sent from the client out of the
'request object.
objXMLDocRequest.load Request
'Now that you have the XML data, use the values in the XML
'document to set the local variables.
strCustomerNumber=objXMLDocRequest.SelectSingleNode _
    ("SOAP-ENV:Envelope/SOAP-ENV:Body/UpdatePO/CustomerNumber").Text
```

```
strItem = objXMLDocRequest.SelectSingleNode _
    ("SOAP-ENV:Envelope/SOAP-ENV:Body/UpdatePO/Item").Text
strQuantity = objXMLDocRequest.SelectSingleNode _
    ("SOAP-ENV:Envelope/SOAP-ENV:Body/UpdatePO/Quantity").Text
'Using the name of the object passed in the header, we will
'instantiate the object.
'Because we do not actually have an object called objOrderPO, we
'will comment out the next line of code.
'Set objOrderPO = _
'    server.CreateObject (Request.ServerVariables.Item(strObject))
'Call the correct method passing in the parameters.
Select Case strMethod
    Case "UpdatePO"
'Because we do not actually have an object called objOrderPO, we
'will comment out the next two lines of code. We are also adding
'dummy values for the strReturn and strOrderID variables.
    'strReturn=objOrderPO.UpdatePO _
    '(strCustomerName, strItem, strQuantity, strOrderID)
    strReturn="0"
    strOrderID="100"
    Case "DeletePO"
    strReturn=objOrderPO.DeletePO _
        (strCustomerName, strItem, strQuantity, strOrderID)
End Select
'Create XML that is going back to the client using a string.
objXMLDocResponse.LoadXML _
    "<SOAP-ENV:Envelope xmlns:SOAP-ENV =" & _
"'http://schemas.xmlsoap.org/soap/envelope'" & _
    " xmlns:xsi='http://www.w3.org/1999/XMLSchema/instance' " & _
    " xsi:schemaLocation=" & _
    "'http://www.northwindtraders.com/schemas/NPOSchema.xsd'>" & _
    "<SOAP-ENV:Body xsi:type='northwindBody'><UpdatePO>" & _
    "<OrderID>" & strOrderID & "</OrderID>" & _
    "<return>" & strReturn & _
    "</return></UpdatePO></SOAP-ENV:Body>" & _
    "</SOAP-ENV:Envelope>"
'Return the XML.
Response.Write objXMLDocResponse.xml
</SCRIPT>
```

In this example, you can see how tightly bound the client-side code is to the object that is being called. The client-side object has to build an XML document that contains the correct parameters and also has to create a header with the right object and method names.

XML PARSER VERSION 2.6 AND VERSION 3.0

The XML parser version 2.6 and version 3.0 extend the older version that came with Internet Explorer 5. The XML parser version 2.6 is a separate DLL (Msxml2.dll) that can be installed in addition to the original XML parser. Various options are available for running the two DLLs together, but those options are beyond the scope of this book. You can check the XML SDK 2.5 (which can be viewed on Microsoft's Web site) for more information about the DLLs. Version 3.0 of the parser is installed as a new DLL (Msxml3.dll) with new version-dependent CLSIDs and ProgIDs to protect those applications that use Msxml.dll or Msxml2.dll and allow you to choose the version of the parser to use in your code.

Version 2.6 comes with five additional XML document objects: *XMLDOM-Document2*, *XMLDOMSchemaCache*, *XMLDOMSelection*, *XMLDOMXSLProcessor*, and *XMLDOMXSLTemplate*. We will discuss the *XMLDOMXSLTemplate* and *XMLDOM-XSLProcessor* objects in Chapter 12 when we discuss XSL. Version 3.0 doesn't add any new features to version 2.6. Thus, we'll have a detailed discussion about the *XMLDOMDocument2*, *XMLDOMSchemaCache*, and *XMLDOMSelection* objects in the following section.

XMLDOMDocument2, XMLDOMSchemaCache, and XMLDOMSelection Objects

The *XMLDOMDocument2* object implements the *IXMLDOMDocument2* interface. This interface is an extension of the *IXMLDOMDocument* interface that supports schema caching and validation. The *IXMLDOMDocument2* interface inherits all the original properties and methods of the *IXMLDOMDocument* interface and adds the following new properties:

EXTENDED *IXMLDOMDOCUMENT2* PROPERTIES

Name	Description
namespaces	Returns a list of all of the namespaces in the document as an *XMLDOMSchemaCollection*(*schemaCache* object)
schemas	Locates all the schema documents using the *XMLDOMSchemaCollection* (*schemaCache* object)

The *XMLSchemaCache* object which implements the *IXMLDOMSchemaCollection* interface contains information about the schemas and namespaces used by an XML document. This interface has the following property and methods:

IXMLDOMSCHEMACOLLECTION PROPERTY

Name	Description
length	Returns the number of namespaces that are currently in the collection

IXMLDOMSCHEMACOLLECTION METHODS

Name	Description
add (namespaceURI, schema)	Adds a new schema to the schema collection. The specified schema is associated with the given namespace URI.
addCollection (XMLDOMSchemaCollection)	Adds all the schemas from another collection into the current collection.
get (namespaceURI)	Returns a read-only DOM node containing the <Schema> element.
namespaceURI (index)	Returns the namespace for the specified index.
remove (namespaceURI)	Removes the specified namespace from the collection.

Now that we've examined the properties and methods in the *IXMLDOM-Document2* interface and the *IXMLDOMSchemaCollection* interface, it's time to see how they are used in the application. Create a new Visual Basic Standard EXE project, and name the default form *frmTestDOM2*. In the form *frmTestDOM2*, place a command button with the name *cmdSchemas* and the caption *Schemas*. Place the following code in the click event handler of this button:

```
Private Sub cmdSchemas_Click()
    Dim objXMLDoc As DOMDocument26
    Dim objXMLSchemas As XMLSchemaCache
    Dim lngSchemaCounter As Long
    Set objXMLDoc = New DOMDocument
    objXMLDoc.async = False
    objXMLDoc.Load ("c:\Books.xml")
    Set objXMLSchemas = objXMLDoc.namespaces
    For lngSchemaCounter = 0 To objXMLSchemas.length - 1
        Debug.Print "URL: " & _
            objXMLSchemas.namespaceURI(lngSchemaCounter)
        Debug.Print "Type: " & _
            objXMLDoc.selectSingleNode("//author").dataType
    Next
    Set objXMLSchemas = Nothing
    Set objXMLDoc = Nothing
End Sub
```

This application loads the Books.xml document that contains a reference to the Books.dtd. If you run this program and click the *Schemas* button when the XML document is referencing the DTD, you will get the following result:

```
URL: www.northwindtraders.com/PO
Type:
```

Looking back at the original XML document, you have the following two lines of code:

```
<!DOCTYPE northwind:BOOKS SYSTEM "c:\Books.dtd">
<northwind:BOOKS xmlns:northwind ="www.northwind.com/PO">
```

You can see that the !DOCTYPE declaration defined the location of the DTD. Because XML documents are aware of namespaces, the parser recognized that the prefix *northwind* was a namespace prefix for the *BOOKS* element. In the next line of code, the parser finds the declaration that associates a namespace with that name and with that declaration. There is no data type information in the result above because this is a DTD.

We will now use a BizTalk schema instead of a DTD. Create the following schema file called Books.xsd:

```
<Schema name="BOOKS" xmlns="urn:schemas-microsoft-com:xml-data"
   xmlns:dt="urn:schemas-microsoft-com:datatypes">
   <ElementType name="BOOKS" content="eltOnly" model="closed">
      <element type="item"/>
   </ElementType>
   <ElementType name="item" content="eltOnly" model="closed">
      <element type="title"/>
      <element type="author"/>
      <element type="price"/>
      <element type="quantity"/>
   </ElementType>
   <ElementType name="title" content="mixed" model="closed">
      <AttributeType name="language" dt:type="string"/>
      <attribute type="language"/>
   </ElementType>
   <ElementType name="author" content="textOnly" model="closed"
      dt:type="string"/>
   <ElementType name="price" content="textOnly" model="closed"
      dt:type="string"/>
   <ElementType name="quantity" content="textOnly" model="closed"
      dt:type="string"/>
</Schema>
```

Create a new XML document called Books2.xml and add the following code:

```
<?xml version="1.0" ?>
<northwind:BOOKS xmlns:northwind="x-schema:c:\Books.xsd">
   <northwind:item>
      <northwind:title language="English">Number, the
            Language of Science</northwind:title>
      <northwind:author>Danzig</northwind:author>
      <northwind:price>5.95</northwind:price>
      <northwind:quantity>3</northwind:quantity>
   </northwind:item>
</northwind:BOOKS>
```

Notice that you need to change the code so that it references Books.xsd. To get a reference to the schema we must use *x-schema* in the namespace declaration. The x-schema syntax is used by Internet Explorer 5 to identify where the schema is. The namespace prefix had to be added to all the elements in order for this code to work. While that should not have been necessary, errors would result if the namespace prefix was not added. This is a reminder that the way things are implemented might not always be what you expect. Finally, change the Visual Basic code so that it references Books2.xml and the namespace prefix is included in the XSL statement:

```
Private Sub cmdSchemas_Click()
    Dim objXMLDoc As DOMDocument26
    Dim objXMLSchemas As XMLSchemaCache
    Dim lngSchemaCounter As Long
    Set objXMLDoc = New DOMDocument
    objXMLDoc.async = False
    objXMLDoc.Load ("c:\Books2.xml")
    Set objXMLSchemas = objXMLDoc.namespaces
    For lngSchemaCounter = 0 To objXMLSchemas.length - 1
        Debug.Print "URL: " & _
            objXMLSchemas.namespaceURI(lngSchemaCounter)
        Debug.Print "Type: " & objXMLDoc.selectSingleNode _
            ("//northwind:author").dataType
    Next
End Sub
```

After you make the changes, running the program and clicking the *Schemas* button will result in the following output:

```
URL: x-schema:c:\Books.xsd
Type:
```

With the current release of the XML parser, the string data type is not being returned.

The *XMLDOMSelection* object represents a list of nodes that match an XSL pattern or an XPath expression. The *XMLDOMSelection* object can be created by using the *selectNodes* method of the *IXMLDOMDocument2* interface that is included in version 2.6 and later of Microsoft XML parser. This object implements the *IXMLDOM-Selection* interface, which inherits from the *IXMLDOMNodeList* interface. In Visual Basic, the *XMLDOMSelection* object can be used as follows:

```
Dim objXMLDoc As DOMDocument26
Dim objXMLSelection As IXMLDOMSelection

Set objXMLDoc = New DOMDocument26
objXMLDoc.async = False
objXMLDoc.Load ("C:\Books.xml")
Set objXMLSelection = objXMLDoc.selectNodes("//item [quantity=3]")
Debug.Print objXMLSelection.expr
```

In this example, we select the *item* element that has an attribute with a value of *3*. The *expr* property of *IXMLDOMSelection* is used to retrieve the XPath expression string. In this case, *"//item [quantity=3]"* is returned.

SUMMARY

In this chapter, you reviewed the majority of the XML DOM objects. These objects allow you to manipulate an XML document in virtually any way that might be required by an application. These objects provide a powerful set of tools that allow you to begin building complete XML applications. You can also use the DOM objects to both send messages to and receive messages from a Web server, which allows you to create SOAP messages as shown in the example in this chapter. In the next chapter, we will look at XSL and learn how the DOM can be used with it.

Chapter 12

XML Presentation with XSL and CSS

In the next two chapters, we will discuss how to use XML with user services components—that is, with the components that run on the client and interact with the user. This chapter will focus specifically on creating *static* user services components that can be used to present information to the user. In Chapter 13, we'll move beyond simply presenting information to the user and begin building dynamic user services components that can interact with the user without having to go to a Web server for each response. As you know, XML data that is brought to a client generally comes in two forms. The first form of data contains elements that define how the content of the document should be displayed. The XHTML document we created in Chapter 5 is an example of the first form of data. The second form of data contains elements that do not define how the document's content should be presented. Since XML was not designed to be a presentation language, the majority of XML documents contain the second form of data—that is, data without specific presentation instructions. XML's strength lies not in its ability to present data, but in its ability to package data into a format that can be validated and easily moved. If we want to present XML data in a Web browser, it would make sense to transform this XML into another language that is designed for presentation and is in XML format, such as XHTML. Extensible Stylesheet

Language (XSL) is designed to transform XML into XHTML and other XML formats so that the XML can be presented in a browser. Currently, XSL primarily transforms XML into XHTML. In the future, though, we could see XSL transforming XML into speech or other formats. This chapter will cover the presentation of data using cascading style sheets (CSS), XSL, and XSL Transformations (XSLT). Let's begin by looking at XHTML and CSS.

XHTML AND CASCADING STYLE SHEETS

One of the most important principles of Web design is creating a uniform look and feel for the entire site. To do this, you can create a standard to define how each of the HTML elements will be presented in the browser. When we created our XHTML template in Chapter 5, we defined a DTD that placed restrictions on the values of certain elements. For example, we used enumerated types to define the possible values for the *font* element's color and size. The problem with using DTDs to define certain elements when designing a Web site is that every developer who creates a page must know the standards and must write the appropriate values in every page.

Cascading style sheets (CSS) enable you to apply a uniform look to all the documents belonging to a Web site. Now we'll look at CSS documents briefly and then see how they can be applied to XHTML documents.

CSS Documents

CSS documents allow you to define a style for any HTML element. Thus, you can define the style for an *h1* element to be red with a font size of 6. This style can then be applied to every *h1* element on your Web site. CSS documents allow you to create a uniform style throughout your Web documents without having to enter specific information for each *h1* element in each page. If you need to change the style for an *h1* element, you need to change it only in the CSS document. If you need to override the style defined in the CSS document for one or more of your *h1* elements in a specific page, you can do this, too.

One major problem with using CSS documents is that they are not supported in every browser. Microsoft Internet Explorer 5 supports nearly all the features of CSS documents, and Internet Explorer 4 also supports most of the CSS features. Netscape has released version 6 that supports CSS level 1 and the DOM. At the time this book goes to print, it is too early to tell how well these features are actually supported. If there are problems with the final release of Netscape 6, it is likely that you will find information on these problems on these Web sites: *http://hotwired.lycos.com/webmonkey/*, *http://webreview.com/pub/guides/style/style.html*, and *http://www.utoronto.ca/ian/style/cssbugs/toc.html*.

If you were to create an XHTML document, you could use CSS documents to define the presentation of the XHTML information. While CSS documents can work for XHTML, they will not work for XML documents that do not contain presentation information. For XML documents without presentation information, you must use XSL.

USING XSL TO PRESENT XML DOCUMENTS

XSL documents are similar to CSS documents in that they both define styles that apply to certain elements, but there are a few differences. CSS defines the typographical style of only XHTML elements, whereas the styles defined in XSL documents apply to entire XML documents. Moreover, XSL might use the styles specified in CSS to produce the output code from XML data. The XSL document must be placed on the same Web server as the file that references it.

As mentioned, most XML data does not contain elements that define how the data should be presented; therefore, you must use XSL documents to transform this XML data into a form that can be presented to the user. In this way, XSL provides a powerful tool to transform XML documents in virtually any way that is necessary.

In this section, we will look at transforming a BizTalk document's body section from XML to XHTML so that it can be displayed in a browser.

We will use the following code, which came from an earlier code sample for BizTalk, to transform XML to XHTML using XSL.

```
<?xml version='1.0' ?>
<biztalk_1 xmlns="urn:biztalk-org:biztalk:biztalk_1">
    <header>
        <delivery>
            <message>
                <messageID>xyzzy:8</messageID>
                <sent>1999-01-02T19:00:01+02:00</sent>
```

(continued)

```
                    <subject>Purchase Order</subject>
            </message>
            <to>
                <address>http://www.fabrikam.com/recv.asp</address>
                <state>
                    <referenceID/>
                    <handle/>
                    <process/>
                </state>
            </to>
            <from>
                <address>mailto:foo@contoso.com</address>
                <state>
                    <referenceID>123</referenceID>
                    <handle>7</handle>
                    <process>myprocess</process>
                </state>
            </from>
        </delivery>
        <manifest>
            <document>
                <name>PO</name>
                <description>Purchase Order</description>
            </document>
        </manifest>
    </header>
    <body>
        <PO xmlns=
        "x-schema: http://schemas.biztalk.org/BizTalk/zi0124pf.xml">
            <POHeader>
                <poNumber>12345</poNumber>
                <custID>100200300</custID>
                <description>Order for 200 desktop PCs
                </description>
                <paymentType>Invoice</paymentType>
                <shipType>Express2d</shipType>
                <Contact>
                    <contactName>John Doe</contactName>
                    <contactEmail>jdoe@fabrikam.com</contactEmail>
                    <contactPhone>4250001212</contactPhone>
                </Contact>
                <POShipTo>
                    <attn>Fabrikam Receiving</attn>
                    <street>10 Main Street</street>
```

```
                <city>Anytown</city>
                <stateProvince>WA</stateProvince>
                <postalCode>98000</postalCode>
                <country>USA</country>
            </POShipTo>
            <POBillTo>
                <attn>Fabrikam Payables</attn>
                <street>101 Headquarters Road</street>
                <city>Anytown</city>
                <stateProvince>WA</stateProvince>
                <postalCode>98000</postalCode>
                <country>USA</country>
            </POBillTo>
        </POHeader>
        <POLines>
            <count>2</count>
            <totalAmount>192000.00</totalAmount>
            <Item>
                <line>1</line>
                <partno>pc1010</partno>
                <qty>200</qty>
                <uom>EACH</uom>
                <unitPrice>800.00</unitPrice>
                <discount>10</discount>
                <totalAmount>144000.00</totalAmount>
            </Item>
            <Item>
                <line>1</line>
                <partno>monitor17</partno>
                <qty>200</qty>
                <uom>EACH</uom>
                <unitPrice>300.00</unitPrice>
                <discount>20</discount>
                <totalAmount>48000.00</totalAmount>
            </Item>
        </POLines>
    </PO>
  </body>
</biztalk_1>
```

Rename this file NorthwindPO.xml. (You can also find this file on the companion CD.)

There is nothing in the NorthwindPO.xml XML document that specifies how it should be presented in a Web browser. With XSL, you can create an XSL template document that will transform every document with our example's structure into XHTML. Let's look at how we could build an XSL document that will transform our example into XHTML.

> **NOTE**   It's important to realize that at this point, Internet Explorer 5 doesn't distinguish a BizTalk document with special presentation. If you change the element *biztalk_1* to some other name, such as say *DaffyDuck*, it will have no effect on how this document is presented in Internet Explorer 5. The only part of this document that is actually being validated against a schema is the *PO* element and its child elements. The schema associated with the *PO* element is located in the BizTalk repository. Currently, nothing is validating the BizTalk elements. If you wanted to validate both the BizTalk elements and the *PO* element and its child elements, you would have to write your own schema for BizTalk as we did for SOAP in Chapter 8. You could then override the BizTalk *body* element's content using the *xsi* namespace as we did with SOAP. For this discussion, we will not be validating the BizTalk elements.

XSL Patterns

XML documents represent a tree of nodes. XSL patterns provide a query language for locating nodes in XML documents. After the nodes in the XML document are identified using a pattern, the nodes will be transformed using a template. The XSL patterns we will be using have the same format as the patterns we used with XPath, such as */ (child)*, *// (ancestor)*, *.(current node)*, *@ (attribute)*, and ** (wildcard)*. In addition to the patterns we already mentioned, XSL also has filter operators to manipulate, sort, and filter XML data.

XSL Filter Operators

The filter operators are similar to the SQL *Where* clause. A filter is evaluated as a Boolean on every node that is within the current context. If the Boolean evaluates to true, the node is included in the returned set; otherwise, it's excluded. Filters are enclosed in brackets. Remember, in our discussion of XPath in Chapter 6, we used the following path to select certain elements:

```
/child::customer [attribute::customerID= c1] [position() = 1]
```

This path selects the first *customer* element from those *customer* elements that are siblings to the *root* element that has an attribute equal to *c1*. The first filter, *[attribute::customerID=c1]*, filters out all the nodes that do not have a *customerID* attribute equal to *c1*. The second filter, *[position()=1]*, filters out all the nodes except the node at position one. With XPath, we could rewrite the previous example as follows:

```
/child::customer [@customerID= c1] [1]
```

We will use this abbreviated form in XSL. There are also some expression operators that we can use when working with XSL. The expression operators are listed in the following table:

XSL EXPRESSION OPERATORS

Operator	Alternative syntax	Description
and	and	Logical-and, shortcut is &&
or	or	Logical-or, shortcut is ||
not()	not	Negation
=	eq	Equality
	ieq	Case-insensitive equality
!=	ne	Not equal
	ine	Case-insensitive inequality
<	lt	Less than
	ilt	Case-insensitive less than
<=	le	Less than or equal
	ile	Case-insensitive less than or equal
>	gt	Greater than
	igt	Case-insensitive greater than
>=	ge	Greater than or equal
	ige	Case-insensitive greater than or equal
	all	Set operation; returns TRUE if the condition is true for all items in the collection
	any	Set operation; returns TRUE if the condition is true for any item in the collection
|		Set operation; returns the union of two sets of nodes

Using these operators, we can create filter patterns that are based on comparisons. We will do this in an example in the section "XSL Document Elements," which begins on the next page.

Transforming XML Using XSL

An XSL document is very similar to an ASP or JSP document in that it can contain a mixture of text (usually XHTML) and scripting code. The XSL document can contain HTML code that will be displayed in a browser and programming instructions that can transform information in an XML document. Putting these two together, you can transform any XML document into XHTML.

To transform the BizTalk document on page 261 into XHTML, you will need to add a processing instruction declaring the location of the XSL document that will be used to transform this XML document. To accomplish this, add the following processing instruction to the top of the NorthwindPO.xml document after the XML declaration:

```
<?xml-stylesheet type="text/xsl" href="NorthwindPO.xsl"?>
```

The *type* attribute declares that the document referenced by the *href* attribute is a style sheet and should be used to determine the styles for the elements in the HTML document.

You now need to create the NorthwindPO.xsl document. The XSL document will be a well-formed XML document. In its simplest form, the content of the XSL document is shown in the following code:

```
<?xml version="1.0"?>
<xsl:stylesheet xmlns:xsl="http://www.w3.org/TR/WD-xsl">
   <xsl:template match="/">
      <xsl:value-of />
   </xsl:template>
</xsl:stylesheet>
```

As you can see, the XSL template in this example is defined using a small set of XML elements. We'll have a detailed discussion of these elements in the next section.

XSL Document Elements

The most commonly used XSL document elements are *stylesheet*, *copy*, *value-of*, *template*, and *apply-templates*. All these elements must be preceded by a namespace when used in an XSL document, as was shown in the NorthwindPO.xsl document. The namespace must be used exactly as it was declared in NorthwindPO.xsl for the XSL document to work in Internet Explorer 5.

The *stylesheet* element

The *stylesheet* element is the root of the XSL document, and there can be only one instance of it in the document. The *stylesheet* element contains the *template* element and the *script* element. It can have the following attributes: *default-space*, *indent-*

result, language, and *result-ns*. The *default-space* attribute can be set to *preserve* to keep the white space in the source document. The *indent-result* attribute specifies whether you want to preserve white space in the output document. If you like, set this attribute to *yes*. You can place script within an XSL style sheet. If you do this, the *language* attribute defines the language you are using, such as Microsoft VBScript or Microsoft JScript. The *result-ns* attribute tells the processor what the output should be. In the case of Internet Explorer 5, all output will be XHTML, so this attribute will be ignored.

The *value-of* and *template* elements

The *value-of* element selects a node and returns the value of the node as text. The syntax for the *value-of* element is as follows:

```
<xsl:value-of select="pattern">
```

The *value-of* element will find the pattern within the current context. If the *select* attribute is not included, *select* will be set equal to "/", which selects the element and its children. This is what we saw in the previous XSL example document. The *value-of* element may be a child of the following XSL elements: *attribute, comment, copy, element, for-each, if, otherwise, pi, template,* and *when*.

The *template* element defines a template for the output of a particular type of node. It has the following syntax:

```
<xsl:template language="language-name" match="Node-context">
```

The *language* attribute specifies the scripting language used within the template. The *Node-context* in the *match* attribute is a pattern that is also used with XPath. The default pattern is *node( ) |/|@**, which includes all the nodes in the document. The *template* element can be a child of only the *stylesheet* and *apply-templates* elements.

Using the *template* element, you can set the context for the elements contained within the *template* element. Using patterns, you can set the context to any element, and its child elements, in the XML document. You can also use a *template* element to create templates that define how an element should be transformed.

The *template* element in the previous XSL example document defines an element that we want to match to—in this case, the *root* element (/ returns the root). Once we have the element, the *value-of* element will return all the elements specified in a pattern as HTML. Since a pattern was not specified, the default will be used. The default will return everything included in the match, which is the root and all its children, as text. If you try to display the NorthwindPO.xml in a browser, the browser will ignore the XSL elements because they are not HTML elements and will output the content of the elements. The output will appear as shown in Figure 12-1.

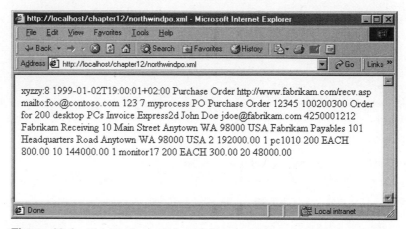

Figure 12-1. *The NorthwindPO.xml document transformed into XHTML.*

Now we need to tell Internet Explorer 5 how we want the content displayed in the browser by adding XHTML elements and using styles. Let's look more closely at the elements that can be used in an XSL file.

We could rewrite the XSL document example to create a template that defines how elements should look after transformation as follows:

```
<?xml version="1.0"?>
<xsl:stylesheet xmlns:xsl="http://www.w3.org/TR/WD-xsl">
   <xsl:template match="/">
      <html>
         <style type="text/css">
            body {font-family:Arial;
                  font-size:12pt; font-weight:normal;
                  color:blue;
                  line-height:150%}
         </style>
         <body>
            <xsl:value-of select="//body" />
         </body>
      </html>
   </xsl:template>
</xsl:stylesheet>
```

This document will now look as shown in Figure 12-2.

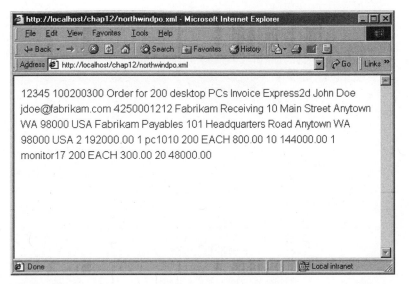

Figure 12-2. *The transformed NorthwindPO.xml document with styles.*

We have now created an XSL template that will take any XML document that is valid according to the schema located at *http://schemas.biztalk.org/BizTalk/zi0124pf.xml* and convert it to XHTML according to the styles and transformations defined in the XSL document.

NOTE Recall that a schema or DTD defines an entire class of documents. An XSL document will be able to transform any document that is included in that class.

In the previous code, you inserted some HTML into the template, defined a style for the *body* element, and placed the transformed XML into the *body* element. In addition, you used the *select* attribute to select only the text within the *body* element and its child elements. Unfortunately, the document still appears as one large blob of text. To break the text apart, you would need to rewrite the template as follows:

```
<?xml version="1.0"?>
<xsl:stylesheet xmlns:xsl="http://www.w3.org/TR/WD-xsl">
<xsl:template match="/">
    <html>
        <style TYPE="text/css">
            body {font-family:Arial;
                font-size:12pt; font-weight:normal;
                color:blue;
                line-height:55%}
        </style>
```

(continued)

```
<body>
   <p>
   <strong>Message ID: </strong>
      <xsl:value-of select="//messageID" /><br></br>
   <strong>Sent: </strong>
      <xsl:value-of select="//sent" /><br></br>
   <strong>Subject: </strong>
      <xsl:value-of select="//subject" /><br></br>
   <strong>To: </strong>
      <xsl:value-of select="//to/address" /><br></br>
   <strong>From: </strong>
      <xsl:value-of select="//from/address" /><br></br>
   <strong>PO Number: </strong>
      <xsl:value-of select="//body//poNumber" />
      <br></br>
   <strong>Customer ID: </strong>
      <xsl:value-of select="//body//custID" /><br></br>
   <strong>Description: </strong>
      <xsl:value-of select="//body//description" />
      <br></br>
   <strong>Contact: </strong>
      <xsl:value-of select="//body//contactName" />
      <br></br>
      <xsl:value-of select="//body//contactEmail" />
      <br></br>
      <xsl:value-of select="//body//contactPhone" />
      <br></br>
   <strong>POShipTo: </strong>
      <xsl:value-of select="//body//attn" /><br></br>
      <xsl:value-of select="//body//street" />
      <br></br>
      <xsl:value-of select="//body//city" />
      <xsl:value-of select="//body//stateProvince" />
      <xsl:value-of select="//body//postalCode" />
      <xsl:value-of select="//body//country" /><br></br>
   <strong>count: </strong>
      <xsl:value-of select="//body//count" /><br></br>
   <strong>Total Amount: </strong>
      <xsl:value-of select="//body//totalAmount" />
      <br></br>
   <strong>Item:<br></br>Line Number: </strong>
      <xsl:value-of select="//body//line" /><br></br>
   <strong>Part Quantity: </strong>
      <xsl:value-of select="//body//qty" /><br></br>
```

```
        <strong>Part Unit Of Measurement: </strong>
            <xsl:value-of select="//body//uom" /><br></br>
        <strong>Part Unit Price: </strong>
            <xsl:value-of select="//body//unitPrice" />
            <br></br>
        <strong>Part Discount: </strong>
            <xsl:value-of select="//body//discount" />
            <br></br>
        <strong>Part Total Amount: </strong>
            <xsl:value-of select="//body//totalAmount" />
            <br></br>
        </p>
    </body>
  </html>
  </xsl:template>
</xsl:stylesheet>
```

This XML document will now appear as shown in Figure 12-3.

Figure 12-3. *The formatted NorthwindPO.xml document.*

As you can see, this document is now approaching a form that can be easily read. There are still a few problems, such as only one *Item* element being shown. We will solve this problem with the *apply-templates* element that will be discussed later in this chapter.

The *copy* element

The *copy* element copies the current node into the output without any changes. The node's child nodes and attributes will not be copied automatically. Essentially, this element doesn't convert the XML into XHTML and could be useful if you are already using XHTML.

For example, you could use the *copy* element as follows:

```
<xsl:template match="//body">
   <xsl:copy />
</xsl:template>
```

This code will output all the body as text without any changes. Thus you can use this element to transform identical data.

The *for-each* and *apply-templates* elements

The *for-each* element has the following syntax:

```
<xsl:for-each order-by="sort-criteria-list" select="pattern">
```

The *for-each* element will iterate over a set of nodes determined by the *pattern* value of the *select* attribute. The default value of the *select* attribute is *node()*—that is, all nodes that are currently in context. The *order-by* criteria can be a semicolon-separated list. If the first *sort* order results in two items that are identical, the second *sort* criterion, if listed, will be used to determine the order. This pattern will continue throughout the number of criteria listed. You can place a + or − sign before the *sort* criterion to indicate ascending (the default) or descending order. The *for-each* element can be a child of the following XSL elements: *attribute*, *comment*, *copy*, *element*, *for-each*, *if*, *otherwise*, *pi*, *template*, and *when*.

The *apply-templates* element has the following syntax:

```
<xsl:apply-templates order-by="sort-criteria-list" select="pattern">
```

The pattern can be the same as the pattern used in XPath, or you can reference a *template* element that defines a transformation of an element in the XML document. The *order-by* element allows you to order the results by a pattern. The *apply-templates* element will tell the processor to search for and apply any templates that match the *select* attribute. The search will begin within the XSL document. If a *template* element is defined that matches the value in the *select* attribute's pattern, this *template* element will be used first. Using the *template* elements, you can create your own templates. We can now place all the *Item* child elements into a table as follows:

```xml
<?xml version="1.0"?>
<xsl:stylesheet xmlns:xsl="http://www.w3.org/TR/WD-xsl">
   <xsl:template match="/">
      <html>
         <style TYPE="text/css">
            body {font-family:Arial;
                  font-size:12pt; font-weight:normal;
                  color:blue;
                  line-height:55%}
         </style>
         <body>
            <p>
            <strong>Message ID: </strong>
               <xsl:value-of select="//messageID" /><br></br>
            <strong>Sent: </strong>
               <xsl:value-of select="//sent" /><br></br>
            <strong>Subject: </strong>
               <xsl:value-of select="//subject" /><br></br>
            <strong>To: </strong>
               <xsl:value-of select="//to/address" /><br></br>
            <strong>From: </strong>
               <xsl:value-of select="//from/address" />
               <br></br>
            <strong>PO Number: </strong>
               <xsl:value-of select="//body//poNumber" />
               <br></br>
            <strong>Customer ID: </strong>
               <xsl:value-of select="//body//custID" />
               <br></br>
            <strong>Description: </strong>
               <xsl:value-of select="//body//description" />
               <br></br>
            <strong>Contact: </strong>
               <xsl:value-of select="//body//contactName" />
               <br></br>
               <xsl:value-of select="//body//contactEmail" />
               <br></br>
               <xsl:value-of select="//body//contactPhone" />
               <br></br>
            <strong>POShipTo: </strong>
```

(continued)

```
    <xsl:value-of select="//body//attn" /><br></br>
    <xsl:value-of select="//body//street"/>
    <br></br>
    <xsl:value-of select="//body//city" />
    <xsl:value-of select="//body//stateProvince" />
    <xsl:value-of select="//body//postalCode" />
    <xsl:value-of select= "//body//country" />
    <br></br>
<strong>count: </strong>
    <xsl:value-of select="//body//count" />
    <br></br>
<strong>Total Amount: </strong>
    <xsl:value-of select="//body//totalAmount" />
    <br></br>
<strong>Item</strong>
<table>
<td><strong>Line Number: </strong></td>
<td><strong>Part Number: </strong></td>
<td><strong>Part Quantity: </strong></td>
<td><strong>Part Unit Of Measurement: </strong></td>
<td><strong>Part Unit Price: </strong></td>
<td><strong>Part Discount: </strong></td>
<td><strong>Part Total Amount: </strong></td>
<!--Above, a template element was used to define
    the context. This template element used the
    backslash as its match attribute. Thus, the
    context for the for-each element is the root
    document--that is, the for-each element
    can iterate through any element in the
    document. In this case, it is iterating
    through the Item elements-->
<xsl:for-each select="//Item">
<tr>
    <!-- uses default line template-->
    <xsl:apply-templates select="line" />
    <!-- uses default partno template-->
    <xsl:apply-templates select="partno" />
    <!-- uses default qty template-->
    <xsl:apply-templates select="qty" />
    <!-- uses default uom template-->
    <xsl:apply-templates select="uom" />
    <!-- uses default unitPrice template-->
    <xsl:apply-templates select="unitPrice" />
    <!-- uses default discount template-->
    <xsl:apply-templates select="discount" />
```

```
                    <!-- uses default totalAmount template-->
                    <xsl:apply-templates select="totalAmount"/>
                </tr>
                </xsl:for-each>
                </table>
                </p>
            </body>
        </html>
    </xsl:template>
    <!--Below are the templates for the table cells.-->
    <!--The line template uses the default text template.-->
    <xsl:template match="//body//line">
        <td><xsl:apply-templates /></td>
    </xsl:template>
    <!--The partno template uses the default text template.-->
    <xsl:template match="partno">
        <td><xsl:apply-templates /></td>
    </xsl:template>
    <!--The qty template uses the default text template.-->
    <xsl:template match="qty">
        <td><xsl:apply-templates /></td>
    </xsl:template>
    <!--The uom template, uses default text template.-->
    <xsl:template match="//body//uom">
        <td><xsl:apply-templates /></td>
    </xsl:template>
    <!-- The unitPrice template uses the default text template.-->
    <xsl:template match="//body//unitPrice">
        <td><xsl:apply-templates /></td>
    </xsl:template>
    <!--The discount template uses the default text template.-->
    <xsl:template match="//body//discount">
        <td><xsl:apply-templates /></td>
    </xsl:template>
    <!--The totalAmount template uses the default text template.-->
    <xsl:template match="//body//totalAmount">
        <td><xsl:apply-templates /></td>
    </xsl:template>
    <!--The default text template.-->
    <xsl:template match="text()"><xsl:value-of /></xsl:template>
</xsl:stylesheet>
```

We have made several changes to the code to allow the multiple *Item* elements to be presented in a table. Figure 12-4 shows what the bottom of this XML document will look like in the browser. As you can see, two items are listed at the bottom of the figure.

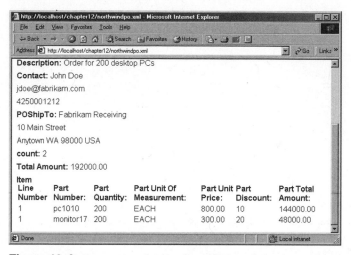

Figure 12-4. *Presenting the NorthwindPO.xml document items in a table.*

Look at the bottom of the previous code listing; you can see the following line of code:

```
<xsl:template match="text()"><xsl:value-of /></xsl:template>
```

This line of code defines a template that handles the text nodes. The XSL draft considers this template one of two built-in templates. The other built-in template is:

```
<xsl:template match="/|*"><xsl:apply-templates/></xsl:template>
```

Internet Explorer 5 does not have these templates built in, but you can add them to your XSL documents. These built-in templates enable you to create style sheets for irregular data by passing text from the source document to the output automatically.

The *xsl:template match="text()"* template is used quite often in the XSL documents when an *apply-templates* element does not have a *select* attribute, such as in the following declaration:

> *<td><xsl:apply-templates /></td>*

Let's look at the following template from the previous code listing, which we will call the *totalAmount* template, and see what it does:

```
<xsl:template match="//body//totalAmount">
    <td><xsl:apply-templates /></td>
</xsl:template>
```

The *<xsl:template match="//body//totalAmount">* line of code will create a new *totalAmount* template. Any *apply-templates* element that has its *select* attribute set to *totalAmount* will be instructing the parser to select this *totalAmount* template.

Because *match* is set to *//body//totalAmount*, the content of the *totalAmount* template will be able to use XSL to transform the *totalAmount* element in the XML document. The value of *match* also defines the content of this template element. The content of the *totalAmount* template includes the start HTML *td* tag for the table, followed by an XSL *apply-templates* element and the end *td* tag. The *apply-templates* element will use the *text* template to return the current content as text. Since the current content is the *totalAmount* element and its attributes and content, the *apply-templates* element will return the text contents of the *totalAmount* element. Thus, the *totalAmount* template will return the start *td* tag, the text content of the *totalAmount* element, and the end *td* tag.

Using this combination of *apply-templates* elements with *template* elements, you can create XSL documents that can do virtually anything you require. The *template* element can contain far more than just HTML elements and the XSL *apply-templates* element; they can also contain other XSL elements such as *choose*, *when*, *otherwise*, *if*, *script*, and *eval*. Let's look at some of these other elements.

The *choose, when, and otherwise* elements

The *choose*, *when*, and *otherwise* elements work together to create something similar to what is commonly called a *select case* statement in other programming languages. The *choose* element has the following syntax:

```
<xsl:choose>
```

Either a *when* or *otherwise* element will follow the *choose* element that will allow for the choice between different options. The *choose* element can be a child element of the following elements: *attribute, comment, copy, element, for-each, if, otherwise, pi, template*, and *when*.

The *when* element provides the testing conditions for the *choose* element. If the *discount* element was not already defined in the previous example, we could replace *<xsl:apply-templates select="discount" />* with this code:

```
<td>
   <xsl:choose>
   <xsl:when test="unitPrice[. $lt$ 500]">
      10
   </xsl:when>
   <xsl:when test="unitPrice[. $ge$ 500]">
      5
   </xsl:when>
   <xsl:otherwise>
      15
   </xsl:otherwise>
   </xsl:choose>
</td>
```

> **NOTE** We could not place this code in a *template* element in our example XSL documents because the *template* element would have to refer to the *discount* element, which would define the content as being only the *discount* element. Since the *unitPrice* element is not included within the context of a *discount* element, a template would not work.

Let's look at how to use the *when* element in a template. In our example XSL document, you can give a different color to an item depending on its unit price by changing:

```
<xsl:template match="//body//unitPrice">
   <td><xsl:apply-templates /></td>
</xsl:template>
```

to this code:

```
<xsl:template match="//body//unitPrice">
   <xsl:choose>
      <xsl:when test=".[. $lt$ 500.00]">
      <td style="color:green"><xsl:apply-templates /></td>
      </xsl:when>
      <xsl:otherwise>
      <td style="color:red"><xsl:apply-templates /></td>
      </xsl:otherwise>
   </xsl:choose>
</xsl:template>
```

In this example, we used the *test* attribute with the *when* element. This example will make the unit price green for items priced under 500 and red for all other items.

The *if* element

You can use the *if* element to selectively choose output as shown here:

```
<xsl:if test=".[. $lt$ 500.00]">do something if true</xsl:if>
```

In the above line of code, *test* is the condition in the source data that will be tested for being either *true* or *false*. In this case, we are testing whether the current element is less than 500. The content of the *if* statement is a template that will be applied if the test is *true*. If the expression in this content identifies at least one node in the current source document, the content of *xsl:if* is placed in the output.

The *eval* element

The *eval* element allows you to evaluate a script expression. This element can be used only by a style sheet with the *xsl* namespace, *http://www.w3.org/TR/WD-xsl*. You cannot use this element in a style sheet that uses the XSLT namespace, *http://www.w3.org/*

1999/XSL/Transform. We'll examine the XSLT namespace in detail later in this chapter. The *eval* element can be a child element of the following elements: *attribute*, *comment*, *copy*, *element*, *for-each*, *if*, *otherwise*, *pi*, *template*, and *when*. You can find the code that illustrates how to use this element in the section "Using the XML DOM to Work with XSLT and XSL" later in this chapter.

The XSL elements for creating XML nodes

You can also use XSL elements to create new nodes that will result in an updated XML document. The elements that are used for creating nodes are: *attribute*, *cdata*, *comment*, *element*, *entity-ref*, and *pi*. If we wanted to create an HTML link attribute for the *Item* element whose *itemID* is 0001, we could do the following:

```
<xsl:template match="//Item[@itemID=0001]/a">
   <xsl:attribute name="href">
      http://www.northwindtraders.com/item0001.gif
   </xsl:attribute>
</xsl:template>
```

The other node elements will work in a similar manner.

XSLT, XPATH, AND XSL FORMATTING OBJECTS

The main difficulty in working with a new and evolving technology such as XML is keeping up with the many changes being made to the specifications. For example, XSL is now being split into three different specifications: XSLT, XPath, and XSL Formatting Objects (XSL FO). XPath originated from XSL; therefore, as you saw earlier in this chapter, XSL uses essentially the same syntax as XPath. Because we've discussed XPath in detail in Chapter 6, we won't repeat the discussion here. The formatting object specification (the *fo* namespace) defines a set of formatting semantics developed as an XML vocabulary for working with documents such as PDFs.

■ XSLT is a language for transforming an XML document to any other text-based document, such as an XHTML document. You can use XSLT to define templates for your output so that your XML data can be delivered to the templates. However, the existing Internet Explorer 5 XSL style sheets are not compliant with the final W3C XSLT recommendation. XSLT introduced many new features after Internet Explorer 5 was released. Therefore, we must update the style sheets to XSLT conformance to utilize these new features. Before we discuss how to update the XSL style sheets, let's take a look at the elements in XSLT.

XSLT Elements

XSLT uses several of the elements that we used with XSL in the same manner. For example, the following elements have not changed: *apply-templates*, *attribute*, *element*, *comment*, *copy*, *for-each*, *if*, *choose*, *when*, and *otherwise*. The *pi* element used in XSL is called *processing-instruction* in XSLT.

The following elements that exist in XSL do not exist in XSLT: *script*, *cdata*, *entity-ref*, and *eval*. If you are converting an XSL document into an XSLT document and these elements are used in the XSL document, you will have to write script that will replace these elements. This is what the Microsoft XSL to XSLT Converter did for the *eval* element. We'll discuss this converter in the next section.

The *stylesheet* element still exists in XSLT, but the attributes have been changed. The attributes for the *stylesheet* element are now: *extension-element-prefixes*, *xmlns:xsl*, and *version*. The *extension-element-prefixes* attribute is used to designate an extended namespace. The *xmlns:xsl* namespace must be *http://www.w3.org/1999/XSL/Transform*. You can include other namespaces.

The following table lists XSLT elements that are not part of XSL:

XSLT ELEMENTS

Name and Syntax	Description
<xsl:include href = *uri/*>	The XSLT resource located by the *href* attribute value is parsed as an XML document, and the children of the *xsl:stylesheet* element in this document will replace the *xsl:include* element in the including document. This element is supported in the Internet Explorer 5 DOM.
<xsl:import href = *uri/*>	Imports another XSLT style sheet. Importing a style sheet is the same as including it except that definitions and template rules in the importing style sheet take precedence over template rules and definitions in the imported style sheet.
<xsl:call-template name = *Name/*>	A *template* element with a *name* attribute specifies a named template. An *xsl:call-template* element invokes a template by name; it has a required *name* attribute that identifies the template to be invoked. Unlike *xsl:apply-templates*, *xsl:call-template* does not change the current node or the current node list.

Name and Syntax	Description
<xsl:text disable-output-escaping = "yes" | "no" />	Creates a text node with the string-value of the content of the *text* element in the result tree. Adjacent text nodes in the result tree are automatically merged. A template can also contain *text* nodes. Each *text* node in a template remains after white space has been stripped. The value of the *disable-output-escaping* attribute can be either *yes* or *no*.
<xsl:number level = "single" | "multiple" | "any" count = *pattern* from = *pattern* value = *number-expression* format = { *string* } lang = { *nmtoken* } letter-value = { "alphabetic" | "traditional" } grouping-separator = { *char* } grouping-size = { *number* } />	Insert a formatted number into the result tree. The number to be inserted may be specified by an expression.
<xsl:sort select = "string" lang = "nmtoken" datatype = {"text" | "number"} order = {"ascending" | "descending"} case-order = {"upper-first" | "lower-first"} />	The XPath expression in *select* indicates the node on which the sort should be based. The *sort* element is supported in Internet Explorer 5, but only with the *select* and *order* attributes.
<xsl:variable name = *qualified-name* select = "*XPath expression*" />	Sets a variable for use within an XSLT style sheet. The *name* attribute is the name of the variable to be used within variable references. To reference the value of the variable, use the $*variable-name* syntax. This element is supported in the Internet Explorer 5 DOM.
<xsl:param name = *qualified-name* select = "*XPath expression*" />	Declares a parameter for use within an XSLT style sheet. To reference the value of the parameter, use the $*parameter-name* syntax. This element is supported in Internet Explorer 5 DOM.
<xsl:copy-of-select select = "*XPath expression*" />	Inserts a result tree fragment or node-set into the result tree. This element is supported by the Internet Explorer 5 DOM.

(continued)

XSLT Elements *continued*

Name and Syntax	*Description*
<xsl:with-param name = "*qualified-name*" select = "*XPath expression*" />	Passes a parameter to a template. This element is supported by the Internet Explorer 5 DOM.
<xsl:key name = *qualified-name* match = *pattern* use = *node-set-expression* />	The *key* element is used to declare keys. This element provides information about the keys of the node that matches the pattern given in the *match* attribute.
<xsl:decimal-format name = *qualified-name* decimal-separator = *char* grouping-separator = *char* infinity = *string* minus-sign = *char* NaN = *string* percent = *char* per-mille = *char* zero-digit = *char* digit = *char* pattern-separator = *char* />	Declares a decimal-format, which controls the interpretation of a format pattern used by the *format-number* function. If there is a *name* attribute, the element declares a named decimal-format; otherwise, it declares the default decimal-format.
<xsl:message terminate ="yes"|"no"/>	Sends a message in a way that is dependent on the XSLT processor. The content of the message instruction is a template. You can instantiate the message by instantiating the content to create an XML fragment. This XML fragment is the content of the message. An XSLT processor might implement the message element by popping up an alert box or by writing to a log file. If the *terminate* attribute has the value *yes*, then the XSLT processor should terminate processing after sending the message.

Name and Syntax	Description
<xsl:fallback />	Normally, instantiating an *xsl:fallback* element does nothing. However, when an XSLT processor performs fallback for an instruction element, if the instruction element has one or more *xsl:fallback* children, then the content of each of the *xsl:fallback* children must be instantiated in sequence; otherwise, an error must be signaled.
<xsl:output method = "xml" | "html" | "text" version = nmtoken encoding = string omit-xml-declaration = "yes" | "no" standalone = "yes" | "no" indent = "yes" | "no" media-type = string />	Allows style sheet authors to specify how they want the result tree to be output. This element is allowed only as a top-level element, and it is supported by the Internet Explorer 5 DOM.

Converting XSL to XSLT

As mentioned previously, we need to update the XSL style sheets to make them compliant to the W3C XSLT specification. Specifically, we'll need to change XSL and related namespaces. A new official XSLT namespace is available: *http://www.wc.org/ 1999/XSL/Transform*. The 2.6 and higher versions of the XML parser can recognize both the new namespace and the existing namespace *http://www.w3.org/TR/WD-xsl*. Since *<xsl:eval>* and *<xsl:script>* blocks are not supported in XSLT, they have to be converted to an XSLT-conformant mechanism. We'll also need to add JScript implementations of *XTLRuntime* functions where necessary, since the *XTLRuntime* object extends the W3C standard. What's more, we will also have to replace all the operators with their XML equivalents. For example, *lt* will need to be replaced with *<*, *gt* will have to be replaced with *>*, and so forth. The operators that have no XML equivalent, such as *ieq*, will require you to write special functions.

Although this sounds like it can be a lot of work, Microsoft actually provides a converter called XSL to XSLT Converter. The converter is zipped into a file named Xsltconv.exe. The file can be downloaded at Microsoft's Web site. The zip file contains three files: Xsl-xslt-converter.xslt, Readme-xslt.txt, and Convert.js. You can run the Convert.js program from the DOS prompt. The format is as follows:

```
PathToConvert.js/convert.js PathToXSLFile/
    XSLFileName [XSLTFileName]
```

The parameter is optional. The program will perform the required conversion from an XSL file to an XSLT file. The version that was used at the time this book was being written had a few minor quirks, such as raising an error if there were any comments in the XSL document. If you convert the XSL document discussed in "The *for-each* and *apply-templates* elements" section of this chapter to an XSLT document, you will find some minor changes as described below. You can also find the XSLT document on the companion CD.

The *stylesheet* element has been changed to the following:

```
<xsl:stylesheet xmlns:xsl="http://www.w3.org/1999/XSL/Transform"
    version="1.0"
    xmlns:msxsl="urn:schemas-microsoft-com:xslt"
    xmlns:local="#local-functions"
    xmlns:xql="#xql-functions"
    xmlns:auto-ns1="http://www.w3.org/TR/WD-xsl">
<!-- [XSL-XSLT] Updated namespace, added the required
  version attribute, and added namespaces necessary for
  script extensions. -->
```

Since Internet Explorer 5 was released prior to the current standard, there was no way to know what the final namespace would be in the standard. Thus, the namespace we have been using with the Internet Explorer 5 XSL documents is different from the W3C namespace.

When working with Internet Explorer 5, you can use the Internet Explorer 5 namespace in your XSL document (*<xsl:stylesheet xmlns:xsl="http://www.w3.org/TR/WD-xsl">*); but when you use this namespace, your XSL documents will not work with other applications that recognize XSLT. On the other hand, if you use XSLT documents with the namespace from the W3C standard, these documents will not currently work in Internet Explorer 5.

You can also see the *msxsl* and *local* namespaces in the *stylesheet* element above. These namespaces will be used to define a set of default functions that will replace all the functions in the Microsoft XSL documents that are not part of the standard. In this case, we are not using any of these functions.

The next two additions from the converter are as follows:

```
<!-- [XSL-XSLT] Explicitly apply the default (and only)
    indent-result behavior -->
<xsl:output method="xml" indent="yes" omit-xml-declaration="yes" />

<!-- [XSL-XSLT] Simulate lack of built-in templates -->
<xsl:template match="@*|/|node()" />
```

The XSLT document has an *output* element that can be used to define how the information should be output. This element has been added to the document. Values for this element have also been added, as well as a default *template* that will select all nodes in the tree.

These are the only changes that were made to the original document. When we discussed XSL above, we used the XPath syntax. As mentioned previously, the XPath syntax was also the same as the XSL syntax. Therefore, nothing needed to be changed since XSLT uses XPath. Thus, for a simple XSL document you will only need to make minor changes. This means that you can currently write XSL documents that work with Internet Explorer 5, and they will only require minor changes when you convert them to XSLT documents.

If you are using more complex XSL documents, such as documents referencing the Internet Explorer 5 *XTLRuntime* extended methods, you will find that you have to make major modifications to your document. If you try to convert the XSL document we made to test the *XTLRuntime* object using the conversion program, you will find that there are major changes. This is because this entire XSL document uses the *XTLRuntime* object, which contains functions that are not part of the W3C standard. One of the conversions looks as follows:

```
nodeName: <!-- [XSL-XSLT] Converted xsl:node-name to
    xsl:value-of --><xsl:value-of select="name()" />
Absolute Child Number:
    <!-- [XSL-XSLT] Converted xsl:eval to xsl:value-of -->
    <xsl:value-of select="local:eval_1_2_2_2_2_2_4(.)" />
```

In XSLT, the *nodeName* function is no longer used; instead, we use the *name* function as the criteria for the *select* attribute of the value element. The second change looks very weird, but it's actually very simple. The value for the *select* attribute of the *value-of* element is *local:eval_1_2_2_2_2_2_4(.)*. The *local* prefix defines the namespace, which points to a location at the bottom of the generated XSLT document. The base *eval_1_2_2_2_2_2_4* is a Java function that is defined in the *local* namespace. The *parameter* that is being passed into the function is the dot (.), or the current element. The *eval_1_2_2_2_2_2_4* function looks as follows:

```
function eval_1_2_2_2_2_2_4(_contextNodeList)
    {
      var __this = _contextNodeList.item(0);
      return absoluteChildNumber(__this);
    }
```

The function takes the first element from the node and returns the *absoluteChildNumber* using another Java function, as shown below:

```
function absoluteChildNumber(pNode)
    {
      var n = 1;
      while (pNode == pNode.nextSibling)
         n++;
      return n;
    }
```

Notice that the *eval_1_2_2_2_2_2_4* function takes a *NodeList* object, while the *absoluteChildNumber* takes a *node* object. The *absoluteChildNumber* function uses the DOM object to get the correct number. Any application that uses a DOM object as specified in the W3C DOM standard, and also is capable of reading XSLT documents, will be able to use these Java script functions. Thus, these are generic XSLT documents.

You can use XSLT with Internet Explorer 5 today, but you will have to do a little work either on the server or on the client. You can use Microsoft's implementation of DOM to transform an XML document using an XSLT document. We will do that in the section "Using the XML DOM to Work with XSLT and XSL" later in this chapter. First we'll take a look at the XPath and XSLT Functions.

XPath Functions

The XPath functions can be used in XSLT documents. We have already seen the *name* function being used as a parameter for the *select* attribute of the *value-of* element. The XPath functions can be divided into four groups: Boolean, string, node-set, and number functions.

Boolean functions

The Boolean functions can be used with comparison operators in filter patterns and return strings or numbers. They are as follows:

BOOLEAN FUNCTIONS

Name	Description
boolean (XPathObject)	Converts the argument to a Boolean. A number is *true* if it's not positive, negative zero, or NaN. A node-set is *true* if it's non-empty. A string is *true* if its length is non-zero.
false ()	Returns *false*.
true ()	Returns *true*.
lang (string)	Used to determine what language should be used for characters; not currently implemented in the Internet Explorer 5 DOM.

String functions

The string functions are used to convert XPath objects to strings and to manipulate strings. They are shown in the following table:

STRING FUNCTIONS

Name	Description
concat (string, string, [string])	Concatenates strings. Can be passed to any number of string parameters.
contains (string1, string2)	Returns *true* if the first argument contains the second argument. Returns *false* otherwise.
normalize-space (string)	Returns the argument with all the white space normalized.

(continued)

String Functions *continued*

Name	Description
starts-with (string1, string2)	Returns *true* if the first argument starts with the second. Returns *false* otherwise.
substring (string1, number1, number2)	Returns the substring of the first argument starting at the second argument with length *number2*. If *number2* is omitted, the function will continue to the end of the string.
substring-after (string1, string2)	Returns the substring of the first argument that follows the first occurrence of the second argument in the first argument.
substring-before (string1, string2)	Returns the substring of the first argument that precedes the first occurrence of the second argument in the first argument.
string (object)	Converts an object to a string.
string-length (string)	Returns the number of characters in a string.
translate (string1, string2, string3)	Returns the first argument with occurrences of characters the second argument replaced by the character at the corresponding position in the third argument.

Node-set functions

The XPath node-set functions are used for filtering and selecting node-sets. The following functions are node-set functions:

NODE-SET FUNCTIONS

Name	Description
count (node-set)	Returns the number of nodes in the node-set.
id (object)	Selects an item by its unique ID. The object is an XPath object. Returns a node-set consisting of node/nodes with ID/IDs corresponding to the parameter passed after it is converted to a string.
last ()	Returns the number of nodes in the node-set.
local-name (node-set)	Returns the local part of the expanded name.
name (node-set)	Returns the expanded name as a string.
namespace-uri (node-set)	Returns the namespace URI of the expanded-name of the node-set.
postion ()	Returns the index number of the node. The first node returns a position of 1.

Number functions

The number functions can be used with comparison operators and can return strings or numbers. They are shown in the following table:

NUMBER FUNCTIONS

Name	Description
number (object)	Converts its argument to a number. This function is not supported in the Internet Explorer 5 DOM.
ceiling (number)	Returns the smallest (closest to negative infinity) number that is not less than the argument and that is an integer. This function is not supported in the Internet Explorer 5 DOM.
floor (number)	Returns the largest (closest to positive infinity) number that is not greater than the argument and that is an integer. This function is not supported in the Internet Explorer 5 DOM.
round (number)	Returns the number that is closest to the argument and that is an integer. If there are two such numbers, the one that is closest to positive infinity is returned. This function is not supported in the Internet Explorer 5 DOM.
sum (node-set)	Returns the sum for each node in the argument node-set. The nodes are first converted to number values before summing. This function is not supported in the Internet Explorer 5 DOM.

XSLT Functions

There are numerous XSLT functions that give information about nodes in a collection. The Microsoft XML parser 2.0 only supports the *node-set* function.

XSLT FUNCTIONS

Name	Description
current ()	Returns the current context node.
document (object, node-set)	Allows access to XML documents other than the main source document. This function is not supported in the Internet Explorer 5 DOM.

(continued)

XSLT Functions *continued*

Name	Description
element-available (string)	Returns *true* if the expanded-name is the name of an instruction. If the expanded-name has a namespace URI equal to the XSLT namespace URI, then it refers to an element defined by XSLT. Otherwise, it refers to an extension element. If the expanded-name has a null namespace URI, the element-available function will return *false*. It can be used with the *choose* and *if* elements. This function is not supported in the Internet Explorer 5 DOM.
format-number (number, string, string)	Converts its first argument to a string using the format pattern string specified by the second argument and the decimal-format named by the third argument, or the default decimal-format, if there is no third argument. The format pattern string is in the syntax specified by the JDK 1.1 *DecimalFormat* class.* This function is not supported in the Internet Explorer 5 DOM.
generate-id (node-set)	Returns a string that uniquely identifies the node in the argument node-set that is first in document order. This function is not supported in the Internet Explorer 5 DOM.
key (string, object)	Selects items by a key and returns all the nodes with the specified key.
system-property (string)	Returns an object representing the value of the system property identified by the name. If there is no such system property, the empty string should be returned.
unparsed-entity-uri (string)	Returns the URI of the unparsed entity with the specified name in the same document as the context node. This function is not supported in the Internet Explorer 5 DOM.
function-available (string)	Returns *true* if and only if the expanded-name is the name of a function in the function library. It can be used with the *choose* and *if* elements. This function is not supported in the Internet Explorer 5 DOM.

---

* See *http://java.sun.com/products/jdk/1.1/docs/api/java.text.DecimalFormat.html* for information on the class DecimalFormat.

XSL AND XSLT SUPPORT IN XML DOM

Now that we have covered XSL and XSLT documents, we can cover the *XTLRuntime* object from the XML parser that shipped with Internet Explorer 5. The *XTLRuntime* object is an extension to the W3C DOM. As we mentioned in Chapter 11, the *XTLRuntime* object works with XSL. This object implements the *IXTLRuntime* interface. The methods implemented by the *IXTLRuntime* interface can be called from within XSL or XSLT documents. Let's look at the properties and methods of the *IXTLRuntime* interface first.

IXTLRuntime Interface

The *IXTLRuntime* interface inherits the *IXMLDOMNode* object interface. In addition to the properties and methods of the *IXMLDOMNode* interface, *IXTLRuntime* extends the *IXMLDOMNode* interface with a set of methods that are accessible to style sheets. The extended methods are as follows:

EXTENDED *IXTLRUNTIME* METHODS

Name	Description
absoluteChildNumber (node)*	Returns the index of the node relative to all its siblings within its parent's child node list. The first node in the child node list is number 1.
ancestorChildNumber (nodeName, node)*	Returns the index of the nearest ancestor of a node in the child node list with the name *nodeName*.
childNumber (node)*	Returns the first node in the child node list with the same node name.
depth (startNode)*	Returns the depth of a level within the document tree at which the *startNode* appears.
formatDate (date, format, locale)	Formats the supplied date using the specified formatting options. The following formats are allowed: m – Month (1-12) mm – Month (01-12) mmm – Month (Jan-Dec) mmmm – Month (January – December) mmmmm – Month, first letter d – Day (1-31) dd – Day (01-31) dddd – Day (Sunday-Saturday)

(continued)

Extended *IXTLRuntime* Methods *continued*

Name	Description
formatDate (date, format, locale), continued	yy – Year (00-99) yyyy – Year (1900-9999) The locale determines the sequence of values in the date. The default is month-day-year.
formatIndex (number, format)	Formats the supplied integer using the specified numerical system. The format can be one of the following: 1 – Standard numbering system 01 – Standard numbering with leading zeros A – Uppercase letter sequence "A" to "Z", then "AA" to "ZZ" a – Lowercase letter sequence "a" to "z", then "aa" to "zz" I – Uppercase Roman numerals, such as I, II, III, and IV i – Lowercase Roman numberals, such as i, ii, iii, and iv
formatNumber (number, format)	Formats the supplied number using the specified format. The format string can have one or more of the following characters: # - Displays only significant digits and omit the insignificant digits. 0 – Displays insignificant zeros if a number has fewer digits than there are zeros in the format. ? – Adds spaces for the insignificant zeros on either side of the decimal points, so that decimal points align when using a fixed-point font. . – Indicates the position of the decimal point. , – Displays a thousands separator or scales a number by a multiple of one thousand.

Name	Description
	% - Displays the number as a percentage. E or e – Displays the number in scientific format. E- or e- – Places a negative sign by negative exponents. E+ or e+ – Places a negative sign by a negative exponent and a plus sign by a positive exponent.
formatTime (time, format, locale)	Formats the supplied time using the specified formatting options. The format can be the following values: h – Hours (0-23) hh – Hours (00 – 23) m – Minutes (0-59) mm- Minutes (00-59) s – Seconds (0-59) ss – Seconds (00-59) AM/PM – Adds AM or PM and displays value in a 12 hour format am/pm – Adds am or pm and displays value in 12 hour format A/P – Adds A or P and displays the value in a 12 hour format a/p – Adds a or p and displays the value in a 12 hour format [h]:mm – Displays the elapsed time in hours [mm]:ss – Displays the elapsed time in minutes [ss] - Displays the elapsed time in seconds ss.00 – Displays fractions of a second The locale is used to determine the correct separator characters.
uniqueID (node)	Returns the unique identifier for the supplied node.

To reference these methods in an XSL or XSLT document, you need to use the *eval* element in your style sheets.

As mentioned, the *eval* element evaluates a script expression and generates a text string. We can create a new XSL document named NorthwindPODOM.xsl for the NorthwindPO.xml document that uses the methods of the *IXTLRuntime* interface as follows:

```
<?xml version="1.0"?>
<xsl:stylesheet xmlns:xsl="http://www.w3.org/TR/WD-xsl">
    <xsl:template match="/">
        <xsl:for-each match="//">
            <html>
            <body style="{color:black}">
                nodeName: <xsl:node-name />
                Absolute Child Number:
                <xsl:eval>absoluteChildNumber(this)</xsl:eval>
                Depth:
                <xsl:eval>depth(this)</xsl:eval>
                <br></br>
                <xsl:for-each match=".//">
                    <p style="{color:blue}">
                        nodeName: <xsl:node-name />
                    Absolute Child Number:
                    <xsl:eval>absoluteChildNumber(this)</xsl:eval>
                    Depth:
                    <xsl:eval>depth(this)</xsl:eval>
                    <br></br>
                    </p>
                    <xsl:for-each match=".//">
                        <p style="{color:green}">
                            nodeName: <xsl:node-name />
                            Absolute Child Number:
                            <xsl:eval>absoluteChildNumber(this)
                            </xsl:eval>
                            Depth:
                            <xsl:eval>depth(this)</xsl:eval>
                            <br></br>
                        </p>
                </xsl:for-each>
```

```
            </xsl:for-each>
          </body>
          </html>
        </xsl:for-each>
    </xsl:template>
</xsl:stylesheet>
```

In this code, we use three *for-each* element loops to apply templates to all the nodes in the top-three levels of the XML document. We also retrieve the name of the selected node, the absolute child number of the selected node, and the depth within the document tree at which the selected node appears. The results of applying this XSL document to the NorthwindPO.xml document is shown in Figure 12-5.

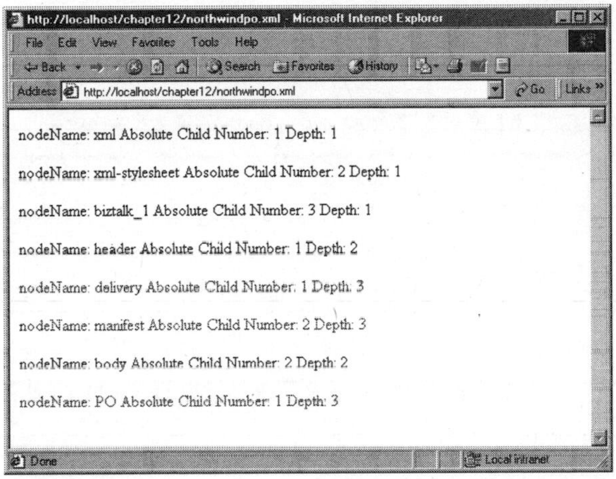

Figure 12-5. *The NorthwindPO.xml document using the XTLRuntime object in the style sheet.*

XMLDOMXSLTemplate and *XMLDOMXSLProcessor* **Objects**

Beginning with the third release of the Microsoft XML parser, the *XMLDOMXSLTemplate* object can be used to hold an instance of an XSL or XSLT template. You can create an *XMLDOMXSLTemplate* object variable in an ASP application for XSL or XSLT documents that may be used frequently or by multiple ASP documents. Since the XSL or

XSLT documents will be stored in the *XMLDOMXSLTemplate* object variable, they will not need to be reloaded or compiled when they are needed. The *XMLDOMXSLProcessor* object is designed to work with the *XMLDOMXSLTemplate* object to transform a given document. The *XMLDOMXSLTemplate* object implements the *IXMLDOMXSLTemplate* interface and the *XMLDOMXSLProcessor* object implements the *IXMLDOMXSLProcessor* interface. The methods and properties of the *IXMLDOMXSLTemplate* and *IXMLDOM-XSLProcessor* interfaces are as follows:

IXMLDOMXSLTEMPLATE PROPERTY

Name	Description
Stylesheet	Allows an XSL style sheet to compile to an XSL template

IXMLDOMXSLTEMPLATE METHOD

Name	Description
CreateProcessor	Creates an *XMLDOMXSLProcessor* object that can use the template

IXMLDOMXSLPROCESSOR PROPERTIES

Name	Description
input	Sets the XML document that will be transformed.
output	Retrieves the output object that will hold the results of the transformation. Can be any object that supports *IStream* interface, *IPersistStream* interface, *IXMLDOMDocument* interface, ASP *Response* object, and *ADODB.stream* object.
readyState	The current state of the processor object.
startMode	The base name of the start mode.
startModeURI	Returns the namespace URI of the start mode.
stylesheet	The XSL style sheet that will be used to perform the transformation.
ownerTemplate	Returns the style sheet template that was used when creating the XSL processor object.

IXMLDOMXSLPROCESSOR **METHODS**

Name	Description
addObject (object, namespaceURI)	Used to pass objects (such as an *XMLDOMDocument* object) to a style sheet.
AddParameter (baseName, parameter, namespaceURI)	Used to pass variables into a style sheet. The variables will be referenced by the base name. The parameter can be a number, Boolean, string, *XMLDOMNodeList* object or *XMLDOMNode* object. The namespace is optional. You can reference these variables in the style sheet by using *<xsl:param>*.
Reset()	Resets the processor object back to the state the object was in prior to calling the *transform* method.

SetStartMode (mode, namespace)	This method allows you to perform subsets of a larger XSL transformation. Using this method is the same as adding the following to the XSL style sheet:
	`<xsl:template match="/">`
	   `<xsl:apply-templates select="*"`
	      `mode="{mode}"/>`
	`</xsl:template>`
	The namespace is optional.

Transform()	Used to begin the transformation or resume a transformation that returned *VARIANT_FALSE*.

To see how to use these objects in ASP pages, create a new ASP application. In the global ASP page add the following code:

```
Sub Application_OnStart
Dim l_oXSLDoc
Dim g_oAcmePOXSLTemplate
Set l_oXSLDoc = CreateObject("Msxml2.FreeThreadedDOMDocument")
Set g_oNorthwindPOXSLTemplate=CreateObject("Msxml2.XSLTemplate")
l_oXSLDoc.async = false
l_oXSLDoc.load("C:\chapter 12\NorthwindPODOM.xsl")
Set g_oNorthwindPOXSLTemplate.stylesheet = l_oXSLDoc
Set Application("template") = g_oNorthwindPOXSLTemplate
End Sub
```

In this example, we created a local document object variable and an *XML-DOMXSLTemplate* object variable that will have application wide scope, and then we loaded the NorthwindPODOM.xsl XSL document. This document will be compiled and stored in the *g_oNorthwindPOXSLTemplate* variable and can be used by multiple ASP documents and clients at the same time. To reference this document in an ASP document named NPODOM.asp, we would need to add the following code to the ASP document:

```
<%@ Language="VBScript" %>
<SCRIPT LANGUAGE="VBScript" RUNAT="Server">
Dim l_oXMLDoc
Dim l_oXMLProccessor
Set l_oXMLDoc = CreateObject("Msxml2.DOMDocument")
l_oXMLDoc.async = false
l_oXMLDoc.load("C:\chapter 12\NorthwindPO.xml")
set l_oXMLProccessor = Application("template").createProcessor()
l_oXMLProccessor.output = Response
l_oXMLProccessor.input = l_oXMLDoc
l_oXMLProccessor.transform()
</SCRIPT>
```

In this case, the NorthwindPO.xml document has been transformed in the ASP page using the XSL document stored in the application variable named template.

PROGRAMMING WITH XSL AND XSLT

Although Internet Explorer 5 cannot identify the namespace in an XSLT document, versions 2.6 and higher of the XML parser can use XSLT documents to transform XML documents. We will use the same BizTalk document we used earlier in this chapter, with some minor changes that will fix errors in the document, to perform the transformation using XSLT documents. Even though we did not receive any error messages when we used the BizTalk document, two errors do exist in the code. The following two elements are not defined in the schema as being children of the *POlines* element:

```
<count>2</count>
<totalAmount>192000.00</totalAmount>
```

If you try to work with the BizTalk document using the XML DOM, the *load* method of the *IXMLDOMDocument* interface will fail. It's important to note this, as we have come this far with no hint that there was an error in the document. This stresses the importance of validating your documents. To correct the error, delete the above two elements from the XML document and rename the document Northwind-

POXSLT.xml. You can also delete the references to these two elements in your XSL and XSLT document. Let's now look at a code sample, which you could use in your production systems, that shows how to code with the XML DOM.

Using the XML DOM to Work with XSLT and XSL

Since the XML DOM is capable of working with XSLT and XSL, we can write an application that uses the DOM to transform an XML document using either an XSLT or an XSL document. This application can be placed on the server and used by an ASP page. If you know that the client has the DOM installed, you can also use this component on the client. In our case, we'll write the application to work on the server.

When a document is requested, the ASP document will call the application, and then the application will transform the XML document using an XSL or XSLT document. After the XML document is transformed, the application will return the document to the ASP document, which will return the transformed document to the client. We will write the application in Microsoft Visual Basic.

> **NOTE** This Visual Basic component will need to run under Microsoft Transaction Server (MTS) to work properly with an ASP document. We won't discuss how to write MTS components in Visual Basic as that would go beyond the scope of this book.

To write the application, you must start by creating a new Visual Basic ActiveX DLL project. Name the project *TransformXML*, and name the default class *Transform*. You will need to get a reference to Microsoft XML version 2.6 and the MTS library. In Microsoft Windows 2000, this library will be the COM+ Services Type Library. In the Properties Window change the *MTSTransactionMode* property to *1 – No Transactions*.

Now that Visual Basic has properties, you should use properties instead of global variables. Properties allow you to have more control over the variables in your project than using global variables. We will use properties in this example, even for private variables.

This example will use three document objects. The first document object, *m_oDOMDocumentSource*, will be used to get a reference to the XML document. The second document object, *m_oDOMDocumentStylesheet*, will be used to get a reference to the XSL or XSLT document. The third document object, *m_oDOMDocumentResult*, will hold the transformed XML document.

Add the following declarations and properties to the Visual Basic project named TransformXML.vbp:

```
Option Explicit
'Document Object for the source
Private WithEvents m_oDOMDocumentSource As MSXML2.DOMDocument26
```

(continued)

```
'Document object for the XSL or XSLT document
Private WithEvents m_oDOMDocumentStylesheet As MSXML2.DOMDocument26
'Document object for transformed XML document
Private m_oDOMDocumentResult As MSXML2.DOMDocument26
'Variable used by StyleSheetURL property
Private m_sStyleSheetURL As String
'Variable used by ReturnHTML property
Private m_sReturnHTML As String
'Get a reference to the MTS Object Context Events
Implements ObjectControl

'Property to get and set StyleSheetURl property
Private Property Get StyleSheetURL() As String
    StyleSheetURL = m_sStyleSheetURL
End Property
Private Property Let StyleSheetURL
    (ByVal v_sNewStyleSheetURL As String)
    m_sStyleSheetURL = v_sNewStyleSheetURL_
End Property

'Property to get and set return HTML
Private Property Get ReturnHTML() As String
    ReturnHTML = m_sReturnHTML
End Property
Private Property Let ReturnHTML(ByVal v_sNewReturnHTML As String)
    m_sReturnHTML = v_sNewReturnHTML
End Property
```

Now we will actually implement the *objectControl* interface:

```
Private Sub ObjectControl_Activate()
    Set m_oDOMDocumentSource = New DOMDocument26
    Set m_oDOMDocumentStylesheet = New DOMDocument26
    Set m_oDOMDocumentResult = New DOMDocument26
End Sub

Private Function ObjectControl_CanBePooled() As Boolean
    ObjectControl_CanBePooled = False
End Function

Private Sub ObjectControl_Deactivate()
    Set oDOMDocumentSource = Nothing
    Set oDOMDocumentStylesheet = Nothing
    Set oDOMDocumentResult = Nothing
End Sub
```

This application is complex because we must wait for the XML document and the XSL or XSLT document to be loaded before we can perform the transformation. We declare the *m_oDOMDocumentSource* and *m_oDOMDocumentStylesheet* with events to get the events of these objects. Using these events, we can trap when the document is actually loaded. When both documents are loaded, we can do the transformation and return the transformed document.

We will now add a function that will return the transformed XHTML string. This function can be called from an ASP page, or it can be called from any application. Add the following function to the project:

```
Public Function ApplyXSLStyle(ByVal v_vXMLDocument As Variant, _
                 ByVal v_vXMLStyleSheet As Variant) As String
    On Error GoTo ApplyStyleError

    StyleSheetURL = v_vXMLStyleSheet
    m_oDOMDocumentResult.async = False
    m_oDOMDocumentSource.async = False
    m_oDOMDocumentStylesheet.async = False
    m_oDOMDocumentSource.Load (v_vXMLDocument)
    'Check for an error
    If m_oDOMDocumentSource.parseError.errorCode <> 0 Then
        DOMError
    End If
    'We will not get to this next line of code until the
    'document is loaded, and the code in
    'm_oDOMDocumentSource_onreadystatechange is executed.
    ApplyXSLStyle = ReturnHTML
    GetObjectContext.SetComplete
    Exit Function
ApplyStyleError:
    Err.Raise Err.Number, Err.Source, _
        "The following error has occured:" & vbCrLf & _
        "Error Description: " & Err.Description & vbCrLf & _
        "Error Source: " & Err.Source & _
        "XSLXSLT:ApplyStyle" & vbCrLf & _
        "Error Number: " & Err.Number
End Function
```

Once we call the *load* function, the next event fired is the *onreadystatechange* event. The *onreadystatechange* event is called four times. The first time the event is raised is when the document is loading. While the document is loading, the *readystate* variable of the *IXMLDOMDocument* object will be 1. The event is raised for a second time when the document is loaded but not yet in the document object. When the document is loaded but not in the document object, the *readystate* variable will have a value of 2. The event is raised for a third time when the document is loaded and partially loaded into the document object. When the document is partially loaded the *readystate* property will have a value of 3. The fourth time the event is raised the document is completely loaded into the document object and ready to use. When the document is fully loaded, the *readystate* property will be 4. Thus, using the *onreadystatechange* event and the *readystate* property, we can determine when the object is actually loaded.

Because we will need to handle any errors loading documents for three document objects, we have moved the error handler into a separate function called *DOMError*. Add the following into the project:

```
Private Sub DOMError()
    Dim objXMLParseError As IXMLDOMParseError
    If m_oDOMDocumentResult.parseError.errorCode <> 0 Then
        Set objXMLParseError = m_oDOMDocumentResult.parseError
    End If
    If m_oDOMDocumentSource.parseError.errorCode <> 0 Then
        Set objXMLParseError = m_oDOMDocumentSource.parseError
    End If
    If m_oDOMDocumentStylesheet.parseError.errorCode <> 0 Then
        Set objXMLParseError = m_oDOMDocumentResult.parseError
    End If

    With objXMLParseError
        Err.Raise .errorCode, _
            "XMLStylesheet.XSLXSLT", _
            "The following error occured:" & vbCrLf & _
            "error code: " & .errorCode & vbCrLf & _
            "error file position: " & .filepos & vbCrLf & _
            "error line: " & .Line & vbCrLf & _
            "error line position: " & .linepos & vbCrLf & _
            "error reason: " & .reason & vbCrLf & _
            "error source Text: " & .srcText & vbCrLf & _
            " XSLXSLT:ApplyStyle"
    End With
End Sub
```

The error handler is essentially the same code we used in the last chapter for the *parserError* object.

Once the source document is loaded (when its *readystate* is equal to 4), we will want to load the XSL or XSLT document. We will do this in the *onreadystatechange* event of the source document. Add the following code to the *onreadystatechange* event of the *m_oDOMDocumentSource* object:

```
Private Sub m_oDOMDocumentSource_onreadystatechange()
   On Error GoTo m_oDOMDocumentSourceORSCError
   If m_oDOMDocumentSource.readyState = 4 Then
      m_oDOMDocumentStylesheet.Load (StyleSheetURL)
      If m_oDOMDocumentStylesheet.parseError.errorCode <> 0 Then
         DOMError
      End If
   End If
   Exit Sub
   m_oDOMDocumentSourceORSCError:
   Err.Raise Err.Number, Err.Source, _
      "The following error has occurred:" & vbCrLf & _
      "Error Description: " & Err.Description & vbCrLf & _
      "Error Source: " & Err.Source & _
      "XSLXSLT:m_oDOMDocumentSource:onreadystatechange" & _
      vbCrLf & "Error Number: " & Err.Number
End Sub
```

In this example, we will load the XSLT or XSL document when the source document is loaded.

Because we have now begun the load for the *m_oDOMDocumentStylesheet* object, the next four steps in the program will be raising the *onreadystatechange* event of the *m_oDOMDocumentStylesheet* object. Once the stylesheet document has been loaded, we can apply it to the source object using the *transformNodeToObject* method of the *IXMLDOMDocument* interface. As we've learned in Chapter 11, the *transformNodeToObject* method will take a document object as its first parameter that contains either an XSL or XSLT document. The second parameter of the *transform-NodeToObject* method will be an object that the transformed document will be placed in. Thus, the *transformNodeToObject* method will work perfectly to transform our XML documents using either XSL or XSLT. Add the following code to the *onreadystatechange* event of the *m_oDOMDocumentStylesheet* object:

```
Private Sub m_oDOMDocumentStylesheet_onreadystatechange()
   On Error GoTo m_oDOMDocumentStylesheetORSCError
   If m_oDOMDocumentStylesheet.readyState = 4 Then
      m_oDOMDocumentSource.transformNodeToObject _
```

(continued)

```
            m_oDOMDocumentStylesheet, m_oDOMDocumentResult
            If m_oDOMDocumentSource.parseError.errorCode <> 0 Then
                DOMError
            Else
            ReturnHTML = m_oDOMDocumentResult.xml
            End If
        End If
        Exit Sub
    m_oDOMDocumentStylesheetORSCError:
            Err.Raise Err.Number, Err.Source, _
                "The following error has occurred:" & vbCrLf & _
                "Error Description: " & Err.Description & vbCrLf & _
                "Error Source: " & Err.Source & _
                "XSLXSLT:m_oDOMDocumentStylesheet:onreadystatechange" & _
                vbCrLf & "Error Number: " & Err.Number
    End Sub
```

When this event is called for the fourth time—that is, when the *m_oDOM-DocumentStylesheet* object is fully loaded, the program will continue execution in the *ApplyXSLStyle* method after the line of code that called the *m_oDOMDocumentSource* object *load* method, which is *ApplyXSLStyle = ReturnHTML*.

You will need to compile this DLL and run it under an MTS package in Microsoft Windows NT 4 or configure it as a COM+ application in Windows 2000, as shown in Figure 12-6.

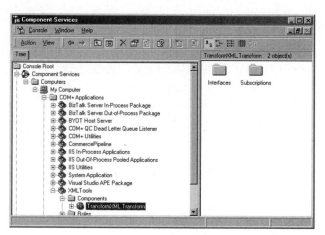

Figure 12-6. *The component registered under COM+ Component Services.*

In this case, the COM+ application XMLTools was called. Once you have registered the component under MTS or COM+ component services, you can create an ASP page named NorthwindPO.asp that can use this object as follows:

```
<%@ Language=VBScript %>
<SCRIPT LANGUAGE=vbscript RUNAT=Server>
   Dim objXSLXSLT, sreturn
   Set objXSLXSLT = server.CreateObject ("TransformXML.Transform")
   sreturn = objXSLXSLT.ApplyXSLStyle _
     ("http://localhost/Chapter12/NorthwindPOXSLT.xml", _
        "http://localhost/Chapter12/NorthwindPO3.xslt")
   Response.Write sreturn
</SCRIPT>
```

You will need to change the parameters of the *ApplyXSLStyle* function so that it references the files in the correct location (in the example case, the files were located on the localhost under Chapter12). This code will work with either an XSL or an XSLT document. The page will display the same format as before.

SUMMARY

For XML that does not contain elements that define the presentation of the XML documents, you can use CSS, XSL, or XSLT documents to transform the document. XSL provides a powerful tool to transform XML documents in virtually any way that is necessary. Currently XSL focuses on the transformation of XML into XHTML. It is likely that XSL will provide more powerful transformations in the future.

CSS, XSL, and XSLT allow us to transform XML into user services components that present XML data in a manner that would provide users with the information they require. Up to this point, the browser-based user services components we have built were not dynamic—that is, they did not allow the user to interact with the information being presented in the interface. If we want to allow users to input information, select the information they want to view, and interact with the interface, we need to add code to our user services components that will perform these functions and update the user interface. We'll discuss how to create the dynamic user services components in Chapter 13.

Chapter 13

Creating Dynamic User Services Components

In Chapter 12, we discussed ways to present XML data in a Web browser using XSL, XSL Transformations (XSLT), and cascading style sheets (CSS). These technologies allowed us to create user services components that could present users with information located in XML documents. Up to this point, the browser-based user services components we have built were not dynamic—that is, they did not allow the user to interact with the information being presented in the interface. If we want the user to be able to interact with the browser-based interface, we will need to add script to our user services components that can respond to the user's input and provide information to the user based on this input.

In this chapter, we'll discuss how to use Dynamic HTML (DHTML) to create dynamic Web-based user services components. DHTML allows you to embed scripts written in either the VBScript or JScript programming languages into an HTML page. Using DHTML, you can create Web pages that contain fully functioning user services components that allow information to be passed back and forth between the user and the system. We'll also use the XML Data Source Object (DSO) in DHTML pages. The XML DSO, which shipped as part of Microsoft Internet Explorer 5, is specifically designed for creating Web-based XML applications. The XML DSO enables you to bind HTML elements to structured XML data using DHTML's data-binding facility. First let's take a look at DHTML.

DHTML

DHTML has made it possible for Web-based user services components to respond directly to input from users without having to make calls to the Web server. Before developers began to use DHTML, they had to rely on server-side applications to process the information inputted by the user and to send the result back to the client. These applications were often written using Common Gateway Interface (CGI) or, more recently, using Active Server Pages (ASP) or Java Server Pages (JSP). Although these programs transferred information to the client, the data was still being formatted and selected on the server. Each time the client needed new information or a different view of the data, another request had to be sent to the server.

Web-based user services components that respond directly to the user's input without having to go back to the server contain DHTML that is embedded in the HTML page. The DHTML code accesses the objects belonging to the Web browser that is hosting the HTML page. The ability to access the browser's objects is what allows DHTML to read and change the content in the Web page and respond to events created by objects in the page. Thus, DHTML creates dynamic Web-based user services components by accessing the browser's objects.

> **NOTE**   Starting with version 4, Microsoft Internet Explorer included DHTML in its technology to allow developers to create Web-based user services components that could respond to the user's input. Netscape Navigator also included a version of DHTML in its Web browser that gave access to the Netscape objects. In addition to including code within HTML pages, Internet Explorer 4 introduced *scriptlets* that allow developers to separate the code from the Web page. The scriptlets are Web pages that contain functions or subroutines that can be accessed and used by a Web page.

DHTML Object Model

DHTML uses an object model to give developers programmable access to the components in a Web page, from the HTML tags to the document itself. The document object can be accessed through script in the HTML page. The DHTML object model uses collections to contain elements in the HTML document. The elements are contained in a hierarchical fashion. Let's use the following HTML code as an example of using DHTML elements and collections in a DHTML document:

```
<html>
    <head>
        <title>
```

```
            DHTML
            </title>
            <script language="vbscript">
                Function showTags()
                    dim strTagNames, intCounter
                    strTagNames=""
                    For intCounter=0 to window.document.all.length-1
                        strTagNames=strTagNames & _
                        window.document.all(intCounter).tagName & " "
                    Next
                    MsgBox "The tags are: " & strTagNames
                End Function
            </script>
</head>
<body onload="showTags()">
    <h1>
    This page demonstrates DHTML.
    </h1>
    <p>
    This document contains several <br></br><b>tags</b>
    </p>
</body>
</html>
```

The function could have also been written in JScript as follows:

```
<script language = "JScript">
function showTags()
    {
    var strTagNames = "";
    for (intCounter = 0; intCounter < document.all.length;
        intCounter++)
        {
        strTagNames = strTagNames +
            window.document.all(intCounter).tagName + " ";
        }
    alert ("This document contains the following tags: " +
        strTagNames);
    }
</script>
```

This DHTML document appears as shown in Figure 13-1.

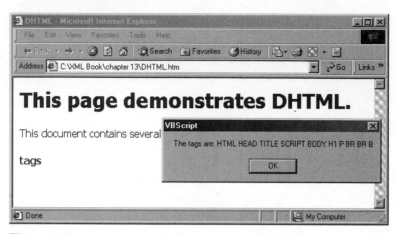

Figure 13-1.   *The DHTML page in Internet Explorer 5.*

The s*howTags* function shown in the preceding code uses the *window* object, which is the top level DHTML object. Contained within the *window* object is the *document* object. Contained within the *document* object is the *all* collection. The *all* collection contains all the elements within the document. The first item in the *all* collection has an index of zero. You can access this item by using *all(0)*. The *length* property of the *all* collection is the number of items in the collection. Thus, the preceding code will go through the *all* collection and get the name of each item in the collection. Notice that the closing *br* tag that we added to make the document compatible with XHTML was considered another tag. We could have also written just *document.all(intCounter)* instead of *window.document.all(intCounter)*, as *window* is the default object.

> **NOTE** Netscape Navigator does not support the Internet Explorer DHTML object hierarchy. There are some similarities between the two, but currently you can write DHTML for either Netscape Navigator or Internet Explorer or write code that works with the few objects that they both share. We will work with only the Internet Explorer DHTML object model, as it is most similar to the W3C DOM standard.

Events Associated with DHTML Objects

Another important part of the HTML code sample in the previous section is the use of events. When working with DHTML, events will form the foundation of your programming model. Using events, we can write code that responds to a user's actions. The events that are supported in most current browsers are: *onblur, onchange, onclick, ondbclick, onfocus, onkeydown, onkeypress, onkeyup, onload, onmousedown, onmousemove, onmouseout, onmouseover, onmouseup, onreset, onselect, onsubmit,* and *onunload.*

> **NOTE** We will not have a detailed discussion of the events and objects in the DHTML object model as it goes beyond the scope of an XML book. Many excellent references on DHTML are available, such as *Dynamic HTML Reference and Software Development Kit*, published by Microsoft Press, 1999.

The *Event* Object

The events listed in the previous section do not have any parameters. To get access to information such as which key was pressed and which mouse button was selected, you can use the *event* object. The *event* object contains a set of properties that can be used with these events. A partial list of the properties associated with the *event* object are: *altKey, button, clientX, clientY, ctrlKey, fromElement, keyCode, offsetX, offsetY, screenX, screenY, shiftKey, srcElement, x*, and *y*.

By using the events associated with DHTML objects and the *event* object's properties, you can have full control of an Internet Explorer 4 or Internet Explorer 5 Web-based interface.

You can also use the *ID* attribute when working with HTML element objects. This attribute represents the actual element object and can be used to get access to the element object's properties. You can manipulate the attributes for an element object by using the *getAttribute, setAttribute*, and *removeAttribute* methods and the *ID* attribute, as shown in the following example:

```
<html>
    <head>
        <title>
            DHTML
        </title>
        <script language="vbscript">
            Function RealignHeader()
                If FirstHeader.getAttribute("align")="middle" Then
                    FirstHeader.setAttribute "align", "center"
                End If
                MsgBox "The alignment for the h1 element is: " & _
                        Document.all("FirstHeader").align
            End Function
        </script>
    </head>
    <body>
        <h1 align="middle" id="FirstHeader">
            This page demonstrates DHTML.
        </h1>
```

(continued)

```
        <p>
            This document contains several <br></br><b>tags</b>
            <br></br>
            <button type="button"  onclick="RealignHeader">
                Click Me </button>
        </p>
    </body>
</html>
```

This page is shown in Figure 13-2.

Figure 13-2. *The DHTML page showing the h1 element's new attribute.*

In this code, we used the *onclick* event of a button to change the alignment of the header. When you click the button, the header content *This page demonstrates DHTML* will become centered. Thus, we have changed the user interface with an event that was triggered by the user clicking a button.

It's possible to write DHTML that will work in both Netscape Navigator and Internet Explorer 4 and Internet Explorer 5 because both browsers share some common objects in their object hierarchy. The W3C DOM Level 2 specification includes a section on a set of objects used for the manipulation of HTML that essentially includes DHTML. We can hope that when the DOM standard is complete, all future browsers will support the DOM and code can be written to a standard set osf objects. Internet Explorer 5 introduced a new feature called DHTML Behaviors, which are based on W3C standards and can be used to handle the events raised by DHTML objects. Let's take a look at DHTML Behaviors.

DHTML Behaviors

Internet Explorer 4 introduced DHTML scriptlets—components written in script that are an extension of the DHTML object model. Although scriptlets will still work with Internet Explorer 5, they are being replaced by DHTML Behaviors that offer functionality that scriptlets do not have. DHTML Behaviors allow us to associate behaviors to the events belonging to the HTML elements. Just as we associated DHTML script functions with the HTML element events, we will associate DHTML Behaviors with HTML element events. As is the case with DHTML, you can either include DHTML Behaviors in your HTML code or place them in separate files.

DHTML Behaviors are lightweight components that extend the functionality of the HTML elements and enable encapsulation and code reuse. DHTML Behaviors can be referenced in Internet Explorer 5 by using styles. A behavior can be defined anywhere a style is defined—for example, in a separate document, in a special section in the *head* element, or as an attribute of an HTML element. You can implement DHTML Behaviors in script using HTML Components (HTC). Let's look at an example of an HTC containing two behaviors. First create an HTC file called Color.htc using the following code:

```
<component>
    <attach event="onmouseover" for="element"
        handler="MouseOver"/>
    <attach event="onmouseout" for="element" handler="MouseOut"/>
    <script language="JScript">
        function MouseOver()
            {
            element.color="blue";
            element.align="center";
            }

        function MouseOut()
            {
            element.color="red";
            element.align="left";
            }
    </script>
</component>
```

This file is written in XML. All the example files discussed in this chapter are available on the companion CD. The root element of the HTC file is the *component* element. Next, two *attach* elements allow us to create two behaviors: one to attach the *MouseOut* function to the *onmouseout* event and one to attach the *MouseOver* function to the *onmouseover* event. The rest of the HTC file is just regular JScript, which will appear as text content of the *script* element. The JScript functions define what the behaviors will do. Below is an example that uses the HTC document:

```
<html>
<head>
<title>Behaviors</title>
    <style type="text/css">
                .colorchange { behavior:url(color.htc);}
    </style>
</head>
<body>
    <font color="green" class="colorchange">
        <h1>Behaviors</h1>
    </font>
    </body>
</html>
```

When you open this document in a browser, the color of the text in *h1* will change to blue as you move your mouse within the *h1* text area and to red when you move out of the text area. The two behaviors we have defined have allowed us to change the color of the text in response to the *onmouseover* and *onmouseout* events.

Notice that the behavior was also supposed to change the *align* attribute, but this did not work. The behavior did not work as it was supposed to because we associated the style with the *font* element that contains the *h1* element. The *font* element allows us to set the color of the content of the *h1* element. Since the *font* element does not have an *align* attribute, it is just ignored. To fix this problem, change the HTML code so that you add the style to the *h1* element as follows:

```
<h1 class="colorchange">
```

You will now find that when the mouse cursor is over the *h1* text it will jump from being left justified to center justified, and from center justified to left justified. The second part of the behavior is working because *align* is the attribute of the *h1* element. We can use behaviors to extend the functionality of any of the elements in the HTML document. We will use HTC to create business services components in Chapter 14.

Now that we've examined how to use DHTML to create dynamic user services components, we'll look at how to use the XML DSO to bind elements in a DHTML page to XML data.

THE XML DSO

The XML DSO allows you to bring data over to the client as XML and then manipulate the XML data directly on the client. As mentioned earlier in the chapter, the XML DSO is a Microsoft technology available in Internet Explorer 5.

> **NOTE** The XML DSO does not make or maintain any connection to a data source. Therefore, any changes that are made to the XML data on the client will not be reflected on the server. To update a data store on the server, a special application would have to be written that could read the updated XML data and then update the data source. Writing such an application is very difficult. A better method to update the data is to use the Microsoft Remote Data Services (RDS) control, which is designed for both reading and updating data on the server. The RDS can connect directly to a database using either a SQL string or a stored procedure.

The XML DSO allows you to work with XML data that is embedded directly in your HTML code. This embedded XML code creates *data islands*.

To create a data island, you will use the new HTML *xml* element. This element is not part of the W3C HTML standard. Only Internet Explorer 5 recognizes the *xml* element. The DSO will find the data located in the *xml* element and use it as a data island. The *xml* element includes an *id* attribute that will be used to reference the data island. The *xml* element looks as follows:

```
<xml id="orderDSO">
<!--XML data goes here -->
</xml>
```

You can also reference XML data in an external XML document by using the *xml* element and the *src* attribute as follows:

```
<xml id="orderDSO" src="NorthwindOrder.xml"></xml>
```

As mentioned above, the XML DSO gives you the ability to read and manipulate XML data islands. You can also bind certain *form* elements to XML data using the XML DSO, which means that the data in the XML DSO will be displayed in the element. Once an element is bound to XML data using the XML DSO, any manipulation of the data you make using the XML DSO will be reflected in the elements that are bound to the XML Data. This will greatly simplify your coding of Web-based user services components. Let's begin by looking at how to bind HTML elements to XML data using the XML DSO.

Binding HTML Elements to XML Data Using the XML DSO

Once you have created a reference to an XML data source using the *xml* element, you can bind this data to some of the HTML elements in a document. With some of the elements, you can display the content that is within the element as either text or as HTML. You would display it as HTML when the content contains HTML elements that you want to be rendered as HTML. The following elements can be bound to XML data using the XML DSO in Internet Explorer 5:

HTML Element	Bound Property
a	*href*
*applet**	*param*
*button***	*innertext, innerhtml*
*div***	*innertext, innerhtml*
frame	*src*
iframe	*src*
img	*src*
input type=checkbox*	*checked*
input type=hidden*	*value*
input type=label*	*value*
Input type=password*	*value*
input type=radio*	*checked*
input type=text*	*value*
*label***	*innertext, innerhtml*
*marquee***	*innertext, innerhtml*
*object**	*param*
*select**	*option*
*span***	*innertext, innerhtml*
table	*-*
*text**	value

*   Content in this element can be updated
** Element can be displayed as HTML

The *table* element is the only HTML element that allows *tabular data binding*. Tabular data binding allows you to bind all the content of an element in an XML document.

XML DSO EXAMPLES

In this section, we will create an example that allows a user to view the data stored in a data island in an HTML page using the XML DSO. This example creates a user services component that is contained within Internet Explorer 5 and that performs all the normal movement through records, such as move next, move previous, and so forth. To begin, we must create the XML data, a DTD for the XML data, and an HTML page to embed the XML data. We will then need to add DHTML script to the HTML page. The DHTML script works with the DSO and allows the user to move through the records using a Web browser. For this example, you will use the XML data from the BizTalk example in Chapter 12. Create a file called NorthwindPO.xml, and add the following XML data to the file:

```
<?xml version="1.0" standalone="no" ?>
<!DOCTYPE POLines SYSTEM "NorthwindPO.dtd">
<POLines>
    <Item>
        <line>1</line>
        <partno>pc1010</partno>
        <qty>200</qty>
        <uom>EACH</uom>
        <unitPrice>800.00</unitPrice>
        <discount>10</discount>
        <totalAmount>144000.00</totalAmount>
    </Item>
    <Item>
        <line>1</line>
        <partno>monitor17</partno>
        <qty>200</qty>
        <uom>EACH</uom>
        <unitPrice>300.00</unitPrice>
        <discount>20</discount>
        <totalAmount>48000.00</totalAmount>
    </Item>
</POLines>
```

Create a DTD for this XML document called NorthwindPO.dtd with the following declarations:

```
<!ELEMENT POLines  (Item+)>
<!ELEMENT Item  (line , partno , qty , uom , unitPrice ,
              discount , totalAmount)>
```

(continued)

```
<!ELEMENT line  (#PCDATA)>
<!ELEMENT partno  (#PCDATA)>
<!ELEMENT qty  (#PCDATA)>
<!ELEMENT uom  (#PCDATA)>
<!ELEMENT unitPrice  (#PCDATA)>
<!ELEMENT discount  (#PCDATA)>
<!ELEMENT totalAmount  (#PCDATA)>
```

You could also create the following BizTalk schema called NorthwindPO.xsd to validate NorthwindPO.xml:

```
<?xml version = "1.0"?>
<Schema name = "NorthwindPO.xsd"
    xmlns = "urn:schemas-microsoft-com:xml-data"
    xmlns:dt = "urn:schemas-microsoft-com:datatypes">
    <ElementType name = "POLines" content = "eltOnly"
                order = "seq">
        <element type = "Item" minOccurs = "1" maxOccurs = "*"/>
    </ElementType>
    <ElementType name = "Item" content = "eltOnly" order = "seq">
        <element type = "line"/>
        <element type = "partno"/>
        <element type = "qty"/>
        <element type = "uom"/>
        <element type = "unitPrice"/>
        <element type = "discount"/>
        <element type = "totalAmount"/>
    </ElementType>
    <ElementType name = "line" content = "textOnly"/>
    <ElementType name = "partno" content = "textOnly"/>
    <ElementType name = "qty" content = "textOnly"/>
    <ElementType name = "uom" content = "textOnly"/>
    <ElementType name = "unitPrice" content = "textOnly"/>
    <ElementType name = "discount" content = "textOnly"/>
    <ElementType name = "totalAmount" content = "textOnly"/>
</Schema>
```

Notice that the *Item* element is defined such that it can appear either one time or several times. This is exactly the type of element we want to bind to a table. Once bound to a table, each instance of the *Item* element will be placed into a row in the table. Let's look at how this can be done.

You can create the following HTML document that uses the XML DSO to render the NorthwindPO.xml XML document in the browser:

```html
<html>
    <xml src="NorthwindPO.xml" id="NorthwindDSO"></xml>
    <body>
    <table  border="2" width="100%" datasrc="#NorthwindDSO"
            cellpadding="5">
        <thead>
            <th>Line Item</th>
            <th>Part No</th>
            <th>Quantity</th>
            <th>UOM</th>
            <th>Unit Price</th>
            <th>Discount</th>
            <th>Total</th>
        </thead>
            <tbody>
                <tr>
                    <td valign="top"><span datafld="line"></span>
                    </td>
                    <td valign="top"><span datafld="partno"></span>
                    </td>
                    <td valign="top"><span datafld="qty"></span>
                    </td>
                    <td valign="top"><span datafld="uom"></span>
                    </td>
                    <td valign="top"><span datafld="unitprice">
                        </span></td>
                    <td valign="top"><span datafld="discount">
                        </span></td>
                    <td valign="top"><span datafld="totalAmount">
                        </span></td>
                </tr>
            </tbody>
    </table>
    </body>
</html>
```

This HTML document will appear as shown in Figure 13-3.

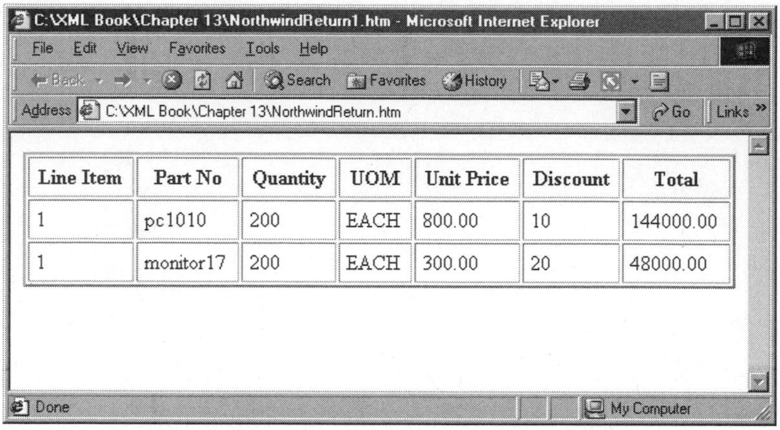

Figure 13-3. *NorthwindReturn.htm showing how the XML DSO data binding works.*

In this example, you used the *xml* element to place the XML data in the NorthwindPO.xml XML document into a DSO object called *NorthwindDSO*. You also bound the table to the *NorthwindDSO* object using the table element's *datasrc* attribute. You have accomplished essentially the same task as you did using XSL, except now we are using a technique that currently works with only Internet Explorer 5.

> **NOTE**   Style sheets and other elements could have been included to further improve this example, but they were left out so that you could focus on how the XML DSO data binding works.

We would presume that each line item in the previous code represents items that go together. In this particular example, there was only one line item (a *line* element equal to 1), which included a computer and a monitor that were sold together. What if there were two line items? If we add the following two *Item* elements to the NorthwindPO.XML document, the page will look as shown in Figure 13-4 in the Web browser. Add the following to the NorthwindPO.XML document:

```
<Item>
    <line>2</line>
    <partno>pc2010</partno>
    <qty>100</qty>
    <uom>EACH</uom>
    <unitPrice>1200.00</unitPrice>
    <discount>10</discount>
    <totalAmount>108000.00</totalAmount>
</Item>
<Item>
    <line>2</line>
    <partno>monitor19</partno>
```

```
        <qty>100</qty>
        <uom>EACH</uom>
        <unitPrice>500.00</unitPrice>
        <discount>10</discount>
        <totalAmount>45000.00</totalAmount>
</Item>
```

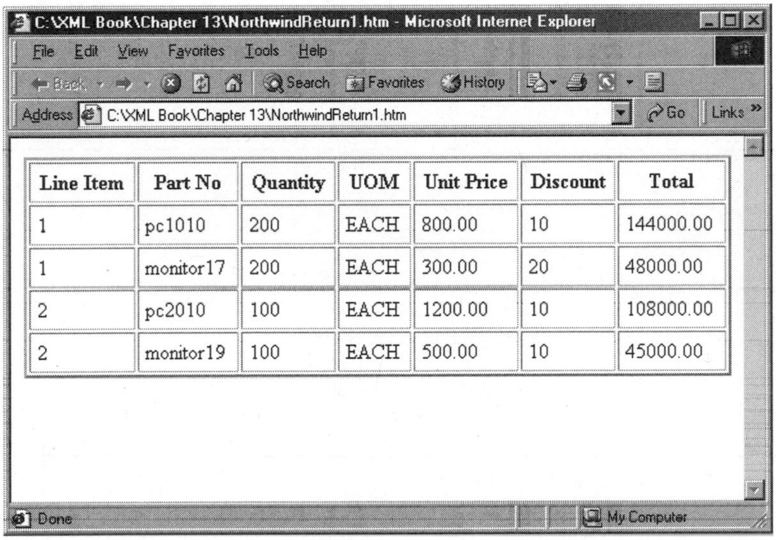

Figure 13-4. *NorthwindReturn.htm with the two new items.*

Although this change is acceptable, you might want to create separate sections for each line item by making some minor changes to the XML document and the DTD. First let's make a few changes to the XML document: add a new element called *po,* and make it the root element of the document; replace the *POLines* element with the *POLine* element; move the *line* element out of the *Item* element's content, and place it within the *POLine* element. The revised NorthwindPO.XML document now looks as follows:

```
<?xml version="1.0" standalone="no" ?>
<!DOCTYPE po SYSTEM "NorthwindPO2.dtd">
<po>
    <POLine>
        <line>1</line>
        <Item>
            <partno>pc1010</partno>
            <qty>200</qty>
            <uom>EACH</uom>
            <unitPrice>800.00</unitPrice>
```

(continued)

```
                <discount>10</discount>
                <totalAmount>144000.00</totalAmount>
            </Item>
            <Item>
                <partno>monitor17</partno>
                <qty>200</qty>
                <uom>EACH</uom>
                <unitPrice>300.00</unitPrice>
                <discount>20</discount>
                <totalAmount>48000.00</totalAmount>
            </Item>
        </POLine>
        <POLine>
            <line>2</line>
            <Item>
                <partno>pc2010</partno>
                <qty>100</qty>
                <uom>EACH</uom>
                <unitPrice>1200.00</unitPrice>
                <discount>10</discount>
                <totalAmount>108000.00</totalAmount>
            </Item>
            <Item>
                <partno>monitor19</partno>
                <qty>100</qty>
                <uom>EACH</uom>
                <unitPrice>500.00</unitPrice>
                <discount>10</discount>
                <totalAmount>45000.00</totalAmount>
            </Item>
        </POLine>
    </po>
```

Next we need to make revisions to the DTD to reflect the changes we made to the XML document. Specifically, delete the declaration for the *POLines* element and declare two new elements: *po* and *POLine*; make *POLine* the child element of *po,* and declare it to occur one or more times; and make the *line* element a child element of *POLine* instead of a child element of *Item*. The new DTD looks as follows:

```
<!ELEMENT po   (POLine+)>
<!ELEMENT POLine   (line , Item+)>
<!ELEMENT Item (partno , qty , uom , unitPrice , discount ,
               totalAmount)>
<!ELEMENT line   (#PCDATA)>
<!ELEMENT partno   (#PCDATA)>
<!ELEMENT qty   (#PCDATA)>
```

```
<!ELEMENT uom    (#PCDATA)>
<!ELEMENT unitPrice  (#PCDATA)>
<!ELEMENT discount  (#PCDATA)>
<!ELEMENT totalAmount  (#PCDATA)>
```

You can now rewrite NorthwindReturn.htm as follows:

```
<html>
<xml src="NorthwindPO2.xml" id="NorthwindDSO"></xml>
    <body>
        <table  border="2" width="100%" datasrc="#NorthwindDSO"
            cellpadding="5">
            <thead>
                <th>Line Item</th>
                <th>Details</th>
            </thead>
            <tbody>
                <td valign="top"><span datafld="line"></span>
                </td>
                <td>
                <table  border="1" width="100%"
                    datasrc="#NorthwindDSO"
                    datafld="Item" cellpadding="5">
                    <thead>
                        <th>Part No</th>
                        <th>Quantity</th>
                        <th>UOM</th>
                        <th>Unit Price</th>
                        <th>Discount</th>
                        <th>Total</th>
                    </thead>
                    <tbody>
                        <tr>
                            <td valign="top">
                            <span datafld="partno"></span></td>
                            <td valign="top">
                            <span datafld="qty"></span></td>
                            <td valign="top">
                            <span datafld="uom"></span></td>
                            <td valign="top">
                            <span datafld="unitprice"></span>
                            </td>
                            <td valign="top">
                            <span datafld="discount"></span>
                            </td>
                            <td valign="top">
```

(continued)

323

```
                              <span datafld="totalAmount">
                              </span></td>
                       </tr>
                    </tbody>
                 </table>
                 </td>
             </tbody>
         </table>
      </body>
</html>
```

You just created two tables, one nested within the other. The first table uses the element *POLine* for the repeating element, as this element can occur one or more times. You did not specify the *datasrc* attribute for the top-level table. The embedded table will need to specify the element that can appear one or more times, which is *Item* in this example. This document will look as shown in Figure 13-5.

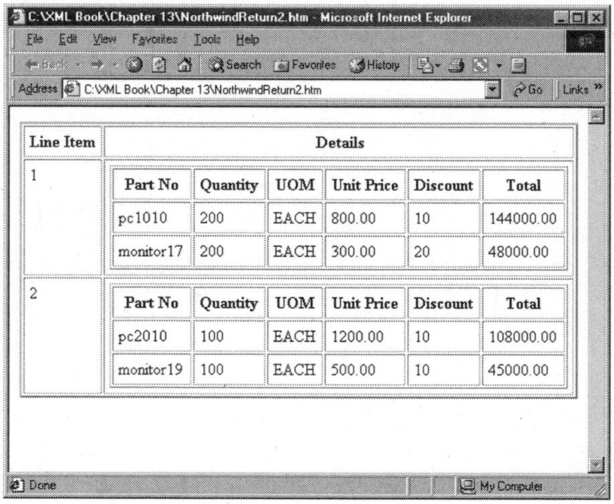

Figure 13-5. *NorthwindReturn2.htm with separate line items.*

The DSO also presents the XML data it contains as an ADO recordset. A recordset is a table of data in memory. You can use an ADO recordset to programmatically manipulate the data. We will discuss ADO in more detail in Chapter 15. For our purposes in this chapter, we can simply view the ADO recordset as an object that has a set of methods that we will be using. The primary methods we will be looking at are *moveFirst*, *moveLast*, *movePrevious*, *moveNext*, and *Fields*. After examining how to code these methods, you can easily code additional methods such as *delete* or *addNew*. Before we can discuss using these methods, we need to discuss the events associated with the XML DSO.

XML DSO Events

The XML DSO has events just as HTML elements have events. The events associated with the XML DSO are as follows:

XML DSO EVENTS

Event	Description
ondataavailable	Raised when data comes in from the data source
ondatasetcomplete	Raised when all the data has arrived from the data source
ondatasetchanged	Raised when data changes
onreadystatechange	Raised when the *readystate* property of the DSO changes
onrowenter	Raised when a row is entered
onrowexit	Raised for a recordset before another row is entered
onrowsdelete	Raised when rows are about to be deleted from the current recordset
onrowsinserted	Raised after rows are inserted into the current recordset
oncellchange	Raised when the data in a bound control or table cell has been changed and the focus has been moved away from the cell

You can use these events to manage XML data in the DSO object. In addition to these events, new properties associated with the *event* object can also be used within the DSO events. The following table shows the new properties associated with the *event* object:

PROPERTIES ASSOCIATED WITH THE *EVENT* OBJECT

Property	Description
bookmarks	Returns a collection of bookmarks that identify the records being inserted or deleted. It can also contain cells that have been changed.
boundElements	Returns a collection of elements in the HTML page that are bound to the DSO and have raised the event.
dataFld	Returns the name of the column or field in the ADO recordset that was affected by an *oncellchanged* event. Thus, it can be used in the *oncellchanged* event to identify which field has been changed.
recordset	Returns a reference to the ADO recordset that is bound to the DSO that raised the event.

```xml
<?xml version="1.0" standalone="yes" ?>
<POLine>
   <Item>
      <partno>pc1010</partno>
      <qty>200</qty>
      <uom>EACH</uom>
      <unitPrice>800.00</unitPrice>
      <discount>10</discount>
      <totalAmount>144000.00</totalAmount>
   </Item>
   <Item>
      <partno>monitor17</partno>
      <qty>200</qty>
      <uom>EACH</uom>
      <unitPrice>300.00</unitPrice>
      <discount>20</discount>
      <totalAmount>48000.00</totalAmount>
   </Item>
   <Item>
      <partno>pc2010</partno>
      <qty>100</qty>
      <uom>EACH</uom>
      <unitPrice>1200.00</unitPrice>
      <discount>10</discount>
      <totalAmount>108000.00</totalAmount>
   </Item>
   <Item>
      <partno>monitor19</partno>
      <qty>100</qty>
      <uom>EACH</uom>
      <unitPrice>500.00</unitPrice>
      <discount>10</discount>
      <totalAmount>45000.00</totalAmount>
   </Item>
</POLine>
```

In the above code, the four items represent one order that includes four items. We will now create the following HTML document:

```html
<html>
   <head>
   <xml src="NorthwindPO3.xml" id="NorthwindDSO"></xml>
      <style type="text/css">
         .FieldName  {font-family:Arial,sans-serif;
         font-size:12px; font-weight:normal}
```

```
                .DataButtons {behavior:url (MoveButtons.htc);}
        </style>
<script language="vbscript">
<!--
Sub NorthwindDSO_ondatasetcomplete()
End Sub
Sub UpdateTextBoxes()
    txtPartNo.value=NorthwindDSO.recordset.Fields("partno")
    txtQuantity.value=NorthwindDSO.recordset.Fields("qty")
    txtUOM.value=NorthwindDSO.recordset.Fields("uom")
    txtUnitPrice.value=NorthwindDSO.recordset.Fields("unitPrice")
    txtDiscount.value=NorthwindDSO.recordset.Fields("discount")
    txtTotal.value=NorthwindDSO.recordset.Fields("totalAmount")
End Sub
Sub MoveNext()
    NorthwindDSO.Recordset.MoveNext
    If NorthwindDSO.Recordset.EOF Then
        NorthwindDSO.Recordset.MoveFirst
    End If
    UpdateTextBoxes
End Sub
Sub MovePrevious()
    NorthwindDSO.Recordset.MovePrevious
    If NorthwindDSO.Recordset.BOF Then
        NorthwindDSO.Recordset.MoveLast
    End If
    UpdateTextBoxes
End Sub
Sub MoveLast()
If (Not NorthwindDSO.Recordset.EOF) And _
    (Not NorthwindDSO.Recordset.BOF) Then
        NorthwindDSO.Recordset.MoveLast
    End If
    UpdateTextBoxes
End Sub
Sub MoveFirst()
If (Not NorthwindDSO.Recordset.EOF) And _
    (Not NorthwindDSO.Recordset.BOF) Then
        NorthwindDSO.Recordset.MoveFirst
    End If
    UpdateTextBoxes
End Sub
-->
</script>
</head>
```

(continued)

```
<body>
    <table  cellpadding="5">
        <tr>
            <td>
                <div class="FieldName">Part No</div>
            </td>
            <td>
                <div class="FieldName">
                    <input id="txtPartNo" name="txtPartNo">
                </div>
            </td>
        </tr>
        <tr>
            <td>
                <div class="FieldName">Quantity</div>
            </td>
            <td>
                <div class="FieldName">
                    <input id="txtQuantity"
                        name="txtQuantity">
                    </div>
            </td>
        </tr>
        <tr>
            <td>
                <div class="FieldName">UOM</div>
            </td>
            <td>
                <div class="FieldName">
                    <input id="txtUOM" name="txtUOM"></div>
            </td>
        </tr>
        <tr>
            <td>
                <div class="FieldName">Unit Price</div>
            </td>
            <td>
                <div class="FieldName">
                    <input id="txtUnitPrice"
                        name="txtUnitPrice">
                </div>
            </td>
        </tr>
```

```
        <tr>
            <td>
                <div class="FieldName">Discount</div>
            </td>
            <td>
                <div class="FieldName">
                    <input id="txtDiscount"
                        name="txtDiscount">
                </div>
            </td>
        </tr>
        <tr>
            <td>
                <div class="FieldName">Total</div>
            </td>
            <td>
                <div class="FieldName">
                    <input id="txtTotal" name="txtTotal">
                </div>
            </td>
        </tr>
    </table>
    <table>
        <td><input id="cmdRetrieveData" name="cmdRetrieveData"
            type="button" value="Retrieve Data"
            onClick="UpdateTextBoxes" ></input></td>
        <td><input id="cmdMoveNext" name="cmdMoveNext"
            type="button" value="Move Next"
        onClick="MoveNext" ></input>
        </td>
        <td><input id="cmdMovePrevious" name="cmdMovePrevious"
            type="button" value="Move Previous"
            onClick="MovePrevious" ></input></td>
        <td><input id="cmdMoveFirst" name="cmdMoveFirst"
            type="button" value="Move First"
            onClick="MoveFirst" ></input></td>
        <td><input id="cmdMoveLast" name="cmdMoveLast"
            type="button" value="Move Last"
            onClick="MoveLast" ></input></td>
    </table>
</body>
</html>
```

Figure 13-6 shows what this document looks like in Internet Explorer 5.

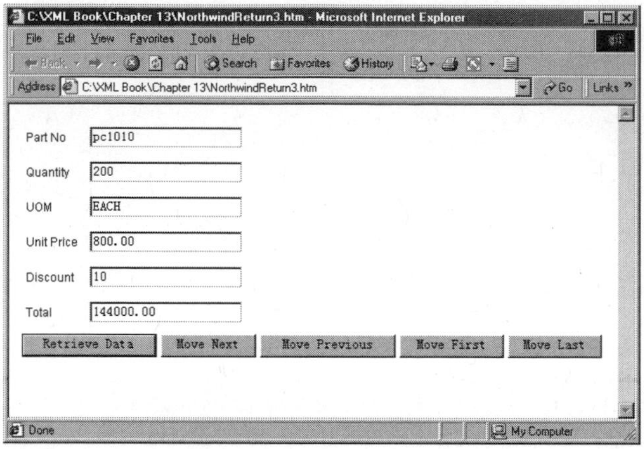

Figure 13-6. *A Web-based user services component for viewing data.*

As you can see, subroutines written in Microsoft Visual Basic were added to the code that will use the XML DSO to move the recordset. These subroutines have been associated to the *onClick* events of the buttons. This is how DHTML code is normally written.

In this example, you did not bind the XML DSO to any of the text boxes. Instead, you used DHTML code and the DSO to fill the text boxes using the *UpdateTextBoxes* function. The *move* functions all perform the appropriate move and then call the *UpdateTextBoxes* to update the text boxes.

SUMMARY

Using DHTML and the XML DSO, you can create dynamic Web-based user services components that use XML. Since DHTML runs on the client machine, it can manipulate the user services components without making a trip to the Web server. The DHTML object model provides access to the components of the Web documents. Combined with the events associated with DHTML objects, this access enables Web developers to create Web applications that contain executable scripts and react to user input. DHTML Behaviors make DHTML functionality more accessible and easier to use in a document. You can also use XML DSO to bind XML data to HTML elements so that you can display the elements and attributes contained in the XML data.

In Chapter 14, we will use DHTML and HTCs together to create client-side business services components that can validate user input.

Chapter 14

Business Services Components

As mentioned in Chapter 10, business services components encapsulate the business rules of a system. Since there are many different types of business rules, there are also many different types of business services components. When we work with XML, the two types of business rules we'll be most concerned with are the rules that validate user input in user services components and the rules that define how XML data will be returned to the client from the server. These two types of rules require two completely different types of business services components.

The components that define how XML data is returned to the client run on a server machine. In a Web application, these components usually run on the Web server. Using the DOM objects, we can create and retrieve data either in XML format or in other formats that can be easily transformed to XML. The business services components can be called by an Active Server Page (ASP) that can then return the data to the client. For example, you could create a Microsoft Visual Basic business services component that retrieves data from a database, manipulates the data and converts it to an XML data island, builds the appropriate DHTML script, and embeds the XML data in the DHTML script. This Visual Basic component can then be used by an ASP to return the data to the client. Because we have already discussed the DOM at great length in Chapter 11, we will not discuss these types of business services components here.

The business services components that we will discuss in this chapter are the components that validate the user's input. This type of component should be placed on the client whenever possible so that the user's input can be validated immediately. As we mentioned in Chapter 10, if these business services components are placed on the server, a delay in the application can occur every time a request is sent to the server for validation. These delays can affect performance.

When you build a standard nonbrowser-based application, it can be relatively easy to create business services components that validate the user's input. For example, you can create a wide range of components in Visual Basic that can perform the validation. Visual Basic has a special type of object called a data source class that can be used to create objects that automatically bind to objects on a form such as a text box or a grid control. If you are working with a Web-based application, you can also use programming languages such as Visual Basic to build business services components, but there is another option. You can use HTML Components (HTC) to create an application that is completely Web based. At the moment, HTCs are supported only by Internet Explorer 5, but it's likely that in the future they will be supported by other browsers in different environments. An HTC can also be used to write code for the events that are raised by the business services components in the browser. Since these events are raised by the user's input, an HTC can be ideal for validating the user's input. Let's look at how to build business services components using the HTC.

USING THE HTC TO CREATE BUSINESS SERVICES COMPONENTS

If you know that the client machines you'll be working with have Internet Explorer 5 installed on them, you will be able to build extremely powerful Web applications for these client machines using HTC and DHTML. The example code we created in Chapter 13 performed only a few simple tasks, but the DHTML code in these examples was becoming fairly long and complex. If we want to add more functionality to our Web-based applications without making the code too long and complicated, we need to remove the DHTML code from the HTML page and place it in a separate component that can be referenced by an HTML page. This removal also makes the HTML document easier to read and update.

Let's take a look at how to extend the capabilities of our Web-based application from Chapter 13 so that it allows the user to edit and review the XML data. If we allow the user to change the values of the XML data, the new values will need to be validated. If the data is validated on the server, this validation can be done as each field is typed in or after all the data has been input. Performing server-side validation as data is input often creates time delays on the client as each field is validated. On the other hand, sending data to the server when all the information is input makes it difficult for the user to find the exact fields that were incorrect. The best solution is to create business services components that run on the client that can validate the data after it has been entered.

> **NOTE** If you validate data on the client, you would still have to validate the data on the server a second time for security reasons, as a malicious hacker could submit invalid data.

HTC enables Web developers to implement behaviors that expose properties, methods, and custom events. As you will see in the example later in this chapter, properties placed inside an HTC will allow us to perform validation whenever the value of a property is changed.

Using an HTC for our validation code offers us several advantages. To begin with, the code we will use to validate a particular XML document can be reused in every Web application that uses XML based on the same schema or DTD. Also, the HTC will be located on the client, so this validation will not require any trips to the server. Finally, if the validation rules change, only the HTC needs to be changed, not the HTML application that uses the HTC.

Before we create our example, let's look at the different elements that can be used in an HTC document. These elements are listed in the following table:

HTC ELEMENTS

Element	*Description*
COMPONENT	Defines the document as being an HTC document; is the root element of an HTC document (HTC can also be used.)
ATTACH	Attaches an event in the source document to a function in the component
METHOD	Defines a method that can be called by the source document
EVENT	Defines an event that can be raised by the HTC
PROPERTY	Defines a property that can be accessed by the source document
GET	Defines the function that will be called when retrieving the value of a property
PARAMETER	Defines a parameter for a function
PUT	Defines the function that will be called when setting the value of a property

The example we will create saves the values of each of the fields in properties in an HTC. The put functions associated with the properties in the HTC will validate each new value. Thus, we will use the HTC to validate any changes to a field. If the change is invalid, we will reset the value of the field to its original value by using the value that is currently in the property. We'll prefix the elements with the public namespace to identify the properties in the HTC as public properties. Public properties can be get or put by external documents. Let's begin by creating a document called ValidatePO.htc that includes the following code:

```
<public:COMPONENT>
   <public:PROPERTY NAME="PartNo"  PUT="putPartNo"
      GET="getPartNo"/>
   <public:PROPERTY NAME="Quantity"  PUT="putQuantity"
      GET="getQuantity"/>
   <public:PROPERTY NAME="UOM"  PUT="putUOM" GET="getUOM"/>
   <public:PROPERTY NAME="UnitPrice"  PUT="putUnitPrice"
      GET="getUnitPrice"/>
   <public:PROPERTY NAME="Discount"  PUT="putDiscount"
      GET="getDiscount"/>
   <public:PROPERTY NAME="Total"  PUT="putTotal" GET="getTotal"/>
   <public:PROPERTY NAME="Error"  PUT="putError" GET="getError"/>
<script language="VBScript">
   Dim strPartNo
   Dim strQuantity
   Dim strUOM
   Dim strDiscount
   Dim strTotal
   Dim strUnitPrice
   Dim strError

   Function putPartNo (newValue)
      If newValue = "" Then
         strError = "The part number is invalid."
      Else
         strPartNo = newValue
      End If
   End function
   Function putQuantity (newValue)
      If newValue = "" Then
         strError = "The quantity is invalid."
      Else
         If IsNumeric(newValue ) Then
            strQuantity = newValue
```

```
        Else
            strError = "The quantity must be numeric."
        End If
    End If
End function
Function putUnitPrice (newValue)
    If newValue = "" Then
        strError = "The unit price is invalid."
    Else
        If IsNumeric(newValue) Then
            strUnitPrice = newValue
        Else
            strError = "The unit price must be numeric."
        End If
    End If
End function
Function putUOM (newValue)
    If newValue = "" Then
        strError = "The UOM is invalid."
    Else
        If (LCase(newValue) = "each") or _
            (LCase(newValue) = "case") Then
            strUOM = newValue
        Else
            strError = "The UOM can only be each or case."
        End If
    End If
End function
Function putDiscount (newValue)
    If newValue = "" Then
        strError = "The discount is invalid."
    Else
        If IsNumeric (newValue) Then
            strDiscount = newValue
        Else
            strError = "The discount must be numeric."
        End If
    End If
End function
Function putTotal (newValue)
    If newValue = "" Then
        strError = "The total is invalid."
    Else
```

(continued)

```
                   If IsNumeric (newValue) Then
                      strTotal = newValue
                   Else
                      StrError = "The total must be numeric."
                   End If
               End If
           End function
           Function putError (newValue)
              StrError = newValue
           End function

           Function getPartNo ()
              getPartNo = strPartNo
           End function
           Function getQuantity ()
              getQuantity = strQuantity
           End function
           Function getUOM ()
              getUOM = strUOM
           End function
           Function getDiscount ()
              getDiscount = strDiscount
           End function
           Function getTotal ()
              getTotal = strTotal
           End function
           Function getUnitPrice ()
              getUnitPrice = strUnitPrice
           End function
           Function getError ()
              getError = strError
           End function
       </script>
       </public:COMPONENT>
```

This document can also be found on the companion CD. As you can see, public properties are used in the document. The advantage of using properties is that they allow us to validate values when a user attempts to change the value of the property. If the value is invalid, we do not allow the property's value to change and raise an error. In the case of the HTC above, we do not actually raise an error but instead set the error property to a string that explains the error.

The *put* functions in this code are used to check that the new values are valid. If they are not valid, the functions set *strError* to a value that explains the error. If the value is valid, the functions set a private variable to the value. Each *put* function is associated with the *PUT* attribute of the corresponding property. For example, the *putPartNo* function is associated with the *PUT* attribute of the *PartNo* property. When you assign a value to the *PartNo* property, the function *putPartNo* is called.

The *get* functions will be used when a certain value is set equal to the property. For example, when you use the *partNo* property, the *getPartNo* function will be called. *PartNo* will return the private variable. Although we do not perform any validation in the *get* functions, you can add validation to these functions too.

In the source document that will use the HTC, we will not use data binding for our text boxes. Instead, we will use DHTML to give us full control of the form as we did in the example in Chapter 13. We will write script to fill the text boxes with user input, to move through the records, and to set and get the properties in the HTC document. Here is the first part of the HTML document, showing the *FillText* function and the *ondatasetcomplete* event:

```
<html>
<head>
<xml src="NorthwindPO2.xml" id="NorthwindDSO"></xml>
<style type="text/css">
   .FieldName  {font-family:Arial,sans-serif; font-size:12px;
                font-weight:normal}
   .POValidate {behavior:url (ValidatePO.htc);}
</style>
<script language="JScript">
function FillText()
   {
   txtPartNo.value=NorthwindDSO.recordset.fields("partno").value;
   txtQuantity.value=NorthwindDSO.recordset.fields("qty").value;
   txtUOM.value=NorthwindDSO.recordset.fields("uom").value;
   txtDiscount.value=NorthwindDSO.recordset.fields
      ("discount").value;
   txtUnitPrice.value=NorthwindDSO.recordset.fields
      ("unitPrice").value;
   txtTotal.value=NorthwindDSO.recordset.fields
      ("totalAmount").value;
   }

function NorthwindDSO.ondatasetcomplete()
   {
   htcSpan.PartNo=NorthwindDSO.recordset.fields("partno").value;
```

(continued)

```
    if (!htcSpan.Error=="")
       {
       alert(htcSpan.Error);
       }
    htcSpan.Quantity=NorthwindDSO.recordset.fields("qty").value;
    if (!htcSpan.Error=="")
       {
       alert(htcSpan.Error);
       }
    htcSpan.UOM=NorthwindDSO.recordset.fields("uom").value;
    if (!htcSpan.Error=="")
       {
       alert(htcSpan.Error);
       }
    htcSpan.UnitPrice=NorthwindDSO.recordset.fields
       ("unitPrice").value;
    if (!htcSpan.Error=="")
       {
       alert(htcSpan.Error);
       }
    htcSpan.Discount=NorthwindDSO.recordset.fields
       ("discount").value;
    if (!htcSpan.Error=="")
       {
       alert(htcSpan.Error);
       }
    htcSpan.Total=NorthwindDSO.recordset.fields
       ("totalAmount").value;
    if (!htcSpan.Error=="")
       {
       alert(htcSpan.Error);
       }
    htcSpan.Error="";
    FillText();
}
```

The *FillText* function is used to place the values of the recordset into the text boxes. It is called when the data has been loaded and when the user moves to another row. The DSO object raises the *ondatasetcomplete* event when all the data has arrived on the client. When this event is raised, we first set all the properties equal to the field values. Because we are setting the properties, the *put* functions in the HTC are used. As mentioned previously, the *put* functions also validate the new values. If there is an error, the property isn't set to the new value and the user gets an error message. This code doesn't fix the error; it only alerts the user to the problem.

To use the HTC document, we need to bind it to a tag on the form. We use the *span* tag named *htcSpan* to bind the HTC document. The *htcSpan* tag is bound by setting its class attribute to *POValidate*, the style linked to the HTC document. Once the *span* tag is bound to the HTC document, it inherits the properties and methods contained in the HTC document. Thus, the properties can be referenced by using the name for the tag followed by a dot followed by the name of the property. For example, *htcSpan.PartNo* refers to the *PartNo* property in the document.

In the second part of the HTML document, we'll use functions that will be associated with the *onBlur* event of all the text boxes. When the user tabs out of a text box, the *onBlur* event will be called. If the value in the text box is different from the value of the field in the recordset, the user has changed the value. If the value has been changed, we will set the field to this new value. Changing the value of the field will result in the *oncellchange* event being raised by the DSO object. We will validate the change in the *oncellchange* event.

```
function partNoChange()
    {
    if(NorthwindDSO.recordset.fields("partno").value!=
        txtPartNo.value)
        {
        NorthwindDSO.recordset.fields("partno").value=
            txtPartNo.value;
        }
    }
function QuantityChange()
    {
    if (NorthwindDSO.recordset.fields("qty").value!=
        txtQuantity.value)
        {
        NorthwindDSO.recordset.fields("qty").value=
            txtQuantity.value;
        }
    }
function UOMChange()
    {
    if (NorthwindDSO.recordset.fields("uom").value!=txtUOM.value)
        {
        NorthwindDSO.recordset.fields("uom").value=txtUOM.value;
        }
    }
function UnitPriceChange()
    {
```

(continued)

```
    if (NorthwindDSO.recordset.fields("unitPrice").value!=
       txtUnitPrice.value)
       {
       NorthwindDSO.recordset.fields("unitPrice").value=
          txtUnitPrice.value;
       }
    }
function DiscountChange()
    {
    if (NorthwindDSO.recordset.fields("discount").value!=
       txtDiscount.value)
       {
       NorthwindDSO.recordset.fields("discount").value=
          txtDiscount.value;
       }
    }
function TotalChange()
    {
    if (NorthwindDSO.recordset.fields("totalAmount").value!=
       txtTotal.value)
       {
       NorthwindDSO.recordset.fields("totalAmount").value=
          txtTotal.value;
       }
    }
```

The third part of the HTML document shows how to use the *oncellchange* event that is fired whenever a field is changed. We will use the *dataFld* property of the *event* object to get the name of the field that has changed. Using a *switch* statement, we will find which field has been changed and set the property for that field equal to the new value. If the change is valid, the property will be set to the new value. If the value is not valid, the property will not be changed and the error property will be set to a string describing the error. If the change is invalid, we will also reset the value in the text box to the original value that is still stored in the property and then use the *select* method of the text box to move focus back to the field that was in error.

```
function NorthwindDSO.oncellchange()
    {
    switch (event.dataFld)
       {
       case "partno":
          htcSpan.PartNo=txtPartNo.value;
        if (!htcSpan.Error=="")
```

```
        {
        txtPartNo.value=htcSpan.PartNo;
        txtPartNo.select();
        }
break;
case "qty":
    htcSpan.Quantity=txtQuantity.value;
    if (!htcSpan.Error=="")
        {
        txtQuantity.value=htcSpan.Quantity;
        txtQuantity.select();
        }
break;
case "uom":
    htcSpan.UOM=txtUOM.value;
    if (!htcSpan.Error=="")
        {
        txtUOM.value=htcSpan.UOM;
        txtUOM.select();
        }
break;
case "unitPrice":
    htcSpan.UnitPrice=txtUnitPrice.value;
    if (!htcSpan.Error=="")
        {
        txtUnitPrice.value=htcSpan.UnitPrice;
        txtUnitPrice.select();
        }
break;
case "discount":
    htcSpan.Discount=txtDiscount.value;
    if (!htcSpan.Error=="")
        {
        txtDiscount.value=htcSpan.Discount;
        txtDiscount.select();
        }
break;
case "totalAmount":
    htcSpan.Total=txtTotal.value;
    if (!htcSpan.Error=="")
        {
        txtTotal.value=htcSpan.Total;
        txtTotal.select();
        }
```

(continued)

```
            break;
      default:
         htcSpan.Error = "Invalid element text";
      }
      if (!htcSpan.Error=="")
         {
         alert (htcSpan.Error);
         htcSpan.Error="";
         }
   }
```

The last part of the HTML document shows the *move* functions and the rest of the HTML code. We will code the *move* functions using JScript instead of using VBScript as we did in Chapter 13 so that we can see how to code in both scripting languages. First the DSO object is moved, and then the *FillText* function is called to set the values in the text boxes.

```
function MoveNext()
   {
   NorthwindDSO.recordset.moveNext();
   if (NorthwindDSO.recordset.eof)
      {
      NorthwindDSO.recordset.moveFirst();
      }
   FillText();
   }
function MovePrevious()
   {
   NorthwindDSO.recordset.movePrevious();
   if (NorthwindDSO.recordset.bof)
      {
      NorthwindDSO.recordset.MoveLast();
      }
   FillText();
   }
function MoveLast()
   {
   if (!NorthwindDSO.recordset.eof && !NorthwindDSO.recordset.bof)
      {
      NorthwindDSO.recordset.moveLast();
      FillText();
      }
   }
```

```
function MoveFirst()
    {
    if (!NorthwindDSO.recordset.eof && !NorthwindDSO.recordset.bof)
        {
        NorthwindDSO.recordset.moveFirst();
        FillText();
        }
    }
</script>
</head>
<body>
    <!--This is the span element that gives the reference to the
        HTC component.-->
        <span id="htcSpan" class="POValidate"> </span>
        <!--We place the values in a table to make them look
            neater.-->
        <table  cellpadding="5">
        <tr>
            <td>
            <div class="FieldName">Part No</div>
            </td>
            <td>
            <!--The onBlur event is associated with the partNoChange
                listed above.-->
            <div class="FieldName"><input type="text" id="txtPartNo"
                onBlur="partNoChange()"></div>
            </td>
        </tr>
        <tr>
            <td>
            <div class="FieldName">Quantity</div>
            </td>
            <td>
            <div class="FieldName"><input id=txtQuantity
                name=txtQuantity onBlur="QuantityChange()"></div>
            </td>
        </tr>
        <tr>
            <td>
            <div class="FieldName">UOM</div>
            </td>
            <td>
                    <div class="FieldName"><input id=txtUOM name=txtUOM
                        onBlur="UOMChange()"></div>
            </td>
```

(continued)

```
      </tr>
      <tr>
         <td>
         <div class="FieldName">Unit Price</div>
         </td>
         <td>
         <div class="FieldName"><input id=txtUnitPrice
            name=txtUnitPrice onBlur="UnitPriceChange()"></div>
         </td>
      </tr>
      <tr>
         <td>
         <div class="FieldName">Discount</div>
         </td>
         <td>
         <div class="FieldName"><input id=txtDiscount
            name=txtDiscount onBlur="DiscountChange()"></div>
         </td>
      </tr>
      <tr>
         <td>
         <div class="FieldName">Total</div>
         </td>
         <td>
         <div class="FieldName"><input id=txtTotal name=txtTotal
            onBlur="TotalChange()"></div>
         </td>
      </tr>
      </table>
   <!--The buttons are also placed in a table so that
      they appear neater in the document.-->
      <table>
   <td><input id=cmdMoveNext name=cmdMoveNext type=button
      value="Move Next" onClick="MoveNext()"></input></td>
   <td><input id=cmdMovePrevious name=cmdMovePrevious
      type=button value="Move Previous"
      onClick="MovePrevious()"></input></td>
   <td><input id=cmdMoveFirst name=cmdMoveFirst type=button
      value="Move First" onClick="MoveFirst()"></input></td>
   <td><input id=cmdMoveLast name=cmdMoveNext type=button
      value="Move Last" onClick="MoveLast()"></input></td>
   </table>
</body>
</html>
```

The whole example code can be found on the companion CD. This example will prompt the user if he or she types in a new value that is invalid. If we used this example in a real application, we would need some way to submit the changes back to the server, where the new XML data is processed. As you can see, creating a fully working application using a browser interface is still a good deal of work.

We could have also used a method in our example to validate the fields. To do this, we could have added the following method to the HTC document:

```
<public:METHOD NAME="CheckValidity">
   <PARAMETER name="FieldName" />
   <PARAMETER name="NewValue" />
</public:METHOD>
```

The *CheckValidity* function written in VBScript would look as follows:

```
Function CheckValidity (FieldName, NewValue)
   Select Case FieldName
   Case "PartNo"
     If NewValue = "" Then
        strError = "The PartNo is invalid."
     End If
   Case "Quantity"
     If Not IsNumeric (NewValue) Then
        strError = "The Quantity is invalid."
     End If
     End Select
End Function
```

You would have to use the *select case* statement to test the *FieldName* and verify whether the *NewValue* is valid for that field. You can write the complete code for this function as an exercise.

COMPILED COMPONENTS

In addition to writing business services components that use HTC, we could write business services components in Visual Basic, Java, or C++ and create compiled objects that are used by the HTML page. (It is also possible to create a compiled HTC, but this can only be done with C++, and the process is extremely complex.)

For example, you could create a business services component using a Visual Basic object that uses the DOM object to work with the XML data. We will not demonstrate how to do this here as the code we used to work with the DOM in Chapter 11 can be used to make either client or server components.

A compiled business services component might run more quickly than an HTC, but a compiled component might need to be installed on the client computer. In a controlled environment where you can be certain that a compiled component will easily install on every client, a compiled component may be the better choice. In an environment in which every client has Internet Explorer 5 installed but there are many different types of clients, it might be better to use HTC.

SUMMARY

In this chapter, we have created a business services component using an HTC running on the client that will validate the values of XML data located in a data island. This component will immediately tell users whether they have entered an invalid field and reset the text box to its previous value. We have also used the DSO to create an application that can allow the user to view the data contained within a data island. Using the DSO, we can create a Web-based user services component that can interact with the user using an HTC that encapsulates the business rules for the application.

Chapter 15

Data Services Components and XML

In the last several chapters, we have discussed user and business services components. In this chapter, we will look at data services components. Recall that data services components are used to exchange business information with business partners, integrate data from other systems, and store and retrieve business data. We'll examine two Microsoft technologies that can be used to build data services components that can perform these tasks. We will start by examining Microsoft ActiveX Data Objects (ADO) 2.5 and its ability to work with XML data. ADO 2.5 simplifies programmatic access to data. In the second half of this chapter, we'll discuss two Internet Server Application Programming Interface (ISAPI) extensions for Microsoft Internet Information Server (IIS). The first ISAPI extension allows you to retrieve data directly from a Microsoft SQL Server 6.5 or 7.0 database in XML format using a Web browser. The second extension enables

IIS to pass the XML directly to the client computer. It can also automatically transform XML documents to other formats using an XSL document on the server if the client does not have Microsoft Internet Explorer 5 installed. Although the second ISAPI extension won't be used to build data services components that can access data, it's included in this chapter so that it can be discussed along with the first ISAPI extension. Let's begin by looking at the XML features found in ADO 2.5.

ADO 2.5 AND XML

Using ADO 2.5, you can read data from nearly any data source, place the data into an ADO recordset (which is similar to a virtual table containing the data in memory), and transform the data to XML. Once the data has been transformed to XML, it can be placed into a data stream and used as output to various sources, such as a file, the ADO ASP *Response* object (which is used to return information to the Web client), and the XML DOM. Outputting the data as XML can be accomplished by using the COM *IStream* interface. The *IStream* interface is an interface designed to support reading and writing data to ADO *Stream* objects. ADO 2.5 requires support for the *IStream* interface.

On the other hand, XML data can be used as a data source of a read-only or read/write recordset in ADO 2.5. For example, you can use ADO 2.5 in an ASP page on a Web server to retrieve data from a database by placing the data into an ADO recordset. The data will then be transferred as XML output to the ASP *Response* object using ADO 2.5. Once the XML data arrives on the client, it can be read into an ADO recordset on the client using DHTML. Using the client-side ADO recordset and DHTML, the user can read and update the data. Let's look at several examples of inputting and outputting data as XML in ADO 2.5 to see how this works.

Outputting Data as XML Using ADO 2.5

In this example, we will retrieve data from the SQL Server 7.0 Northwind Traders database and save the data as XML in a text file. We'll use ADO 2.5 in a Visual Basic application to perform this task. To create the example application, follow these steps:

1. Open Visual Basic, create a standard EXE application, and change the name of the default form to *frmADOXML*.

2. Choose Reference from the Project menu, and add a reference to *Microsoft ActiveX Data Objects 2.5 Library*.

3. Add a command button called *cmdSave* to the form with a caption *Save*.

4. Add the following code to the click event handler of the command button *cmdSave*:

```
Private Sub cmdSave_Click()
    Dim objNWRecordset As ADODB.Recordset
    Dim objNWConnection As ADODB.Connection
    Set objNWRecordset = New ADODB.Recordset
    Set objNWConnection = New ADODB.Connection

    objNWConnection.CursorLocation = adUseClient
    'You will need to replace IES-FUJI with the
    'appropriate data source in the
    'following statement.
    objNWConnection.Open "Provider=SQLOLEDB.1; " & _
        "Integrated Security=SSPI;Persist Security Info=False;" & _
        " User ID=sa;Initial Catalog=Northwind;
        " Data Source=IES-FUJI"
    objNWRecordset.CursorLocation = adUseClient
    objNWRecordset.CursorType = adOpenStatic
    Set objNWRecordset.ActiveConnection = objNWConnection
    objNWRecordset.Open "Products"
    'Save the recordset to a file as XML.
    objNWRecordset.Save "C:\Products.xml", adPersistXML
End Sub
```

This code initially creates an ADO *Connection* object called *objNWConnection* and a *Recordset* object called *objNWRecordset*, and then sets the properties for these objects and opens them. A *Connection* object provides a connection to any data source. A *Recordset* object is a virtual table in memory that contains the data that is retrieved from a data source. The *CursorLocation* property of the *Recordset* object determines whether the data will be located on the client or on the server. The *CursorLocation* property also determines whether the connection must be maintained with the database (server cursor) or the connection can be broken (client cursor) while creating a disconnected recordset. The *Open* method of the ADO *Connection* object contains the connection string as a parameter. The connection string includes the catalog, which is the database that is going to be used, the data source, which is the name of the SQL Server, and the user ID, which is a valid user name to use when opening the connection. This connection string is connecting to a SQL Server database. You will have to change the name of the data source to the name of your SQL Server database that contains the Northwind Traders database.

The ADO *Connection* object connects to the Northwind Traders database, and the *Recordset* object connects to the *Products* table of the Northwind Traders database. Once these connections are made, the S*ave* method of the *Recordset* object is called to save the data as XML.

As you can see, the *Save* method uses the *adPersistXML* parameter to save the data as XML. The XML file that is created will have two main sections. The first section contains a BizTalk schema for the data, and the second section contains the actual data. There are four namespace prefixes that are used in the file. The first namespace prefix is *s*, which is used to prefix the schema definition for the data. The second namespace prefix is *dt,* which is used for the datatype definitions in the schema. The third namespace prefix is *rs*, which references the properties and methods of the ADO recordset. The fourth namespace prefix is *z*, which references the actual data. The Products.xml XML file that was generated from the previous code looks as follows:

```xml
<xml xmlns:s='uuid:BDC6E3F0-6DA3-11d1-A2A3-00AA00C14882'
    xmlns:dt='uuid:C2F41010-65B3-11d1-A29F-00AA00C14882'
    xmlns:rs='urn:schemas-microsoft-com:rowset'
    xmlns:z='#RowsetSchema'>
<s:Schema id='RowsetSchema'>
    <s:ElementType name='row' content='eltOnly'>
        <s:AttributeType name='ProductID' rs:number='1'>
            <s:datatype dt:type='int' dt:maxLength='4'
                rs:precision='10' rs:fixedlength='true'
                rs:maybenull='false'/>
        </s:AttributeType>
        <s:AttributeType name='ProductName' rs:number='2'
            s:writeunknown='true'>
            <s:datatype dt:type='string' dt:maxLength='40'
                rs:maybenull='false'/>
        </s:AttributeType>
        <s:AttributeType name='SupplierID' rs:number='3'
            rs:nullable='true' rs:writeunknown='true'>
            <s:datatype dt:type='int' dt:maxLength='4' rs:precision='10'
                rs:fixedlength='true'/>
        </s:AttributeType>
        <s:AttributeType name='CategoryID' rs:number='4'
            rs:nullable='true' rs:writeunknown='true'>
            <s:datatype dt:type='int' dt:maxLength='4' rs:precision='10'
                rs:fixedlength='true'/>
        </s:AttributeType>
```

```
            <s:AttributeType name='QuantityPerUnit' rs:number='5'
               rs:nullable='true' rs:writeunknown='true'>
               <s:datatype dt:type='string' dt:maxLength='20'/>
            </s:AttributeType>
            <s:AttributeType name='UnitPrice' rs:number='6'
               rs:nullable='true' rs:writeunknown='true'>
               <s:datatype dt:type='i8' rs:dbtype='currency'
                  dt:maxLength='8' rs:precision='19'
                  rs:fixedlength='true'/>
            </s:AttributeType>
            <s:AttributeType name='UnitsInStock' rs:number='7'
               rs:nullable='true' rs:writeunknown='true'>
               <s:datatype dt:type='i2' dt:maxLength='2' rs:precision='5'
                  rs:fixedlength='true'/>
            </s:AttributeType>
            <s:AttributeType name='UnitsOnOrder' rs:number='8'
               rs:nullable='true' rs:writeunknown='true'>
               <s:datatype dt:type='i2' dt:maxLength='2' rs:precision='5'
                  rs:fixedlength='true'/>
            </s:AttributeType>
            <s:AttributeType name='ReorderLevel' rs:number='9'
               rs:nullable='true' rs:writeunknown='true'>
               <s:datatype dt:type='i2' dt:maxLength='2'
                  rs:precision='5' rs:fixedlength='true'/>
            </s:AttributeType>
            <s:AttributeType name='Discontinued' rs:number='10'
               rs:writeunknown='true'>
               <s:datatype dt:type='boolean' dt:maxLength='2'
                  rs:fixedlength='true' rs:maybenull='false'/>
            </s:AttributeType>
            <s:extends type='rs:rowbase'/>
         </s:ElementType>
      </s:Schema>
      <rs:data>
      <z:row ProductID='1' ProductName='Chai' SupplierID='1'
         CategoryID='1' QuantityPerUnit='10 boxes x 20 bags'
         UnitPrice='18' UnitsInStock='39' UnitsOnOrder='0'
         ReorderLevel='10' Discontinued='False'/>
      <z:row ProductID='2' ProductName='Chang' SupplierID='1'
         CategoryID='1' QuantityPerUnit='24 - 12 oz bottles'
         UnitPrice='19' UnitsInStock='17' UnitsOnOrder='40'
         ReorderLevel='25' Discontinued='False'/>
      ⋮
      </rs:data>
      </xml>
```

Using ADO 2.5, we have created an XML document that contains the schema and the data for the Products table of the Northwind Traders database.

NOTE For more information about ADO 2.5, look at the Microsoft Data Access Components (MDAC) 2.5 SDK on Microsoft's Web site.

In some cases, you will have to make changes to the generated data before it can be used as XML. For example, if there is an invalid character in the column name, such as a space, you will have to change the name to a valid XML name. You would do this by changing the name attribute and adding an *rs:name* attribute that contains the original name of the field. Thus, if you had a column in the database called *Shipper Name* you could end up with the following *AttributeType*:

```
<s:AttributeType name='Shipper Name' rs:number='9'
   rs:nullable='true' rs:writeunknown='true'>
   <s:datatype dt:type='i2' dt:maxLength='2' rs:precision='50'
       rs:fixedlength='true'/>
</s:AttributeType>
```

You would have to change the AttributeType as follows:

```
<s:AttributeType name='ShipperName' rs:name='Shipper Name'
   rs:number='9' rs:nullable='true' rs:writeunknown='true'>
   <s:datatype dt:type='i2' dt:maxLength='2' rs:precision='50'
       rs:fixedlength='true'/>
</s:AttributeType>
```

This document can then be presented in Internet Explorer 5 as XML or transformed to XHTML or other formats using an XSL document.

The original file that is generated can be used only to create a read-only ADO recordset. If you want to create an updatable client-side disconnected recordset, you must add an *rs:updatable* attribute to the *ElementType* definition. A client-side disconnected recordset has no connection to the original data source. A user can review, edit, delete, update, and add records to the recordset, but a connection to the database must be reestablished in order for the changes to be saved to the database. To save the changes, the *UpdateBatch* method of an ADO recordset must be called after the disconnected recordset is reconnected to the database. The *UpdateBatch* method is used to send multiple recordset updates to the server in one call.

To make the data updatable, you would change the *ElementType* definition to the following:

```
<s:ElementType name='row' content='eltOnly' rs:updatable='true'>
```

Inputting Data as XML Using ADO 2.5

Reading the XML data generated by ADO 2.5 is just as easy as outputting the data. To examine how to input data as XML using ADO 2.5 in the example application, add another command button to the *frmADOXML* form and call it *cmdRetrieve* with a caption *Retrieve&Add*. Add the following code to the click event handler of the command button *cmdRetrieve*:

```
Private Sub cmdRetrieve_Click()
    Dim objNWRecordset As ADODB.Recordset
    Set objNWRecordset = New ADODB.Recordset

    'Open the recordset to a file as XML.
    objNWRecordset.Open "C:\Products.XML", Options:=adCmdFile
    'Add a new record.
    objNWRecordset.AddNew
    objNWRecordset.Fields("ProductName") = "Test"

End Sub
```

> **NOTE**   An error will be raised if you run this code without adding the *rs:updatable* =*'true'* attribute to the schema section of the generated XML file.

Setting *Options* to *adCmdFile* tells ADO that this data will be coming from a regular file and not from a database.

Once you add a new record, edit a record, or delete a record, you must call the *Update* method of the ADO recordset. Each time you call the *Update* method, the updated record is marked within the recordset. If you make changes to the recordset and save the changes to a file, you can see the actual changes. These changes are being made only to the recordset, not to the actual data in the database, as there is no connection to the database.

Making Changes to the Data

Now that we have seen how to save data as XML and how to open XML data using ADO, we will look at how to make changes to the XML data. We will start by writing code to open the Products.xml file we created, and then we'll make changes to the data. Once the changes are made, we will call the *Update* method of the recordset. When the changes are complete, we will save the new data to a file called

ProductsUpdate.xml. First add another command button called *cmdMakeChanges* to the form with a caption *Make Changes*. Add the following code to the click event handler of the command button *cmdMakeChanges*:

```
Private Sub cmdMakeChanges_Click()
    Dim objNWRecordset As ADODB.Recordset
    Set objNWRecordset = New ADODB.Recordset
    'Open the recordset to a file as XML
    objNWRecordset.Open "C:\Products.XML", Options:=adCmdFile
    objNWRecordset.Fields("ProductName") = "Test"
    objNWRecordset.Update
    objNWRecordset.MoveLast
    objNWRecordset.Delete
    objNWRecordset.Update
    objNWRecordset.Filter = adFilterPendingRecords
    objNWRecordset.Save "c:\ProductsUpdate.xml", adPersistXML
End Sub
```

In this case, we have changed the product name of the first record to *Test* and deleted the last record. The changed recordset is then saved to the ProductUpdate.xml file. You can see the following new additions in the ProductUpdate.xml file after clicking the *Make Changes* command button:

```
⋮
<rs:update>
   <rs:original>
      <z:row ProductID='I' ProductName='Chai' SupplierID='1'
         CategoryID='1' QuantityPerUnit='10 boxes x 20 bags'
         UnitPrice='18' UnitsInStock='39' UnitsOnOrder='0'
         ReorderLevel='10' Discontinued='False'/>
   </rs:original>
   <z:row ProductName='Test'/>
</rs:update>
⋮
<rs:delete>
<z:row ProductID='77' ProductName='Original Frankfurter grüne Soße'
   SupplierID='12' CategoryID='2' QuantityPerUnit='12 boxes'
   UnitPrice='13' UnitsInStock='32' UnitsOnOrder='0'
   ReorderLevel='15' Discontinued='False'/>
</rs:delete>
```

With the updated XML file, ADO can reconstruct a recordset that has the original and new values for fields that are edited and can determine which rows have been deleted. Now let's look at how we would actually update the data source.

UPDATING THE DATA SOURCE

Currently, the data we have been working with has been saved only to a local file. This data will still have to be saved to the original data source (the Northwind Traders database, in this case). To save the updated data, add another command button to the form called *cmdSaveUpdate* with a caption *Save Update* and add the following code to the click event handler of the command button *cmdSaveUpdate*:

```
Private Sub cmdSaveUpdate_Click()
Dim objNWRecordset As ADODB.Recordset
Dim objNWConnection As ADODB.Connection
Dim objXMLRecordset As ADODB.Recordset
Dim lngFieldCounter As Long

Set objNWRecordset = New ADODB.Recordset
Set objXMLRecordset = New ADODB.Recordset
Set objNWConnection = New ADODB.Connection


objNWConnection.CursorLocation = adUseServer
'You will need to replace IES-FUJI with the appropriate data
'source in the following statement.
objNWConnection.Open _
    "Provider=SQLOLEDB.1;Integrated Security=SSPI;" & _
    "Persist Security Info=False;" & _
    "User ID=sa;Initial Catalog=Northwind;Data Source=IES-FUJI"
objNWRecordset.CursorLocation = adUseServer
objNWRecordset.CursorType = adOpenDynamic
objNWRecordset.LockType = adLockPessimistic
Set objNWRecordset.ActiveConnection = objNWConnection
objXMLRecordset.Open "C:\ProductsUpdate.XML", Options:=adCmdFile
objXMLRecordset.Filter = adFilterPendingRecords
Do Until objXMLRecordset.EOF
    If objXMLRecordset.EditMode <> adEditAdd Then
        objNWRecordset.Open _
           "Select * From Products Where ProductID=" _
           & objXMLRecordset.Fields.Item("ProductID").OriginalValue
        If objXMLRecordset.EditMode = adEditDelete Then
           'Delete
           objNWRecordset.Delete
        Else
```

(continued)

```
            'Edit
        For lngFieldCounter = 0 To objXMLRecordset.Fields.Count-1
            'Can Not Change Primary Key
        If UCase(objXMLRecordset.Fields.Item( _
            lngFieldCounter).Name) _
            <> "PRODUCTID" Then
            objNWRecordset.Fields.Item(lngFieldCounter).Value = _
                objXMLRecordset.Fields.Item(lngFieldCounter).Value
        End If
    Next
    End If
Else
    objNWRecordset.Open _
        "Select * From Products Where ProductID=" & 0
    objNWRecordset.AddNew
        'Add New
    For lngFieldCounter = 0 To objXMLRecordset.Fields.Count - 1
        'Auto Increment field for productID
        If UCase(objXMLRecordset.Fields.Item( _
            lngFieldCounter).Name) _
            <> "PRODUCTID" Then
            objNWRecordset.Fields.Item(lngFieldCounter).Value = _
                objXMLRecordset.Fields.Item(lngFieldCounter).Value
        End If
    Next

End If
objNWRecordset.Update
objNWRecordset.Close
objXMLRecordset.MoveNext
Loop
End Sub
```

Once again, we create a *Connection* object called *objNWConnection* to connect to the Northwind Traders database, and a *Recordset* object called *objNWRecordset* to hold the data from the ProductsUpdate.xml file. You will need to configure the data source and change the connection string again, just as in the previous example. *ObjNWRecordset* is used to get a reference to the record that is being updated using a SELECT statement with a WHERE clause.

The second *Recordset* object called *objXMLRecordset* is used to retrieve the XML data, which contains the data that has been added, edited, or deleted. You can also get the XML data from an ADO data stream, which we'll cover in the section "Working with Streams" later in this chapter.

Once we have obtained the XML data stored in the *objXMLRecordset* recordset, we apply a filter so that the only visible records are the ones that have had changes done to them or are new records. We then move through each record in *objXML-Recordset* that is new or has been changed and retrieve that record from the database using *objNWRecordset*.

Once we have only the records that are about to be changed, we can perform the correct operations: *AddNew*, *Delete*, and *Edit*. We begin by checking the *EditMode* property of *objXMLRecordset* to find out which operation was being done on this record, and then perform the operation accordingly.

If you have worked with disconnected ADO recordsets before, you might have expected that we would use the *UpdateBatch* method of the ADO recordset. Unfortunately, the disconnected ADO recordset created using XML has no reference to the original table that was used to get the data. Thus, even though you can create an ADO connection to the correct database and set the recordset's *ActiveConnection* property to this connection, there is simply no way of connecting the recordset to the right table. Because the recordset cannot be connected to the correct table, the *UpdateBatch* method cannot work. As you can see from the previous example, we have created two *Recordset* objects: *ObjXMLRecordset* and *objNWRecordset*.

> **NOTE** In order to keep the code simple, the example we have been working with does not include error handling. Remember that all production code should have error handlers. In this example, you would need to check the record that is about to be changed to make sure it actually exists in the database and has not been changed by someone else. You can check the status of the data by using the *PreviousValue* property of the *Recordset* object for each field. The *PreviousValue* property will give the value of the field before it was changed. We have used query strings containing table and field names in the code; however, in production code, we would use constants so that only the value of the constant would need to be changed if the table or field names changed.

Working with Streams

In the previous examples, we have been saving information to data files. It's likely that you will not want to do this for most of your applications. Instead, you can work directly with data streams that can pass the data into a DOM object or pass it back to the client in an ASP *Response* object. Now we'll look at an example that shows how we can use a stream to place the data directly into the DOM objects.

This example will load data from a text file and place it into an ADO *Stream* object. The data will then be loaded into a DOM object. Once you have the data in the DOM object, you can do almost anything you want to it, including transforming it with XSL. To place the data into an ADO *Stream* object, add another command button to the form. Name it *cmdStream* with a caption *Stream* and add the following code to the click event handler of the command button *cmdStream*:

```
Private Sub cmdStream _Click()
    Dim objNWRecordset As ADODB.Recordset
    Dim objADOStream As ADODB.Stream
    Dim objDOM As DOMDocument
    Dim strXML As String
    Dim objNWConnection As ADODB.Connection
    Set objADOStream = New ADODB.Stream
    Set objDOM = New DOMDocument
    Set objNWRecordset = New ADODB.Recordset
    Set objNWConnection = New ADODB.Connection
    objNWConnection.CursorLocation = adUseClient
    'You will need to replace IES-FUJI with the appropriate data
    'source in the following statement.
    objNWConnection.Open _
    "Provider=SQLOLEDB.1;Integrated Security=SSPI;" & _
    "Persist Security Info=False;" & _
    "User ID=sa;Initial Catalog=Northwind;Data Source=IES-FUJI"
    objNWRecordset.CursorLocation = adUseClient
    objNWRecordset.CursorType = adOpenStatic
    Set objNWRecordset.ActiveConnection = objNWConnection
    objNWRecordset.Open "Products"
    objADOStream.Open
    objNWRecordset.Save objADOStream, adPersistXML
    strXML = objADOStream.ReadText
    objDOM.loadXML strXML
End Sub
```

Just as in our other examples, this code creates an ADO *Connection* object and a *Recordset* object. Once the connection to the Northwind Traders database has been made and the recordset contains the data from the Products table, the XML data is saved to an ADO *Stream* object called *objADOStream*. The information is passed from the ADO *Stream* object to a string variable called *strXML*, and then the XML data is placed into a DOM document object called *objDOM* using the *loadXML* method of the document object. In this way, we have opened data from a regular database and passed the data as XML into a DOM document object. As you can see, the ADO recordset is versatile and can be used on both the client and the server to build powerful data access components in distributed applications.

XML SQL SERVER ISAPI EXTENSION

The SQL Server extension allows you to send a SQL query to a SQL Server 6.5 or 7.0 database through IIS in the HTTP query string of the request and get the data back as XML. The extension will give you a preview of the functionality that will be in SQL Server 2000. You can download this tool from the Microsoft Web site at *http://msdn.microsoft.com/xml/articles/xmlsql/sqlxml_prev.asp,* where you can find the link *Download Microsoft SQL Server XML Technology Preview.* Right-click this link and choose Save Target As from the context menu to open the Save As dialog box. You will see the Sqlxmlsetup.exe file in the File Name box. Save this file to the local drive of a server running IIS. To install this extension, follow these steps:

1. Run Sqlxmlsetup.exe. The ISAPI DLL will be copied to your server and a menu entry named XML Technology Preview for SQL Server will be created.

2. Choose Programs from the Start menu, XML Technology Preview for SQL Server, and then Registration Tool. This will open a vrootmgt MMC snap-in that can be used to set up a SQL database so that the database can be accessed directly through the Web.

3. You will need to create a virtual root on the IIS Web server using the vrootmgt MMC snap-in. As an example of how this works, right click on the Default Web Site, choose New, and then choose Virtual Directory to open the New Virtual Directory Properties window, as shown in Figure 15-1.

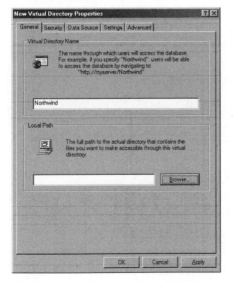

Figure 15-1. *The New Virtual Directory Properties window.*

4. In the General tab, change the default name of the virtual directory to a name such as *Northwind* and specify a local path to the actual directory that contains the files you want to make accessible through this virtual directory.

5. Click the Security tab. You can choose any of the security mechanisms that are appropriate for your server, including Windows Integrated security and SQL Server account. Select a security mechanism that will give you access to the Northwind Traders database on a SQL Server database that you have access to. If you select the Always Log In As option, you must supply a user ID that has access to the Northwind Traders database.

6. Next select the Datasource tab, choose the correct data source, and pick the Northwind Traders database.

7. Select the Setting tab, and then select Allow URL Queries.

8. Click OK to close the New Virtual Directory Properties window.

Accessing SQL Server

You should now be able to access SQL Server in a URL that specifies HTTP as the protocol. Place the following query into the navigation bar in Internet Explorer 5 and get back the appropriate results:

```
http://localhost/northwind?sql=SELECT+*+FROM+Customers+FOR+XML+AUTO
```

Figure 15-2 shows what this query returns.

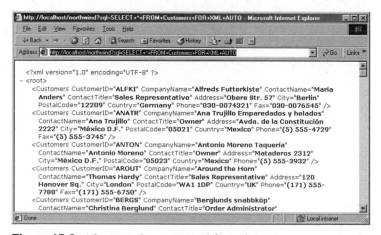

Figure 15-2. *The XML data returned from the query.*

As you can see, this ISAPI extension allows you to rapidly and easily retrieve data from a SQL Server database. The format of the XML data can be specified in several ways by using the FOR XML clause in the SELECT statement. The FOR XML clause can specify one of the three modes: AUTO, RAW, and EXPLICIT. In Figure 15-2, we used the AUTO mode to allow the ISAPI extension to format the data as a nested tree. The RAW mode takes the query result and transforms each row in the result set into an XML element with a generic row identifier as the element tag. Figure 15-3 shows what the results would look like using the RAW mode.

Figure 15-3. *Using the RAW mode in the query.*

The EXPLICIT mode allows you to define the shape of the XML tree that is returned.

Using URLs to Execute Queries

You can use a URL and SQL statements to access SQL Server and execute stored procedures. Besides SQL statements, you can also specify templates using a URL. A template is a SQL query string formatted as an XML document. It contains one or more SQL statements. The general format for the query strings are as follows:

```
http://NameOfIISServer/
 NameOfVirtualRoot?SQL=SQLQueryString| template=XMLTemplate]
 [&param=value[&param=value]…]
```

or

```
http://NameOfIISServer/NameOfVirtualRoot [/filepath]/
 filename.xml [?param=value[&param=value]…]
```

If a SQL statement is used, you can use the FOR XML clause and specify one of the three modes mentioned above.

The *param* value in the above query string is a parameter or a keyword. Keywords can be of three types: *contenttype*, *outputencoding*, and *_charset_*. The *contenttype* keyword describes the content type of the document that will be returned. The content type can be images such as JPEG and text. The *contenttype* value will become part of the HTTP header that is returned. The default is text/XML. If you are returning XHTML, you should set *contenttype* to text/html. If you do not want the browser to perform any formatting, you can use text/plain. For images and other SQL Server binary large object (BLOB) fields, you can use one of the registered MIME types. The registered MIME types can be found at *ftp://ftp.isi.edu/innotes/iana/assignments/media-types/media-types*.

The *outputencoding* keyword is the character set that will be used for the returned document. The default is UTF-8. The *_charset_* keyword is the character set for decoding the parameters that are passed in; its default is also UTF-8.

When writing out the queries you must use the defaults for HTML query strings. For example, we used the plus sign (+) for spaces. You will need to use a percentage sign (%) followed by the hex value for the following characters: /, ?, %, #, and &.

You can also specify an XSL file to transform the XML data, as shown in the following URL:

```
http://localhost/northwind?sql=SELECT+CompanyName,+ContactName
+FROM+ Customers+FOR+XML+AUTO&xsl=customer.xsl&contenttype=text/html
```

The file Customer.xsl can be placed in any subdirectory that is part of the virtual root subdirectory tree. The code for the XSL file would look as follows:

```
<?xml version="1.0"  encoding="ISO-8859-1" ?>
<xsl:stylesheet xmlns:xsl="http://www.w3.org/TR/WD-xsl">
   <xsl:template match = "*">
      <xsl:apply-templates />
   </xsl:template>

   <xsl:template match = "Customers">
      <TR>
      <TD><xsl:value-of select = "@CompanyName" /></TD>
      <TD><B><xsl:value-of select = "@ContactName" /></B></TD>
      </TR>
   </xsl:template>

   <xsl:template match = "/">
      <HTML>
      <HEAD>
```

```
        <STYLE>th { background-color: #CCCCCC }</STYLE>
      </HEAD>
      <BODY>
        <TABLE border="1" style="width:300;">
          <TR><TH colspan="2">Customers</TH></TR>
          <TR><TH>CompanyName</TH><TH>Contact Name</TH></TR>
          <xsl:apply-templates select = "root" />
        </TABLE>
      </BODY>
      </HTML>
  </xsl:template>
</xsl:stylesheet>
```

This document will look as shown in Figure 15-4.

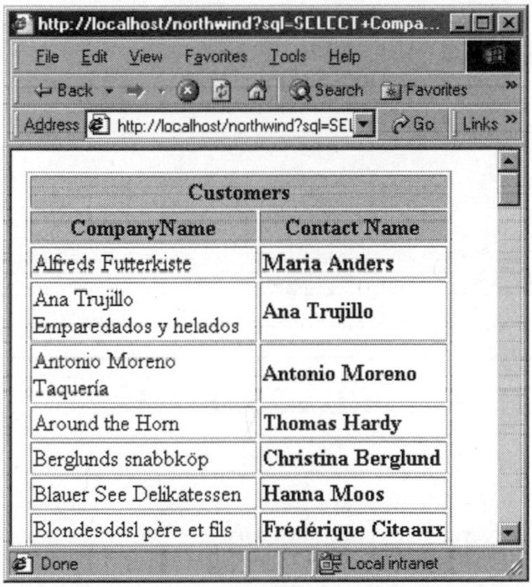

Figure 15-4. *The transformed XML data.*

You can execute a stored procedure using the EXECUTE command. For example, the Northwind Traders SQL Server database comes with a stored procedure called CustOrderHist. The stored procedure looks as follows:

```
CREATE PROCEDURE CustOrderHist @CustomerID nchar(5)
AS
SELECT ProductName, Total = SUM(Quantity)
FROM Products P, [Order Details] OD, Orders O, Customers C
```

(continued)

```
WHERE C.CustomerID = @CustomerID
AND C.CustomerID = O.CustomerID AND O.OrderID = OD.OrderID
AND OD.ProductID = P.ProductID
GROUP BY ProductName
```

This stored procedure takes one parameter, the ID of the customer. To execute this query we can use the following HTTP query string:

```
http://localhost/northwind?sql=EXECUTE+CustOrderHist+
 "ALFKI"+FOR+XML+AUTO
```

This query gets the order history for the customer with an ID of *ALFKI*. The results of this query are shown in Figure 15-5.

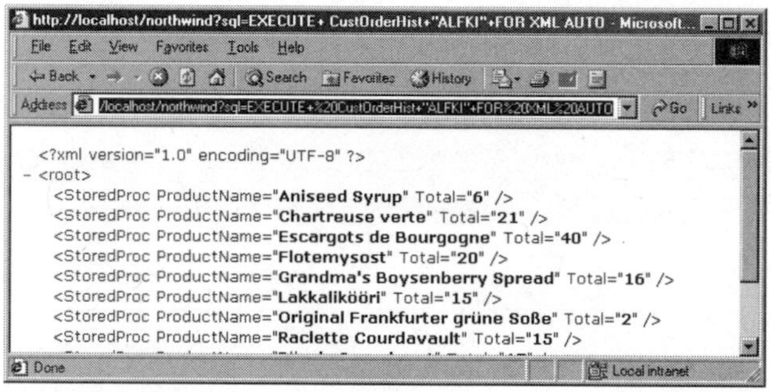

Figure 15-5. *Sales for customer with ID ALFKI.*

Using the SQL ISAPI Extension to Update Data

You can also update data to a database using the SQL ISAPI extension. To perform an update you must create an *update gram*. An update gram is a template that is sent in an HTML query string. The general format of an update gram is shown below:

```
<sql:sync xmlns:sql="urn:schemas-microsoft-com:xml-sql">
   <sql:before>
      <TABLENAME [sql:id="value"] col="value" col="value".../>
   </sql:before>
   <sql:after>
      <TABLENAME [sql:id="value"] [sql:at-identity="value"]
         col="value" col="value".../>
   </sql:after>
</sql:sync>
```

Using this format, you can perform inserts, updates, and deletes. When performing an insert you would leave out the *before* element, when performing a delete you would leave out the *after* element, and when performing an update you would include both the *before* and *after* elements and list the columns that have changed.

For example, to add a new product to the Northwind Traders' Products table we could create the following HTML file called InsertProd.htm:

```
<HTML>
<SCRIPT>
   function InsertXML(ProdName, UInStock)
   {
   myTemplate = "http://localhost/northwind?template=" +
      "<ROOT xmlns:sql='urn:schemas-microsoft-com:xml-sql'>" +
         "<sql:sync>" +
         "<sql:after>" +
         "<Products ProductName=\"" + ProdName +
         " UnitsInStock=\"" + UInStock + " \"/>" +
         "</sql:after>" +
         "</sql:sync>" +
         "<sql:query>select * from Products FOR XML AUTO " +
         "</sql:query>" +
      "</ROOT>";
   alert(myTemplate);
   document.location.href = myTemplate;
   }
</SCRIPT>
<BODY>
   Product Name:<INPUT type="text" id="ProductName" value="">
      <br></br>
   Units In Stock:<INPUT type="text" id="UnitInStock" value="">
      <br></br>
   <INPUT type="button" value="insert"
      OnClick="InsertXML(ProductName.value, UnitInStock.value);"/>
</BODY>
</HTML>
```

You can also find this HTML file on the companion CD. This HTML page uses a Java script function that builds the template. The backslash (/) is required for including a quote within a quote. You must place quotes around the new values or you will get an error. Unfortunately, there are some fields, such as money, which will not be accepted by SQL Server this way. These fields would need to be updated using a stored procedure as described below. Notice that we also included a *sql:query* element that is used to determine what is returned to the client. This will allow us to see whether the data was actually added to the database. Figure 15-6 shows what the HTML page and the query string look like.

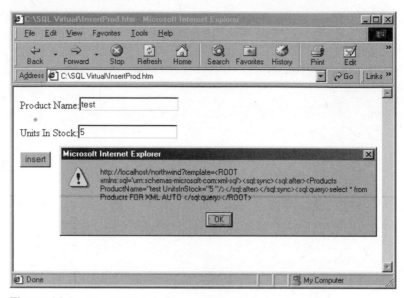

Figure 15-6. *The HTML page for updating with query string.*

There are other more advanced features of the SQL ISAPI extension that extend beyond the level of this book. If you are interested in these features, you can look at the documentation that comes with the SQL ISAPI extension.

XSL ISAPI EXTENSION

In Chapter 12, we created an ASP page that used the DOM to transform an XML page to XHTML on the server using an XSL document. Instead of writing your own code to perform XSL transformations on the server, you can use the XSL ISAPI extension to automatically transform an XML page that includes a reference to an XSL page if the browser is not Internet Explorer 5. If the browser being used is Internet Explorer 5, the XML page is sent to the client as is, and the transformation is done on the client. For the most part, the XSL ISAPI will be working with data and transforming it according to a set of rules defined in an XSL document.

The Xslisapi.exe file is a zipped file that contains the files for the ISAPI extension. This file can be found at *http://msdn.microsoft.com/downloads/webtechnology/xml/xslisapi.asp*. To install this extension on a server running IIS, follow these steps:

1. Expand the files into a folder in your local drive. You will see numerous headers for C++, but we are interested in only Xslisapi.dll.

2. Copy the Xslisapi.dll file into the %SystemRoot%\SYSTEM32\INETSRV directory.

3. Open the Internet Services Manager console, right click on the default Web site, and select Properties as shown in Figure 15-7.

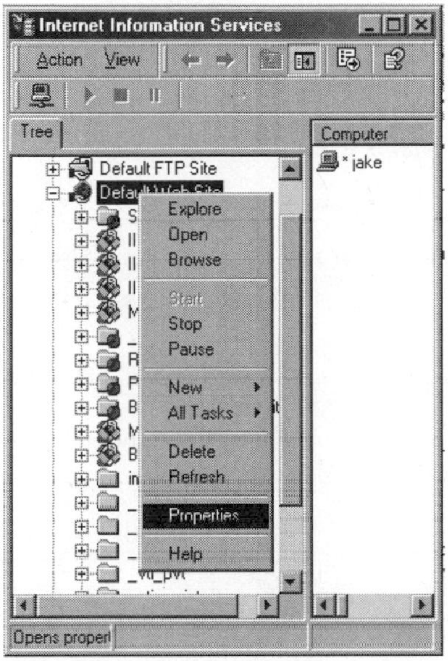

Figure 15-7. *Opening Properties Window in the default Web site.*

4. In the Properties window, select the Home Directory tab and then click on the Configuration button.

5. Select the App Mappings tab and click Add.

6. Type in *xslisapi.dll* as the executable and *.xml* as the extension. If you are using IIS 5 (Microsoft Windows 2000), click Limit To and add *HEAD, GET*. If you are using IIS 4, enter *PUT, POST>, DELETE* in the method exclusions box.

7. Finally, clear the Script engine check box and select the Check That File Exists check box. If you are using Internet Explorer 5 in Windows 2000, the configuration would appear as shown in Figure 15-8. Click OK twice.

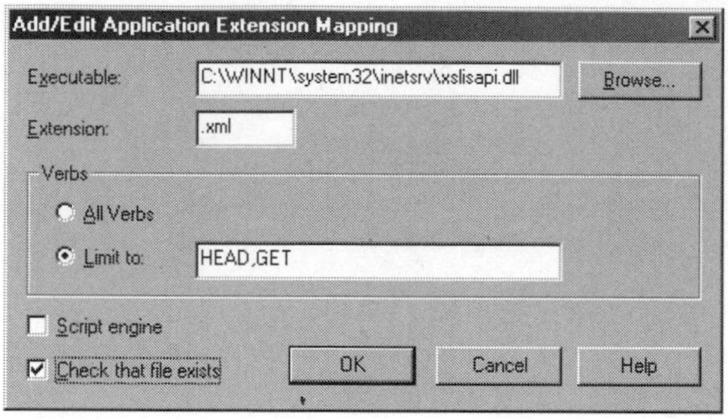

Figure 15-8. *Application Mappings for Internet Explorer 5.*

8. In the Home Directory tab's Execute Permissions box, select Scripts And Executables so that the xslisapi DLL is allowed to execute over any XML document on your Web site.

9. Click OK, and close the Properties window.

At this point, each request for an XML file that contains the processing instruction *<?xml-stylesheet type="text/xsl" href="*yourstyle.xsl*"?>* will go through the xslisapi DLL.

If the requesting browser is Internet Explorer 5, the xslisapi DLL will pass the XML document directly to the client. Otherwise, the xslisapi DLL will perform the XSL transformation on the server.

You can use a different style sheet for server-side processing and client-side processing by using a *server-href* attribute within the same processing instruction. If the xslisapi DLL needs to do server-side processing, it will first look for the *server-href* attribute. If the attribute is there, it will use the XSL page referenced by *server-href*. If the client doesn't have Internet Explorer 5 installed, the style sheet referenced by the *server-href* attribute will be used to transform the document. Thus, we would rewrite the processing instruction as follows:

```
<?xml-stylesheet type="text/xsl"
    server-href="serversideStyle.xsl" href="yourstyle.xsl"?>
```

You can also add a special Config.xml file into the same directory as the xslisapi DLL. This configuration file is optional and gives additional instructions to the xslisapi DLL.

SUMMARY

In this chapter, we discussed two Microsoft technologies that we can use to create data services components that can access data: ADO 2.5 and the SQL ISAPI extension. ADO will allow you to access data in any data store, whereas the SQL ISAPI extension allows you to access data in a SQL 6.5 or 7.0 database. Using ADO and the SQL ISAPI extension, you can create XML data that can be presented to the user and used for updating data.

The XSL ISAPI extension allows you to automatically transform XML documents using XSL on the server when the client does not have Internet Explorer 5 installed. This can be used if you do not want to write ASP pages that use the DOM to perform these translations. In the next chapter, we will look at Microsoft BizTalk Server 2000, a new technology that enables business partners to exchange information.

Chapter 16

Microsoft BizTalk Server 2000

The new Microsoft BizTalk Server 2000 provides powerful tools for the exchange of information between businesses. The tools included with BizTalk Server 2000 allow you to create BizTalk schemas, to map fields and records from one specification to another, and to move data from one corporation to another using XML. These tools are based on the XML technology and standard and provide the data translation for an application-integration server. You can visit the Microsoft BizTalk Server 2000 Web site at *http://www.microsoft.com/biztalkserver/* to download the BizTalk Server 2000 Technology Preview. The site includes instructions on how to install and set up a BizTalk server.

The five main tools in BizTalk Server are BizTalk Editor, BizTalk Mapper, BizTalk Management Desk, BizTalk Server Administration Console, and BizTalk Server Tracking. These tools can provide you with the ability to receive and send documents in a variety of formats, validate and create documents, work with multiple protocols, and ensure document delivery. In this chapter, we will discuss the tools of BizTalk Server 2000.

> **NOTE**   As this book goes to press, the first beta version of BizTalk Server 2000 was released. It's likely that some minor changes and fixes will be made to this product before the final release.

THE BIZTALK EDITOR

The BizTalk Editor allows you to edit BizTalk documents and schemas. Using the BizTalk Editor, you can import existing document definitions, including DTDs, BizTalk schemas, electronic data interchange (EDI) specifications such as American National Standards Institute (ANSI) X12 and electronic data interchange for administration, commerce, and transport (EDIFACT), flat files, well-formed XML, structured document formats, and XML-based templates. You can also create new *specifications* from blank templates. A specification is a structured document that tells BizTalk Server 2000 how to format data. All specifications are stored as XML. Let's take a look at how the BizTalk Editor works.

If you have installed BizTalk Server 2000, click the Start button, point to Programs, Microsoft BizTalk Server 2000, and then choose BizTalk Editor to open the BizTalk Editor. We will work with the Northwind.biz document we created in Chapter 9 to see how to use the BizTalk Editor to edit this document. First take the following code in the Northwind.biz document and save it as Categories.xml (we have removed the *customer* element because the BizTalk Editor currently imports only one component at a time):

```
<Schema name = "NorthwindSchema"
    xmlns = "urn:schemas-microsoft-com:xml-data"
    xmlns:dt = "urn:schemas-microsoft-com:datatypes">
    <ElementType name = "Categories"
        xmlns:Categories = "urn:northwindtraders.com.Categories"
        content="eltOnly" model="closed">
        <group order = "seq">
            <element type = "Categories.CategoryID"
                minOccurs = "1" maxOccurs = "1" />
            <element type = "Categories.CategoryName"
                minOccurs = "1" maxOccurs = "1" />
            <element type = "Categories.Description"
                minOccurs = "0" maxOccurs = "1" />
            <element type = "Categories.Picture"
                minOccurs = "0" maxOccurs = "1"/>
        </group>
    </ElementType>
```

```
    <ElementType name = "Categories.CategoryID"
        xmlns:Categories = "urn:northwindtraders.com.Categories"
        dt:type = "int">
        <description>
            Number automatically assigned to a new category
        </description>
    </ElementType>
    <ElementType name = "Categories.CategoryName"
        xmlns:Categories = "urn:northwindtraders.com.Categories"
        dt:type = "string">
        <description>Name of food category</description>
    </ElementType>
    <ElementType name = "Categories.Description"
        xmlns:Categories = "urn:northwindtraders.com.Categories"
        dt:type = "string"/>
    <ElementType name = "Categories.Picture"
        xmlns:Categories="urn:northwindtraders.com.Categories"
        dt:type = "bin.base64">
        <description>
            Picture representing the food category
        </description>
    </ElementType>
</Schema>
```

To import a well-formed XML document, a DTD, or a BizTalk schema, from the Tools menu choose Import. The Select Import Module screen will appear as shown in Figure 16-1.

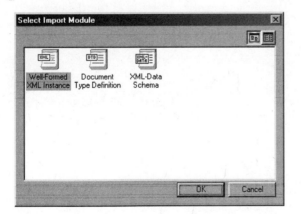

Figure 16-1. *The Select Import Module screen.*

Since we are working with a BizTalk schema, choose XML-Data Schema and then select the Categories.xml file. At this point, a dialog box will appear informing you that *group* elements are not supported; just click OK. The records and fields of the imported schema will appear in the BizTalk Editor specification tree, as shown in Figure 16-2.

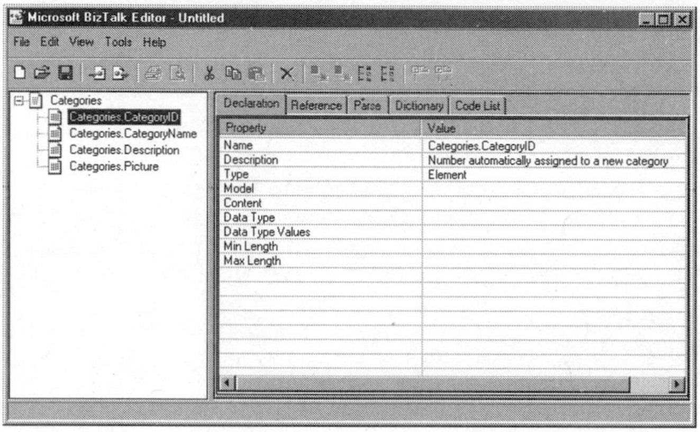

Figure 16-2. *Imported schema in BizTalk Editor.*

As you can see, the BizTalk Editor has imported most of the information, such as the elements and their child elements and the values of these elements. However, it did not import the data types. You will need to add the data types. For the *CategoryID* element, click on the right column next to Data Type and a list box will appear. Select *integer[int]* from the drop-down list. Add the data types for the other elements.

Records and Fields

The BizTalk Editor uses records and fields to present a document structure. Records and fields represent two types of components found in EDI documents: segments and elements. A field corresponds to an EDI element and a record corresponds to an EDI segment. In regards to XML, we can think of a field as an element that either contains text or has no content at all, and a record as an element that can contain text, content, or other elements. As you can see in Figure 16-2, the root node was a record that contained four fields. The BizTalk Editor interprets the data contained in the records and fields of a document specification and creates a specification that is an XML representation of the document.

In Figure 16-2, you can also see that the BizTalk Editor has five tabs: Declaration, Reference, Parse, Dictionary, and Code List. Let's examine these tabs in more detail.

The Declaration Tab

The Declaration tab can be used to set declaration property values, add a custom declaration, and delete a custom declaration. The properties listed in the Declaration tab are shown in the following table:

DECLARATION TAB PROPERTIES

Property	Description
Name	Name of the element.
Description	Description of the element. This property can be used as a comment.
Data Type	Data type of the element.
Model	Can be *closed* or *open*. If the model is *closed*, the structure of a document that uses the specification currently being defined in the BizTalk Editor must conform to this specification. If the model is *open*, a document that uses this specification does not have to conform to this specification.
Type	Determines whether this component is an attribute or an element. For the root node, it can only be an element.
Content	Defines the type of content for an element. The root node and any record with child elements are *Element Only*, which means they can contain only elements. All other records can be either *Empty* or *Text Only*. If an element is empty, it contains no content.
MinLength, MaxLength	Used for fields or records that contain string content. These properties define the length of the field.

The Reference Tab

The Reference tab can be used to set reference property values. It provides properties for each BizTalk Editor component. The properties of the root node, records that are not the root, and fields are all different from each other for the Reference tab. The available Reference tab properties for the root node are shown in the table that follows.

REFERENCE TAB PROPERTIES FOR THE ROOT NODE

Property	Description
Schema Name	Name of this particular specification.
Standard	Name of an industry standard, such as XML, X12, or EDIFACT, that was used to create this standard (if one exists).
Standards Version	Version of the standard (if a standard was used).
Document Type	The document type of the specification (if a specification was used).
Version	Version number of the specification.
Default Record Delimiter	Determines which character you want to use to delimit records. You can use different characters for different records. This only applies to non-EDI standards.
Default Field Delimiter	Determines which character you want to use to delimit fields. You can use different characters for different fields. This only applies to non-EDI standards.
Default Subfield Delimiter	Determines which character you want to use to delimit child fields. You can use different characters for different fields. This applies only to non-EDI standards.
Default Escape Character	Can be set to Tab (0x9), LF (0xa), and CR (0xd). This applies only to non-EDI standards.
Unicode	If you set this property to *Yes*, the data associated with this specification uses the Unicode character set. If you don't specify the value for this property, it works with both Unicode and non-Unicode data. If you set this property to *No*, the data cannot be Unicode. If you are working with ASCII data, you must set this property to *No*.
Receipt	If this property is set to *Yes*, you'll receive an interchange receipt acknowledgement, which will tell you that the message arrived at its destination. If this property is set to *No,* the documents built from this specification will be validated, but no receipt will be delivered if the message is received.
Envelope	If this specification belongs to an interchange specification, choose *Yes;* otherwise choose *No*.
Target Namespace	If you are working with a BizTalk framework document that uses a namespace, you must list the namespace here.

REFERENCE TAB PROPERTIES FOR RECORDS

Property	Description
Min Occurs	Minimum number of times that a record can occur. The value can be either *0* or *1*.
Max Occurs	Maximum number of times a record can occur. The value can be either *1* or *. If you use either a star or don't specify a value for this property, BizTalk Mapper will define this record as a loop, if the specification is used in BizTalk Mapper.

REFERENCE TAB PROPERTIES FOR FIELDS

Property	Description
Required	If the field is required, set this property to *Yes*.
Start Position	If the property is positional (contains a position in the record where a field starts), a number that indicates the starting position of the field in the record.
End Position	If the property is positional, a number that indicates the ending position of the field in the record.

Figure 16-3 shows the Reference tab for the root node.

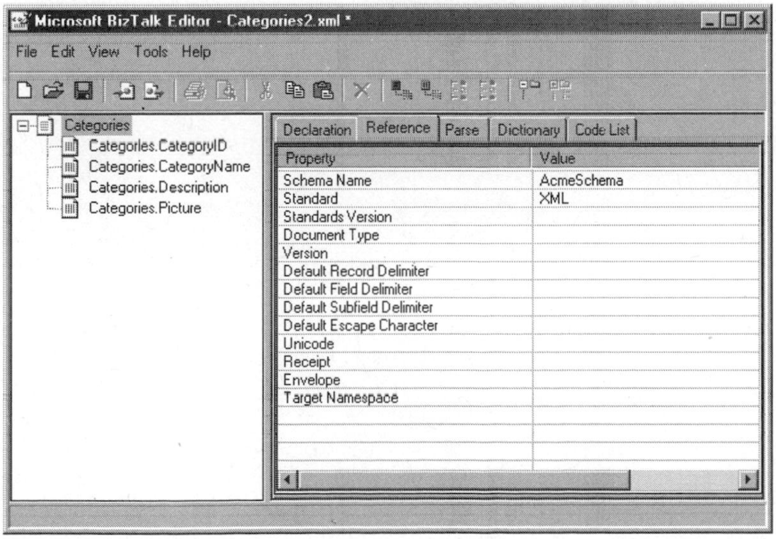

Figure 16-3. *The BizTalk Editor showing the Reference tab properties for the root node.*

Notice in the figure that we are missing the namespace that we had originally included. Add the following namespace to the root node *Target Namespace* property on the Reference tab: *urn:northwindtraders.com.Categories*.

The Parse Tab

The Parse tab is used to determine how the fields are defined in a document that uses the specification created by the BizTalk Editor. The Parse tab is used for documents that are delimited in some way, such as a comma delimited text file. The actual properties that are available will depend on whether you are working with a field or record and on the standard (such as X12, EDIFACT, or XML) and *Structure* property on the Parse tab you are using. If you have chosen to use XML as your standard, no properties will be available in the Parse tab. Because the schema we imported earlier used an XML specification, we cannot see or set any values of the Parse tab properties using the BizTalk Editor. If you choose either the X12 or EDIFACT standard, you will be able to set up properties for the Parse tab with delimited documents.

PARSE TAB PROPERTIES FOR ROOT NODES AND RECORDS

Property	Description
Structure	Can be delimited or positional. If left blank, the file is considered to be delimited.
Source Tag Identifier	Name of the source tag that is used to match the record with the data.
Source Tag Position	Used in positional records; indicates the beginning of the tag.
Field Order	Either *Prefix* (a delimiter is placed before each component, for example, *aa *bb *cc), *Postfix* (a delimiter is placed after each component, for example, aa* bb* cc*), *Infix* (a delimiter is placed between components, for example, aa*bb*cc), or *Blank* (unknown order). This property is used only for delimited records.
Delimiter Type	Can be set to *Character* (the actual character to use as the delimiter is defined in the *Delimiter Value* property), *Inherit Record* (use the delimiter designation of the previous record), *Inherit Field* (use the delimiter designation of the previous field), or *Inherit Subfield* (use the delimiter designation of the previous subfield). This property is used only for delimited records.

Property	Description
Delimiter Value	The character that is used to delimit the text if the value of the *Delimiter Type* property is *Character*. This property is used only for delimited records.
Escape Type	Can be *Character* (tells the parser to suspend the delimiter designation if this character is found in the document; the character is specified in the *Escape Value* property), or *Inherit Escape* (for inheriting the previous record's escape type).
Escape Value	If the value of the *Escape Type* property is *Character*, this property specifies the escape character.
Append New Line	If set to *Yes,* indicates that when the record delimiter is found, begin the next record on a new line. If set to *No*, all records are on the same line.
Skip Carriage Return	If set to *Yes*, the parser will skip the carriage return (CR) value after a delimiter.
Skip Line Feed	If set to *Yes*, the parser will skip the line feed (LF) value after a delimiter.
Ignore Record Count	If set to *Yes*, tells the parser not to count any *CR* or *LF* values when counting characters.

PARSE TAB PROPERTIES FOR FIELDS

Property	Description
Custom Data Type	Used for specifications that are based on an X12 or EDIFACT standard. Only applies if the structure type is delimited.
Custom Date/Time Format	Used for specifications that are based on an X12 or EDIFACT standard. Only applies if the structure type is delimited.
Justification	For positional and delimited files. If set to *Left*, the data that is less than the maximum length is aligned left. If set to *Right*, the data is aligned right.
Pad Character	A character that will be used to pad blank spaces in a field.

The Dictionary Tab

The Dictionary tab is used to set up the properties for *agreements*. Agreements will be discussed in more detail in the section "BizTalk Management Desk" later in this chapter, but in simple terms, an agreement is used to define the rules for passing documents between two corporations. Using agreements, pipelines can be created that pass documents back and forth between two servers. (We will discuss pipelines in more detail later in this chapter.) The Dictionary tab defines the location of the agreement that is used for a field.

DICTIONARY TAB FIELD PROPERTIES

Property	Description
Source Type	Indicates the document instance value for the source type.
Source Value	Indicates the actual data in the document instance that will be used to validate a document. For example, an ID number.
Destination Type	Indicates whether the sender or receiver data located in the document instance will be used to validate the document.
Destination Value	Indicates whether the actual destination data in the document instance will be used to validate the actual document.
Document Type	Indicates that the document name in the document instance is to be used to validate the document.
Document Node	When using an envelope schema, the document node indicates the body record that will hold the actual document.
Version	Indicates the document version that will be used to validate the document.

BIZTALK MAPPER

BizTalk Mapper allows you to map fields and records from one specification to fields and records in another specification. BizTalk Mapper uses *links* and *functoids*. A link is a simple copy operation from the value in one field to the value in another field. A link can also copy to a functoid. A functoid is an object that allows for complex structural manipulation operations between source elements and destination elements. Before a specification can be used in BizTalk Mapper, it needs to be defined in the BizTalk Editor. BizTalk Mapper supports EDI, flat files, XML files, schemas, and even ADO recordsets. BizTalk Mapper can also create XSL style sheets for mapping.

As an example of how to use BizTalk Mapper, we will use two PO specifications that come with BizTalk Server 2000. To see how BizTalk Mapper works, follow these steps:

1. Click the Start button, point to Programs, Microsoft BizTalk Server 2000, and then choose BizTalk Mapper.

2. From the File menu, choose New. You will see the Select Source Specification Type screen where you can choose either Local Files, which is a specification on your local computer or network; Templates, which are templates that came with BizTalk Server; or WebDav (Web Distributed Authoring and Versioning) Files, which refers to specifications on shared servers. For our example, we will imagine that we are transferring a purchase order file from a local XML file to an XML purchase order file located in a common WebDav location.

3. In the Select Source Specification Type screen, click Templates, choose XML, and then choose CommonPO.xml. You will now see the Select Destination Specification Type screen.

4. For the destination, choose WebDav Files. The Retrieve Destination Specification screen will appear. In this screen choose Microsoft, and then choose CommonPO.xml. In this case, both specifications use fields with the same name. In other cases, the fields might have completely different names.

5. Expand the POHeader on both the source specification and destination specification. You can see the fields contained in the POHeader. Drag the Purpose field from the source to the destination. The map should now look as shown in Figure 16-4.

By connecting source and destination fields, you can create a map between a source and a destination specification. If you now connect other fields, you can go to the Tools menu and choose Compile Map to produce XSL code that will create the transformation between the two specifications. Figure 16-5 shows the XSL code generated in the Output tab on the bottom of the BizTalk Mapper after linking several other fields and then compiling.

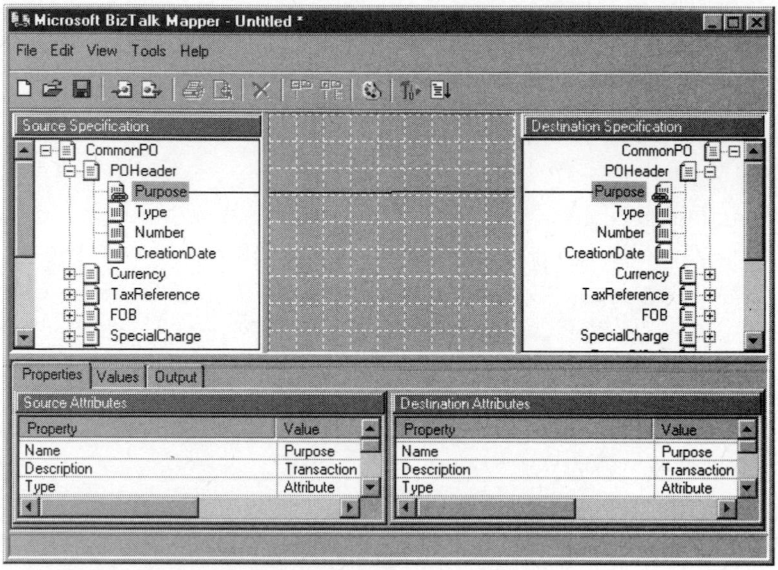

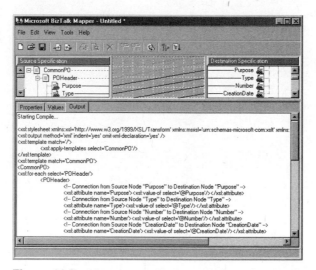

Figure 16-4. *Microsoft BizTalk Mapper.*

Figure 16-5. *The Output tab showing the XSL code after compiling.*

As mentioned, you can use functoids to perform complex structural transformations between source elements and destination elements. Functoids use predefined formulas and specific values to perform calculations. You can select functoids from the Functoid Palette. To work with functoids, follow these steps:

1. On the View menu, choose Functoid Palette to open the Functoid Palette screen.

2. From the Functoid Palette screen, you can choose a functoid and drag it to the mapping grid area. The mapping grid area is the gray grid area between the source and destination in Microsoft BizTalk Mapper. As an example, select the Mathematical tab of the Functoid Palette screen, click the X (multiplication) functoid, and drag the X onto the grid. Connect a field to the functoid, right click the functoid, and then select Properties to open the Functoid Properties window. In this window, select the Script tab. You can see that a function is created in this tab, as shown in Figure 16-6.

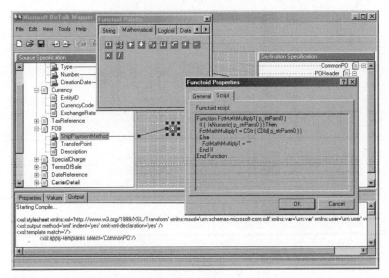

Figure 16-6. *The Script tab in the Functoid Properties window.*

In our case, the function *FctMathMultiply1* is defined in the following code:

```
Function FctMathMultiply1( p_strParm0 )
  If ( IsNumeric( p_strParm0 ) ) Then
  FctMathMultiply1 = CStr ( CDbl( p_strParm0 ) )
  Else
    FctMathMultiply1 = ""
  End If
End Function
```

As you can see, the function is just a template. You will need to fill in the necessary functionality to make this function work. In the pre-release version of the BizTalk Mapper, this script cannot be edited in the Functoid Properties window. However, you can go to the Advanced tab of the Functoid Palette to edit the script. (You might need to scroll over to see the Advanced tab.) Get the Custom Visual Basic Script from the Advanced tab and drop it on the grid, make a connection from a field in the source document to a field in the destination document, and then edit the script. A custom transformation will be created between the source field and the destination field.

As you can see, functoids make it easy to do transformations. When the map is compiled by choosing Compile Map from the Tools menu, the XSL script will include functions to perform these transformations.

BizTalk Management Desk

The BizTalk Management Desk is used to create, establish, and maintain relationships within a corporation and between a corporation and its partners. These relationships are built on *agreements*, which are rules that determine how information is exchanged. Each agreement has a source organization and a destination organization, or an internal organization and one of its applications. The first step in creating an agreement is designating a default organization, which can be either the source or the destination for every agreement. Applications can also be either the source or the destination, but not both. If an application is used, it must be part of the default organization. There must be at least one document definition defining which documents the source can send to the destination. An *open agreement* means that either the receiver or the sender, but not both, are open. An open-source agreement always has the designated default organization as its destination organization; an open-destination agreement always has the designated default organization as its source organization.

An agreement defines the movement of information in one direction. If the default organization is the source, it is an outbound agreement. If the default organization is the destination, it is an inbound agreement. Outbound agreements oversee the movement of information out of BizTalk Server 2000, and inbound agreements control the movement of information into BizTalk Server 2000.

Using BizTalk Management Desk

In this section, we are going to look at how BizTalk Management Desk works. Follow these steps:

1. Click the Start button, point to Programs, Microsoft BizTalk Server 2000, and then choose Microsoft BizTalk Management Desk. You will see a Help window displayed that describes the steps you need to take in order to move information between corporations. The first time you use the BizTalk Management Desk, you'll need to select a default organization.

2. In the upper right corner, click the Select button in the Default Organization box. This will bring up the Select An Organization screen. If you do not have an organization yet, click New. This will bring up the Organization Editor. For this example, we'll create an organization for Northwind Traders Corporation.

3. In the General Tab, type *Northwind Traders* for the Organization Name in the Organization Identifiers section. In the Identifiers tab you will see that there already is a default Organization identifier named Organization. All organizations get this default, do not delete or change it. You can create as many identifiers as you want, but if you are using an X12 format, you should create a two-character identifier as the default.

4. To create a new identifier, type *NWT* in the Value field of the Identifier tab, and check Set As Default.

5. Click Refresh to add the new value to the list of identifiers.

   NOTE BizTalk Management Desk also allows you to create custom names with a qualifier and to associate applications with the default organizations, but we will not go into this in this example. Refer to the Microsoft BizTalk Server 2000 Help file for the detailed information.

6. Click OK in the Organization Editor, and then click OK in the Select An Organization box. You should see Northwind Traders listed as the default organization.

7. The next step is to create an agreement. On the File menu click New, and then click Agreement. This will bring up the Agreement Editor. We will make this a movement of information within the Northwind Traders Corporation from its central location to its European location.

8. Type *Northwind Traders Europe* in the Agreement Name field in the Agreement Editor.

9. Click the Destination icon. This will bring up the Select An Organization screen again.

10. Click New, and create an organization called Northwind Traders Europe. In the Identifiers tab, give it a value of *NWTE,* and set this as the default. After you create Northwind Traders Europe, select it as the destination.

Now that we've created the agreement, the next step will be to create a *document definition*. A document definition provides a reference to a specification, which can be created using BizTalk Editor. The outbound and inbound documents will both be associated with a document definition. A *pipeline* connects the document definition of an outbound document with the document definition of an inbound document. Pipelines are defined in agreements and distribution lists.

You can use the predefined document definitions, or you can use a specification, such as one that is created with BizTalk Editor, to create a new definition. To create a new definition, from the View menu, choose Document Definitions. This will open the Document Definitions Viewer. You can use any specification that is published to a server. For this example, click New to display the Document Definition Editor screen. Click Browse in the Document Definition Editor screen, choose Microsoft, and then choose Common PO.xml in the local server. Type *CommonPO.xml* in the Document Definition Name field. You can select the Tracking tab if you want to log any of the fields. You can add two of the following types of fields to log: integer, real, date, and text. You can select multiple fields as a custom data type. These fields will become an XML concatenated string. You can only track fields that have a data type specified. You can use the information that is logged to perform tracking of certain business operations. The quantity field for a particular item or the total for purchase orders are two examples of fields that you might want to track and could use to perform an analysis of various business processes.

You can also add selection criteria in the Document Definition Editor. BizTalk Server 2000 determines what document definition to associate a document with by getting information from the document. For X12 and EDIFACT documents, it is not possible to obtain this information from the document. Thus, the information concerning which document definition to use must be placed in the functional group header of the X12 or EDIFACT document. The selection criteria is used to uniquely identify the document definition when processing an inbound EDI document. The selection criteria can also be used to create functional group header information for outbound EDI document envelopes. When working with X12 and EDIFACT, you'll need to add the following selection criteria: application_sender_code, application_receiver_code, and functional_identifier. The X12 format will also need the standards_version selection criteria, and the EDIFACT will need the standards_version_type and the standards_version_value selection criteria. We will not add any selection criteria for tracking, therefore just click OK in the Document Definition Editor and then click Close on the Document Definition Viewer. Next, go to the Agreement Editor and click on the Document Definition icon. This will bring up the Select Document Definition screen. Click on the CommonPO.xml file that you just selected and then click Add. Click OK. You should now see that the text below the Document Definition icon reads *Complete*.

You will now need to select a Transport method. Click on the Transport icon. This will bring up the Transport screen. In this screen, select a transport type. For this example, select HTTP. For the Address field, type *http://localhost*, where *localhost* is the name of your local server. Then click OK to close the Transport screen.

At this point, we have completed all the required steps for creating agreements. There are some optional things we can do. We can create an envelope that creates headers and sometimes footers for the document. BizTalk Server 2000 currently supports Custom XML, ANSI X12, UN/EDIFACT and flat file (either delimited or positional) envelope formats. You can also create your own custom envelope formats.

We will not create an envelope or set security properties in this example, so you can now click Save in the Agreement Editor to open the Save As screen. Click Save Agreement As Complete and then click OK. In the BizTalk Management Desk you can see that this is an outbound agreement because the default organization is the sender.

Now let's create an inbound agreement:

1. On the File menu, click New, and then choose Agreement. This will bring up the Agreement Editor. Name the agreement Internal Order.

2. Click the Source icon to open the Select An Organization screen. In this screen, click New to open the Organization Editor.

3. In the Organization Editor, type *Northwind Traders Order Dept* for the Organization Name field.

4. Click the Identifiers tab, type *NWTOD* for the value, and then click Set As Default. Click Refresh, and then click OK in the Organization Editor. Close the Select An Organization screen.

5. In the Agreement Editor, click the Source icon to open the Select An Organization screen. In this screen, choose the *Northwind Traders Order Dept* and then click OK.

6. Click the Document Definition icon to open the Select Document Definition screen. In this screen, choose CommonPO.xml and then click OK.

7. Click the Transport icon, choose HTTP for the Transport Type field, and then type *http://localhost*. The destination should be Northwind Traders.

8. Click Save to open the Save As screen. Choose the Save Agreement As Complete option. You should now see that this agreement is listed as an inbound agreement in the BizTalk Management Desk.

Pipelines

Pipelines connect an inbound agreement to an outbound agreement. For example, you could have an inbound agreement created from an order application that takes orders and sends them to BizTalk Server 2000. Once they arrive on BizTalk Server 2000, an outbound agreement is used to send these orders to a distributor. The connection of the inbound and outbound agreements creates a pipeline.

To create a pipeline, you must always select the outbound agreement first. Click on the Northwind Traders Europe Outbound agreement. On the File menu, choose New, and then choose Pipeline. The Pipeline Editor opens in the lower-right pane of the BizTalk Management Desk. In this example, orders will be sent from the Internal Orders department to BizTalk Server 2000 and then forwarded to the European offices. We will use the two agreements we have created to do this.

In the Pipeline Editor, type *PO Pipeline* as the pipeline name. Click the Inbound Agreement icon to open the Select An Inbound Agreement screen. Choose Northwind Internal, and then choose CommonPO.xml as the inbound and outbound document definitions. Click Save. To view the pipeline you have created, go to the View menu and choose Pipeline. This will open the Pipeline Viewer, where you can view the available pipelines.

Distribution Lists

A distribution list consists of a set of complete outbound agreements that you can use to send the same document to a group of different trading partner organizations. A distribution list can support only one outbound document definition. When a distribution list is created, the default organization automatically becomes the source organization. To create a distribution list, on the File menu, click New, and then click Distribution List to open the Distribution List Editor. Type *Northwind Distribution List* for the Distribution List Name field. Click the Browse button and select the CommonPO.xml document definition in the Select An Outbound Document Definition screen. Click OK. This will enable the Refresh button for the agreements. In the Distribution List Editor, click Refresh. The only outbound agreement that we have created is Northwind Traders Europe. Click this agreement in the Available Agreements window and click Add. If we had other agreements, we could add them, too. Click OK.

SUBMITTING AND RECEIVING BIZTALK DOCUMENTS

Once a document has been placed into BizTalk Server 2000, BizTalk Server 2000 will route the message properly. You can use an application for the source or destination as long as the source or the destination is the default. You can also write an application that retrieves inbound BizTalk documents from the server and passes outbound documents to BizTalk Server 2000. BizTalk Server 2000 comes with the *IInterchange* interface, which can be used by the applications you write to communicate to BizTalk Server 2000.

When working with Microsoft Visual Basic, you will need to get a reference to the Microsoft BizTalk Server Interchange 1.0 Type Library. You can then get a reference to an Interchange object. This object implements the BizTalk Server *IInterchange* interface that has the following methods:

METHODS IN THE *IINTERCHANGE* INTERFACE

Method	Description
CheckSuspendedQueue ([DocName As String], [SourceName As String], [DestName As String])	Used to get a reference to a list of document handles for documents that are in the Suspended Queue.
DeleteFromSuspendedQueue (DocumentHandleList)	Deletes all specified documents in the Suspended Queue.
GetSuspendedQueueItemDetails (ItemHandle As String, SourceName, DestName, DocName, ReasonCode, ItemData)	Returns the details on a document in the Suspended Queue.
Submit (lOpenness As MODELDB_OPENNESS_TYPE, [Document As String], [DocName As String], [SourceQualifier As String], [SourceID As String], [DestQualifier As String], [DestID As String], [PipelineName As String], [FilePath As String], [EnvelopeName As String]) As String	Submits a document as a string to BizTalk Server 2000 for a synchronous processing. The MODELDB_OPENNESS_TYPE is used to determine if the document is open and can be the following constants: MODELDB_OPENNESS_TYPE_ DESTINATION, MODELDB_ OPENNESS_TYPE_NOTOPEN, and MODELDB_OPENNESS_ TYPE_SOURCE.
SubmitSync (Openness As MODELDB_OPENNESS_TYPE, [Document As String], [DocName As String], [SourceQualifier As String], [SourceID As String], [DestQualifier As String], [DestID As String], [PipelineName As String], [FilePath As String], [EnvelopeName As String], SubmissionHandle, ResponseDocument)	Submits a document as a string to BizTalk Server 2000 for synchronous processing and returns a response if one is provided.

The BizTalk SDK, which comes with BizTalk Server 2000 and is part of the BizTalk Server 2000 Help file, includes a complete tutorial and Visual Basic example that shows how to use this interface.

BizTalk Server Administration Console

The BizTalk Server Administration Console can be used to manage BizTalk servers; configure global server group properties such as shared locations and queues for document tracking; configure and manage *receive* functions such as FTP, File, and Message Queuing; and view and manage business document queues. The BizTalk Server Administration Console is a Microsoft Management Console (MMC) snap-in. The console can be used by the system administrator.

To view the properties of a BizTalk Server group, right-click BizTalk Server Group and choose Properties from the context menu to display the BizTalk Server Group Properties window. There are four tabs on the Properties window: General, Connection, DTA, and Errors. The General tab is used to view the name of the server, the SMTP host (if there is one), and the WebDAV URL. The Connection tab is used to define the SQL Server database that will be used for the Document Tracking and Activity (DTA) database and also the Queue database that is shared by all BizTalk servers in the group. The DTA tab is used to set up tracking for incoming and outgoing messages and track when the log will be cleaned up. The Errors tab is used to set whether the server will or will not stop when a severe error occurs.

The WebDAV repository is a file system that uses HTTP. All of the specifications and maps used to translate and manipulate documents can be stored in a WebDAV repository and shared by all the BizTalk servers in a group.

BizTalk Server can move documents from any queue into the Suspended Queue, where they can be deleted, resubmitted, or retransmitted. The action that is taken on the Suspended Queues depends on the processing instructions for the business document. The following queues are available in the BizTalk Server Administration Console:

Queues in the BizTalk Server Administration Console

Queues	Description
Work Queue	Contains all the items that are currently being worked on by BizTalk Server 2000. An administrator can manually move a document in this queue to the Suspended Queue.
Retry Queue	Contains any items that are in the process of being retransmitted for delivery. An administrator can manually move a document in this queue to the Suspended Queue.

Queues	Description
Scheduled Queue	Contains all documents that have been processed and are waiting to be sent to their distribution list. An administrator of BizTalk Server 2000 can manually move a document in this queue to the Suspended Queue.
Suspended Queue	Contains any items that failed processing, including parse errors, serialization errors, the inability to find a pipeline configuration, and so forth. Items in this queue can be selected and the administrator can view the error description or the document itself, or delete the document. See the table below for a list of parser errors and actions that can be taken for these errors.

QUEUE ERRORS AND ACTIONS

Processing State Value	Description of Error	Suspended Queue Action
Parser Failure	The business document could not be parsed by BizTalk Server 2000	The contents of the document can be viewed. The document should not be resubmitted until the error is found and corrected.
Pipeline Failure	The business document was successfully parsed, but a failure occurred after parsing	The document can be viewed and resubmitted
Transmission Failure	The document could not be transmitted	The document can be viewed and resubmitted
User Move From Another Shared Queue	A BizTalk Server administrator manually moved the document from another queue	The document can be viewed and resubmitted
Unknown	There is an unknown error	The contents of the document can be viewed. The document should not be resubmitted until the error is found and corrected.

BizTalk Server Tracking User Interface

BizTalk Server 2000 will be released with a user interface (UI) used for tracking all of the documents that move through BizTalk Server 2000. At the time this book is going to press, however, the tracking UI has not yet been released. This UI can be used by both business analysts and system administrators. The business analyst can monitor and analyze the documents that come through BizTalk Server 2000 to create new business strategies for the corporation. For example, by analyzing the customer data in the BizTalk documents, business analysts can determine customers' buying patterns, customer types, and so on. You can perform these tasks by creating custom fields that are used to analyze the information. System administrators can set up what is being tracked, establish activity-logging settings, purge settings, and perform troubleshooting analysis.

Both source documents and destination documents can be tracked as they move through BizTalk Server 2000. You can choose to track a single document or batches of documents and then log the processing activity related to the tracked document. The tracking UI also enables you to locate a document's exact location and capture information about the source and destination document's name and type, user-defined fields, and date and time parameters. In addition, you can use the tracking UI to save the data in either XML format or a native format and view the details of the document activity information.

SUMMARY

BizTalk Server 2000 provides a set of tools that enable you to share documents among different corporations and within a corporation and edit specifications on which those documents are based. Although BizTalk Server 2000 works with a wide range of document formats, the native format for BizTalk is XML documents that are defined in schemas. BizTalk Server will help make it possible for XML to become the standard format used for moving information through corporations. Because BizTalk Server 2000 works with different formats, it is capable of working with existing systems while still being capable of integrating with systems that will be built over the next several years.

Index

Note: Italicized page references indicate figures, tables, or code listings.

Symbols and Numbers

& (ampersand)
  preceding an internal general entity, 76
  preceding external parsed general entities, 97
  referencing general entities, 77
  representing in content sections, 47
&#, preceding Unicode character values in XML documents, 75
* (asterisk) element marker for child elements, 59, 60
. (dot) pattern in XPath, 118
.. (double dots) pattern in XPath, 118
" (double quotation mark), 48–77
// (double slash) pattern in XPath, 118
entities, predefined
  &amp, 47, 75
  &apos, 64, 75
  &gt, 47, 75
  &lt, 47, 75
  &quot, 48, 75
= (equality) operator, *265*
> (greater than) operator, *265*
>= (greater than or equal) operator, *265*
< (less than) operator, *265*
<= (less than or equal) operator, *265*
!= (not equal) operator in XSL, *265*
% (percent sign), referencing parameter entities, 77, 78
+ (plus sign) marker for child elements, 59, 60, 61
# (pound sign)
  identifying a special predefined name in a DTD, 57
  preceding a PCDATA declaration within a group of child elements, 62
* (processing instruction) pattern in XPath, 118
? (question mark) marker for child elements, 59
@* (select all) pattern in XPath, 118
@attr (select attribute) pattern in XPath, 118
; (semicolon)
  following an internal general entity, 76
  following external parsed general entities, 97
' (single quotation mark), 48–77

/ (slash)
  pattern in XPath, 118
  representing the *root* element, 114
| (vertical bar separator)
  with child elements, 61
  in a DTD, 145, 193
  overriding with markers, 62
  in XSL, *265*
200 status code, 170
405 status code, 170
501 status code, 170
510 status code, 170

A

a element
  adding to *CellContent*, 37
  associating unique IDs with, 64
  completing for an XML document, 36
  declaring in conformance with the XHTML standard, 92
  in a DTD, 67
  entering values for, 42
  marking child elements in, 59
  modifying the definition of, 64
abort method, *224, 248*
absoluteChildNumber Java function, 286
absoluteChildNumber method, *291*
absolute location, 112
abstract attribute for the *simpleType* element, 131
Active Server Pages (ASP), 308
ActiveX Data Objects (ADO) 2.5. *See* ADO 2.5
ActiveX Data Objects (ADO) disconnected recordset, 218
actuate attribute, 122
addCollection method, *255*
add method, *255*
addObject method, *297*
AddParameter method, *297*
address child element, 183
ADO 2.5, 347
  information about, 352
  inputting data as XML, 353
  making changes to XML data, 353–54

393

Index

Index

JAKE STURM

Jake Sturm has extensive experience in all levels of enterprise development. Jake has built a wide range of solutions, including Web applications, by using Microsoft Visual Basic, Microsoft Internet Information Services (IIS), Microsoft Transaction Server (MTS), and Microsoft SQL Server. He helped develop a Microsoft Windows DNA workshop and is the author of several technical books, including *Data Warehousing with Microsoft SQL 7.0 Technical Reference* (Microsoft Press, 2000), *VB6 UML Design and Development* (Wrox Press, 1999), and *Visual Basic Project Management* (Wrox Press, 1999).

Currently, Jake is working for Innovative Enterprise Solutions, Inc., as an Enterprise Systems Architect and conducts workshops on various topics, including XML and Windows DNA. His e-mail address is *jakes@gti.net,* and his company Web site address is *http://ies.gti.net.* Jake resides in New Jersey with his wife, Gwen; her two daughters, Jillian and Lynzie; his son, William; and his daughter, Maya.

MICROSOFT LICENSE AGREEMENT

Book Companion CD

IMPORTANT—READ CAREFULLY: This Microsoft End-User License Agreement ("EULA") is a legal agreement between you (either an individual or an entity) and Microsoft Corporation for the Microsoft product identified above, which includes computer software and may include associated media, printed materials, and "online" or electronic documentation ("SOFTWARE PRODUCT"). Any component included within the SOFTWARE PRODUCT that is accompanied by a separate End-User License Agreement shall be governed by such agreement and not the terms set forth below. By installing, copying, or otherwise using the SOFTWARE PRODUCT, you agree to be bound by the terms of this EULA. If you do not agree to the terms of this EULA, you are not authorized to install, copy, or otherwise use the SOFTWARE PRODUCT; you may, however, return the SOFTWARE PRODUCT, along with all printed materials and other items that form a part of the Microsoft product that includes the SOFTWARE PRODUCT, to the place you obtained them for a full refund.

SOFTWARE PRODUCT LICENSE

The SOFTWARE PRODUCT is protected by United States copyright laws and international copyright treaties, as well as other intellectual property laws and treaties. The SOFTWARE PRODUCT is licensed, not sold.

1. **GRANT OF LICENSE.** This EULA grants you the following rights:

   a. **Software Product.** You may install and use one copy of the SOFTWARE PRODUCT on a single computer. The primary user of the computer on which the SOFTWARE PRODUCT is installed may make a second copy for his or her exclusive use on a portable computer.

   b. **Storage/Network Use.** You may also store or install a copy of the SOFTWARE PRODUCT on a storage device, such as a network server, used only to install or run the SOFTWARE PRODUCT on your other computers over an internal network; however, you must acquire and dedicate a license for each separate computer on which the SOFTWARE PRODUCT is installed or run from the storage device. A license for the SOFTWARE PRODUCT may not be shared or used concurrently on different computers.

   c. **License Pak.** If you have acquired this EULA in a Microsoft License Pak, you may make the number of additional copies of the computer software portion of the SOFTWARE PRODUCT authorized on the printed copy of this EULA, and you may use each copy in the manner specified above. You are also entitled to make a corresponding number of secondary copies for portable computer use as specified above.

   d. **Sample Code.** Solely with respect to portions, if any, of the SOFTWARE PRODUCT that are identified within the SOFTWARE PRODUCT as sample code (the "SAMPLE CODE"):

      i. **Use and Modification.** Microsoft grants you the right to use and modify the source code version of the SAMPLE CODE, *provided* you comply with subsection (d)(iii) below. You may not distribute the SAMPLE CODE, or any modified version of the SAMPLE CODE, in source code form.

      ii. **Redistributable Files.** Provided you comply with subsection (d)(iii) below, Microsoft grants you a nonexclusive, royalty-free right to reproduce and distribute the object code version of the SAMPLE CODE and of any modified SAMPLE CODE, other than SAMPLE CODE, or any modified version thereof, designated as not redistributable in the Readme file that forms a part of the SOFTWARE PRODUCT (the "Non-Redistributable Sample Code"). All SAMPLE CODE other than the Non-Redistributable Sample Code is collectively referred to as the "REDISTRIBUTABLES."

      iii. **Redistribution Requirements.** If you redistribute the REDISTRIBUTABLES, you agree to: (i) distribute the REDISTRIBUTABLES in object code form only in conjunction with and as a part of your software application product; (ii) not use Microsoft's name, logo, or trademarks to market your software application product; (iii) include a valid copyright notice on your software application product; (iv) indemnify, hold harmless, and defend Microsoft from and against any claims or lawsuits, including attorney's fees, that arise or result from the use or distribution of your software application product; and (v) not permit further distribution of the REDISTRIBUTABLES by your end user. Contact Microsoft for the applicable royalties due and other licensing terms for all other uses and/or distribution of the REDISTRIBUTABLES.

2. **DESCRIPTION OF OTHER RIGHTS AND LIMITATIONS.**

   - **Limitations on Reverse Engineering, Decompilation, and Disassembly.** You may not reverse engineer, decompile, or disassemble the SOFTWARE PRODUCT, except and only to the extent that such activity is expressly permitted by applicable law notwithstanding this limitation.

   - **Separation of Components.** The SOFTWARE PRODUCT is licensed as a single product. Its component parts may not be separated for use on more than one computer.

   - **Rental.** You may not rent, lease, or lend the SOFTWARE PRODUCT.

   - **Support Services.** Microsoft may, but is not obligated to, provide you with support services related to the SOFTWARE PRODUCT ("Support Services"). Use of Support Services is governed by the Microsoft policies and programs described in the user manual, in "online" documentation, and/or in other Microsoft-provided materials. Any supplemental software code provided to you as part of the Support Services shall be considered part of the SOFTWARE PRODUCT and subject to the terms and conditions of this EULA. With respect to technical information you provide to Microsoft as part of the Support Services, Microsoft may use such information for its business purposes, including for product support and development. Microsoft will not utilize such technical information in a form that personally identifies you.

- **Software Transfer.** You may permanently transfer all of your rights under this EULA, provided you retain no copies, you transfer all of the SOFTWARE PRODUCT (including all component parts, the media and printed materials, any upgrades, this EULA, and, if applicable, the Certificate of Authenticity), **and** the recipient agrees to the terms of this EULA.

- **Termination.** Without prejudice to any other rights, Microsoft may terminate this EULA if you fail to comply with the terms and conditions of this EULA. In such event, you must destroy all copies of the SOFTWARE PRODUCT and all of its component parts.

3. **COPYRIGHT.** All title and copyrights in and to the SOFTWARE PRODUCT (including but not limited to any images, photographs, animations, video, audio, music, text, SAMPLE CODE, REDISTRIBUTABLES, and "applets" incorporated into the SOFTWARE PRODUCT) and any copies of the SOFTWARE PRODUCT are owned by Microsoft or its suppliers. The SOFTWARE PRODUCT is protected by copyright laws and international treaty provisions. Therefore, you must treat the SOFTWARE PRODUCT like any other copyrighted material **except** that you may install the SOFTWARE PRODUCT on a single computer provided you keep the original solely for backup or archival purposes. You may not copy the printed materials accompanying the SOFTWARE PRODUCT.

4. **U.S. GOVERNMENT RESTRICTED RIGHTS.** The SOFTWARE PRODUCT and documentation are provided with RESTRICTED RIGHTS. Use, duplication, or disclosure by the Government is subject to restrictions as set forth in subparagraph (c)(1)(ii) of the Rights in Technical Data and Computer Software clause at DFARS 252.227-7013 or subparagraphs (c)(1) and (2) of the Commercial Computer Software—Restricted Rights at 48 CFR 52.227-19, as applicable. Manufacturer is Microsoft Corporation/One Microsoft Way/Redmond, WA 98052-6399.

5. **EXPORT RESTRICTIONS.** You agree that you will not export or re-export the SOFTWARE PRODUCT, any part thereof, or any process or service that is the direct product of the SOFTWARE PRODUCT (the foregoing collectively referred to as the "Restricted Components"), to any country, person, entity, or end user subject to U.S. export restrictions. You specifically agree not to export or re-export any of the Restricted Components (i) to any country to which the U.S. has embargoed or restricted the export of goods or services, which currently include, but are not necessarily limited to, Cuba, Iran, Iraq, Libya, North Korea, Sudan, and Syria, or to any national of any such country, wherever located, who intends to transmit or transport the Restricted Components back to such country; (ii) to any end user who you know or have reason to know will utilize the Restricted Components in the design, development, or production of nuclear, chemical, or biological weapons; or (iii) to any end user who has been prohibited from participating in U.S. export transactions by any federal agency of the U.S. government. You warrant and represent that neither the BXA nor any other U.S. federal agency has suspended, revoked, or denied your export privileges.

DISCLAIMER OF WARRANTY

NO WARRANTIES OR CONDITIONS. MICROSOFT EXPRESSLY DISCLAIMS ANY WARRANTY OR CONDITION FOR THE SOFTWARE PRODUCT. THE SOFTWARE PRODUCT AND ANY RELATED DOCUMENTATION ARE PROVIDED "AS IS" WITHOUT WARRANTY OR CONDITION OF ANY KIND, EITHER EXPRESS OR IMPLIED, INCLUDING, WITHOUT LIMITATION, THE IMPLIED WARRANTIES OF MERCHANTABILITY, FITNESS FOR A PARTICULAR PURPOSE, OR NONINFRINGEMENT. THE ENTIRE RISK ARISING OUT OF USE OR PERFORMANCE OF THE SOFTWARE PRODUCT REMAINS WITH YOU.

LIMITATION OF LIABILITY. TO THE MAXIMUM EXTENT PERMITTED BY APPLICABLE LAW, IN NO EVENT SHALL MICROSOFT OR ITS SUPPLIERS BE LIABLE FOR ANY SPECIAL, INCIDENTAL, INDIRECT, OR CONSEQUENTIAL DAMAGES WHATSOEVER (INCLUDING, WITHOUT LIMITATION, DAMAGES FOR LOSS OF BUSINESS PROFITS, BUSINESS INTERRUPTION, LOSS OF BUSINESS INFORMATION, OR ANY OTHER PECUNIARY LOSS) ARISING OUT OF THE USE OF OR INABILITY TO USE THE SOFTWARE PRODUCT OR THE PROVISION OF OR FAILURE TO PROVIDE SUPPORT SERVICES, EVEN IF MICROSOFT HAS BEEN ADVISED OF THE POSSIBILITY OF SUCH DAMAGES. IN ANY CASE, MICROSOFT'S ENTIRE LIABILITY UNDER ANY PROVISION OF THIS EULA SHALL BE LIMITED TO THE GREATER OF THE AMOUNT ACTUALLY PAID BY YOU FOR THE SOFTWARE PRODUCT OR US$5.00; PROVIDED, HOWEVER, IF YOU HAVE ENTERED INTO A MICROSOFT SUPPORT SERVICES AGREEMENT, MICROSOFT'S ENTIRE LIABILITY REGARDING SUPPORT SERVICES SHALL BE GOVERNED BY THE TERMS OF THAT AGREEMENT. BECAUSE SOME STATES AND JURISDICTIONS DO NOT ALLOW THE EXCLUSION OR LIMITATION OF LIABILITY, THE ABOVE LIMITATION MAY NOT APPLY TO YOU.

MISCELLANEOUS

This EULA is governed by the laws of the State of Washington USA, except and only to the extent that applicable law mandates governing law of a different jurisdiction.

Should you have any questions concerning this EULA, or if you desire to contact Microsoft for any reason, please contact the Microsoft subsidiary serving your country, or write: Microsoft Sales Information Center/One Microsoft Way/Redmond, WA 98052-6399.

Register Today!

0-7356-0796-6

Return the bottom portion of this card to register today.

Developing XML Solutions

FIRST NAME   **MIDDLE INITIAL**   **LAST NAME**

INSTITUTION OR COMPANY NAME

ADDRESS

CITY   **STATE**   **ZIP**

( )

E-MAIL ADDRESS   **PHONE NUMBER**

U.S. and Canada addresses only. Fill in information above and mail postage-free.
Please mail only the bottom half of this page.

**For information about Microsoft Press®
products, visit our Web site at
mspress.microsoft.com**